Missile Contagion

Missile Contagion

Cruise Missile Proliferation and the Threat to International Security

Dennis M. Gormley

PRAEGER SECURITY INTERNATIONAL
Westport, Connecticut · London

Library of Congress Cataloging-in-Publication Data

Gormley, Dennis M., 1943–
    Missile contagion : cruise missile proliferation and the threat to international security /
    Dennis M. Gormley.
        p. cm.
    Includes bibliographical references and index.
    ISBN-13: 978–0–275–99836–3 (alk. paper)
1. Cruise missiles. 2. Ballistic missiles. 3. Arms race. 4. United States—Military policy. I. Title.
UG1312.C7G67   2008
358.1'7—dc22   2008000195

British Library Cataloguing in Publication Data is available.

Library of Congress Catalog Card Number: 2008000195
ISBN-13: 978–0–275–99836–3

First published in 2008

Praeger Security International, 88 Post Road West, Westport, CT 06881
An imprint of Greenwood Publishing Group, Inc.
www.praeger.com

Printed in the United States of America

The paper used in this book complies with the
Permanent Paper Standard issued by the National
Information Standards Organization (Z39.48–1984).

10 9 8 7 6 5 4 3 2 1

To Sonia
Ma partenaire et épouse extraordinaire

Contents

Preface and Acknowledgments

Writing is such a solitary endeavor. Where—and with whom—it is accomplished naturally eases the loneliness and facilitates the objective. Spending three virtually uninterrupted months during the summer of 2007 in our house on Little Mulky Mountain, nestled in the foothills of the Blue Ridge Mountains in Rappahannock County, Virginia, accompanied by my wife and partner Sonia, and joined midway by a Labrador retriever named Rappy, had to be this side of heaven. Other than occasional visits by a local black bear searching for and supping on low-hanging fruit from our peach, pear, and apple trees, we were left alone to attend to the business at hand. My only disappointment, which frankly redounded to finishing the book as planned, was not getting out on the Rapidan or Rose rivers to cast a fly or two in pursuit of our native brook trout. Rather than personal discipline, a summer drought kept me on schedule.

Inspiration for this book came from several sources. From the late Albert Wohlstetter, with whom I worked off and on for over a decade, I learned the importance of persistence in effecting changes in government policy, especially when dealing with problems perennially afflicted by the fallacy of the "lesser-included case." Just two examples illustrate the point. Nonproliferation policy is supposed to address both ballistic and cruise missiles, but cruise missiles were left out of the Hague Code of Conduct, the only extant normative treatment addressing missile proliferation today. Also, America's Patriot missile defense interceptors, which are designed to combat both ballistic and cruise missiles, batted one thousand against Iraq's ballistic missiles in the 2003 war in Iraq but went zero for five against Iraq's primitive cruise missiles, not even detecting, much less intercepting, one of them. These two shortcomings, together with other policy missteps examined in the book, are fueling a dangerous missile contagion in the Middle East, South Asia, and Northeast Asia alike. Albert Wohlstetter foretold of that spread when, two years before his passing in January 1997, he graciously wrote a long foreword to my first effort at understanding cruise missile proliferation.[1]

Another source of inspiration came from Albert's wife, the late Roberta Wohlstetter, a superb analyst and historian in her own right. For the last five years, I've taught my graduate students at the University of Pittsburgh the lessons derived from Roberta's brilliant 1962 book, *Pearl Harbor: Warning and Decision*. Influential in shaping my approach to the book was Roberta's reminder that warning of war is a two-sided game. That is, we should never assume that the foreign activities we are observing are impervious to outside influence—most notably, actions taken by the United States. This reminder certainly applies to intelligence analysis, where too often there is an exclusive fixation on pursuing better and better intelligence capabilities in order to clarify the enemy's intentions and capabilities when in fact the enemy may be waiting to see what we will do next. As Greg Treverton aptly put it, we "co-create" the threat with our enemies.[2] But the notion is also equally applicable to missile proliferation, where state behavior is frequently shaped more powerfully than we first might imagine by U.S. behavior. My previous work on cruise missile proliferation certainly considered the co-creation factor, but I've more systematically examined its importance in the treatment at hand.

Finally, and no less important, is the impact that Malcolm Gladwell's book, *The Tipping Point: How Little Things Can Make a Big Difference* (2000), had on my thinking about how to make sense of seemingly contagious events. Although Gladwell's book deals with how small-scale social events shape human behavior, it prodded my thinking about what might be shaping the sudden outbreak of cruise missile proliferation that commenced roughly four years ago, particularly since virtually all analysts thought a tipping point would be reached much sooner. Of course, applying the notion of a tipping point in proliferation is nothing new.[3]

Over the years many people were instrumental in supporting my research on cruise missile proliferation. I am especially grateful to Tom Swartz, formerly of the Defense Advanced Research Projects Agency, who got me started in the early 1990s, and later on to Matt Ganz and Jim Carlini, who kept the fires burning. Teddy Winkler of the Swiss Ministry of Defense also generously allowed me to pursue a different angle on the subject early on. More recently, I have benefited greatly from the support of the Smith-Richardson Foundation and The Ploughshares Fund. I want to particularly thank Paul Carroll of the latter organization for believing that seemingly small investments could result in measurable impact.

Journal editors have also been central agents in enabling debate and discourse on the topic at hand. Dana Allin has been especially generous in allowing me ample space in the quarterly journal *Survival*. Thanks also to Jonas Siegel at the *Bulletin of the Atomic Scientists* and Scott Parrish at the *Nonproliferation Review* for their editorial guidance and helpful comments.

Numerous people helped by provoking my thinking, answering questions, pointing me to unfamiliar material, or allowing me a forum to discuss and debate the subject of cruise missile proliferation. They include Charley Beck, Greg Cirincione,

Greg DeSantis, Michael Krepon, Mark Lazaroff, Tom Mahnken, Tim McCarthy, Scott McMahon, Matt Norman, Henry Sokolski, Richard Speier, David Whelan, and Phil Williams. None of their comments or guidance should be construed as endorsement of the views I've taken in the book.

For the especially heavy lifting I am in debt to several people. Jonathan Stevenson and Jack Mendelsohn read and commented upon every draft chapter. Without their sane advice and wisdom, the book would not be nearly as coherent as I hope it is. I am also most grateful that Dick Clarke, John Newhouse, and Janne Nolan found time to read portions of the book and comment accordingly. My former student and current colleague at Monterey Institute's James Martin Center for Nonproliferation Studies, Anya Loukianova, was truly indispensable in fact checking, graphics support, and reading and commenting on several chapters. I also want to thank Elizabeth Claeys for her sharp eye and the disciplined approach she brought to copy-editing my manuscript.

In the end, however, this book would not be without my associate and spouse, Sonia Ben Ouagrham-Gormley, whose love, patience, and support steadied me at several difficult points along the way. A scholar herself, Sonia kindled my interest in specialized knowledge skills by introducing me to the field of science and technology studies and allowing me to mate what I intuitively knew from seven years at Harry Diamond Laboratories to an academically rigorous literature. What's more, she read every word and gave order and clarity to an otherwise unruly first draft. Most important of all, her heart was in this difficult project no less than mine, giving meaning to Antoine de Saint-Exupéry's notion that love best consists of "looking together in the same direction."

Dennis M. Gormley
Flint Hill, Virginia
October 2007

Abbreviations

ADSAM	air-directed surface-to-air missile
AESA	active electronically scanned array
ASCM	anti-ship cruise missile
ATBM	anti-tactical ballistic missile
ATM	Airborne Tactical Missile (Russia)
AWACS	Airborne Warning and Control System (U.S.)
BMD	ballistic missile defense
CALCM	conventional air-launched cruise missile
CBM	confidence-building measure
CEP	circular error probability
CPMIEC	China Precision Machinery Import and Export Corporation
CSIST	Chung-Shan Institute of Science and Technology (Taiwan)
DARPA	Defense Advanced Research Projects Agency (U.S.)
DPRK	Democratic People's Republic of Korea
DRDO	Defense Research and Development Organization (India)
DSMAC	digital scene-matching area correlation
EU	European Union
EXBS	Export Control and Related Border Security program (U.S.)
G7	Group of Seven
GEM	Patriot Guidance-Enhanced Missile (U.S.)
GLONASS	Global Navigation Satellite System (Russia)
GPS	Global Positioning System (U.S.)
ICBM	intercontinental ballistic missile
IGMDP	Integrated Guided Missile Development Program (India)
INF	Intermediate-Range Nuclear Forces Treaty
INS	inertial navigation system
IRBM	intermediate-range ballistic missile
IRGC	Islamic Revolutionary Guard Corps (Iran)

JASSM	Joint Air-to-Surface Standoff Missile (U.S.)
JDAM	Joint Direct Attack Munition (U.S.)
JLENS	Joint Land-Attack Cruise Missile Defense Elevated Netted Sensor (U.S.)
JSSEO	Joint SIAP System Engineering Organization (U.S.)
JSTARS	Joint Surveillance and Target Attack Radar System (U.S.)
JTAMDO	Joint Theater Air and Missile Defense Organization (U.S.)
LACM	land-attack cruise missile
MC2A	Multi-Sensor Command and Control Aircraft (U.S.)
MDA	Missile Defense Agency (U.S.)
MEADS	Medium Extended Air Defense System (multinational)
MP-RTIP	Multi-Platform Radar Technology Insertion Program (U.S.)
MRBM	medium-range ballistic missile
MTCR	Missile Technology Control Regime
NASIC	National Air and Space Intelligence Center (U.S.)
NATO	North Atlantic Treaty Organization
NCRI	National Council of Resistance of Iran
NDC	National Development Complex (Pakistan)
NORAD	North American Air Defense Command (U.S.-Canada)
NPR	Nuclear Posture Review (U.S.)
NSC	National Security Council (U.S.)
NSG	Nuclear Suppliers Group
OIF	Operation Iraqi Freedom
PAC	Patriot Advanced Capability (U.S.)
PLA	People's Liberation Army (China)
PRC	People's Republic of China
PSLV	Polar Satellite Launch Vehicle (India)
RPV	remotely piloted vehicle
SALT	Strategic Arms Limitation Treaty
SAM	surface-to-air missile
SDF	Self-Defense Force (Japan)
SDI	Strategic Defense Initiative (U.S.)
SIAP	single integrated air picture (U.S.)
SLAMRAAM	Surface-Launched Advanced Medium-Range Air-to-Air Missile (U.S.)
SLBM	submarine-launched ballistic missile
SLV	space-launch vehicle
SM	Standard Missile (U.S.)
SRBM	short-range ballistic missile
STRATCOM	Strategic Command (U.S.)
TEL	transporter-erector-launcher
TERCOM	terrain contour-matching
THAAD	Terminal High-Altitude Area Defense (U.S.)
TSMFS	Tactical Shore-based Missile for Fire Suppression (Taiwan)
UAE	United Arab Emirates
UAV	unmanned aerial vehicle
UCAV	unmanned combat air vehicle
UN	United Nations
VLS	vertical launch system
WMD	weapons of mass destruction

Part One ——————————————

The Proliferation Context

1 —————————————————————————————————————

Introduction

In the early morning hours of August 11, 2005, in a remote and arid part of Pakistan's western Baluchistan province, Pakistani engineers test-launched a weapon like no other in their country's ambitious missile development program. Instead of employing a large solid- or liquid-fueled rocket as ballistic missiles do, the new weapon was propelled off its launcher by a small solid-rocket booster on the missile's tail. Compared with the huge plume and readily detectable infrared signature produced by a ballistic missile's rocket engine, the booster's plume was so small that it avoided detection by early warning satellites stationed above Earth in geosynchronous orbits. Once the missile, called Babur, was safely away from its launcher, the solid-rocket booster quickly dropped away. A mechanical engine then took over and propelled the missile to an altitude of only 610 meters (m), or 2,000 feet, after which it dipped back down and, like a low-flying airplane, followed the folds of the earth along a highly unpredictable preprogrammed course to its designated target area.

Had Pakistani officials wished to keep the test a secret, they could have readily done so, but they were keen to tell the world that Pakistan had just joined an elite club of nations that possess land-attack cruise missiles (LACMs).[1] Immediately after the successful test, Pakistan's President Pervez Musharraf announced the achievement to a television audience, declaring, "The biggest value of this system is [that] it is not detectable. It cannot be intercepted."[2]

States have long seen the value of acquiring LACMs capable of delivering conventional as well as mass-destruction payloads, but they faced major hurdles in doing so.[3] Chief among them were designing and building a suitable navigation and guidance system and obtaining a propulsion system capable of achieving the desired range.

Through the 1980s, only the United States and the Soviet Union had mastered the demanding task of accurately navigating unmanned missiles over long distances to within meters of the intended target area. This was achieved by employing a radar altimeter in the missile's nose that compared what it detected on the ground with an onboard digital map, derived from highly classified satellite reconnaissance, showing the missile's programmed path to the target. As the missile approached the target area a tiny camera in the missile's nose viewed the target scene and, after comparing it with a highly precise stored target scene, adjusted the missile's flight path accordingly to achieve unprecedented accuracy. Not only was it enormously expensive to develop the needed targeting infrastructure, but such contour- and scene-matching technology was also subject to strict export controls.

The advent of the U.S. Global Positioning System (GPS) in 1978 eliminated this hurdle by providing unmanned missiles with precise information about their locations. Though originally conceived to provide the U.S. military alone with precise timing and location information, as a result of decisions made by Presidents Ronald Reagan and Bill Clinton, GPS has become a permanent and indispensable fixture of unrestricted commerce.[4] What is more, fearing that the United States might curtail access to its 30-satellite GPS constellation during wartime, others have decided to build their own space-based position-location systems. The European Union's, called Galileo, is a 30-satellite constellation intended to begin operating by 2013, while China hopes to expand upon its currently limited 5-satellite system, called Beidou 1, to deploy eventually a 35-satellite constellation, called Beidou 2, with separate services for its military and worldwide commercial users. Moscow's original plans for its Global Navigation Satellite System (GLONASS) were sidetracked by the breakup of the Soviet Union, but Russia now plans to have a full constellation of 24 satellites operating by 2009. The myriad applications that these systems will facilitate will be largely for the public good. But while technology itself is often neutral, it can also be used to do harm.

The other prime hurdle to membership in the LACM club is developing a suitable propulsion system. To be sure, the kind of highly efficient turbofan engines that propel American and Russian long-range LACMs well beyond 1,000 kilometers (km) to their targets remain beyond the technological grasp of most aspiring missile developers. Yet, because manned aircraft are not subjected to the comparatively tight export controls that LACMs encounter, LACM aspirants could turn to unrestricted, if less highly efficient, turbojet engines produced by a broad array of industrial and even some developing countries. This fact has certainly been the case since GPS and its subsidiary technologies became commercially available over 15 years ago.

SIGNS OF CONTAGION

Pakistan is not the only new LACM aspirant. India, together with Russia, is developing the BrahMos supersonic cruise missile, which will have the capability to strike targets at sea or over land to a range of 290 km. And in the summer of 2007, India disclosed officially that it had at least two other LACM programs underway, including one similar to the U.S. Tomahawk with a range of 1,000 km and another co-developed with Israel's help. Not to be outdone by its rival, Pakistan tested another new LACM, called Raad, in late August 2007. In East Asia, China, Taiwan, and South Korea are rushing to deploy new LACMs with ranges of 1,000 km or more, while Japan is contemplating acquiring a LACM for "preemptive" strikes against enemy missile bases. In the Middle East, Israel was once the sole country possessing LACMs, but now Iran appears to be pursuing cruise missile programs for both land and sea attack. Iran has also provided the terrorist group Hezbollah with unmanned aerial vehicles (UAVs) and sophisticated anti-ship cruise missiles (ASCMs), one of which severely damaged an Israeli vessel and killed four sailors during the 2006 war in Lebanon. In April 2005, Ukraine's export agency unveiled plans to market a new LACM, called Korshun. The design of this new missile appears to be based solely on the Russian Kh-55, a nuclear-capable, 3,000-km-range LACM, which Ukrainian and Russian arms dealers had illegally sold to China in 2000 and to Iran in 2001.

Such rapid and unexpected developments suggest that the proliferation of missiles capable of delivering WMD and highly accurate conventional payloads is approaching a critical threshold. The surprising fact is that cruise missiles, not ballistic missiles, constitute the primary problem. While India, Iran, North Korea, and Pakistan have developed new medium-range ballistic missiles (1,000–3,000 km in range), overall trends since the end of the Cold War show a significant net decrease in worldwide ballistic missile arsenals largely due to U.S.-Soviet arms control treaties.[5] Even though the range of ballistic missiles has slowly increased, their horizontal spread has been largely kept under check. Yet ballistic missiles, and defenses against them, still command virtually the exclusive attention of decisionmakers and analysts.

Flying under the radar, both literally and figuratively, cruise missiles add a dangerous new dimension to protecting U.S. security interests and preventing regional military instability. Cruise missiles are not destined to supplant ballistic missiles. But when both are employed together, they could severely test even the best missile defenses. Perversely, the U.S. quest to sell ballistic missile defenses may be hastening this eventuality. Knowing that such defenses are not nearly as effective against LACMs as they are against ballistic missiles, some states—including China, Pakistan, and Iran—are now developing new LACM programs to complement their ballistic missile arsenals. Others that are planning to purchase missile defenses, like Taiwan and Japan, have decided to complement them with much cheaper offensive systems that include LACMs. Worse yet, they are linking LACM use to preemptive doctrines. In either case, the unintended by-product is likely to be regional arms races and crisis instability.

ARGUMENT IN BRIEF

For at least 15 years, analysts have been arguing that LACMs were likely to proliferate rapidly. In the first authoritative treatment of the subject, published in 1992, Seth Carus concluded: "It now appears inevitable that Third World countries will begin to acquire land-attack cruise missiles during the 1990s."[6] While cautioning that analysts had focused on technology spread at the expense of systems integration challenges, K. Scott McMahon and I concluded in early 1995: "Overall, we judge Third World incentives to acquire land-attack cruise missiles to be sufficiently compelling to suggest a threat of some considerable magnitude probably emerging by the end of this decade."[7] Indeed, several LACM development programs probably commenced in the mid- to late 1990s, but only now, roughly a decade later, has a series of seemingly small events nudged LACM growth toward a dangerous "tipping point" in missile proliferation.[8]

Understanding why, despite the dilatoriness of acquiring nations, an epidemic of cruise missile proliferation only now appears imminent is the primary objective of this book. To that end, it explores the role of three factors in shaping the spread of LACMs: the critical importance of access to specialized *knowledge; narrative* messages about reasons for acquiring cruise missiles; and *norms* of state behavior relating to nonproliferation policy and defense doctrine affecting state acquisition behavior. Rather than supplanting ballistic missiles, LACMs may eventually join them to become complementary means of assuring—barring the deployment of advanced and considerably more expensive missile defenses—that offensive missiles threaten enemies with a high probability of arriving safely, with increasing effectiveness.

KNOWLEDGE

The most prominent argument about the spread of scientific knowledge and science-based technology is a decidedly simplistic one. By virtue of employing a universally understood methodology, scientific knowledge spreads steadily, aided by globalization and the internet. Technology, in turn, diffuses easily and smoothly into complex systems, including weapons. This reductionist view is no less popular regarding matters of weapons proliferation. The Pentagon's Defense Science Board, in a 2006 report on U.S. nuclear capabilities, argued that the desirability of a nuclear-free world was irrelevant because nuclear weapons cannot be "erased from history."[9] In effect, the nuclear genie is out of the bag and can never be put back.

But there is an alternative view, held by scholars in the field of science and technology studies. They argue that there are actually two kinds of knowledge at work in the construction of any complex science and technology endeavor: explicit and tacit knowledge.[10] Whereas explicit knowledge consists of information or engineering formulations that can be recorded and passed easily from one place to another, tacit knowledge cannot be written down or passed via digital media. Rather, it is acquired through the laborious and lengthy process of apprenticeship. Tacit knowledge, then, is the product of a uniquely fertile social and intellectual environment composed of mentors and protégés.[11] Obtained as it is under these narrowly bounded circumstances, tacit knowledge skills are not widely diffused in the way that explicit knowledge is.

Thus, to the extent that new design and development work is terminated and tacit knowledge skills are not passed on directly to the next generation of designers, it will require a substantial amount of "reinvention" to recreate any complex weapon system.[12] The fact that states or terrorist groups can easily acquire all the component technologies comprising the basic ingredients of a cruise missile does not necessarily mean that they can readily develop militarily useful missile systems. Developing any complex military system depends on a small number of key individuals who possess certain tacit knowledge skills—the most important of which are systems engineering or integration skills. In the case of missile development, systems engineering skills are critical to fabricate, integrate, and produce a turbofan engine, or to integrate all the component parts of a land-attack navigation and guidance system so that it can repetitively and confidently perform its intended function.

Early assessments of cruise missile proliferation gave insufficient weight to these specialized skills and concentrated instead on export control shortcomings and the blizzard of dual-use technologies flooding the marketplace between 1990 and 2000. For example, a presentation I and a colleague made to members of the Rumsfeld Commission in June 1998 showed the results of our study of how a first-generation cruise missile, the Chinese HY-2 Silkworm, could be transformed from a short-range (about 100 km) anti-ship missile into a longer-range (about 1,000 km) land-attack missile using only commercially available component technology.[13] The study was based solely on gathering explicit knowledge; nothing was actually built and tested. Because of this limitation, the study team devoted considerable effort to analyzing how long it might take developing countries to accomplish such a feat, including building a serial production capability as well as integrating the new missile into the existing force structure. The study's conclusion was that it would take six to ten years, a time that could conceivably be cut in half depending on the extent and nature of foreign assistance—most notably the provision of experienced systems engineers. The commission's chairman, Donald Rumsfeld, disagreed, saying that it would take not more than a year to achieve the desired objective. Fortuitously, in searching for Iraq's WMD programs after the 2003 invasion, the Iraq Survey Group discovered that Iraq had attempted, beginning in June 2002 in a project called Jinin, to convert the HY-2 anti-ship cruise missile into a 1,000-km-range LACM, intending to complete a development cycle of three to five years. Importantly, Iraq was not starting from scratch. Engineers had devoted years of work on an HY-2 project that extended the missile's range from 100 to 150 km, which, noted Survey Group inspectors, directly contributed to the Jinin project. In nearly six months of activity, little was accomplished aside from computer simulations to test the prospect of successfully integrating a surplus helicopter engine into the missile's airframe. An apparent test of a candidate engine failed to demonstrate sufficient thrust. No work on navigation, guidance, or control was even planned until after successful integration of the engine, which Iraqi engineers admitted was a challenging proposition in the first place.[14] On arguably simpler UAV programs, Iraqi engineers produced indigenous designs that depended heavily on foreign procured components (including engines and guidance components) but achieved only modest progress in most cases, over as much as seven years of development work.[15] In short, even the three- to five-year estimate for Iraq's HY-2 conversion programs seems overly optimistic.

The kinds of specialized knowledge that Iraq could have used appear essential in helping to explain the recent spike in cruise missile proliferation. For example, Chinese fingerprints are all over Pakistan's Babur LACM, while Russian engineering is known to have enabled China to produce a workable propulsion system for its new LACMs. Russian technical assistance, formalized in a joint production agreement, has helped India to produce and deploy its first cruise missile, the supersonic BrahMos, which can fulfill both anti-ship and land-attack missions. And Israeli assistance is manifest in New Delhi's quest to produce subsonic LACMs. Iran's three new cruise missile programs reportedly depend on foreign-trained engineers who honed their skills in France, Germany, Russia, China, and North Korea.[16] And even though the United States has thus far apparently sought to forestall Taiwan's cruise missile ambitions, Taiwan has already obtained critical U.S. cruise missile technology and is working to convince its patron—so far without any reported success—to provide a more advanced turbofan engine to extend its missile's range. Thus, while the flow of technology components is necessary, it is not sufficient to enable cruise missile proliferation without the critical support of a small and exceptionally skilled group of engineering practitioners in an equally small number of industrial countries. This reality, in a sense, represents the good news related to the unfolding LACM contagion. If states can more effectively control the spread of these "black art" skills, there is hope that the worse features of the contagion can be checked.

NARRATIVE

Just as the specialized knowledge of a small number of engineers can help foster the spread of LACMs, a seemingly inconsequential event can embellish the narrative message associated with LACMs and their consequent appeal. During the Iraq War, five crude Iraqi LACMs managed to evade otherwise successful U.S. missile defenses. Because they did not produce any casualties, or derail coalition military operations, Iraq's surprise use of LACMs was generally viewed as a footnote to an otherwise swift and successful military campaign. But to specialists within the U.S. government and elsewhere, the chief lesson became that ballistic missile defenses alone cannot address the threat of low-flying cruise missiles. And because they are significantly less expensive than missile defenses, LACMs, alongside existing ballistic missile arsenals, will make defending against all types of missile threats an increasingly daunting and costly challenge.

Since the launch of the first operational German V-2 rocket in 1944, ballistic missiles have furnished their owners with the symbolic cachet of military sophistication —not to mention the confidence that comes with possessing a delivery means capable of arriving reasonably close to its target without prospect of interception. Against Germany's slow, high-flying V-1, the progenitor of today's LACMs, Britain had managed by war's end to greatly improve its defenses. By the last week of V-1 attacks, Britain's air defenses intercepted 79 percent of incoming V-1s. Still, roughly 21,000 V-1s were launched against the Allies during the war, causing more than 18,000 casualties in London alone.[17]

Modern low-flying LACMs present decidedly more attractive offensive options. Compared with ballistic missiles, LACMs are expected to be much more accurate (by a factor of at least ten), less costly (by at least half) and, because of their aerodynamic stability and larger footprint, substantially more effective in delivering chemical and biological agents (enlarging the lethal area for biological attacks by at least ten times, conservatively).[18] Also in contrast to larger ballistic missiles, LACMs provide more flexible and survivable launch options from air, land, and sea platforms, while offering easier maintenance in harsher environments. And surely the success of American Tomahawk cruise missiles in both the 1991 and 2003 wars with Iraq burnished their appeal. Still, until recently, the symbolic and psychological power of ballistic missiles trumped LACMs' superior efficiency and effectiveness. As long as ballistic missiles were not seriously threatened by effective missile defenses, they maintained this apparent advantage over cruise missiles no matter how problematic their true military utility proved to be.

By 2003, circumstances had changed. Whereas U.S. missile defenses performed poorly against Iraq's ballistic missiles during the 1991 Gulf War (the Government Accountability Office generously attributed them a 9 percent interception rate), greatly improved Patriot missile defenses intercepted all nine of the ballistic missiles Iraq launched in 2003. That the Patriot batteries failed to detect or intercept any of the five primitive Iraqi LACMs only bolstered their value as a difficult-to-defeat delivery system. In fact, the addition of LACMs to the Iraqi missile threat sowed such confusion among U.S. forces that it contributed to a series of friendly-fire casualties: Patriot batteries erroneously shot down two friendly aircraft, killing three crew members, while an American F-15 crew destroyed a Patriot radar, in the belief they were being targeted.[19] That a mere handful of primitive LACMs could achieve such an impact seems to have sunk in quickly. "This was a glimpse of future threats. It is a poor man's air force," the chief of staff of the 32nd U.S. Army Air and Missile Defense Command told the *New York Times* shortly after the fall of Baghdad. "A thinking enemy will use uncommon means such as cruise missiles and unmanned aerial vehicles on multiple fronts."[20]

During the 1990s, when many of the cruise missile development programs examined in this book were launched, the LACM narrative rarely if ever fixed on the appeal of surviving missile defenses. But in the aftermath of 2003's events, a new cruise missile narrative is beginning to stick with virtually every new cruise missile program. For example, President Musharraf's characterization of Pakistan's new cruise missile as undetectable and incapable of interception seemed destined for Indian ears. It came less than a month after Washington reportedly had agreed to permit New Delhi to acquire Israel's Arrow missile defense system.[21] Pakistan repeated this narrative emphasis in the aftermath of its March 22, 2007 test launch of its Babur LACM, when it released the following press statement: "Babur . . . is a terrain hugging, radar-avoiding cruise missile, whose range has now been enhanced to 700 km. It is a highly maneuverable missile with pinpoint accuracy."[22] Iran, too, confronted with Israel's substantial investment in ballistic missile defenses, appears to view a cruise missile arsenal as an efficient way to increase the return on investment in its Shihab ballistic missile program.[23] And even South Korea has focused public attention on the assured penetration potential of its four new LACM development programs.

NORMS

Seemingly insignificant events can often produce surprising results, or simply reinforce already weakly established norms. Norms against missile proliferation do not have nearly the robustness or legal standing of those pertaining to the proliferation of nuclear, biological, and chemical weapons, yet there have been recent attempts to strengthen them.[24] In 1999, the 34-nation Missile Technology Control Regime (MTCR), a supplier cartel launched in 1987 by the United States and its Group of Seven (G7) partners to curb missile proliferation, initiated work that eventually led, in November 2002, to the adoption of the Hague Code of Conduct against Ballistic Missile Proliferation. Open to all states and meant to complement the MTCR's supply-side restrictions on the transfer of technology and missiles, the Hague Code established a broad international norm against the spread of ballistic missiles. As of late 2006, 125 nations had become code signatories. Despite the fact that the MTCR covers both ballistic and cruise missiles, the regime's members regrettably left cruise missiles out of the Hague Code's normative content. In so doing, they have inadvertently contributed to fostering an epidemic of LACMs.

Three months prior to the launch of the Hague Code, the George W. Bush administration issued its new national security strategy of preemption. The doctrine moved U.S. policy away from deterrence and containment toward attacking enemies before they could attack the United States. From the purely military point of view, there are obvious advantages to decisive and successful preemption. But from the policy point of view, there is equally the danger that brandishing such an aggressive strategy will establish a precedent for others to follow and generate unwanted instability during regional crises.[25] Indeed, it is worrisome to see the emulation of the U.S. preemption doctrine interact with weak missile nonproliferation norms to make cruise missiles the "first strike" weapon of choice in several volatile regions of the world.

Shortly after the U.S. invasion of Iraq, President Putin said Russia retained the right to launch preemptive strikes to defend its interests. Israel, too, cited U.S. preemption doctrine when it attacked an alleged terrorist camp in Syria in October 2003. North Korea announced that "a preemptive strike is not the monopoly of the United States."[26] The Indian external affairs minister avowed that India had a more persuasive case to launch preemptive strikes against Pakistan than did the United States against Iraq.[27] In October 2004, a Japanese Defense Agency panel report stipulated a requirement for launching preemptive strikes against enemy ballistic missile launch installations with a ballistic missile of its own.[28] Under pressure from its coalition partner, the Liberal Democratic Party decided to drop its ballistic missile study plan. But it subsequently became evident that Japanese planners had turned instead to considering LACMs. According to Japanese defense officials, they anticipate fewer obstacles, both inside and outside Japan, to acquiring cruise missiles rather than ballistic missiles.[29] Further, the high cost of purchasing land- and sea-based U.S. missile defenses, particularly in light of the ever-growing size of Chinese and North Korean offensive missile arsenals, furnishes economic and strategic logic for LACM acquisition. Cheaper offensive missile options allow the Japanese to mimic the U.S. military's doctrinal preference for "attack operations," or counterforce strikes to reduce the enemy's capacity to overwhelm missile defenses.[30]

Elsewhere in Northeast Asia, the United States has long sought to curb the missile ambitions of South Korea and Taiwan. Worried about a North-South arms race as well as sowing suspicion in Tokyo and Beijing if South Korea commenced a missile buildup, Washington persuaded Seoul to accept a 300-km-range/500-kilogram (kg) payload limit on ballistic missiles as a condition of South Korea's entry into the MTCR in 2001. Yet, despite the MTCR's equal treatment of ballistic and cruise missiles, Washington gave Seoul the go-ahead to develop LACMs no matter the range, as long as the payload was under 500 kg.[31] Shortly after Pyongyang's October 2006 nuclear test, South Korean military authorities leaked the existence of four LACM programs, with ranges between 500 and 1,500 km. The South Korean press took immediate note of the fact that not just all of North Korea but also Japan and China would be within range of these missiles.[32] The South Korean military nearly simultaneously rolled out a new defense plan, involving preemptive use of "surgical strike" weapons, including its LACMs, against enemy missile batteries.[33] For cost reasons, South Korea has also rejected America's wish to sell it its Patriot missile defense system.[34] Offensive solutions are clearly winning out over missile defense in South Korea.

A similar story is unfolding in Taiwan. Since the mid-1970s, Washington has pressured Taiwan to steer clear of ballistic missile development, while allowing Taipei to pursue a short-range anti-ship cruise missile. To cope with China's relentless buildup of ballistic missiles facing Taiwan, Washington preferred that Taipei purchase Patriot missile defenses. Taiwan finally did so in the mid-1990s but has thus far balked against purchasing the latest American "hit-to-kill" missile defenses due to their extraordinarily high cost and the realization that they won't alone suffice against China's new LACM developments. Increasingly openly, Taiwan now appears headed toward emphasizing offensive missiles as its best option. In early 2005, Taiwan test-fired its first LACM, initially to a range of 500 km, but with intentions to expand to 1,000 km and to deploy 500 of them on mobile launchers.[35] Taiwanese military analysts also spoke of a "preventive self-defense" strike option, entailing early preemptive use of cruise missiles to sow confusion in China's strike plans.[36] The U.S. State Department has pressured Taiwan to terminate its LACM program, but with little sign of success. Washington's long-standing policy against Taiwan's acquisition of ballistic missiles is showing signs of failure too. Taiwan told a visiting U.S. delegation in April 2007 that it is converting its Tien Kung air defense interceptor into a ballistic missile to complement its growing LACM ambitions.[37]

Nor is South Asia immune from the contagion. In early 2004, the Indian military rolled out a new offensive strategy, called "Cold Start," involving the capacity to conduct lightning strikes across the Line of Control in Kashmir followed by withdrawal before Pakistan had a chance to react.[38] Precision, long-range strikes, including India's new BrahMos LACM slated for deployment with Indian army units, would play a featured role in such a strategy. But Indian strategists have reacted to Pakistan's Babur LACM, which has a substantial range advantage over BrahMos (initially by 200 km, now 400 km, achieved in Pakistan's March 2007 test), by suggesting that

India approach its missile partner, Russia, to obtain certain "restrictive technologies" to match, or even greatly exceed, Babur's range. Such an expansion of BrahMos' capabilities is seen as feasible because, unlike Indian ballistic missile programs, the BrahMos cruise missile is "not under the global scanner."[39] The discrepancy in missile norms also came into play after Pakistan's surprise test launch of its Babur cruise missile in August 2005. Only a few days earlier, Pakistan and India had agreed in principle to notify each other before missile tests. But the agreement—like the Hague Code—dealt only with ballistic missiles.

IMPLICATIONS

Ballistic missiles have dominated the missile proliferation scene thus far. They emblematized ultimate military power during the Cold War. Iraq's use of modified Scud ballistic missiles during the 1991 Gulf War mesmerized the public with lasting images of duels between Iraqi ballistic Scuds and U.S. Patriot missile defenses. Ballistic missiles based on Scud technology have spread widely to potential American adversaries and, as a potential means of WMD delivery, they represent significant impediments to U.S. force projection and a potent means of future coercive diplomacy. An epidemic of cruise missile proliferation would aggravate matters gravely. If the use of large numbers of low-cost LACMs becomes a major feature of future military operations, a combination of cruise and ballistic missile attacks, even with conventional payloads, could make early entry into regional bases of operation increasingly problematic.[40] Nuclear, and possibly biological, payloads would produce catastrophic consequences.

By fixating on the familiar threat of ballistic missiles, strategic planners and nonproliferation specialists are in danger of overlooking the broader implications of cruise *and* ballistic missile proliferation. As far back as December 1996, a congressionally mandated independent review panel chaired by Robert Gates, former director of the Central Intelligence Agency and current secretary of defense, chided the intelligence community and, by implication, policymakers for "an inconsistency in . . . treatment of ballistic and cruise missiles."[41] While the Gates panel found ample reason for concern about cruise missile threats to the American homeland, it disclosed that the intelligence community had dismissed LACMs, despite their technological feasibility, largely because it could not imagine reasons and scenarios for their use. The intelligence community has since sought to treat missile threats with greater balance, but evenhandedness is far less evident in nonproliferation policy and missile defense planning.

Faulty nonproliferation policies need urgent attention. The second-class treatment of cruise missiles will not change until the Hague Code gives equal normative status to both ballistic and cruise missiles. A more progressive approach to addressing missile proliferation within the MTCR is also required to stanch the LACM epidemic. Given the cardinal importance of specialized knowledge in enabling indigenous development of LACMs—particularly those skills transferred through direct, face-to-face engagement between skilled practitioners and novice engineers—much better thinking is needed on ways and means of preventing, or interfering with, intangible technology transfers.

Better prospects for dampening intangible technology transfers would clearly flow from practices that encourage U.S. cooperation with Russia and China. One important priority for the next U.S. administration would be greatly increased transparency measures vis-à-vis both Russia and China in regard to U.S. defense programs —particularly on ballistic missile defenses, the U.S. nuclear posture, and growing U.S. reliance on conventionally armed global strike concepts. The new administration should work closely with Moscow on developing joint ballistic missile defense and early warning systems, which would eliminate a source of great tension between the two countries over the past two years.

The United States correctly points its finger at Russia and China (not a formal regime member but an avowed adherent to its principles) for their inconsistent export practices. Most notably, China's suspected support to Pakistan's new LACM program, if true, egregiously violates MTCR principles. On balance, however, it would be better to have China operating from within the MTCR than operating as a mere adherent, but only on the condition that Beijing adjust its behavior particularly in regard to accepting changes in the regime incorporated since 1993 that improve its treatment of cruise missile and UAV transfers. MTCR members should also encourage Russia to ignore any Indian requests for technological assistance to help India develop strategic-range LACMs in response to Pakistan's new cruise missile. And Russia should exercise extreme caution in selling the Russo-Indian Brah-Mos cruise missile to interested countries in Latin America and Southeast Asia, among others.

U.S. export behavior warrants adjustment as well. Unless the United States decides to add cruise missiles to the Hague Code, normative change is doomed. Washington should also reverse course in regard to its reported wish to loosen MTCR rules governing the sale of both large UAVs and missile defense interceptors and possibly remove interceptors altogether from MTCR consideration. Though the Bush administration has grand plans for global missile defenses and views UAVs as tools that allow for precision delivery of conventional weapons rather than WMD, it is foolish to view interceptors or large UAVs as purely defensive systems, incapable of offensive use. Large UAVs can deliver nuclear payloads or large quantities of biological or chemical agents, and the Soviet-era SA-2 interceptor has been widely used as a basis for building offensive ballistic missiles. In the end, incautious missile defense and UAV exports could accelerate rather than abate the LACM epidemic.

While improved defenses against short- and medium-range ballistic missiles have made LACMs more attractive offensive options for several states, cruise missile defense programs remain stalled. Fighters equipped with advanced detection and tracking radars will eventually possess some modest capability to deal with low-volume attacks. But existing U.S. programs are underfunded, while interoperability, doctrinal, and organizational issues discourage the military services from producing joint and effective systems for defending U.S. forces and allies in regional military campaigns. Homeland defense is even more sadly lacking: an August 2006 Pentagon assessment identified nine "capability gaps" that may not be rectified until 2015.[42]

Looming large in any missile defense debate is the question of affordability. During the height of the Reagan-era Strategic Defense Initiative, defense strategist Paul Nitze, no critic of missile defenses, argued that they should be "cost effective at the margin," meaning that it should be less expensive to make incremental improvements to missile defenses than it would be to achieve offensive gains. Whereas such a proposition always seemed dubious with respect to ballistic missiles, it appears inconceivable when large arsenals of relatively cheap cruise missiles are added to the mix. In a new era in which denying one's adversaries their military objectives has superseded mutual assured nuclear destruction as a strategic imperative, the missile defense challenge will stiffen immeasurably if LACMs spread. At the very least, the United States, as the predominant if not exclusive purveyor of missile defenses globally, should carefully remind its friends and allies of what its missile defenses can—and cannot—be expected to accomplish against current and prospective missile threats, ballistic and cruise missiles alike.

Though new weapons do not inherently increase the risk of conflict, when coupled with preemptive doctrines, advanced weapons that are difficult to detect and that could allow for a surprise attack—especially those seen as capable of producing decisive results without recourse to WMD—may tempt states to take risks. Past wars in the Middle East come readily to mind, and so too does China's increasing reliance on a doctrine espousing "actively taking the initiative" to catch the enemy unprepared.[43] That Taiwan, South Korea, and Japan, driven by the high costs of missile defenses and the perceived benefits of cruise missiles, have also turned to preemptive strike notions, ought to be a matter of great concern. By tying precision conventional strike weapons to truly offensive war doctrines, a number of states—including several great powers—may inadvertently be moving closer to lowering the vital threshold between peace and war. These developments suggest the urgent need for the United States to cut a path back to strategic stability by toning down, if not entirely eliminating, the preemption option.

ORGANIZATION

The book is divided into three parts. In Part One, *The Proliferation Context,* Chapter 1 has introduced the book's main arguments in brief and surveyed their implications for nonproliferation and defense planning. Chapter 2 examines broad trends in ballistic missile proliferation, particularly as they have begun to intersect with missile defenses, while Chapter 3 focuses on regional ballistic missile competitions. Chapter 4 first traces the development and use of LACMs in combat since World War II and then assesses the principal pathways by which they have expanded widely in recent years. Chapter 5 turns to examining the recent spate of new cruise missile programs that augurs a contagious spread of LACMs in the Middle East, South Asia, and Northeast Asia.

In Part Two, *Proliferation Instrumentalities,* Chapter 6 sizes up the role of special-ized knowledge, notably systems integration skills, as a critical factor in enabling the spread of LACMs. Chapter 7 examines recent changes in the narrative underpin-ning the appeal of LACMs—most importantly, the extent to which cruise missiles increase the cost and reduce the effectiveness of missile defenses. Chapter 8 explores the normative context within which states are making choices about missile acquisi-tion and employment. Two areas here merit special attention: missile nonprolifera-tion norms and preemptive military doctrines for missile use.

Part Three, *Policy Responses,* addresses the policy adjustments needed to stanch the spread of LACMs in the first place, or, barring that, to cope militarily with an increasingly toxic mix of ballistic and cruise missiles. Chapter 9 focuses on both non-proliferation and defense policy responses to the contagious spread of cruise missiles. The first line of defense in coping with signs of a missile epidemic is repairing missile nonproliferation policies, most notably developing improved ways to control intan-gible technology transfers. The chapter next examines alterations in current missile defense priorities needed to improve cruise missile defenses. Both regional and homeland defense requirements are explored. Chapter 9 concludes with a set of rec-ommendations designed to avert the unintended consequences of poorly crafted pol-icy choices. Most importantly, it suggests ways to engage Russia and China in efforts to dampen the missile contagion.

The Ballistic Missile Context

This book is largely about factors shaping the spread of land-attack cruise missiles (LACMs). But this phenomenon is by no means occurring in a vacuum. While it is conceivable that some countries will decide to acquire only cruise, rather than ballistic, missiles, or that cruise missiles will supplant existing ballistic missiles over time, the preponderance of evidence suggests that most nations will acquire a mix of the two. Sadly, there is no simple template against which nations choose the weapons they develop or acquire. Decisions to acquire weapons must be judged in the unique context of the acquiring state's security interests and needs, bureaucratic processes and politics, assessments of adversary strengths and weaknesses, and, because proliferation is not merely the product of raw technological determinism, access to specialized knowledge, which is most often provided by foreign sources. To set the stage for examining why an epidemic in cruise missile proliferation is on verge of occurring, it is essential to consider the context in which changes in knowledge, narrative, and norms are operating: that of an already substantial and potentially destabilizing level of ballistic missile proliferation.

The Nazi German V-1 cruise missile may have preceded its ballistic missile cousin, the V-2, into combat by three months, but once V-2 ballistic missiles began to fly towards Allied cities and ports in September 1944, they immediately eclipsed cruise missiles as the most fearful of Nazi "vengeance" weapons. On a purely objective basis neither the V-1 nor V-2 missile was particularly effective. According to an analysis by Steve Fetter, each V-2's one-ton warhead landing in London produced on average 5 deaths and 13 injuries, while damaging 40 buildings. Fetter also calculated that V-1 cruise missiles produced just over 2 deaths and 6 injuries per attack, lower than the V-2's casualties, since the V-1's noisy engine and slow speed furnished better warning than did the fast-traveling V-2's.[1]

The introduction of a standoff weapon for which there existed no adequate defense was psychologically demoralizing. Prior to the first V-2 missiles hitting London, R. V. Jones, British head of scientific intelligence for the Royal Air Force, articulated why British politicians so feared the German V-2 program, even though German bombers represented a much greater threat to Britain's population.

The answer is simple: no weapon yet produced has a comparable romantic appeal. Here is a 13-ton missile which traces out a flaming ascent to heights hitherto beyond the reach of man, and hurls itself 200 miles across the stratosphere at unparalleled speed to descend—with luck—on a *defenceless* target.[2] (Emphasis added)

Thus, however ineffective ballistic missiles armed with conventional warheads would prove to be objectively, their capacity to invoke a heavy sense of defenselessness demonstrated that they could take a significant toll psychologically and thus politically, which, after all, is the prime objective of warfare. Furthermore, ballistic missiles can have a comparative advantage over reusable manned aircraft carrying substantially larger payloads in some circumstances. Between September 1944 and March 1945, over 3,000 German V-2 ballistic missiles delivered 2,400 tons of high explosive, killing about 7,000 people. By contrast, on February 23, 1945, in a brief 22 minutes, 361 British Lancaster bombers dropped 1,571 tons of high explosive on the German town of Pforzheim, killing about 17,000 people.[3] But by that late date in the war, the Allies had largely decimated the German Luftwaffe as a defensive force, thereby greatly reducing the risks of such large bomber attacks. Had Germany's air defenses been thicker, Allied bombers might have had to attack lower-value targets instead of higher-value ones furnished with substantial protection. According to Allied Supreme Commander Dwight D. Eisenhower, had the Germans managed to perfect their V-weapons six months earlier, the invasion of Europe might not have been possible.[4]

USE OF BALLISTIC MISSILES AFTER WORLD WAR II

After World War II, ballistic missile acquisition and use would prove appealing to an increasing number of states. Ballistic missiles figured in six different conflicts, including the Egyptian and Syrian missile attacks on Israel in the 1973 Yom Kippur War, the 1985–88 War of the Cities between Iraq and Iran, the Afghan civil war from 1988–1991, the 1991 Persian Gulf War, the Yemen civil war of 1994, and the 2003 U.S.-led invasion of Iraq. The most notable were the War of the Cities and the two Persian Gulf Wars of 1991 and 2003.

In the Iraq-Iran war, both sides sparsely used ballistic missiles until 1985, when Iraq began to attack Tehran with its new al-Hussein missiles. This campaign culminated in a period of six weeks during 1988 in which about 190 Iraqi missiles killed some 2,000 people. More broadly, the missile attacks terrorized the Iranian people, leading to the evacuation of roughly one-half Tehran's population. Iran's responsive attacks on Baghdad, involving about 90 Scud missiles, seemed to have little effect on Iraqi morale.[5] There appears little doubt that Iraq's war-fighting strategy of employing ballistic missiles as terror weapons figured importantly in Tehran's decision to seek a cease-fire and eventual conclusion of the war in 1988. According to some specialists, Iraq's threat of attacking Tehran with chemically armed missiles figured heavily into Iran's decision to accept a less than balanced outcome to the war.[6] Iraq had repeatedly employed blister and nerve agents against Iranian military targets during the war with some notable tactical success, but possible "strategic" use of such potent weapons was quite another matter. Missile use in the War of the Cities also profoundly influenced Saudi Arabia to obtain, from China, 2,500-km-range CSS-2 ballistic missiles—a deal struck reportedly a few months after Iran's Scud attacks on Iraq in March 1985.[7]

In the 1990–91 Persian Gulf War, Iraq threatened to use its Scud and al-Hussein ballistic missiles as both a means of deterrence and escalation control.[8] Iraq's missile threat failed to deter the U.S.-led United Nations Coalition from commencing Operation Desert Storm to retake Kuwait. Once active combat commenced in January 1991, however, Iraq used its ballistic missile force—successfully firing 81 ballistic missiles altogether, 31 of which were fired at Israel—in part to escalate the conflict by disrupting coalition operations and drawing Israel into the war. Iraq nearly achieved the latter objective. Because U.S.-deployed Patriot missile defense batteries could not successfully intercept most of Iraq's ballistic missiles, and U.S. warplanes were unable to find and attack any of Iraq's mobile missile launchers, Israel came perilously close to intervening, which risked splitting the fragile coalition at a decisive point in the war.[9]

The strategic lessons of Iraq's ballistic missile attacks for both Israel and the United States became clear in the war's aftermath. Israel's previous ambivalence about investing in costly ballistic missile defenses was no longer politically viable.[10] After the war, with U.S. financial support, Israel would embark on developing the Arrow missile defense system. America, too, had entered the war unprepared to deal with Iraq's missile threat. When Iraq's divisions dispatched Kuwait with ease in its August 1990 invasion, only three experimental Patriot Advanced Capability-2 (PAC-2) interceptors existed in the U.S. Army's inventory.[11] Fortunately, Saddam Hussein gave the U.S.-led coalition six months, in which the U.S. Army could pull the PAC-2 system out of its test program and undertake an emergency production effort. When the air campaign began in mid-January 1991, enough Patriot missile defense batteries were deployed in Israel and Saudi Arabia to foster the illusion, if not the reality, of some degree of defense capability against Iraq's missile threat. Together with U.S. diplomatic pressure, it was enough to convince Israeli leaders not to intervene. After the war, however, the U.S. Government Accountability Office determined that at best only 9 percent of Iraq's missiles were successfully engaged.[12] Patriot's radar experienced difficulty distinguishing real missiles from missile debris created when Iraqi Scuds broke up after reentering the atmosphere. Patriot interceptors proved much better at knocking incoming missiles off course rather than destroying the warhead, which explains why their success rate in Saudi Arabia (defending small point targets like airbases) was better than in Israel (protecting large urban areas).[13] When an errant Iraqi Scud hit a U.S. military barracks at Dhahran, Saudi Arabia near the war's close, over 100 American soldiers lost their lives. This was more than enough to justify what would become more than a $3 billion investment in improving Patriot missile defenses in the decade after the 1991 war.[14]

The second Gulf War in 2003 at once legitimated U.S. investments in upgrading Patriot missile defenses while also demonstrating the system's continuing weaknesses. Leading up to the war, faulty intelligence assessments of Iraq's WMD holdings included poor appraisals about that nation's missile arsenal. It was fair to assume—

and was proven correct during the war—that Iraq possessed at least a small force of al-Samoud short-range ballistic missiles, capable of ranges between 150 to 200 km. At these short ranges, al-Samouds could not practically threaten regional targets unless Iraq managed to deploy them in the northern or southern fly zones—a dubious proposition. Intelligence assessments, which proved wrong in the end, suggested that Iraq might have possessed a small number of longer-range al-Hussein ballistic missiles, capable of delivering a primitively armed chemical or biological payload to a range of 650 km. Iraq had admitted to the United Nations (UN) Special Commission that before the 1991 war it had filled 25 warheads with anthrax, botulinum toxin, and aflatoxin, and 50 others with the mixed chemical agents sarin and cyclosarin.[15]

Also of concern was knowledge that before the 1991 war Saddam Hussein had handed pre-delegated authority to his commanders to launch biological- and chemical-armed missiles if nuclear weapons were used against his regime or Baghdad was threatened. With regime change a declared U.S. goal this time around, the fear was that Saddam might be more inclined to use WMD-armed missiles against both civilian and military targets. But instead of WMD-armed al-Hussein missiles, Iraq used al-Samoud and Ababil ballistic missiles, which, due to their shorter ranges and slower speeds, proved easier to intercept. In all, of the 19 ballistic missiles Iraq launched at coalition targets in Kuwait and Iraq, only nine threatened potential targets (the others landed in deserted areas). All nine were successfully intercepted and destroyed, vastly exceeding Patriot's performance record in 1991.[16]

But America's missile defenses were not without flaws. While the American missile defense system batted one thousand against ballistic missiles, it struck out entirely when Patriot batteries and missile warning systems, such as the U.S. Air Force's Airborne Warning and Control System (AWACS), failed to detect or intercept any of the five primitive Iraqi cruise missiles launched against coalition targets. One came close to hitting a Marine command post on the first day of the war, while the others landed innocently or produced minor damage to civilian targets. More ominous for the future, however, was the fact that Iraq's use of both ballistic and cruise missiles forced Patriot radars to search for both high- and low-angle missiles, thereby probably contributing to Patriot's unfortunate series of friendly-fire incidents, including the loss of two aircraft, and worse, the deaths of three crew members. None of this should have surprised military planners. Over the preceding decade of the 1990s, the Pentagon had detailed in depth the abysmal state of cruise missile defenses and steps needed to rectify shortcomings.[17] What did surprise American war planners was the unexpected Iraqi use of both ballistic and cruise missiles, which portended more demanding missile defense challenges to come.

THE GROWING UTILITY OF BALLISTIC MISSILES

The preceding partial review of ballistic missile use in combat since World War II certainly suggests that conventionally armed ballistic missiles have yet to demonstrate that they can achieve decisive military effects with any degree of certainty. As Aaron

Karp has wisely observed, the military effects of conventionally armed ballistic missiles are "highly contingent on numerous considerations, mitigated by their unreliability and inaccuracy, by targeting choices, geography, numbers, and an opponent's morale and ability to take countermeasures."[18] War is an uncertain enough pursuit without depending on weapons that inherently add uncertainty to its outcome. Military strategists appreciate the enduring meaning of Prussian strategist Helmuth von Moltke's 19th century admonition, "No plan of operations can look with any certainty beyond the first meeting with major forces of the enemy."[19] Of course, arming ballistic missiles with nuclear weapons—and conceivably biological or more remotely chemical weapons—would surely improve the changes of a decisive outcome, but not without incalculable consequences, most notably should it involve breaking the long-standing taboo on nuclear use. Thus, at least since the early 1980s, military planners have tried to exploit conventionally armed ballistic missiles largely through dabbling with things they have some degree of control over: improving missile reliability and accuracy, thinking more creatively about targeting choices, and integrating missile use into the larger framework of operational art.

One of the most creative and persistent advocates of exploiting the revolution in technologies supporting precision delivery of conventional weapons, including conventionally armed ballistic missiles, was the chief of the Soviet General Staff, Marshal Nikolai Ogarkov (as a Colonel-General in the late 1960s, Ogarkov was the second-ranking and a highly influential member of the Soviet delegation to the first U.S.-Soviet strategic arms limitation talks). In an oft-quoted interview in the Soviet military newspaper Krasnaya Zvezda of May 8, 1984, Marshal Ogarkov summed up the essence of what we call today a "revolution in military affairs":

> Rapid changes in the development of conventional means of destruction and the emergence in the developed countries of automated search and destroy complexes, long-range high-accuracy terminally guided combat systems, unmanned flying machines and qualitatively new electronic control systems make many types of weapons global and make it possible to sharply increase (by an order of magnitude) the destructive potential of conventional weapons, bring them closer, so to speak, to weapons of mass destruction in terms of effectiveness. The sharply increased range of conventional weapons makes it possible immediately to extend active combat operations . . . to the whole country's territory, which was not possible in past wars. This qualitative leap in the development of conventional means of destruction will inevitably entail a change in the nature of the preparation and conduct of operations. This, in turn, predetermines the possibility of conducting military operations using conventional systems in qualitatively new, incomparable, more destructive forms than before. Operations and the role and significance of the initial period of the war and its first operations become incomparably greater.[20]

Marshal Ogarkov's comments about advanced conventional weapons achieving, or at least coming closer to approximating, the effectiveness of nuclear weapons accented the mid-1980s' missile defense wars. Proponents of President Reagan's Strategic Defense Initiative (SDI), pejoratively cast by the media as "Star Wars," tended toward the view that newly deployed Soviet theater ballistic missiles, with ranges of between 300 to 1,000 km, and armed with advanced conventional munitions, were capable of independently destroying complex targets like North Atlantic Treaty Organization (NATO) airbases, which then were assigned either nuclear weapons or several conventionally armed fighter-bombers. Thus, to SDI proponents, such an important threat demanded anti-tactical ballistic missile (ATBM) defenses greatly exceeding what was intended with regard to upgrading the Patriot air defense system.[21] Conversely, SDI's opponents, who had difficulty separating ATBM from SDI (the former were seen as a "stalking horse" for the latter), downgraded the threat of conventionally armed ballistic missiles by simply taking the SDI proponents' exaggerated argument and disproving it.[22]

Starting in the early 1970s, what in fact did occur was the Soviet development of a new generation of short-range ballistic missiles with greatly improved range and accuracy and a significant increase in launchers deployed forward in Eastern Europe. Soviet military specialists at the time claimed that such accuracies were obtained by combining upgraded inertial guidance with either in-flight updates or terminal guidance.[23] After the most prominent of these new ballistic missiles, the Soviet SS-23, was eliminated as part of the 1987 Intermediate-Range Nuclear Forces (INF) Treaty, it was discovered that its guidance system contained improved inertial guidance with an onboard digital computer and a terminal homing system employing an active millimeter wave radar that compared what the missile's radar detected with a stored image of the target. Overall, the missile possessed a 30-m circular error probability (CEP) accuracy, meaning that the missile's payload would be expected to land half the time within the radius of a 30-m circle.[24] From positions in Eastern Europe, Soviet and Warsaw Pact missile batteries could target NATO airbases and nuclear storage facilities throughout the depth of Western Europe, including the United Kingdom. But missiles alone would not be expected to achieve the success desired by Soviet planners. Indeed, their primary role was to leverage the effectiveness of an equally expanding dimension of Soviet conventional firepower: aircraft-delivered conventional weapons. During the 1970s, dramatic improvements were made in Soviet Frontal Aviation, including nearly a doubling in offensive load capacity and 70 percent more versatility in comparison with the predecessor generation of aircraft.[25] By 1978, the Central Intelligence Agency had estimated that Soviet Frontal Aviation's share of Soviet defense spending was about twice that of the Strategic Rocket Forces.[26]

Rather than counting on ballistic missiles alone to achieve decisive military effects, Soviet planners instead viewed these weapons as improving the prospects of a massive conventional "air operation." The goals of the air operation derived from two major problems confronting Soviet military planners in the mid-1980s. On the one hand, NATO airpower was seen as capable of neutralizing the Warsaw Pact's superiority in ground forces. On the other hand, NATO theater nuclear forces threatened escalatory strikes on the Soviet homeland. Alone, conventionally armed aircraft—the heart of the Soviet air operation—were incapable of furnishing the shock and damage effectiveness of nuclear weapons. To remedy this shortcoming, Soviet planners devised a truly combined-arms approach, involving significant contributions from conventionally armed ballistic missiles, aircraft, radioelectronic combat (jamming, chaff, etc.), airborne and heliborne assaults, and special-purpose (Spetsnaz) forces.

The key to achieving success, thought the Soviets, lay in taking preemptive action during the so-called "initial period of war," when one's adversary had yet to fully mobilize. This would have almost certainly been the case in regard to reinforcing Europe with U.S. divisions situated in peacetime in the continental United States. But it applied even more to compounding the inherent tendency of NATO airpower to operate with reduced efficiency in the initial stages of a war, a factor born out in Western historical experience.[27] Of course, the reduced efficiency of airpower during the initial period of war could have affected both NATO and the Warsaw Pact. But, as one Soviet analyst observed:

> even where both opposing sides had considerable forces and means but one of them preempted the other in deploying and launching an attack, the outcome of operations in the initial period placed the nation subjected to surprise attack in an extremely difficult situation.[28]

Thus, the goal of preemption, or usurping control at the outset, is not to win in one blow but to adjust the initial conditions so as to predetermine a favorable outcome.

Traditionally, nuclear-armed missiles played the featured role in Soviet notions of preemption.[29] The conventional air assault became, in effect, an operational substitute for the initial mass nuclear strike. The success of subsequent ground operations depended on the air operation's achieving preemptive shock effect on an unprepared NATO. Timing was critical: the first shots of a war in Europe would have been the air operation's leading edge attacks by conventionally armed ballistic missiles, largely preceding any contact between Warsaw Pact ground units and NATO's covering forces by a couple of hours.

Before the advent of accurate ballistic missiles, if the Soviets sought to commence war in Europe with conventional weapons, they would have had to allocate a majority of their first-wave aircraft to suppressing NATO's air defenses—a daunting task indeed. Furthermore, without the benefit of ballistic missiles a massive air operation's first wave of attacks risked the loss of tactical surprise. Even if Soviet decisionmakers chose to attack without reinforcing Eastern European air bases with aircraft from the Soviet Union, NATO could have still tracked Warsaw Pact aircraft from takeoff. Successful tracking and quick response would have permitted some NATO interceptors to fill potential air corridors, thereby increasing Warsaw Pact aircraft attrition rates during the critical initial mass strike. Moreover, by not being assured that NATO's ground-based air defenses were effectively suppressed, Warsaw Pact pilots would have had to fly low-altitude penetration routes at the risk of suffering losses from traditional low-altitude anti-aircraft guns and missiles. Most important of all, however, the need to suppress enemy air defenses with aircraft would diminish the effectiveness of the initial blow on the primary target set: NATO nuclear weapons and airfields.

A precursor ballistic missile attack, executed minutes before the first-wave air strike, was designed precisely to mitigate the drawbacks just enumerated. The chances of achieving tactical surprise, and thereby catching NATO aircraft on the ground, were materially improved by employing missiles first: their flight times ranged from 30 seconds to five minutes, the latter being roughly half the flight time of aircraft. In the absence of effective NATO missile defenses, Soviet missiles had a greater assurance than aircraft of penetrating to suppress NATO air defenses. Aircraft released from such missions could then fly to the primary target set using higher and deeper routes with heavier payloads. What's more, if missiles succeeded in pinning down the main body of aircraft at NATO airbases, fewer allied interceptors would have entered Warsaw Pact air penetration corridors to meet the first-wave air strike. By assuming primary responsibility for the suppression of NATO air defenses, missiles yielded a predictable enhancement in aircraft performance and overall efficiency. As one Soviet writer put it, "the use of a missile can replace a number of aircraft sorties which are expensive and which stand a chance of being destroyed by the enemy's air defense means."[30]

Thus, while several Western analysts in the early 1990s viewed conventionally armed ballistic missiles as plainly cost ineffective—particularly when compared with aircraft—Soviet analysts saw just the opposite. Missiles didn't simply replace aircraft for certain missions, but enabled more expensive and reusable manned platforms, each of which could deliver on average seven times the payload of a ballistic missile, to achieve decisive results in the critical opening hours of conflict. Missile leveraging of aircraft effectiveness largely came about by virtue of improved missile accuracy, launcher increases, and range enhancement.[31] The lesson is that conventionally armed ballistic missiles are most usefully regarded as an integrated element of combined-arms warfare in a major theater of war, not merely as simple counterforce targeting devices.

The logic and rationale that formed the basis of the Soviet air operation, including the essential role played by conventionally armed ballistic missiles, is reflected in current Chinese military writings. Like their Soviet counterparts, Chinese strategists devote considerable space to the importance of seizing the initiative from the very beginning of a conflict. In an illuminating analysis of contemporary Chinese military strategy based on extensive review of Chinese military literature, RAND Corporation analysts quote one Chinese military analyst as saying that "in a high-tech local war, a belligerent which adopts a passive defensive strategy and launches no offensive against the enemy is bound to fold its hands and await destruction."[32]

Chinese strategy is also conditioned by a recognition that for some time the Chinese are likely to be inferior to their potential adversaries. This clearly is the case in regard to the United States, but it is also true with respect to Taiwan, to the extent that Taiwan has a comprehensively superior air force. If China is prevented from obtaining air superiority, any prospective Chinese cross-strait military campaign is likely to fail. Chinese strategists view their growing arsenal of conventionally armed ballistic missiles as a means of trumping the Taiwanese air force. The sheer shock value of ballistic missiles, not to speak of the possible difficulty of defending against them, can have a successful coercive effect on one's adversary. Thus, exercising them in peacetime or even using them for demonstration purposes, as China in fact did off Taiwan's shores in 1995–96, fits into the Chinese notion of deterrence operations. More provocatively, ballistic missiles could be employed against a small set of targets or used as part of a larger military operation involving a coercive blockade.[33] Most auspiciously, Chinese ballistic missiles could constitute a central component of a surprise attack designed to achieve Chinese air superiority.

First, to credibly threaten airfield runways and other critically important point targets (air defense installations, command-and-control facilities, etc.), the latest Chinese ballistic missiles must be at least as accurate as the Soviet SS-23. This now appears feasible. Over seven years ago, U.S. Defense Secretary William Cohen's "Report to Congress on the Security Situation in the Taiwan Strait" stated that the Pentagon expected China to incorporate satellite-assisted navigation technology into missiles aimed at Taiwan by 2005. Indeed, as noted in Chapter 1, China completed deployment of the Beidou 1 satellite navigation and positioning system in late 2007 and has plans for a 35-satellite constellation with global coverage and much-improved accuracy. Second, the contemplated role of Chinese ballistic missiles would have to remain modest. In his otherwise excellent book published in 2000, Paul Bracken argues that 45 Chinese missiles loaded with conventional warheads could "virtually close the ports, airfields, water works, and power plants, and destroy [Taiwan's] oil storage."[34] The reality is that while highly accurate ballistic missiles with conventional payloads can play a critically important role, aircraft-delivered munitions must be counted on to deliver the most telling blow.

As with the Soviet air operation, China views missiles as a means of temporarily closing Taiwanese airfields, thereby pinning down Taiwan's superior air force and exposing it to aircraft bombardment.[35] Missile strikes would also leverage Chinese aircraft effectiveness by attacking Taiwanese airfield runways, airbase command and control, early warning radar facilities, and ground-based air defenses.[36] Aircraft released from these missions could fly higher and deeper routes with heavier payloads and concentrate on reducing Taiwanese air sorties to a minimum. The Chinese literature closely mimics previously classified lecture materials from the Soviet-era Voroshilov General Staff Academy, which emphasize that the weight of the initial blow, comprising leading-edge missile attacks, can "create favorable conditions for effective actions of friendly air forces, ensure better results of actions against enemy airfields, contain the deployment or redeployment of the enemy air forces [by pinning them down on or out of the airbase], neutralize [their] activity, and deprive [them] of the initiative and the capability to support ground forces."[37] According to Mark A. Stokes, who served as a U.S. military attaché in China, contemporary Chinese literature sees missile strikes against airbase runways and taxiways as designed to "shock and paralyze air defense systems to allow a window of opportunity for follow-on PLAAF [People's Liberation Army Air Force] strikes and rapid achievement of air superiority."[38] Perhaps the major difference between Chinese and Soviet articulation of the role of missiles is that China foresees missile strikes, applied in a combined-arms fashion, affecting not just the achievement of air superiority but also information and sea dominance.[39]

Two other facets relating to the Chinese approach to employing missiles merit brief mention. The first is the challenge of carefully orchestrating the command-and-control arrangements associated with any complex combined-arms campaign. Chinese planners envision creating a Firepower Coordination Center within the Joint Theater Command, which would manage the application of firepower at the theater level of warfare. Separate coordination cells would be created to deal with missile strikes, air strikes, special operations, and ground and naval forces. Most germane to missile-air interaction would be an airspace coordination cell, which would de-conflict and coordinate the delicate execution of integrated strikes from missiles and aircraft.

A second issue regarding the effectiveness of conventionally armed ballistic missiles relates to achieving the required volume of fire within a specific timeframe. Soviet writers referred to the intensity of fire as essential to suppressing the adversary.[40] The notion of compressing firepower into a short period of time saw its most dramatic expression in the development of carrier aviation in the mid-1920s. During that period, war-gaming at the U.S. Naval War College in Newport, Rhode Island demonstrated that discrete pulses of combat power (namely, carrier-based airpower) were more effective than the continuous streams of firepower emanating from battleships. The effectiveness of such pulses depended critically on the number of aircraft a carrier could launch in a given unit of time. Naval analysts also learned from applying pulse power in war games about the advantages of striking first with carrier aviation, which is certainly a lesson demonstrably present in both Soviet and Chinese military writings on achieving air superiority.[41] According to the Pentagon's 2007 annual assessment of Chinese military power, seven missile brigades, with between 180 and 210 DF-11/DF-15 short-range missile launchers, with between 875 and 975 missiles, face Taiwan. This compares with a projected 1990 Soviet deployment of 234 SS-22/SS-23 missile launchers and perhaps 1,400 missiles in East Germany and Czechoslovakia before the breakup of the Soviet Union.[42] Missile launchers, like aircraft launched from a carrier, are the appropriate measure of the intensity of fire within a unit of time. Taiwan, compared with NATO in Central Europe circa 1990, has far fewer important targets against which Chinese missiles might be employed. While NATO had at least 20 main operating bases in its Central Region, Taiwan reportedly concentrates all of its most important combat aircraft on only three main operating bases: roughly 60 Mirage 2000 air defense aircraft are housed at one airfield, while two other airbases support around 120 F-16 air defense/attack aircraft.[43] It is also fair to say that the same disparity in target numbers applies equally as well to other critical target sets, including air defense sites, early warning radars, command-and-control facilities, and logistical storage sites. Thus, China would appear to have a healthy sufficiency of launchers. Overall, China has more than adequately absorbed Soviet doctrinal and planning practices for integrated missile and air operations. These lessons and practices are relevant not only for a potential contingency against Taiwan, but also for an anti-access campaign against U.S. military forces seeking to deploy in the region.[44]

GLOBAL BALLISTIC MISSILE TRENDS

Although there is evidence of qualitative improvements in ballistic missiles that make them relevant to modern warfare, quantitative trends in ballistic missile prolif-eration—at least on the surface—indicate a decline. In early 2005, a prominent American analyst of nonproliferation issues asserted that ballistic missile prolifera-tion and the threat that it engenders have actually abated substantially since the end of the Cold War.[45] Seen through the particular lens that this analyst employed —a decidedly American one concerned primarily with ballistic missiles capable of striking the homeland and the rationale for missile defenses—there is ample truth to such an argument. But were one to view missile proliferation developments from Taipei, Beijing, Tokyo, Seoul, New Delhi, Islamabad, Tel Aviv, Tehran, or the Penta-gon, for that matter, the conclusion would undoubtedly be otherwise.

The primary reason for a declining global ballistic missile arsenal primarily relates to reductions in U.S. and Russian intercontinental-range missile systems. At the start of 2007, Russia deployed 489 intercontinental ballistic missiles (ICBMs), including 76 SS-18s, 123 SS-19s, 243 SS-25s, and 47 SS-27s. Its sea-based missile force included 173 (83 SS-N-18s and 90 SS-N-23s) submarine-launched ballistic missiles (SLBMs) for a total of 662 long-range ballistic missiles. This represents a 72 percent reduction from a Cold War high of 2,380 ICBMs and SLBMs. In early 2007, America deployed 500 Minuteman III ICBMs, of which 50 were slated for elimina-tion by late 2007, and 336 Trident II SLBMs for a total of 836. This is about half of the Cold War deployment of 1,710 long-range ballistic missiles.[46]

Reductions in intermediate-range ballistic missiles (or IRBMs, with ranges between 3,000 and 5,500 km) are even more dramatic, again because of arms con-trol. The INF Treaty of 1987 eliminated an entire class of U.S. and Soviet IRBMs; it covered both nuclear and conventional ground-launched ballistic and cruise mis-siles with ranges of 500 to 5,500 km. France and the United Kingdom eliminated their IRBM systems and replaced them with small inventories of SLBMs. China, for its part, still maintains 20 DF-4 IRBMs. Thus, largely due to the INF Treaty, the IRBM category has undergone a 97 percent decrease in its overall numbers. But other aspirants to IRBMs intend to increase global numbers in the coming years. North Korea has fitfully pursued the Taepodong-2 IRBM/ICBM, which is assessed to have a range somewhere between 3,500 and 6,000 km. More ominous is North Korea's April 2007 parading of a new IRBM (called the BM-25 in the media) which reportedly has a range of between 2,500 and 4,000 km and is based on the former Soviet Union's SS-N-6 SLBM. Rumors circulating in both the German and Israeli press suggest that Iran has acquired the BM-25 from North Korea.[47] India, too, tested its Agni-3 IRBM to a range of 3,500 km on April 12, 2007, and Indian tech-nicians associated with the Agni-3 program now claim that they could extend the missile's reach to intercontinental ranges within a two- to three-year timeframe, should the government wish them to do so.[48] Thus, Northeast Asia, South Asia, and the Middle East appear destined to become worrisome loci of IRBM growth.

The INF Treaty also affected global levels of medium-range ballistic missiles (or MRBMs, with ranges between 1,000 and 3,000 km). But INF reductions were offset by a substantial buildup of MRBMs in key regional settings. China, North Korea, India, Pakistan, Israel, Iran, and Saudi Arabia currently possess MRBMs, while China has deployed a medium-range SLBM force. Thus, while the overall MRBM deployment numbers may have fallen slightly off from Cold War-era numbers (from 547 in combined U.S., French, Russian, and Chinese forces in 1987 to perhaps a number today closing in on 1987's numbers).[49] Viewed from a regional perspective, proliferation of MRBMs shows strong signs of worsening over the next decade and beyond.

Short-range ballistic missiles (SRBMs) of less than 1,000-km range constitute the largest segment of the global ballistic missile arsenal. Twenty-nine nations besides the 5 recognized nuclear-weapon states (United States, Russia, United Kingdom, France, and China) possess ballistic missiles, but 21 of the 29 have only Scud-B (300 km) or related longer-range derivatives. It is true that SRBMs are generally viewed as "non-strategic" delivery systems. But in the confined geographic circumstances of the Middle East or the Taiwan Straits, SRBMs acquire the status of strategic weapons. Were Syrian SRBMs to become as accurate as Chinese SRBMs facing Taiwan, Israel would probably regard them as strategic weapons. Further, the 1998 "Commission to Assess the Ballistic Missile Threat to the United States," chaired by Donald Rumsfeld, argued that "a nation with a well-developed, Scud-based ballistic missile infrastructure would be able to achieve first flight of a long-range missile, up to and including intercontinental ballistic missile range (greater than 5,500 km), within about five years of deciding to do so."[50] This conclusion proved highly controversial in regard to quickly scaling up to ICBM ranges: even though North Korea possessed a "well-developed" ballistic missile infrastructure and Iran was placing "extraordinary emphasis on its ballistic missile and WMD development programs," after nearly a decade neither country appears ready to flight-test an ICBM.[51] But there is far less disagreement over the possibility that a country's Scud inventory could be used to reach the MRBM or even IRBM range levels.[52]

Ballistic Missiles and Regional Competitions

There is no simple way to compare regional ballistic missile programs. Disparate reasons inform the acquisition motivations of regional competitors. Some states are driven by the prestige value of joining an elite club of nations who pursue the "trappings of power" through acquiring or developing their own ballistic missile.[1] Others may view ballistic missiles as a preferred alternative to costly and more vulnerable air forces. More advanced states, which are capable of producing accurate, conventionally armed ballistic missiles, are driven by the desire to improve their own air forces' effectiveness vis-à-vis the perceived vulnerability of their enemies' air forces. And others wish to derive coercive effects from brandishing ballistic missiles capable of delivering conventional or WMD payloads. Whether regional powers are aiming to threaten their neighbors or to deny the United States entry into the region, ballistic missiles have a distinct appeal because a successfully launched ballistic missile has a higher probability of delivering its payload to its target compared with other means. Thus, while the notion of ballistic missile competition differs decidedly from region to region, a new phenomenon affecting regional balances is the introduction of increasingly effective ballistic missile defenses that promise to alter the dynamics of each regional competition.

MIDDLE EAST

Ballistic missiles have become a prized commodity among several belligerent states in the Middle East faced with Israeli technological and military superiority. These states include Syria, Iran, and Saudi Arabia, although the Saudi acquisition of Chinese-supplied DF-3A medium-range ballistic missiles (MRBMs) in 1985 is of far less military significance than Syria's and Iran's growing missile holdings. At present, neither Syria nor Iran has the capacity to undertake military attacks with conventionally armed ballistic missiles aimed at significantly disrupting Israel's decided offensive air superiority over these two adversaries. Both Syria and Iran, whose air forces do not remotely measure up to Israel's, seem more inclined at present toward developing the capacity to threaten Israel with chemical, biological, and eventually, in Iran's case, nuclear weapons.[2]

According to the National Air and Space Intelligence Center (NASIC), Syria's missile arsenal is largely a Scud-based one, the only exception being the SS-21 (100 km). Otherwise, Syria deploys the Scud-B (300 km), Scud-C (500 km), and

Scud-D (700 km).[3] Syria has depended from the 1960s on foreign assistance, first from the former Soviet Union, and more recently from North Korea, China, and Iran.[4] North Korea is believed to have transferred the Scud-D, which is thought to possess a separating warhead and course correction capabilities that could conceivably improve its accuracy.[5] NASIC does not provide estimates of the number of Scuds or SS-21s that Syria has produced or acquired from external sources, but it does show "fewer than 50" launchers available for every system save for the longest-range missile, Scud-D.[6] With what could be as many as 100 launchers facing Israel, there is more than ample potential, in theory, for generating a significant volume of fire. Were Syria somehow to achieve the accuracy of the Chinese missiles facing Taiwan, a more militarily significant threat would face Israel.

In light of the cramped geography of the region (the two nations' capitals are less than 100 km from their common borders), all of Israel is easily within range of Syrian missiles. In the early 1990s, when Israel had yet to commit fully to deploying significant missile defenses, even Syria's inaccurate Scuds (900-m circular error probability [CEP]), together with the more accurate but shorter-range SS-21 (150-m CEP), were seen as a potentially serious threat to Israel's air forces in that they could arrive on their targets with little warning and cause significant damage in a short period of time.[7] But today, any short-term effects from missile attacks—most likely SS-21s, due to their greater accuracy—would probably remain unexploited by Syrian air forces, which may be large but are marked by poor pilot training and low operational readiness.[8] Moreover, orchestrating an effective combined-arms operation would require that Syrian air and missile forces be more skilled in coordinating and executing closely timed missile and air strikes than they appear to be.

Israeli missile defenses further devalue the threat of Syria's ballistic missiles. Since the 1991 Gulf War, Israel has been fully committed, with U.S. cooperation, to deploying missile defenses. Most important is the development of the Arrow-2 missile defense system, which was purposefully designed to handle ballistic missiles with ranges of up to 1,500 km and to intercept incoming missiles at a much higher altitude—up to 50 km—than Patriot missile interceptors. Thus, in theory, Arrow-2 interceptors are far more likely to destroy longer-range missile threats before any inadvertent atmospheric breakup occurs (as in the 1991 war, when Patriot PAC-2 missiles faced 600-km-range al-Hussein ballistic missiles).[9] Insofar as interception could take place over adversary territory, this possibility also raises risks to the adversary—particularly when, as is likely to be the case with Syria or Iran, the ballistic missile is carrying a chemical payload.

Israel intends to have a nationwide missile defense system deployed by 2010.[10] This system will consist of three batteries of Arrow-2 missiles, two of which are deployed thus far. Israel has also enhanced its attack warning capability, which is critical to initiating timely passive defense measures such as donning protective masks in case of chemical attack. Israel has deployed two intelligence satellites—the Eros and Ofeg-5—that provide independent evidence of threat activities. The Arrow's Green Pine target-tracking radar also furnishes Israel with its own source of missile launch evidence, which can be enhanced further with information provided by the American Defense Support Program satellites that detect ballistic missile launch plumes from geosynchronous orbits. The U.S.-furnished Patriot PAC-2, and possibly PAC-3, will complement Israel's Arrow deployments by completing a two-tier missile defense system and will furnish point defenses for Israeli cities and other strategically important targets, such as the Negev Nuclear Research Center, which is now within range of not only Iranian ballistic missiles but also Syria's Scud-D missiles.

It thus seems improbable that Syria will develop a sufficient number of advanced ballistic missiles to counter Israel's missile defense. That is not for want of trying. In 2004, Syria sought to procure the new Russian SS-26 ballistic missile system, known as the Iskander-E, which has a range of roughly 280 km.[11] Designed apparently as a replacement for the Intermediate-Range Nuclear Forces-banned SS-23 ballistic missile, the SS-26's range and accuracy are probably similar to the SS-23's, though it appears that an export version with a MTCR-compliant range of under the regime's 300-km threshold was necessary to ensure that the missile would not antagonize Moscow's fellow MTCR member states.[12] Were Syria to acquire the new SS-26, its advantages relative to Israeli offensive and defensive options would be significant. For one, the SS-26 is designed to perform maneuvers after launch that make accurate tracking more difficult for missile defense radars. The missile is also exceptionally fast, which increases the premium on missile defense reaction time.[13] Moreover, unlike Syria's liquid-fueled Scud missiles, which require time-consuming and dangerous preparation time in the field to prepare for launch, the SS-26 uses a solid-fuel rocket motor. This greatly reduces preparation time and thus the missile's vulnerability to counterforce attacks. While Israel, in its 2006 war in Lebanon, struggled to find and attack Hezbollah's ubiquitous short-range Katyusha rockets, which can be put in place and launched by one man in a matter of moments, Israeli air and ground forces effectively flooded the skies with unmanned aerial vehicles (UAVs) networked together to provide loitering aircraft with precise targeting coordinates of detected medium- and long-range Hezbollah rocket launchers. As a result, Israel managed to destroy between 80 and 90 percent of Hezbollah's longer-range launchers (around 125), all within a timeframe of between 45 seconds to a minute between detection and attack.[14] For the time being, however, Israel will not have to worry about facing the more demanding SS-26 in Syria's hands. Under pressure from both Washington and Tel Aviv, Moscow announced in April 2005 that it would stop plans to export the SS-26 to Syria.[15]

Other Syrian attempts to bolster its missile force's survivability against Israel's preemptive counterforce capabilities include persistent efforts to obtain solid propellant manufacturing technology or complete solid-fuel ballistic missiles from foreign entities, together with constructing underground, hardened structures and tunnel complexes to protect operational missile units and production facilities alike. Syria also sought but apparently did not receive the Chinese M-9 (DF-15) solid-fuel ballistic missile (600 km) in 1991. Secretary of State James Baker reportedly intervened with the Chinese in late 1991 and extracted a commitment not to sell the missiles to Syria. Afterwards, however, reports emerged that China had instead agreed to assist Syria in manufacturing their own version of the Chinese solid-fuel missile.[16] Whether or not this is the case, there is little doubt about Syria's interest in acquiring the necessary production technology to manufacture solid-propellant ballistic missiles.[17] Syria's placing of its operational missile units and production facilities underground comes as no surprise. Increasingly threatened by Israeli and U.S. precision guided weapons possessing pinpoint accuracy, Syria and Iran, among others, have begun to exploit commercially available boring equipment, which can rapidly and efficiently dig a tunnel 18 m wide at the rate of 70 m each per day. Although it is not known what means Syria is employing, apparently it has enlisted the aid of North Korea, China, and Iran to help with two large underground facilities housing its missile production infrastructure.[18] Syria's eventual acquisition of solid-fuel missiles may prove slightly more productive in the end than going underground, as Israel undoubtedly knows where these underground facilities are located, as well as the particular aim points needed to seal off such facilities with multiple attacks.

Clearly, despite Syria's persistent efforts to acquire a formidable force of ballistic missiles, including ones armed with chemical and, potentially, biological agents, Israel remains overwhelmingly dominant in every respect. Besides its vastly superior conventional capability, Israel possesses its own force of nuclear-armed ballistic missiles that would allow it to attack any regional target of interest. The heart of that force consists of 50 single-stage Jericho-1 solid-fuel ballistic missiles (range: 500 km) deployed on mobile launchers, 100 two-stage Jericho-2 (range: 1,500 km) missiles on underground wheeled launchers or railroad flat cars, and an uncertain number of three-stage Jericho-3 (range: 4,800 km) missiles, which reportedly became operational in 2005.[19] These missiles can deliver payloads ranging between 500 and 1,000 kg. Were Israel in need of achieving even longer ranges, it could readily convert its space launcher, the Shavit, into a missile capable of delivering a nuclear weapon to a range over 7,000 km.[20]

Preemption has been an option in Israeli military decisionmaking since its first application in the Six Day War of 1967. The confined geographic circumstances facing both Israel and Syria may increase incentives to strike first during crises. In spite of Israel's clear dominance, Syria's acquisition of more robust missile capabilities, particularly if such capabilities are seen to furnish even a temporary advantage, may only worsen crisis instability. The development of a two-tier ballistic missile defense system should allay Jerusalem's traditional predilection toward preemptive action. Yet some Israeli strategists, while championing multi-layered missile defenses, still strongly affirm the need to act preemptively, especially in light of the increasing threat of WMD-armed missiles.[21]

For a variety of reasons, Iran presents a decidedly different kind of ballistic missile threat than does Syria. Iran has comparative geographic advantages. With roughly nine times the landmass of Syria, Iran is slightly larger than Alaska, while Syria is a shade smaller than North Dakota. Iran's huge area furnishes valuable strategic depth, allowing Iran to deploy its fixed and mobile missile launchers deep within Iran's interior. The distance from Tel Aviv to Tehran (1,598 km) is almost 7.5 times the distance from Tel Aviv to Damascus (214 km). And there is nearly another 900 km of strategic deployment depth to the east of Tehran, where missiles could be based. That said, strategic depth cuts more than one way. While it affords operational breathing room, it also means that short-range ballistic missiles are unlikely to satisfy one's military needs. When Iran extended the striking distance of its 1,300-km-range ballistic missile, called the Shihab-3, which has more than enough capability to strike Tel Aviv or Riyadh from points well within Iran's territory, an Iranian aerospace official suggested that the desired range was 1,500 km, which, unsurprisingly, would allow the Shihab-3 to operate from launch sites outside the reach of Israel's F-15I strike aircraft.[22] To provide an even more comfortable degree of maneuver space, the Shihab-3's extended-range version appears capable of a range of between 1,700 and 2,500 km.[23]

In an evenhanded analysis of Iran's ballistic missile programs published in late 2006, Uzi Rubin offers several useful insights about Iran's missile ambitions. Rubin notes that the number and variety of deployed and developmental missiles in Iran's programs reflect a palpable sense of urgency.[24] Relying on technical support from entities in Russia, China, and North Korea, and compelled by necessity during its 1980–88 war with Iraq, Iran set out essentially from scratch to deploy ballistic missiles today ranging from battlefield short-range systems to MRBMs capable of targeting Israel, Saudi Arabia, and U.S. bases in the Middle East. Moreover, Iran is on the verge of deploying a 3,500-km-range intermediate-range ballistic missile (IRBM), which would enable Tehran to target Berlin. By the end of this decade, all of continental Europe will likely be within range, while Iran's space-launch vehicle (SLV) program appears destined to bring Iran closer to a missile capable of reaching U.S. territory in another five years.[25]

Tehran got its start in 1985 by first purchasing Scud-B missiles from Libya and then quickly turning to North Korea for more extensive support. Iran provided cash to help finance North Korea's missile development in exchange for substantial hard and soft technology transfers and, essentially, the right to buy whatever Pyongyang produced. Initially, Iran acquired over 200 Scud-Bs (called Shihab-1) and Scud-Cs (Shihab-2), but what Tehran really coveted was the capacity to produce ballistic missiles on its own. A U.S. State Department official described the hard technology arrangement as follows: "you first buy entire missiles and the kits to assemble missiles, and then you learn to make them on your own—designs and blueprints come with the package." While hard production equipment and blueprints are certainly necessary to produce Scuds, the key ingredient Tehran sought, and received, according to the same official, was the specialized knowledge provided by North Korean engineers who worked face-to-face with their Iranian counterparts to help them master the Scud production process.[26] This relationship has permitted Iran to expand its holdings of Scud-B and Scud-D missiles. By 1998, based on Nodong technology provided by North Korea, Iran first tested the 1,300-km-range Shihab-3 missile, which could deliver a payload of between 750 to 1,200 kg, but only with an accuracy of 3 km. In 2004 Iran tested an extended-range version of the Shihab-3, which is believed capable of traveling to a range of 2,000 km.[27] Although the

Shihab-3 possessed virtually no military utility it could terrorize nearby states—in particular, Israel, which now was within range of an Iranian ballistic missile.

Most of Iran's ballistic missiles are liquid-fueled. But both solid and storable-liquid systems are either deployed or on track for deployment. In the case of solid systems, Iran obtained the 150-km-range CSS-8 solid-fuel ballistic missile from China in 1989 and is suspected of attempting to purchase M-11 solid-fuel missiles, although evidence is thin.[28] The United States did later impose sanctions on China; however, Chinese assistance in not only solid-propellant production but also in guidance and missile testing has continued.[29] Such support probably aided Iran in its development of the Fateh-110, a 200-km-range solid-propellant missile first tested in 2002 and now deployed widely as an Iranian battlefield delivery system.

Extensive foreign assistance also manifests itself in Iran's acquisition of a new storable-liquid ballistic missile capable of a range of 3,500 km. Storable-liquid fueled ballistic missiles have great virtue because they obviate the need for time-consuming and dangerous prelaunch fueling. Iran again turned to North Korea, which depended heavily on Russian technical assistance to produce this 3,500-km-range ballistic missile based on the Soviet-era SS-N-6 submarine-launched ballistic missile. The missile, initially called the BM-25 but now officially referred to as Musudan (the U.S. intelligence community names foreign missiles based on the place where they are first identified), reportedly depends heavily on technology inputs to North Korea from the Makayev OKB Design Bureau in Russia, which began as early as 1987, during the Gorbachev era.[30] As Israeli missile specialist Uzi Rubin points out, mastery of storable-liquid technology is no easy task. It requires special production equipment and unique expertise to achieve self-sufficiency. "That the North Koreans managed to master this technology on their own from sets of drawings or from the copying of smuggled Russian examples stretches the imagination," argues Rubin.[31] Moreover, storable-liquid technology is not the only complex engineering task involved in Musudan's development. The missile is a ground-mobile version of a submarine-launched missile, which means it must be reinforced to operate in harsher environments. And the original SS-N-6 design had to have its range increased from 2,500 to 3,500 km. The sum total of these changes implies extensive redesign of the airframe, guidance and control system, and requalifying the integrity of internal structures. None of these challenges could be met by either North Korea or Iran without the specialized know-how of Makayev's highly skilled practitioners.

Despite Iran's transparency compared with other emerging missile states, uncertainty shrouds several joint Iranian-North Korean programs. It appears that 18 Musudan IRBMs and their launchers were transferred from North Korea to Iran in late 2005 or early 2006, and that the same missile was paraded in Pyongyang in April 2007. Yet no firm evidence of any missile testing is available. Iran and North Korea's symbiotic relationship suggests that North Korea may have transferred the missile to Iran for testing, or the missile may have been tested in Russia during that country's extensive involvement in the Musudan's development.[32] Shihab-3 testing, while certainly more extensive, does not reflect Western test standards for ballistic missiles.

Roughly half of Iran's 10 launches of the Shihab since 1998 appear to have been total or partial failures. Apparently driven by the necessity to deploy a deterrence-oriented missile threat to its neighbors, however, Iran was satisfied enough to declare the Shihab-3 operational. Unless the Musudan IRBM was covertly tested in Russia, it will have to await several tests before it too becomes operational. Reports in May 2004 and in the second half of 2005 indicate that Iran sought North Korea's Taepodong-2, a missile having a range of between 5,000 and 6,000 km.[33] And not least of all is Iran's ambition to be a spacefaring nation by virtue of acquiring a space-launch vehicle, which also implies a straight, if rocky, path toward development of an intercontinental-range ballistic missile.[34] Iran's interest in North Korea's Taepodong-2 may well reflect its SLV ambitions, but if Tehran's curious "test" of a sounding rocket in February 2007 is any indication—neither Russian nor American early warning systems detected an Iranian space launch—Iran's SLV program may be moving at a glacial pace.[35]

Although Iran has certainly improved its indigenous capacity to execute complex missile programs, it still remains dependent on foreign assistance, particularly to make its ballistic missiles more than just a psychologically effective deterrent against its principal adversaries. To gain any credible military utility with conventional payloads, significant improvements in guidance systems must be made. Without North Korea's substantial assistance—at a substantial cost and with great reciprocal benefit—Iran would not be in a position today to threaten much of Europe and all of the Middle East. But North Korea is not likely to become a near-term source of components or of knowledge about advanced guidance technology. China, on the other hand, could. According to the U.S. intelligence community, China has already "delivered dozens, perhaps hundreds of missile guidance systems and computerized tools to Iran," but whether Iran has sought, or China has been willing to sell, the same level of guidance sophistication found in the latest Chinese ballistic missiles is unknown.[36] According to the Central Intelligence Agency, Russia has "helped Iran save years" in development time for the Shihab-3, while providing missile production equipment to enable Iran to develop newer missiles, inducing the United States to impose sanctions against certain Russian entities.[37] Whether or not Russia is willing to furnish even more advanced technology or sustained systems engineering know-how remains to be seen. Finally, Iran is not entirely dependent on its traditional sources of missile technology support. Tehran has successfully pursued a broadened set of relationships with India, including discussions about closer military ties and the creation of a "joint defense working group."[38] Given India's missile advances as well as New Delhi's close ties to Russia in various cooperative development programs, Iran's emerging relationship with India bears close watching.

SOUTH ASIA

Dr. A. P. J. Abdul Kalam was elevated to the presidency of India in 2002 after having served as head of India's Integrated Guided Missile Development Program (IGMDP) and advancing India's historic quest to acquire one of the primary

symbols of world power: nuclear-capable ballistic missiles. Dr. Kalam's elevation testified to the importance of India's quest to become independent of foreign sources
not only in space-launch activities but also in ballistic missile development. How
Dr. Kalam furthered India's ballistic missile ambitions differs sharply from the norm.
Typically, nations already possessing ballistic missiles transform them into SLVs;
America's Atlas ballistic missile propelled John Glenn into space in 1962. But India
decided from the start to pursue space-launch rockets first and only subsequently
to develop ballistic missiles by exploiting what they had first learned, or acquired,
from abroad to help fashion an SLV.[39] Dr. Kalam led India's development of its first
SLV program (SLV-3), which succeeded in placing a satellite in low earth orbit in
1980. He also was responsible for India's Polar Satellite Launch Vehicle (PSLV)—a
two-stage solid-propellant rocket. Both the SLV-3 and the PSLV are based on technology that came from the United States in the 1960s. Richard Speier, a noted missile expert, argues that the two solid-propellant stages that comprise the PSLV could
readily be employed as the basis for a three-stage ICBM, were India to give its missile
developers the go-ahead.[40] In 1983, Dr. Kalam took responsibility for inaugurating
India's IGMDP, under which India developed the Prithvi and Agni ballistic missile
programs—the heart of its current battlefield and strategic ballistic missile capability.
Working closely with India's Department of Atomic Energy, Dr. Kalam then led
weaponization work related to turning India's ballistic missiles into nuclear-capable
delivery means after their successful series of nuclear tests in May 1998.[41]

The IGMDP represents India's chief mechanism to accomplish self-sufficiency in
military technology. India has military ambitions that go well beyond ballistic missile
acquisition. Its army, air force, and navy customers seek new tanks, aircraft, and ships
to satisfy its conventional military needs. Pakistan, India's principal adversary, has
less than one-seventh India's population and cannot compete with India in conventional military capabilities quantitatively or qualitatively. Pakistan is therefore compelled to fall back on its first-strike, early-use nuclear doctrine to deter India. New
Delhi's strategists would like to achieve the capacity to wage a limited conventional
war without triggering nuclear escalation. Thus, India faces stiff demands in becoming self-sufficient in both missile and other high-tech military systems for conventional as well as nuclear use. To date, however, it has not fared nearly as well in
turning out its own tanks, aircraft, and ships as it has in developing and deploying
ballistic missiles. There is a long list of indigenous developmental setbacks in non-
missile programs, from its Light Combat Aircraft program to its Arjun main battle
tank. These disappointments underscore the higher priority India devotes to ballistic
missile acquisition. India continues to turn largely to Russia for tanks and aircraft,
while the Indo-Israeli defense relationship increasingly shows signs of blossoming.[42]

Foreign technical assistance has played an important role in India's ballistic missile
acquisitions, but such dependence has diminished of late. French sounding rockets
and American solid-propellant technology helped advance India's SLV program,
while Germany and the United Kingdom assisted, respectively, in the areas of payload calculation and ignition systems. Russia's provision of cryogenic engines helped
India immensely in its space-launch program. In late 2006, India said that it had

developed its own indigenous cryogenic engine to help launch its Geosynchronous Satellite Launch Vehicle. Indian scientists and engineers working on basic missile research also depended in part on American supercomputers supplied by IBM and Digital Equipment Corporation.[43] Nevertheless, the proportion of domestic components of India's latest missiles has grown significantly in the last two decades. According to senior Indian defense scientists, about 85 percent of the components of the Agni-3 ballistic missile, which was tested successfully for the first time in April 2007 and is estimated to have a range of 3,500 km (enough to target Shanghai and possibly Beijing), were manufactured domestically.[44]

While India certainly values the prestige and technological spin-offs derived from ballistic missiles, it also needs ballistic missiles to strengthen its military deterrent vis-à-vis both Pakistan and China, India's two strategic rivals. In discussing nuclear-armed aircraft in 1998, retired Air Commodore Jasjit Singh noted that their "limitations of range and susceptibility to interception by hostile systems make it critical that the central component of the nuclear arsenal must rest on ballistic missiles."[45] Neither China nor Pakistan possesses ballistic missile defenses.

India's shorter-range systems can target Pakistan; its longer-range ones China. In the former category are the Prithvi-1 and -2, and its naval counterpart, the Dhanush (or Prithvi-3). The first, an army asset, is capable of 150-km range carrying a 1,000-kg payload; the second, owned by the air force, has a range of 250 km with a 500–750-kg payload; the third, launched from a ship, can fly 400 km carrying a 500-kg warhead. The Prithvi-series of ballistic missiles is based on the Soviet-era surface-to-air SA-2, a missile interceptor propelled by a liquid-fueled engine, although the navy version is believed to use a solid-propellant first stage and a liquid-fueled second stage. The army and air force versions are road mobile, and all three versions are operationally hampered by the lengthy time it takes to fuel and fire the missile. This may explain why some Indian sources have said that India has no plans to deploy a nuclear-capable Prithvi-1.[46] Improving missile accuracy, however, may also suggest that India could employ Prithvi in tandem with its air force, in a manner similar to the way China foresees using its conventionally armed missiles vis-à-vis Taiwan. Indian sources now report that the latest Prithvi modifications include a guidance capability aided by the Global Positioning System (GPS), producing accuracies of 75 m or better.[47]

Also relevant to targeting Pakistan is the Agni-1, a single-stage solid-fueled missile capable of ranges between 700 and 1,200 km, depending on the type of payload, its weight, and the missile's launch angle.[48] This increased range over the Prithvi-series allows the Agni-1 to operate, as one Indian analyst notes, "deployed away from pre-emptive strike zones," meaning that the missile launch units can operate from deep within India, far from most if not all potential Pakistani strike systems.[49] Essentially, the Agni-1 missile appears to be the first stage of the two-stage Agni-2, with improved guidance borrowed as well from the Agni-2 program.

As for longer-range ballistic missiles capable of targeting China, the Agni-2, a two-stage, solid, road-mobile missile, is believed capable of a range of 2,000 km or more, carrying a 1,000-kg warhead. This would allow the Agni-2 to cover parts of western

China. But in order to reach farther into China, including Shanghai and Beijing, India turned to the Agni-3, which can strike targets out to a range of roughly 3,500 km. First successfully tested in April 2007 from a rail-mobile launcher, the Agni-3 appears to have demonstrated Indian success in solving problems with missile staging and reentry vehicle design, which led to the missile's failure during its first test in July 2006.[50]

Indian commentators like to draw a clear distinction between India's and Pakistan's respective approaches to developing their ballistic missile arsenals. While India's is largely indigenous, they say, Pakistan's is heavily dependent on foreign assistance. Pakistan has depended substantially on China first to catapult it into the solid-propellant ballistic missile field. When China's willingness to provide complete missiles or component parts waned in the early 1990s due to U.S. sanctions and diplomatic pressure, Pakistan then turned to North Korea for liquid-fueled ballistic missiles. One interesting facet of these dependencies is the competitive relationship between Pakistan's nuclear weapons development programs. Pakistan's National Development Complex—charged with developing a plutonium-based weapon—pursued the Chinese track; the Khan Research Laboratories—responsible for uranium-based weapons—sought help from North Korea. At least in the case of A. Q. Khan's track, there existed an important reciprocal, perhaps bartering, dimension to the bilateral relationship. It now seems clear that in exchange for North Korean missiles and extensive technical assistance, Pakistan furnished Pyongyang with gas-centrifuge uranium enrichment technology to complement North Korea's otherwise plutonium-dependent approach to nuclear weapons development.[51]

China's support of its ally Pakistan explains its actions in supplying ample missile technology assistance to Islamabad. Chinese assistance began in the early 1980s and eventually influenced virtually each and every Pakistani solid-propellant ballistic missile. The Haft-1 was the first if not the most useful missile; its short range (80 km) limited its utility to only a conventional payload. Fewer than 50 launchers are deployed today. The Haft-2 and Haft-3 benefited greatly from China's provision of the M-11 (DF-11) missile; the Haft-2 has a range of nearly 300 km carrying a 500-kg warhead but is not thought to be nuclear capable, while the Haft-3 (Ghaznavi) can strike deeper (280–400 km) with a 500-kg nuclear payload. The Haft-4 (Shaheen-1) depends heavily on China's M-9 (DF-15) road-mobile missile and has a range of 450 km carrying a 1,000-kg nuclear payload. China's assistance is also reflected in the Haft-6, a 2,000 to 2,500-km-range missile that is still undergoing development.[52]

North Korea's support of its liquid-fueled missile program probably began in the mid-1990s, but it was quickly followed by the first test launch of the Haft-5 (Ghauri-1), which is estimated to have a range of 1,300 km carrying a 500–750-kg payload. The missile is a cutoff of the North Korean Nodong missile, which has also, along with substantial North Korean on-site technical assistance, greatly influenced Pakistani efforts to extend the Haft-5's range even more. Still under development are the Nodong-influenced Ghauri-2, with a 1,500–2,300-km range and 700-kg payload and the Ghauri-3, which appears to be based on North Korea's

Taepodong-1. The Ghauri-3 is believed headed toward achieving a range of between 2,700 and 3,500 km.[53]

India's substantial and growing conventional force advantages over Pakistan explain why Islamabad has so heavily emphasized the acquisition of an assured penetration capability against India. Pakistan also depends on aircraft delivery of nuclear weapons, using American-furnished F-16s, which Islamabad resumed buying after President Bush waived restrictions on their sale in 2005. But aircraft are currently far more vulnerable than ballistic missiles because of existing Indian air defenses compared with only plans for future ballistic missile defenses.

The assured penetration of Pakistan's ballistic missiles could become questionable were India to act on its demonstrated interest in ballistic missile defenses. India has long sought to acquire Israel's Arrow ballistic missile defense system. Both New Delhi and Tel Aviv have lobbied Washington hard to make an exception to extant restrictions regarding Arrow's export to India.[54] The United States has partially funded and transferred restricted technology to Israel to support Arrow's development from the beginning. Moreover, because the Arrow's missile interceptor is considered an export-restricted system under the provisions of the MTCR (theoretically, it is capable of delivering a 500-kg payload to a range of at least 300 km), Washington has felt obliged to discourage Israel from selling the Arrow to India. Under the reported terms of the India-U.S. Civil Nuclear Cooperation agreement, announced in mid-2005, however, in exchange for placing its civilian nuclear facilities under international monitoring, India would obtain a free hand to purchase previously restricted conventional weapons, including Israel's Arrow.[55] No such restrictions apply to the U.S. Patriot missile defense system, which Washington is eager to sell to its close allies and friends, including India.

To promote its goal of a global ballistic missile defense system, since the beginning of the George W. Bush administration, U.S. Defense Department officials have encouraged interest in, and better yet, purchase of, U.S. missile defense systems. With respect to India, Washington linked its missile defense promotional program to its broader quest to establish a strategic relationship with India as, among other things, a long-term bulwark against China. To that end and in cooperation with India, in 2004 the Bush administration prepared a plan, called the Next Step in Strategic Partnership agreement, which envisioned four areas of cooperation: civilian space and nuclear, high-tech trade, and missile defense.[56] In February 2005, a team of specialists from the Pentagon's Defense Security Cooperation Agency visited New Delhi and gave members of India's External Affairs and Defense ministries a classified technical presentation on the Patriot PAC-2 missile defense system.[57] In July 2005, the United States and India announced that they had agreed to expand bilateral activities and commerce in all four areas specified in the Next Step agreement. Meanwhile, Indian technical specialists have called for India to pursue the more advanced version of Patriot, PAC-3, with its hit-to-kill interceptor.

Like Israel, India seems predisposed to pursue a missile defense architecture composed of at least two layers. The Israeli Arrow interceptor can engage missiles up to 50 km in altitude at ranges out to 100 km away from the firing batteries.[58] Flying at nine times the speed of sound, the interceptor does not directly hit the incoming missile (as the Patriot PAC-3 hit-to-kill interceptor is designed to do); rather it comes close enough to allow its warhead fragmentation pattern to destroy the missile warhead (similar to the older Patriot PAC-2 interceptor). But because the Arrow's engagement altitude of 8 km is relatively low, a terminal engagement interceptor like the Patriot PAC-2 or PAC-3 must be employed.

Consistent with its approach to offensive missile development, India does not wish to become entirely dependent on foreign sources to satisfy its quest for ballistic missile defenses. For some time India has experimented with its Akash surface-to-air missile interceptor—which started out designed to intercept low-flying aircraft—to determine its capacity to perform ballistic missile engagements. The Akash thus seems slated, in principle, to perform Patriot's role as the terminal interceptor against shorter-range ballistic missile threats (<1,000-km range) at fairly low intercept altitudes. To engage faster-traveling and longer-range ballistic missiles (>1,000-km range), India's Defense Research and Development Organization (DRDO) has under development a single-stage solid-propellant interceptor which was first tested in November 2006. Among other objectives, future testing will focus on increasing the intercept altitude and testing the performance of various foreign components (comparing a French guidance radar against the Israeli Green Pine acquisition radar, for example), although Indian sources note that they wish to be in a position to replace foreign components with domestically produced ones by 2012.[59] But the competition will be stiff between more proven and tested American and Israeli missile defense systems and India's far less mature development programs.

India's strategic analysts would do well to devote as much examination to the strategic implications of its decision as its DRDO is to the daunting technical demands of ballistic missile defense. Pakistan will not be able to match India's growing conventional force dominance. Its heavy reliance on nuclear deterrence could be threatened over the long run by a combination of India's growing conventional strike capabilities (aircraft-delivered precision guided munitions and conventionally armed ballistic and cruise missiles) paired with a two-tier missile defense system—especially if the two tiers consisted of the more proven Israeli Arrow and U.S. Patriot systems. China, too, will be forced to examine ways to make certain that its core targeting needs vis-à-vis India are met. While China's missile assistance to Pakistan since 2001 has become far less substantial than it was in the late 1990s, which compelled Islamabad to turn more to North Korea, Beijing could see fit to increase the flow of component technologies or even complete offensive missile subsystems in light of India's acquisition of missile defenses. China's involvement in Pakistan's acquisition of land-attack cruise missiles (LACMs) could lead to a wider South Asian regional arms competition.

NORTHEAST ASIA

Northeast Asia is burdened by a legacy of past conflicts and unresolved cultural and territorial tensions. Long-standing contentiousness between mainland China and its "renegade province," Taiwan, represents but one of several prospective flash points in the region, one that would almost inevitably involve not just China and Taiwan but the United States and its close ally, Japan. Sino-Japanese and Japanese-Korean relations remain afflicted by the wartime history of Japanese militarism and imperialism, while the residue of the Cold War manifests itself most prominently in a divided Korean peninsula and the nuclear and missile ambitions of an unpredictable North Korea. While there is hope that the stabilizing effects of regional economic cooperation will ameliorate tensions over the long run—particularly if a war over Taiwan can be avoided—other long-term indicators furnish cause for concern.[60] South Korea's perspective is an important one. From Seoul's standpoint, unless more proactive and imaginative diplomatic initiatives are undertaken in the region, growing security instability is likely to be the case.[61] The clearest signs of concern arise from an escalating Sino-Japanese defense buildup, which, if left unattended, could prevent denuclearization on the peninsula. Fueled by double-digit economic growth and a defense budget that grows even faster, China's missile, air, and naval modernization plans are worrisome. But so are Japan's plans to eliminate constitutional constraints on obtaining offensive military capabilities complemented by increasingly robust missile defenses. Although the U.S. Congress may balk at authorizing the sale of America's most advanced fighter, the stealthy F-22 Raptor, to Japan, the mere fact that Japan wishes to obtain such a potent strike capability, with an operational radius of 2,000 km, in order to attack adversary missile launch sites, is of interest not only in Beijing but Seoul and Pyongyang as well.[62]

At present, of course, although Japan does not possess ballistic missiles it could readily achieve the capacity to produce them based on its extensive development of space-launch vehicles. Japan first became involved in space rockets after an agreement was signed with the United States that conditioned U.S. technological support on the basis that Japan would not support third-party launches without U.S. consent. Later on, Japan decided to develop its own SLV, the H-2, which conducted its first successful launch in 1994. Because the H-2 proved less than cost effective, Japan produced the H-2A SLV, first launched in 2001. Japan's joint venture, called the Rocket Systems Corporation, created to develop and market the original H-2 SLV in 1990, engaged two U.S. satellite developers to launch its systems over the next decade.[63] Thus, in light of this substantial base of SLV experience, had the Japanese political leadership chosen to permit its Defense Agency to pursue its stipulated 2004 requirement for developing a ballistic missile capable of conducting preemptive conventional strikes against adversary ballistic missile launch sites, Japan could have easily produced such a missile. Probably because ballistic missiles are seen as more provocative, Japan seems bent on acquiring either, or perhaps both, LACMs or penetrating manned aircraft—preferably the F-22 Raptor—capable of long-range delivery of precision guided munitions.

Although Japan has not shown clear intent in pursuing offensive missiles as other countries in the region have, the Japanese Defense Agency's tentative interest in offensive missile options suggests an underlying tension between missile offense and defense. North Korea's provocative missile launches over or near Japanese territory together with its 2006 nuclear test only solidified Japan's efforts to build a two-tier missile defense system, despite concerns about the system's costs ($8.26 billion) and potential effectiveness. Four Maritime Self-Defense Force Aegis destroyers, armed with Standard Missile-3 (SM-3) interceptors designed to intercept ballistic missiles in space, will be complemented by a second lower tier comprised of 16 ground-based Patriot PAC-3 missile defense batteries deployed at several Air Self-Defense Force bases scattered around Japan. The PAC-3 second tier would intercept those missiles that escape interception by the first tier of SM-3 interceptors, but analysts worry that the system's high cost will allow the offense to overwhelm the defense.[64] Of course, offensive missile options are not just a cheaper alternative for Japan; their possession could be seen as complementing inadequate defenses to the extent that successful counterforce missile strikes would reduce the adversary's capacity to overwhelm one's missile defenses.

China has no impediments comparable to Japan's to pursuing ballistic missile development. But its goals in that area have been facilitated through significant foreign assistance, most notably from Russia. This assistance proved fortuitous for China when U.S. arms sales to Beijing were terminated in the aftermath of the Tiananmen Square incident and other Chinese human rights violations in 1989. A natural marriage of convenience between Russia and China came into being in the early 1990s. With Russian defense industries suffering palpably from the demise of Soviet-era subsidies, and with China seeking to parlay its growing economic might into military clout, the two nations established a robust military trade relationship.[65] Both countries also plainly shared an interest in balancing, to the extent possible, the growing hegemonic power of the United States.

Russia provided China with substantial technical expertise, production materials, and component technologies in the areas of offensive missiles, missile defenses, and nuclear weapons. Among the most critical items were rocket engines and related technology and missile guidance technology. Because Russia had obligations under the MTCR not to transfer certain complete missile systems or restricted component technologies, its defense entities had to operate surreptitiously to avoid the threat of sanctions. Yet they successfully managed not only to furnish China with extensive component technologies but also to export critically important systems engineering skills. In late 1992, China reportedly recruited skilled Russian technicians to work in their missile plants to help improve the accuracy of China's missiles.[66] A year later, the two countries signed a five-year agreement to cooperate in military technology, which most prominently included exchanging skilled technical specialists. Intelligence sources also state that China has received help in solid-propellant missile fuel and technical aid in improving missile launching from submerged submarines.[67] Especially important for improving ballistic missile guidance for its conventionally armed missiles facing Taiwan, China apparently signed a cooperative agreement with Russia in 2000 on the use and improvement of Russia's Global Navigation Satellite System (GLONASS). Since then, of course, China commenced developing its own

Beidou global navigation system, but the Chinese have likely obtained valuable insight into adapting this technology to improve the accuracy of their ballistic missile systems from their cooperation with Russian specialists.

Given the dramatically different ballistic missile deployment rates China has pursued vis-à-vis Taiwan compared with intercontinental and other regional threats, it is clear that Taiwan represents China's chief military priority. China has deployed around 200 mobile missile launchers capable of delivering nearly 1,000 solid-propellant ballistic missiles (a mix of 300-km-range DF-9/M-1 and 600-km-range DF-15/M-9 missiles) to targets in Taiwan. By comparison, China has taken what some might argue is a decidedly slow and risky approach to deploying ballistic missiles earmarked to defend against other threats. Only 20 DF-5A liquid-fuel ballistic missiles, first deployed in 1981, serve as China's primary ICBM force capable of threatening the United States from a range of 13,000 km. Also currently available are 16 DF-3A liquid-fuel missiles, deployed in 1971 and capable of striking targets out to 3,100 km; 22 DF-4 liquid-fuel missiles, deployed first in 1980 and capable of 5,500-km range; and 35 DF-21A, a solid-propellant mobile missile, first deployed in 1991 and capable of 2,150-km range. None of these missiles are believed to be particularly accurate. Aside from the mobile DF-21A, China's land-based ballistic missiles suffer from low readiness due to the disadvantages of liquid-fueling. Their capacity to survive a surprise attack by U.S. nuclear-armed missiles or even attacks by highly accurate conventional weapons is also questionable, due not only to low force readiness, but also to China's poor early warning capabilities and its placement of forces in well-known and vulnerable caves or missile silos.[68]

The survivability of Chinese land-based ballistic missiles will be greatly improved once long-standing mobile missile development efforts reach fruition. The DF-31, an 8,000-km-range three-stage solid-propellant missile, which was started in 1985, has yet to be fully deployed. Nevertheless, it qualifies for what the Pentagon calls "initial threat availability"—or ready for use in an emergency. Its range does not permit full coverage of the United States. However, the DF-31A, a modification the DF-31, is designed to travel 12,000 km—adequate to cover the entire United States—and might deliver multiple warheads or a single warhead with penetration aids to overcome missile defenses. It may reach full operational capability by the end of this decade.[69]

The Pentagon's 2007 assessment of China's military power indicates that China has five new nuclear-powered missile submarines under development (Jin-class) and that each sub will eventually be outfitted with twelve solid-propellant 8,000-km-range ballistic missiles, called the JL-2.[70] These new subs have been under development since the late 1980s, which suggests that China has experienced several difficulties along the path to operational deployment. China's only current nuclear-powered submarine is a Xia-class boat carrying 12 JL-1 liquid-fueled ballistic missiles capable of delivering a single warhead to a range of 1,700 km. Although the Xia-class sub was commissioned in 1981, it has only occasionally left port due to repeated technical problems.[71]

China's most advanced systems are dedicated to its near-term focus on preparations for offensive combat operations across the Taiwan Strait. Accordingly, Beijing's nascent interest in ballistic missile defense is probably a response to Taiwan's interest in offensive missile options as well as U.S. strike options. Reports of China's acquisition of Russia's S-300 surface-to-air missile system, roughly equivalent to the U.S. Patriot system, began to occur in 1992. The Pentagon's 2007 assessment of China's military power reports that China will soon receive the latest version of that generic system, called the S-300PMU-2, which can intercept missiles and aircraft out to a range of 200 km.[72] Surely China's drive to improve its capacity to intercept ballistic missiles is not just related to mimicking America's pursuit of global missile defenses. A much more immediate concern must relate to Taiwan's revelation, in April 2007, that it is not only pursuing cruise missiles for land attack but also trying to convert its Tien Kung-2 air defense missile into a ground-to-ground ballistic missile, called Tien Kung-2B.[73]

Taiwan's ballistic missile aspirations are long-standing. Until recently, however, Washington has managed to convince Taipei that such a course of action could prove destabilizing. Washington had no such misgivings about Taiwan's interest in anti-ship cruise missiles (ASCMs) and surface-to-air missiles (SAMs), both of which could be turned into offensive land-attack delivery systems. Taiwan produced several hundred Hsiung Feng (HF) ASCMs and Tien Kung-1 (Sky Bow) SAMs starting in the 1970s, while simultaneously nurturing its ballistic missile ambitions by seeking to acquire technical know-how on inertial navigation and guidance by way of an arrangement for training 15 students at the Massachusetts Institute of Technology.[74] After Washington nixed the MIT training, Taiwan turned inward, building missile capacity within its own Chung-Shan Institute of Science and Technology, which grew to over 2,000 professionals.[75] In the meantime, Taiwan developed a 100 +-km-range ballistic missile (Green Bee), first shown in 1981, but then tested Washington's patience when it allocated research money to a 960-km-range missile, called Tien Ma (Sky Horse). Washington's pressure ended the Sky Horse program in 1981. Instead, the Chung-Shan Institute turned to a more acceptable pursuit—building its own Tien Kung-1 (Sky Bow) SAM, seemingly only for defensive purposes. Here Taiwan depended substantially on outside technical assistance. It spent $1.1 billion in 1993 to acquire component technologies from U.S. defense contractor Raytheon needed to produce the Tien Kung (Sky Bow) SAM.[76] Taiwan also started a space launcher program but abandoned it in 1990 due to export control and political restrictions imposed by Washington.

China's ballistic missile buildup and internal political imperatives inevitably combined to reenergize Taiwan's ballistic missile ambitions, despite Washington's protestations to the contrary. While the United States persisted in arguing that missile defenses represented the safest and most effective means to check China's offensive buildup, Taiwanese policymakers repeatedly reverted to offensive options. They argued that ballistic missiles offered a better way to deter China than either air forces or ballistic missile defenses. In the latter case, they calculated that ballistic missiles were immensely cheaper than defensive systems, so that no matter how much Taiwan spent on defense, the offense would always have the advantage. In March 1995, Taiwan's Defense Minister Chiang Chung-ling argued before the legislature: "Undoubtedly, the best defense strategy is to attack . . . . The best defense measure is to destroy the [Chinese] M-class missiles before they are launched."[77] Rumors were then spreading that Taiwan had turned its HF-2 ASCM into a land-attack system, and by March 1999, Taiwan reportedly allocated $600 million for missile development, including converting the HF-2 into a LACM.[78] Washington's fixation on preventing Taiwan from acquiring ballistic missiles moved Taipei toward not only the pursuit of LACMs (HF-2E) but also the acquisition of their own defensive missile interceptors that could subsequently be transformed into offensive ballistic missiles (Tien Kung-2B).

A similar pattern of U.S. pressure affected South Korea's long-standing ballistic missile ambitions.[79] Just as Washington was concerned about Taiwan's offensive ambitions provoking China, it viewed South Korea's missile aspirations as potentially destabilizing insofar as Pyongyang would use them as a pretext for expanding its own missile programs, and China and Japan would perceive them with suspicion. Whereas Washington attempted to steer Taiwan toward cruise missiles and air defense interceptors, it permitted South Korea, under a 1979 memorandum of understanding, to pursue a ballistic missile program with a range cap of 180 km—too short to reach Pyongyang. But even before that agreement, beginning in the early 1970s, Washington had permitted Seoul to obtain specialized missile training from Raytheon and the U.S. military to help turn the Nike-Hercules air defense interceptor into a ballistic missile (called NHK-1) capable of eventually achieving a range of 180 km. By 1995, in the context of North Korea's expanded nuclear activity, Seoul sought to abandon the 1979 range restriction and replace it with a 300-km cap. As pressure for change increased in Seoul, the U.S. and South Korea proceeded to discuss missile matters intensively through the end of the Bill Clinton administration in January 2001. By 1999, Seoul was demanding that it be allowed to develop a 500-km-range ballistic missile. Days before Bush took office, Seoul and Washington reached a "self-declared" adoption (versus a written memorandum of understanding) of missile guidelines that essentially permitted South Korea to build and deploy a 300-km-range ballistic missile, build for "research purposes" a 500-km-range ballistic missile, develop a 500-km-range cruise missile as long as its payload remained under 500 kg, and build an SLV without limits on range and payload as long as it did not depend on solid propellant. Ominously, Washington agreed that Seoul could build these missiles "to the extent needed to meet its security needs."[80] South Korea joined the MTCR two months later.

Since the 2001 "self-declared" adoption, South Korea has energetically sought to meet its security needs through further offensive missile developments as well as acceleration of its space-launch vehicle program. Of course, the NHK-2 ballistic missile program had demonstrated in a 1999 missile test that it was already capable of reaching its 300-km range cap.[81] Apparently, South Korean security concerns extended considerably beyond the range of North Korea, as it unveiled in 2006 the existence of four LACM programs with ranges between 500 and 1,500 km.[82] In May 2007, South Korea's defense minister met with his Indian counterpart in New Delhi and waxed eloquent about India's rapid achievements in missile technology, while expressing interest in collaborating with India on various defense projects.[83] More relevant perhaps to Seoul's long-term missile ambitions was a meeting, two months earlier, between South Korea's deputy prime minister and minister of science and technology and Russian officials to discuss deepening and accelerating scientific cooperation between Seoul and Moscow. The meetings afforded Seoul officials the opportunity to press Moscow to ratify a "Technology Safeguards Agreement" still languishing in Russia's Duma, awaiting its approval. Once approved, the agreement would permit Russia to transfer to South Korea critical technology needed to complete the first stage of their KSLV-1 program, an SLV scheduled to launch a satellite into space in late 2008. U.S. concerns that Seoul may eventually turn its SLV program into a long-range ballistic missile may account for delays in ratification of the agreement. A U.S. delegation visited Russia's Federal Space Agency in early 2006 seeking assurances that any technology transferred to South Korea would include strict end-use monitoring to make certain it would be used only for peaceful purposes.[84] Long gone, it seems, are the days when Washington could employ its security guarantee or promise of technology as leverage to restrain South Korea's missile ambitions.

North Korea's ballistic missile technology and knowledge are reflected prominently in the previously discussed arsenals of Syria, Iran, and Pakistan, but these countries are not the only North Korean customers. Egypt, Libya, and Yemen have all purchased either missiles, missile components, or missile technology from Pyongyang. As for North Korea's own arsenal, most attention focuses on when that nation will possess the capacity to threaten targets on the U.S. landmass. The U.S. national intelligence estimate published in December 2001 stated that while Pyongyang did not yet have its ICBM-capable missiles operational, it was estimated that North Korea's multi-stage Taepodong-2 missile was probably ready for flight testing and capable of delivering a nuclear weapon-sized (several hundred kg) payload to parts of the United States.[85] Of course, that missile was unsuccessfully tested in July 2006, when Pyongyang broke its self-imposed moratorium on missile testing (declared first in September 1999) with a barrage of seven missile launches. Most importantly, the Taepodong-2's first-stage booster rocket failed 42 seconds after ignition, with the missile falling into the sea.

Whereas North Korea's capacity to threaten the United States remains questionable, that is not the case with respect to either targets in Japan or South Korea, including bases from which U.S. forces would operate. North Korea's 1,300-km-range Nodong ballistic missile, of which there are believed to be 200 or so, can cover targets in Japan, as can the 2,200-km-range Taepodong-1, though the latter system is probably not yet operational. Neither missile has sufficient accuracy to be militarily effective, say, in degrading U.S. air bases through conventional attacks, but they would likely cause significant Japanese casualties, especially if they delivered chemical payloads.[86] Once it is deployed, North Korea's 3,500-km-range Musudan missile, based on the Russian SS-N-6, has more than enough range to reach not only Japan but also U.S. bases in Okinawa and possibly Guam. As for South Korea, the lion's share of Pyongyang's more than 800 ballistic missiles appears slated for targets to the south. Even 300-km-range Scud-B missiles can cover about two-thirds of South Korea, while the Scud-C, with a range of 500 km, can strike the entire country. The North's new shortest-range ballistic missile (100–120 km), the KN-02, a new solid-propellant missile apparently based on the Soviet-era SS-21 missile, could hit U.S. military targets at Osan Air Base and Camp Humphreys. The better accuracy —250–300 m—of HN-02 missiles could make them more effective than Scuds, assuming they are armed with conventional payloads and enough missiles are available to achieve a significant volume of fire.

What makes the buildup of ballistic missiles in the region potentially destabilizing is their inevitable interaction with missile defense deployments. Japan feels threatened not just by North Korea but also China. In response, Japan has cooperated extensively with the United States to research, develop, and deploy significant ballistic missile defenses. China, in turn, worries about Japanese missile defenses being employed for Taiwan's protection, which could conceivably nudge Taiwan toward a formal declaration of independence. For decades, but with decreasing success, the United States has used its security guarantees to Taiwan and South Korea to constrain their ballistic missile ambitions. Encouraging both countries to purchase ballistic missile defenses instead of pursuing missile offenses has also been part of the bargain, but not without any clear success. Indeed, one of the unintended consequences of pushing missile defense too hard with close allies has been the fostering of incentives on the part of threatened states to pursue cruise missiles as a way of overcoming missile defenses. When faced with such countermeasures along with the high cost and problematic effectiveness of ballistic missile defenses, some U.S. allies only become more inclined themselves to turn toward ballistic missiles, cruise missiles, or both.

Land-Attack Cruise Missiles—
Signs of Contagion

Given the impressive role played by U.S. Tomahawk cruise missiles in the first Gulf War of 1990–1991, expectations grew that other countries would seek to acquire land-attack cruise missiles (LACMs) during the 1990s. Certainly some nations hatched plans or actually commenced LACM programs in that decade, but only now have signs of a long-expected contagion of interest in and acquisition of LACMs become both conspicuous and arresting.[1]

By the start of the twenty-first century, one could safely observe that while the spread and use of ballistic missiles had dominated policymakers' attention, during the last decade of the twentieth century LACMs had become more prominent instruments of warfare than ballistic missiles. Witness America's use of LACMs in seven different contingencies. As Figure 1 clearly shows, cruise missile use beginning in 1944 to the present (19,645) greatly exceeds that of ballistic missile use (5,880)—by over 3 to 1. Eliminate missile use during World War II, and the number of ballistic missiles and cruise missiles used since then is roughly comparable (2,380 versus 2,645). But because U.S. LACMs accounted for virtually all of the post-World War II cruise missiles used and, conversely, because prospective enemies of the United States employed nearly all of the ballistic missiles, the latter tend to be perceived as the proliferation challenge of most import.[2] If this was ever true, it may no longer be. Whereas in the first year of the twenty-first century, LACMs had not spread widely beyond the arsenals of the United States and Russia, the missile contagion now underway suggests that an entirely different and decidedly more worrisome future is about to unfold.

USE OF CRUISE MISSILES AFTER WORLD WAR II

The story of LACM use after World War II is overwhelmingly an American one. Yet, both the United States and the Soviet Union experimented widely after World War II with cruise missiles based on derivatives of the German V-1. U.S. and Allied engineers had worked unsuccessfully to develop an equivalent to the V-1 during the war, but they came up short. Using recovered German V-1s after the war, U.S. engineers were able to work around prior problems by reverse engineering the V-1.[3] Early designs used standard liquid-fueled aircraft engines and autopilots for guidance and control. Later on, command guidance and inertial navigation systems (INS)

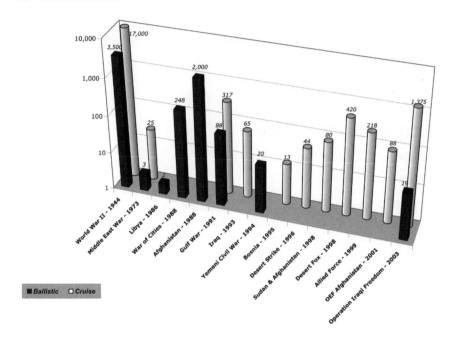

Figure 1   History of Cruise and Ballistic Missile Use. (*Sources:* [1] "Aircraft and Munition Effectiveness in Desert Storm," in *Operation Desert Storm: Evaluation of the Air Campaign,* GAO Report GAO/NSIAD-97-134, June 1997, http://www.fas.org /man/gao/nsiad97134/app_03.htm. [2] "Cruise missiles and 'smart' bombs used in Afghanistan," *Jane's Missiles and Rockets,* November 1, 2001, http://www.janes. com. [3] *Cruise Missiles: Proven Capability Should Affect Aircraft and Force Structure,* GAO Report GAO/NSIAD-95-116, April 1995, 27–28, http://www.gao.gov/archive/1995/ ns95116.pdf. [4] M. L. Cummings, "The Double-Edged Sword of Secrecy in Military Weapon Development," *IEEE Technology and Society Magazine 22,* 4 (Winter 2003– 2004), http://web.mit.edu/aeroastro/www/people/missyc/pdfs/CummingsSSIT.pdf. [5] Michael Dorsey, "Chief calls CALCM a 'very good capability,' " *Air Force News,* May 6, 1999, http://www.fas.org/man/dod-101/sys/smart/docs/n19990505_990883.htm. [6] "Egypt Nuclear, Chemical and Missile Milestones—1960–2000: Risk Report," Wisconsin Project on Nuclear Arms Control, September-October 2000, http://www. wisconsinproject.org/countries/egypt/milestones.htm. [7] "Iran's drive to deploy ballistic missiles," *Jane's Intelligence Review,* June 1, 1995, http://www.fas.org /news/iran/1995/iran-950611.htm. [8] David Isby, "Cruise Missiles Flew Half the Desert Fox Strike Missions," *Jane's Missiles and Rockets,* February 12, 1999, http://www. janes.com. [8] Benjamin Lambeth, *NATO's Air War for Kosovo* (Santa Monica: The RAND Corp., 2001), http://www.rand.org/pubs/monograph_reports/MR1365/. [9] "Missiles, NBC Weapons, and Conflict in the Middle East: An Annotated Chronology," James Martin Center for Nonproliferation Studies, May 1999, http://cns.miis.edu /research/wmdme/chrono.htm. [10] *Operation Enduring Freedom and the Conflict in Afghanistan: An Update,* House of Commons Library, October 31, 2001, http://www. parliament.uk/commons/lib/research/rp2001/rp01-081.pdf. [11] "Operation Deliberate Force," NATO AFSouth Factsheet, December 16, 2002, http://www.afsouth.nato. int/factsheets/DeliberateForceFactSheet.htm. [12] Richard Russell, *Weapons Proliferation and War in the Greater Middle East: Strategic Contest* (New York: Routledge, 2005), 59–76. [13] "Storm Shadow/SCALP EG CM," *Defense Update,* January 27, 2005, http://www.defense-update.com/products/s/storm-shadow.htm. [14] Gregory Treverton, *Framing Compellent Strategies* (Santa Monica: The RAND Corp., 2000), http:// www.rand.org/pubs/monograph_reports/MR1240/.)

replaced autopilots while solid propellants and—preferentially—air-breathing turbojet (and later more efficient turbofan) engines largely supplanted liquid-propelled engines. The U.S. Navy submarine-delivered Regulus missile and the U.S. Air Force ground-launched Matador were built to deliver nuclear weapons, while the Soviet Union focused on heavy nuclear-armed and conventionally armed cruise missiles fired from submarines and strategic bombers intended to destroy U.S. carrier battle groups at sea. These early designs had little or no military utility as conventional means of delivery. The long flight times of early cruise missiles meant that the INS accumulated operationally unacceptable navigation errors, resulting from inertial drift, wind, and thermal updrafts. In addition to impairing terminal accuracy, these shortcomings also precluded cruise missiles from flying low and evading terrain obstacles and thereby avoiding radar detection and ground-based air defenses. By the late 1950s, ballistic missiles and manned aircraft had become the preferred means of weapons delivery—nuclear and nonnuclear alike.

The military utility of LACMs finally blossomed with the development of a new form of guidance know as terrain contour-matching (TERCOM). It depended on a small radar's sensing and comparing the terrain over which the cruise missile flew and comparing it with mapping data stored in the missile's flight control system. TERCOM not only facilitated accurate delivery but also permitted the missile to fly very low and avoid enemy air defenses. An additional, even more advanced technology called digital scene-matching area correlation (DSMAC), wherein images of the target area collected by an onboard camera are compared with stored ones, further improved terminal accuracy. But because these advances depended heavily on highly classified satellite imagery for terrain maps as well as uniquely skilled sensor specialists, they remained the exclusive domain of the United States and Soviet Union—at least until the advent of the Global Positioning System (GPS) and its subsequent global commercialization.[4] Most notably for cruise missile use, this revolution in TERCOM and DSMAC guidance and control technology ushered in a host of new types of cruise missiles, most prominently, the U.S. Tomahawk. The increasing spread of GPS and its Russian, European, and Chinese competitors has greatly reduced the cost of the precise delivery of munitions and removed one of two primary barriers (the other being highly efficient propulsion) to using LACMs for delivery much beyond a range of 300 km.[5]

The cruise missile was by no means easy for platform-centric military institutions to adapt. The U.S. Air Force and U.S. Navy dragged their feet for 20 years before making any solid commitment to procure LACMs and unmanned aerial vehicles (UAVs) in militarily significant quantities. Much is made of the general rule that reusable tactical aircraft can carry seven times the payload of a cruise or ballistic missile. But when the expected rate of attrition and true life cycle costs of aircraft and missiles are factored in, a different picture emerges. Writing in a monograph published by the Air War College in 2000, U.S. Air Force Lt. Col. David Nicholls argued that so long as cruise missile attrition is less than 80 percent, cruise missiles are more cost effective than manned aircraft.[6] While this is an important insight for the U.S. military, it is a much more profound one for developing countries worried about the survivability of their aircraft facing industrialized powers. Given the relative cost advantages of LACMs compared with both aircraft and ballistic missiles, it would not be surprising to find various countries entertaining the notion that LACMs may increasingly offer them a so-called "poor man's air force," or the capacity to conduct a strategic bombing campaign without the need to first achieve air superiority.[7] Indeed, adding LACMs to an existing ballistic missile inventory has the additional advantage of increasing the probability of penetrating missile defenses, thereby assuring that cruise missile attrition will remain substantially less than 80 percent.

Though perhaps initially oversold, cruise missile utility was first demonstrated during Operation Desert Storm beginning in January 1991 when a U.S.-led United Nations coalition commenced its air campaign against Iraq. U.S. Tomahawk cruise missiles played a role similar to the one conceived by Soviet strategists in designing their air operation: during the first hours of the air campaign, LACM strikes (contrasted with ballistic missiles in the Soviet and, later, Chinese plans) leveraged the subsequent effectiveness of manned aircraft by attacks on critical Iraqi leadership, air defense and command-and-control targets, among others. A total of 282 submarine-launched Tomahawks and 35 air-launched cruise missiles were used in 1991. The Joint Chiefs of Staff boasted of an 85 percent success rate, but subsequent analysis by the Center for Naval Analyses and the Defense Intelligence Agency pointed to a substantially lower (but classified) record of success, at least in the case of navy Tomahawks, due in part to the inadequacy of the missile's blast fragmentation warhead against hardened targets and its TERCOM limitations over desert terrain.[8] Because the existence of the U.S. Air Force conventional air-launched cruise missile (CALCM) was classified in 1991, it was not publicly acknowledged until much later that the 35 CALCMs used in the 1991 war were equipped with GPS guidance, suggesting that they performed more effectively by overcoming TERCOM's route planning limitations over desert terrain. After the war, the navy developed a Block III variant that incorporated GPS into the missile's guidance system.

Despite some weaknesses during the Tomahawk's first use, the U.S. military rapidly exploited this real-world battlefield experience. Future upgrades focused on improved accuracy, lighter warheads, extended range, more agile mission and weapons planning systems, and more effective warheads to deal with point, area, and hard targets.[9] These improvements help explain why, twelve years after Operation Desert Storm, operating against a diminished Iraqi target set compared with 1991 and during a war of only three weeks compared to 1991's six week campaign, the U.S. military employed over four times as many LACMs (1,340 versus 317). Broadened LACM utility was also on display in the British effort. The Iraq War saw the U.K. -French-produced Storm Shadow cruise missile used for the first time in combat. Launched from British Tornados, around 30 were reportedly used successfully against high-value, hardened targets, such as communications bunkers.[10] While LACM inventories were no doubt more substantial than they were in 1991, the overall increase in LACM use also resulted from the significant improvements made in precision LACM delivery, making them a critical factor in the rapid achievement of U.S. and British air superiority. Here once again, LACMs helped leverage aircraft effectiveness, which included over 4,000 sorties to degrade Iraqi air defenses.[11] Yet, LACMs were only a small part of the dramatic transformation that had occurred in precision delivery of conventional munitions between 1991 and 2003: of roughly 29,000 bombs and missiles used by the United States in the 2003 war in Iraq, almost 70 percent were precision guided. This compares to only 7 percent during the 1991 war against Iraq—an order of magnitude improvement.[12]

If America's use of cruise missiles in Iraq in 2003 represented the largest use of such weapons in combat since World War II, it was not the only historic marker established in that otherwise lopsided military campaign. Not since Egypt used 25 Soviet-made AS-5 cruise missiles against Israel in the Yom Kippur War had any country other than the United States employed LACMs in combat. Perhaps as a prophecy of future circumstances, Iraq surprised coalition forces when, on the first day of combat, it launched the first of five LACMs, which in this case providentially came within less than a kilometer of striking a U.S. Marine encampment on the Kuwaiti border.[13] Although there existed much prewar uncertainty about the nature of Iraq's ballistic missile threat, coalition air defense and intelligence personnel were well prepared to deal with ballistic missiles. All 9 threatening Iraqi ballistic missiles were intercepted while another 10 nonthreatening missiles landed harmlessly in the desert or Gulf waters. On the other hand, neither the U.S. Army's Patriot ground-based surveillance radars or the U.S. Air Force's Airborne Warning and Control System (AWACS) detected any of the five crude Iraqi cruise missiles. Although none achieved any direct military impact, their use was not without consequence. The sudden emergence of a cruise missile threat caused coalition forces to alter their rules of engagement, which meant that Patriot missile defense units faced both low-angle cruise and high-angle ballistic missile threats. Such a complication contributed to friendly-fire incidents, when Patriot batteries mistakenly shot down two coalition aircraft and one friendly aircraft destroyed a Patriot radar after mistaking its monitoring of the aircraft for hostile target preparation. It was learned after the war that Iraq had worked on converting Chinese-made Seersucker anti-ship cruise missiles (ASCMs) into land-attack systems with the objective of extending a tenfold improvement in range from 100 to 1,000 km. That project was cut short before the war's start but not before Iraq managed to transform a handful of Seersuckers into primitive LACMs with a range of roughly 150 km. Had Iraq been more skilled in fashioning these LACMs or in executing strike missions, their military consequences might have been more significant. Still, the event provided a serendipitous warning of what could come should LACMs spread more widely.

The two wars in Iraq represented only the most prominent examples of LACM use since World War II. In between the first and second wars in Iraq, LACMs became the U.S. weapon of choice because of their accuracy and because they did not place pilots at risk. This was demonstrated in two enforcement missions in January and June of 1993: Operation Desert Strike to protect the Kurds in 1996, and Operation

Desert Fox in 1998 in response to Iraq's interference with United Nations (UN) inspectors, when 420 cruise missiles performed half the strike missions.[14] Despite Desert Strike's involving only 44 cruise missiles, LACMs demonstrated how highly accurate unmanned weapons, some traveling over great distances, could achieve decisive military and political results without risking manned aircraft or producing unwanted collateral damage. Two B-52s armed with 13 CALCMs flew 22,400 km using aerial refueling, and during their 14 hours of flight, reprogrammed CALCM aim points based on the latest intelligence. After two days of successful strikes against thick Iraqi air defenses, and as an additional carrier, several aircraft, and ground units began deploying to the region, Iraq stood down from further actions against the Kurds and agreed to an expanded no-fly zone.

LACMs also figured in contingencies outside of Iraq. They played a minor role when North Atlantic Treaty Organization (NATO) forces undertook Operation Deliberate Force against the Bosnian Serb army in 1995, which led to the Dayton peace accords. More substantial use of LACMs occurred in NATO's nearly three-month-long bombing campaign against Serbia in Operation Allied Force in 1999 during the Kosovo War. Allied Force was designed to force Serbia to stop its ethnic cleansing of Kosovar Albanians. After the conflict, a senior navy admiral testified before Congress that Tomahawks had damaged or destroyed 90 percent of assigned targets, including some mobile targets that demanded unprecedented rates of response.[15] The Royal Navy, in its first use of cruise missiles in combat, reported that 17 of 20 U.S.-furnished Tomahawk cruise missiles fired successfully struck their targets.[16] British officials would later boast that the Royal Navy's LACM helped coerce Slobodan Milosevic eventually to agree to NATO's terms.[17] Two years later, an unknown number of British Tomahawks, along with U.S.-delivered LACMs, also took part in the opening salvoes of Operation Enduring Freedom in Afghanistan.[18] Prior to September 11, 2001 Tomahawks' operational successes had already taken a toll on LACM inventories, forcing the U.S. Navy in 1999 to convert 200 Tomahawk ASCMs into LACMs as well as upgrade another 424 TERCOM-only versions into the GPS variant. In rationalizing these upgrades and inventory increases, a senior navy official in March 2000 noted an average of 110 Tomahawks per year had been expended since 1993.[19]

The most controversial operations involving LACMs were the attacks on the al-Shifa pharmaceutical plant in Khartoum, Sudan and on al-Qaeda camps in Afghanistan in retaliation for the al-Qaeda-sponsored embassy bombings in Tanzania and Kenya in August 1998. Although the al-Shifa strike dominated press scrutiny due largely to questions about the plant's role in producing chemical weapons, the ineffectiveness of cruise missile attacks against Osama bin Laden's Afghan camps underscored the difficult challenges of attacking fleeting targets. While using LACMs stationed on submarines in the Arabian Sea kept troops out of harm's way, it invited enormous operational problems. The most crucial was the long delay between acquiring reliable intelligence on bin Laden's precise location and the execution of the LACM strike—a process normally requiring six hours.[20] This reality generated significant interest in new roles for unarmed and subsequently, armed UAVs.

Unarmed UAVs, with their extended loiter capability, were seen to provide surveillance and communications connectivity superior to that of manned aircraft. But armed UAVs could do much more. In the aftermath of the September 11 terrorist attacks, the United States for the first time effectively employed armed Predator UAVs. By November 2001, two Hellfire missiles launched from a Predator killed Muhammad Atef, al-Qaeda's chief of military operations. By late October 2002, an armed Predator operated by the Central Intelligence Agency flying over Yemen, with Yemen's approval, killed a top al-Qaeda operative and five companions traveling in the same car. Though questions were raised about the action's legality, the notion of combining real-time eyes, by way of several organic surveillance packages, with a weapon allowing for the virtually instantaneous engagement of so-called time-critical targets, was powerfully appealing. Assuming that authorization to fire could be prearranged or achieved quickly, such a combined sensor and weapons-carrying UAV overcame the drawbacks of using LACMs launched from great distances hours after acquiring targeting intelligence.

Tomahawk cruise missiles used in the war with Iraq in 2003 could not be directed remotely after launch like armed Predators, but in early November 2002 the U.S. Navy completed the demonstration test flight phase of a program aimed at enabling the remote redirection of LACMs after launch. Called the Tactical Tomahawk, this new Tomahawk is capable of being reprogrammed in flight not only to attack one of 15 preprogrammed targets but also to switch to a new target based on a last minute change. The navy accepted it for service in September 2004. At a cost of slightly more than $729,000 apiece, or roughly half of a Tomahawk Block III's cost, this new LACM also is equipped with a video camera and can loiter over the battle area for some hours (compared with Predator's days), allowing users to assess battle damage and send entirely new GPS coordinates to redirect the missile to a new target of opportunity.[21] Over 2,200 of these Tactical Tomahawks are being deployed on surface ships and submarines, including on four converted Ohio-class nuclear subs, which previously each carried 24 Trident D-5 nuclear-armed ballistic missiles but will eventually carry as many as 154 Tactical Tomahawks.[22] In 2008, the United Kingdom's Royal Navy attack submarines will begin to be outfitted with Tactical Tomahawks.

More tentative are hopes that a much more sophisticated version of armed Predators, called unmanned combat air vehicles (UCAVs), will someday contribute significantly to unmanned delivery of weapons. The Pentagon's Defense Advanced Research Projects Agency cosponsored with the air force a Boeing Corporation-designed UCAV called the X-45, originally conceived of as an air defense suppression weapon, which would safely open up the skies for manned aircraft to deliver weapons. But many analysts balked at the notion that unmanned aircraft could adequately handle such dynamic and complex missions. In early 2006, the air force cancelled the X-45 program and decided instead to focus on a new long-range bomber. Were the latter system exclusively a means of delivering conventional weapons, it is conceivable that a UCAV might be an acceptable substitute, but if the future bomber is tasked to deliver nuclear weapons, any future bomber would likely require a pilot.

The U.S. Navy and the United Kingdom remain keenly interested in UCAVs, but the likelihood that they will soon become a significant form of unmanned weapons delivery seems doubtful.

New LACMs and armed UAVs with greatly increased operational agility, on the other hand, seem destined for prominence. Even today, they are central to the George W. Bush administration's post-September 11 preemption strategy, which essentially reserved to the United States the right to attack potential enemies before they strike first.[23] This also fit well into former Secretary of Defense Donald Rumsfeld's notion of military transformation—foremost his quest to avoid long force buildups and address crisis circumstances with rapid and agile application of precision attacks against time-sensitive targets. To be sure, there are clear risks associated with substituting smaller but lethally effective forces, supported by long-range sequential attacks so unrelenting that they allow the enemy little or no time to recover, in place of larger force size: America's seemingly insoluble counterinsurgency campaign in Iraq is a sad reminder that U.S. adversaries are smart enough to know that engaging the American military on its terms is bound to fail. Yet, however much future wars may be tilted toward so-called asymmetric conflicts, the U.S. military remains wedded to increasingly more effective forms of long-range precision strike.

Even though Predator's and Tactical Tomahawk's loiter and retargeting capabilities offer much more hope of success against fleeting targets, the next logical step is turning to supersonic LACMs. With U.S. Navy funding, Lockheed Martin is developing a supersonic cruise missile whose turbine-based combined-cycle engine can accelerate the missile from a subsonic launch speed to Mach 3+ for five minutes of the missile overall flight time. The design goal is a quick reaction LACM that can deliver a 340-kg payload to a range of more than 1,000 km.[24] The U.S. Air Force has longer ranges in mind. As part of its longer-term goals for its emerging "Global Strike Force," the air force is supporting a research and development program to develop a reusable hypersonic cruise missile carrying 5,500-kg payloads over 14,500 km within two hours.[25]

The American development and employment of LACMs and latterly armed UAVs promises to allow for more discriminating military operations. But these developments are double-edged. On one hand, such systems foster U.S. goals to execute a preemptively oriented conventional military strategy. On the other, these very systems—and even much cruder versions—in the hands of adversaries of the United States could present overwhelming hurdles to the implementation of such a strategy. Were LACM and UAV proliferation to proceed unimpeded, it could combine with the further spread of ballistic missiles to give multidimensional offensive forces a distinct advantage over layered missile defenses, with jarring consequences not just for America but also for regional stability and perhaps even counterterrorism. Such consequences, signs of which are beginning to appear, combined with the capability of UAVs to deliver nuclear, biological, and chemical payloads, set the stage for a new level of the missile proliferation threat—one sharply at odds with a discriminating use of force.

REVISITING THE PATHWAYS TO ACQUIRING LACMS

In a book published in 2001 I argued that monitoring the LACM threat will be enormously difficult due to the ease with which development programs can be safely hidden from even the most sophisticated technical intelligence systems.[26] As disclosed by the *Washington Times,* a highly classified report to the new U.S. director of national intelligence in 2005 concluded that the U.S. intelligence community had missed more than a dozen Chinese military developments. The first one mentioned was China's development of a new long-range cruise missile.[27] Unlike ballistic missiles, cruise missile tests do not require large rocket motors that can readily be detected from space. And LACM development itself can be intermingled with aircraft production activities, making it difficult to draw firm evidence of a cruise missile program until the developing nation chooses to divulge the program's existence. Pakistan's surprise test of its first LACM, called Babur, in August 2005, need not have been disclosed then, but Pakistan decided to do so largely, it appears, to place India on notice that ballistic missile defenses would be futile against Pakistan's new weapons. South Korea, too, seemed to have a potent political-military message in mind when, in an apparent response to North Korea's flight tests of seven ballistic missiles on July 5, 2006, South Korean officials advised media sources that Seoul had developed a LACM capable of reaching targets deep in North Korea.[28] The exact provenance of the Pakistani and South Korean LACM programs is uncertain, although it would not be surprising to learn that China furnished Pakistan with extensive support and conceivably even wholesale transfer of complete or component missile parts for local assembly. South Korea is far better equipped to develop such a missile indigenously, yet Washington's knowledge of the program hints that some technical assistance might have occurred.

DIRECT SALES BY INDUSTRIAL STATES

The quickest path to becoming a member of the LACM club is through a direct transfer of components or entire systems. Ordinarily, such direct sales or transfers are more likely to be detected than converting ASCMs or UAVs to LACMs, or converting manned airplanes, either military or civilian, into weapons-carrying "missiles." Rogue activities by Russian or Chinese officials, of course, would be harder to detect. Furthermore, there remains cause for concern that industrial suppliers may take advantage of the loose ground rules in the 1987 Missile Technology Control Regime (MTCR) governing the transfer of Category I cruise missiles—that is, those capable of carrying a 500-kg payload at least to 300 km.[29] A degree of regulatory ambiguity over cruise missile ground rules is to some extent inevitable: the technology needed to produce a 1,000-km-range cruise missile is not fundamentally different from that needed for much shorter-range systems. Depending on the payload, amount, and type of fuel used, range can often be improved by a factor of five or more without affecting the missile's airframe and engine. Moreover, variations in a cruise missile's flight profile, especially taking advantage of more fuel-efficient flight at higher altitudes, can lead to substantially longer ranges than manufacturers or countries might wish to acknowledge. By contrast, ballistic missile range can be more readily determined because ballistic missiles are launched from one point to another point, and that range is governed by a maximum-range trajectory. Thus, while the MTCR has largely succeeded in keeping advanced ballistic missiles from proliferating widely, it is less likely to inhibit the spread of advanced LACMs.

In 1998, reason to worry about the cruise missile range issue became more than merely theoretical. The United Arab Emirates, a non-MTCR country, announced that it had signed a contract with the Anglo-French firm Matra BAE Dynamics (MBD), which was aggressively promoting foreign sales of variants of the original French LACM called Apache that had been developed beginning in 1989 to meet French air force requirements. The French claimed the Apache had a range of 140 km while carrying a payload of around 520 kg. A longer-range variant (~300 to 400 km), the aforementioned Storm Shadow, was successfully competed in 1996 to meet a British LACM requirement for a standoff cruise missile, the results of which led to the merger of the missile arms of Matra and BAE, or MBD (later MBDA Missile Systems, following a larger merger of Europe's missiles activities).[30] Underscoring the inherent modularity of LACMs, the French developed a "strategic" version of the same missile for the French air force, called the SCALP-EG, with a range of between 400 and 600 km. All of these Apache variants, from the shortest to the longest ranges, use the same basic airframe and feature a stealthy aerodynamic shape, low-observable materials, low infrared signatures, and a combination of guidance and navigation schemes designed to achieve a high probability of survival and high terminal effectiveness. The announcement of the sale drew a rash of formal and informal protests (including demarches) by Washington to Paris and London, as the U.S. State Department firmly believed that all versions of the Apache, including the Black Shaheen, destined for the United Arab Emirates, could carry a 500-kg payload to at least 300-km-range and therefore fell within MTCR prohibitions.[31] Indeed, in a leaked memorandum on the sale, the chief of staff to the French Minister of Defense Alain Richard argued that the missile had a range of 500 km and there were many more reasons to veto the sale.[32] Internal and external protests fell on deaf ears, as both Paris and London decided to go ahead with the sale, arguing that it represented no proliferation danger. Britain even tried hard to fashion an "export" version of the Black Shaheen, but reportedly failed to allay Washington's concerns.[33]

That France and Britain, two charter members of the MTCR, would exploit the regime's ambiguous rules on cruise missile range, or simply put aside the regime's guidelines that call on all members to exercise a presumption of denial with respect to such Category I missiles, except under rare circumstances, came as a jolt to Washington and other regime members. The fear more broadly was that effectively skirting the MTCR's range limits would create an unfortunate precedent with regard to the future behavior of more unpredictable states—notably Russia, an MTCR member, and China, a purported adherent to the regime's guidelines. Concern about this precedent prompted technology experts from MTCR member states to take up the ambiguities in determining cruise missile range at a meeting in Berlin, in

July 2000. Finally, at their plenary meeting in September 2002 in Warsaw, MTCR member states agreed to a clearer set of definitions for both cruise missile and UAV "range" and "payload."

Storm Shadow returned to center stage once again in 2007. As part of an upgrade to the Royal Saudi Air Force's Tornado strike aircraft, BAE Systems, which owns 37.5 percent of MBDA, began integrating Storm Shadow into the Saudi package, although the British prime minister had yet to make a decision on the transaction and Washington had not formally advised 10 Downing Street of its position on the transaction. Washington's long-standing position regarding LACM sales in the Middle East has been decidedly restrictive, although Israel is well equipped with a variety of its own LACMs. Reportedly, despite the Storm Shadow's ambiguously cast range of greater than 250 km, the version flown by the British Royal Air Force has a range of around 650 km.[34] Testing the limits of the MTCR's already fragile consensus surrounding how to deal with cruise missile transfers is bound once again to raise the fear of establishing an unwanted precedent that will be exploited even more egregiously by other less responsible states.

Is fear of more substantial sales of advanced LACMs legitimate? Russia's behavior suggests that it is. As Russia's military design bureaus struggled to stay afloat in the aftermath of the U.S.S.R.'s collapse, Russian military and export officials decided to hold an inaugural international air show at Moscow's Zhukovskiy airfield in August 1992. Among hundreds of aircraft and missiles on display was an "Airborne Tactical Missile" (ATM), not yet manufactured but appearing in a sales brochure. There the missile was described as having a length of 6.04 m, a diameter of 0.514 m, a wingspan of 3.1 m, and a launch weight of 1,250 kg. Combined with a distinctive engine that was shown in its deployed mode, positioned under the missile's fuselage, the brochure easily revealed the missile's parentage: the Raduga Design Bureau's Kh-55 strategic-range (3,000 km), nuclear-capable LACM, designed for launch from an aircraft. But instead of the Kh-55's range, the ATM's advertised range was only 500–600 km. In spite of the missile's true potential range, one can assume than Russia kept the acknowledged range of the ATM under 600 km because of the 1979 U.S.-Soviet Strategic Arms Limitation Treaty—known as SALT II. Although it never entered into force, SALT II was implemented by both parties voluntarily, and it counted any cruise missiles with range greater than 600 km as "strategic," thereby limiting their number in accord with SALT II's provisions. To avoid any dispute about compliance, Russia apparently announced the ATM's capabilities to keep them below SALT II's handling of "strategic" cruise missiles.

In 1992, when the ATM was first advertised, Russia had yet to adhere to or become a formal member of the MTCR, making it unnecessary to reduce the ATM's range to meet the more stringent standards (300 km/500 kg) of this multilateral accord. But in July 1993, roughly a year after first announcing the ATM at the Moscow air show, Russia agreed to adhere to the MTCR's guidelines beginning on November 1, 1993. Perhaps in anticipation of the constraints associated with the MTCR's guidelines, Russia suddenly chose to display a new "tactical" version of the Kh-55 for export at the February 1993 IDEX Defense Exhibition in Abu Dhabi.

Now called the Kh-65E, this version had an acknowledged range of 280 km, just below the MTCR's 300-km-range parameter.[35] Interestingly, the Chinese Hong Niao-1 (HN-1) LACM is reportedly derived from the Kh-65E, although the HN-1 was supposedly tested to a range of 600 km in 1999, more than twice the distance of its Russian cousin.[36]

Much the same strategy seems evident in Russia's Club family of anti-ship and land-attack cruise missiles, produced by the Novator Design Bureau.[37] In 1984, Novator delivered the Soviet Union's first submarine-launched cruise missile, the 3M-10 (known as the SS-N-21 in the west), which was capable of delivering a nuclear payload to a range of 3,000 km. Borrowing from the 3M-10's technology, Novator fabricated a supposedly MTCR-compliant land-attack cruise missile called the 3M-14E (the "E" model denotes export), capable of being launched from a 533-millimeter (mm) submarine torpedo tube—just like its progenitor, the 3M-10 —while delivering a 400-kg payload to 300 km.[38] China and India have already purchased the 3M-14E LACM, in China's case, as part of a package deal along with eight Russian Kilo-class 636M diesel-electric submarines, and in India's, as the primary delivery system for a refurbished Indian Kilo-class submarine.[39] Ever cautious about Washington's sensitivity with respect to potential Russian violations of MTCR provisions, especially in the context of the 2006 Indian nuclear deal with Washington, the Indian press account claimed that the Club missile only had a range of 200 km, a third under the range claimed by Novator. And India and China are merely the first countries in line. In November 2006, at the INDO Defense Expo & Forum, a Novator Design Bureau official added an extra incentive to boost the Indonesian navy's interest in Russian submarines when he said: "If Indonesia signs a contract to buy Russian-made submarines, we are ready to arm them with the Club-S missile system." Moscow's extension of a $1 billion line of credit to Jakarta right before the INDO exhibition certainly could not have hurt prospects for inking the deal.[40] In early September 2007 the submarine deal appeared to be finalized.[41]

Russia is not the exclusive purveyor of heretofore strategic-range LACMs that have suddenly taken on a conveniently tactical character. In the April 8, 2005 issue of *Air & Cosmos,* a French weekly defense, aviation, and technology magazine, it was disclosed that Ukraine's state arms exporter, Ukrspetsexport, intended to market a new LACM called Korshun.[42] In an apparent effort to avoid a conflict with the export guidelines of the MTCR, of which Ukraine is a member, the Korshun's range of 280 km and payload of 480 kg were acknowledged to be just under the regime's stiffest Category I provisions, implying a presumption to deny sales. Although no details were provided about precisely where the Ukrainian missile project stood regarding potential customers or the stage of the project's development, the article did explain that the Korshun was based on technologies that Ukraine had acquired during the Soviet era from the 3,000-km-range Kh-55 LACM. Of course, the Raduga Design Bureau originally designed the Kh-55; however, a Ukrainian production plant at Kharkiv produced over 1,000 of these missiles until all production was moved exclusively to Russia in 1987. The Kh-55's advanced turbofan engine was also produced in Zaporojie, Ukraine until 1987.[43] This suggests that the infrastructure to support development and production of the Korshun may be in place.

It is noteworthy that the Korshun's unveiling came on the heels of the explosive disclosure in February 2005 by a Ukrainian parliamentary official that a criminal case had been opened charging that Ukrainian and Russian arms dealers (including the former head of Ukrspetsexport), as well as a Ukrainian security official, had conspired in the illegal sale of 12 to 20 Ukrainian Kh-55 LACMs to China and Iran.[44] The transfer occurred during the tenure of Ukrainian president Leonid Kuchma.[45] U.S. and British officials commenced discussions with their Ukrainian counterparts about the proliferation implications of the illegal transfers. Japan registered its concern with both Ukraine and Iran, urging Iran not to transfer any of the Kh-55s to North Korea.[46]

Based on the description and photographs of the Korshun spin-off of the Kh-55 in *Air & Cosmos,* the missile closely resembles its progenitor despite the huge range disparity. They share the same wingspan (3.1 m) and diameter (0.514 m) and have roughly similar launch weights (Korshun: 1,090 kg versus Kh-55: 1,210 kg). Their bodies, wings, and control surfaces appear the same. Their major difference lies in the Korshun's 6.3-m length, 0.26 m longer than the Kh-55's. This slight difference in length results from the placement of the Korshun's engine in the rear of the missile's fuselage, with an air intake underneath, whereas the Kh-55's engine pops out of the rear section after launch and hangs beneath the missile's fuselage during flight. By making the Korshun more streamlined, Ukrainian designers may be seeking to reduce the missile's overall radar cross-section by eliminating the unwanted right angles of the exposed engine on the Kh-55, which reflect telltale radar energy. Certainly, the reason for the Kh-55's added launch weight of 120 kg is the missile's need for more fuel than the Korshun to achieve its desired maximum range of 3,000 km. The slight weight differential between the two LACMs still doesn't explain their range disparity. The Korshun may employ a less efficient engine than the Kh-55's R-95-300 turbofan, which is much more fuel efficient than a turbojet engine.

Russia's Raduga Design Bureau has not discarded the seemingly ubiquitous Cold War-era Kh-55. At a roundtable discussion on the future of the Russian defense industry, held on May 26, 2005 and sponsored by the Russian Academy of Sciences, Aleksandr Rakhmanov, a senior research official of the Russian Federation's Armaments Directorate, bragged: "Literally two months ago there was a demonstration of our precision air-launched missile, the Kh-555, which from a distance of 2,000 km went right through a window." At the same roundtable, Igor Garivadskiy, chairman of the Raduga Design Bureau's board of directors, where the Kh-555 was designed and developed, argued that while the new missile shared the same external appearance, it had little in common with the Kh-55 from a performance standpoint.[47] Other Russian press reports note that the Kh-555 has a substantially longer range (5,000 km) compared with its progenitor, along with new optical and satellite guidance systems, low radar cross-section, and a variable flight profile to enhance the LACM's survivability. The missile has reportedly joined the inventory of the Russian Federation's air force.[48] Because of its nonnuclear precision, President Putin and other senior Russian officials have touted the new cruise missile as offering Russia the capacity to execute preventive pinpoint strikes against terrorist and other targets.[49]

In late May 2007, Russia tested two new missiles, the R-24 intercontinental-range ballistic missile and a ground-launched cruise missile called the R-500, as a means of threatening U.S. plans to deploy elements of a missile defense system in Poland and the Czech Republic.[50] Although these tests became a convenient way for Russia to express its displeasure with Washington's plans to engage Moscow's former allies in U.S. missile defense plans, they also reflected standard steps in the developmental process of proving the merits of two new missile programs. Their conception occurred long before Moscow had reason to worry—reasonably or not—about U.S. missile defense plans in Europe. What makes the R-500 LACM more than a curiosity is its affiliation with the Iskander ballistic missile system. Indeed, the missile was given the name Iskander-K (for "krylataya," meaning cruise). When the dots are connected in an otherwise confused set of press releases following the R-500's inaugural test on May 29, 2007, what emerges is Russian plans to deploy not one but two entirely different surface-to-surface missiles on a standard Iskander transporter-erector-launcher (TEL): the expected Iskander, or SS-26, short-range ballistic; and the surprisingly new R-500 LACM, about which virtually nothing is currently known.

The Iskander's developmental origins leave much room for maneuver in regard to true missile range. It was meant to replace the OTR-23 (SS-23) ballistic missile system, which was eliminated as part of the 1987 Intermediate-Range Nuclear Forces (INF) Treaty. The INF Treaty nominally covered nuclear and conventional ground-launched ballistic and cruise missiles with ranges of 500 to 5,500 km. The Russian military claimed that the SS-23's range did not reach 500 km, so the missile should not have been shoehorned into the INF Treaty, as U.S. negotiators insisted.[51] The SS-23 was slated to replace aging, 300-km-range Scud-B missiles, of which there were many hundreds of launchers and thousands of missiles at the signing of the INF Treaty.[52] The collapse of the Warsaw Pact and then the Soviet Union eliminated the imperative to address this need. Iskander came along in the 1990s to fill the void, at least initially, in two ways. First there was the Iskander-E, or an export variant of the Russian-only Iskander-M. In light of Moscow's new MTCR obligations, the Iskander-E ballistic missile has an advertised range of 280 km carrying a 480-kg payload, conveniently just under the MTCR's range and payload thresholds. As for the domestic Iskander-M, Russia is under no legal obligation to constrain the missile's range except for the INF Treaty's provision stipulating that no ballistic missile should be tested beyond a range of 500 km. Iskander-E became operational in 2007, while the longer-range domestic-only Iskander-M is expected to be deployed in 2009.

Iskander developments took a surprising turn with the addition of the R-500 cruise missile, tested on May 29, 2007. According the press accounts of the test, the subsonic cruise missile flew very low at about 100 m while performing several maneuvers and came within 30 m of the intended target. No range was mentioned but, like its domestic cousin, Iskander-M, the ground-launched LACM can be tested and deployed with a range of 500 km or less. But again, cruise missiles have much more wiggle room with respect to range than ballistic missiles because of their inherent modularity. As seen in both the Anglo-French Storm Shadow (and its derivative, Apache) and the Russian Kh-55 to an even greater extent, there is ample room within the bodies of these cruise missiles to achieve great range variability as long as the missile's center of gravity is not changed to the extent that the missile's aerodynamic flight stability is materially altered.[53] If, in fact, the determination of range is solely the responsibility of the exporting nation, then the fox will surely be guarding the henhouse in regard to cruise missile sales.

China's track record of missile sales also leaves reason for concern. While Beijing no longer operates as recklessly as it once did with ballistic missile transfers to Pakistan, Pakistan's development of the Babur, a missile possessing all the markings of a Tomahawk look-alike, suggests that Pakistan may once again be relying on its former benefactor for missile assistance. Not surprisingly, Indian observers see the Babur as of Chinese origin, with a "label change."[54] The most detailed account of Babur's origin appeared in *New Delhi Force,* an internet-based version of an independent Indian monthly national security magazine, authored by Prasun K. Sengupta.[55] Writing from his home base in Malaysia, Sengupta details the story of a deal struck in August 2004 between Beijing and Islamabad for the China Precision Machinery Import and Export Corporation (CPMIEC) to furnish Pakistan's National Development Complex (NDC) with one regiment of LACMs, comprising 18 road-mobile TELs each carrying four canister-mounted LACMs. The deal also included regimental command posts and logistical support vehicles as well. China's CPMIEC was to act as the prime contractor, responsible for supplying all components to Pakistan's NDC for licensed assembly locally. Sengupta included a long list of Chinese entities supporting this alleged transaction. But six months later, Sengupta's credibility fell apart altogether when he turned to an entirely different, and even more bizarre, accounting of Babur's origin, with new players, including Pakistan's Dr. Abdul Qadeer Khan, setting up a parallel acquisition network to enable China, Iran, and Pakistan to obtain Kh-55s illegally from Ukraine.[56] Perhaps the only thing that can be safely drawn from the existing evidence is that it appears reasonably likely that Pakistan permitted its ally, China, to gain access to a few unexploded U.S. Tomahawk missiles (launched errantly at al-Qaeda targets in Afghanistan in 1998), and, as a result, now must contend with another entrant to a growing LACM club.

One way or the other, China represents a critical wildcard with respect to enabling the further spread of LACMs. Beijing's current adherent status, involving a pledge to stand by the MTCR's general guidelines, is problematic especially in regard to cruise missiles. When China agreed to observe the guidelines in 1994, it took the unusual step of formulating its own version of what adherence meant. China agreed "not to export ground-to-ground missiles featuring the primary parameters of the MTCR," suggesting that air-to-ground cruise missiles are not included in its formulation. When Washington agreed to waive sanctions against Chinese entities involved in missile-related exports to Pakistan and Iran in 2000, China undertook not to export nuclear-capable ballistic missiles and their related technologies and to publish an

MTCR-like export control list. Washington hailed the agreement as a major diplomatic milestone, yet nowhere in the text of either the Chinese or the American statement was there a reference to cruise missiles. Indeed, the State Department's official statement reiterated Beijing's reference to "nuclear-capable ballistic missiles" alone.[57] Early in the Bush administration, Washington admitted that it needed "to do additional work to clarify China's willingness to implement fully the terms of the November 2000 agreement."[58]

There was at least a hint in November 2000 that China's approach to missile export controls might eventually be brought closer in line with the MTCR. In a policy statement on missile nonproliferation made without specifically referring to the MTCR, the Chinese Foreign Ministry promised to issue new export control laws covering missile transfers.[59] China delivered on its promise in August 2002 when it published the "Chinese Missile and Missile Technology Regulations and Export Control List," which included virtually all of the MTCR's Category I (complete systems and subsystems) provisions, but fell significantly short in treating Category II systems and dual-use technologies that require case-by-case review before their sale. Upon its release, China's lead arms control official observed: "There are items not contained in MTCR in the list [sic]. So in this respect, this list covers a wider area than MTCR. Of course there is also a very limited number of MTCR items that are not in the list because they are not really that relevant, either because we don't have them, or they have never come into the picture, or because our experts do not know exactly what they are."[60] Among the "very limited" Category II items not covered were GPS technology and delivery systems with a range equal to or greater than 300 km no matter the weight of the payload, a provision added by MTCR member states in 1993 in order to expand the regime's mandate to include chemical and biological delivery systems. Cruise missiles, so much more effective than ballistic systems for chemical and biological delivery, were foremost on the minds of MTCR members when they expanded their mandate in 1993. In view of China's growing arsenal of short-range delivery systems, ballistic and cruise alike, this important provision of the MTCR was clearly not left out because these missiles are irrelevant, or China doesn't possess them, or their experts don't understand them. Putting aside the whole question of effective enforcement, if Beijing's tendentious formulation of the MTCR remains in place today, there remains ample wriggle room for China to fuel a prospective missile contagion.

CONVERTING ASCMS AND UAVS INTO LACMS

Conversion of ASCMs into LACMs remains more worrisome with respect to older, first-generation missiles than more modern, smaller designs—especially if a substantial increase in range is desired.[61] Much is made in threat circles about the world's inventories of ASCMs as somehow representing a readily accessible source that countries can turn to in order to develop LACMs. Granted, with roughly 75,000 ASCMs in 40 developing nations, and with several developing countries having transformed ASCMs into LACMs, this pathway merits close attention. We have seen, on the one hand, countries like the United States and Russia turn Harpoon and Club ASCMs into land-attack variants. The ubiquitous U.S. Harpoon, exported to at least 24 nations, was turned into a LACM in 1991 but without any increase in the missile's 100-km range. By 1997, a newer version, with about a 250-km-range, became available to navy aircraft. The Russian Club-series of anti-ship and land-attack cruise missiles do not exceed 300 km in range. The same goes for the Indian-Russian BrahMos cruise missile, which can be equipped to double as both an ASCM and LACM.

China achieved a more significant range increase than did Russia. In seeking to produce an air-launched LACM with a range of around 500 km, China used its own 1970s-era C-601 Silkworm ASCM, with a range of roughly 100 km, as a test bed for a much more potent and capable LACM, called the YJ-63, employing inertial and GPS mid-course guidance and possibly an electro-optical television system for terminal homing, achieving a circular error probability (CEP) of 10–15 m while carrying a 500-kg payload.[62] China's lessons learned with the YJ-63 LACM may well have been passed on to Iran, which is reported to be upgrading around 300 Chinese HY-2 Seersucker ASCMs by fitting them with a turbojet engine and new guidance systems.[63] Chinese companies have been accused of having sold Iran the following ASCMs: HY-1 and HY-2, and the C-201, C-601, C-801, and C-802.[64] Both the HY-2 and C-601 are derivatives of the Russian Styx ASCM and are suitable candidates for Iran to convert into a LACM with several times the range of the ASCM.

As a family of first-generation anti-ship missiles, large-bodied ASCMs derived from the Russian Styx probably represent the third largest class of exported ASCMs after the U.S. Harpoon and French Exocet. Such countries as Bangladesh, the Democratic Republic of Congo, Dubai, Egypt, Iran, North Korea, and Pakistan hold them in their missile inventories. Styx-derivative ASCMs generally pack a total weight of 2,500 kg, more than 1,000 kg over a Tomahawk's weight. But size is a virtue in regard to conversion, as conversion entails removing the ancient liquid-propellant rocket engine and bulky radar and replacing them with a much smaller turbojet engine and inertial/GPS guidance system. This exchange would provide ample room within the missile's body for additional fuel to increase the range substantially, possibly even to a range slightly beyond 1,000 km, depending on the missile's chosen payload. Among the principal challenges would be finding a suitable turbojet engine to replace the HY-2 liquid-rocket propulsion system, maintaining the missile's flight stability over these long distances, and furnishing the missile with a guidance and navigation system capable autonomously of directing the missile to the intended target. China—and perhaps Iran with China's help— have achieved LACM capability from this class of first-generation ASCMs.

Prior to the 2003 war, Iraq turned to the HY-2 ASCM for two distinct programs. The first, called Al Faw, appears to have commenced in the early 1990s and was disclosed to inspectors in 1996. It started up again after inspectors left Iraq in 1998. The program's goal was to extend the HY-2's range from 100 to 150 km, which was achieved. This missile was fired five times against coalition targets during Operation Iraqi Freedom. Much more ambitiously, Iraq undertook the Jinin project in 2001, seeking to produce a true LACM with a range of 1,000 km. Anticipating the arrival of UN inspectors, the Jinin project was cancelled in December 2002, but not before Iraq had investigated the choice of a suitable engine. Not having access to a turbojet engine, Iraqi engineers instead resorted to a Russian turbine helicopter engine and attempted to modify it to produce thrust rather than torque—by no means an inconceivable technical path to choose but one posing significant challenges, which Iraqi engineers began to appreciate after starting.[65] Iraq's experience underscores the importance of access to a suitable quantity of turbojet engines if ASCM conversion is to be accomplished. The only existing version of the Chinese HY-series of ASCMs that is equipped with a turbojet engine is the HY-4. HY-4 conversion to a LACM represents a much more straightforward path. Otherwise, a nation would have to turn to acquiring unrestricted gas-turbine engines available in civilian and military markets from Canadian, European, Japanese, U.S., and other manufacturers.

Interestingly, Iraq viewed the propulsion challenge as the long pole in the developmental tent for the Jinin project. Developing a suitable land-attack navigation system would only be accomplished once the propulsion challenge had been met. But from the Iraq Survey Group's account, Iraqi engineers greatly underestimated this requirement. They assumed this task would be easily accomplished by scavenging or adapting guidance systems from other missiles, such as the Chinese C-601 air-launched ASCM, and if this failed, they would acquire components from foreign sources.[66] Iraqi engineers had at least once before counted on a scavenged C-601 component, but it had failed to solve the problem and the program involving conversion of an aircraft trainer into a remotely piloted vehicle was abruptly cancelled after several years of crashes.[67] Turning instead to foreign acquisition of component technologies to develop a serviceable navigation and guidance system and appropriate mission planning would have proven more daunting than Iraqi assumptions about the task implied. Although the component parts can be acquired "off the shelf" or from civilian or military aircraft markets, integrating them into a working whole that achieves the consistently precise results demanded of a land-attack navigation system is not a simple proposition.[68]

Converting unarmed UAVs into weapons-carrying "LACMs" represents another and arguably easier proliferation path. This is particularly the case should the UAV already possess a sophisticated guidance and navigation system, capable of sustaining autonomous flight over long distances. Otherwise, conversion would entail installing such a flight navigation system, a radar altimeter, and a warhead or dispensing system (if biological or chemical agent release were intended).

Both the possibilities of using such converted UAVs and the challenges of detecting and defending against them have been on display in the Middle East since November 2004. Then, the terrorist group Hezbollah reminded Israel of its vulnerability when it launched an Iranian-supplied UAV that flew undetected over northern Israel for at least five minutes before landing out at sea for recovery.[69] Iran is believed to have provided Hezbollah with at least eight of its own Mohajer-4 UAVs, which Hezbollah calls Mirsad-1. These are small UAVs powered by a 10-horsepower (hp) reciprocal engine with a wingspan of about 3 m and a fuselage length of just under that length. Other analysts claim that Hezbollah used the Iranian Ababil UAV, which is slightly larger and employs a 25-hp engine, and flew for a longer period over Israel.[70] Not surprisingly, Israeli officials expressed grave concern about such a threat, fearing that these small UAVs could be armed with explosives. While a surprise attack on an Israeli city employing these armed UAVs probably would not have a significant military effect, the psychological impact would be lasting. As for detecting or intercepting these low- and slow-flying threats, one Israeli official likened the task to "catching a mosquito with a net."[71] Hezbollah succeeded once again, in April 2005, in surprising Israeli air defense forces and flying over Israeli airspace for nine minutes and then returning safely to southern Lebanon. This second successful overflight conjured fears of Hezbollah using these small UAVs to deliver biological or chemical agents. With such a small payload and limited compartment space, perhaps only biological use is feasible. Even that would require modifications eliminating parachute recovery and incorporating a suitable dispenser system, as well as programming of the UAV to dispense the agent upon command from the ground or by means of preprogramming the UAV if it were truly autonomously flown. Iranian engineers could probably accomplish such modifications.

Israel's air force finally mastered the detection and interception of Hezbollah's UAVs during the two-month war in Lebanon during the summer of 2006. But as one press account noted, the challenge only came after "meticulous planning, sky-high readiness and a good bit of luck."[72] As Israel feared, two of the four Hezbollah UAVs—confirmed as Iranian-furnished Ababils—appeared to have been armed. One carried 10 kg of explosives, and the other, which crashed upon launch, may have had a payload of 50 kg. One UAV penetrated Israeli airspace but crashed just south of the Lebanon border, while the other two were shot down by the imaginative "tweaking of multiple radars" and successfully delivered Python air-to-air missiles.[73] Israeli officials acknowledged the extreme difficulty of detecting and intercepting these UAVs. "We could easily have been in a situation where we found the target, but wouldn't have succeeded in striking it," observed Maj. Gen. Elyezer Shkedy, commander of Israel's air force.[74] Unsaid and even more important are the consequences of not finding the target in the first place, which would be likely in the absence of extraordinarily high airborne readiness.

5

Regional Signs of Missile Contagion

Saddam Hussein's regime faced three harsh realities. First, due to sanctions Iraq could not acquire modern fighter and bomber aircraft, traditionally the chief means of delivering large WMD or conventional payloads. Second, even were Iraq successful in acquiring new aircraft, it could not counter its enemies' anti-aircraft missile technology. And third, Iraq's air force had proven extremely vulnerable, especially when it had faced robust counterforce attacks against Iraqi airfields before aircraft could escape. As a consequence, Saddam's "long-arm" policy transferred funds earmarked for the procurement of new aircraft and related equipment to the development of unmanned aerial vehicles (UAVs) and missiles. To Iraq's list of harsh realities might be added another lesson learned during the 2003 war with America and its coalition partners: the increasing likelihood that ballistic missiles will be challenged by greatly improved ballistic missile defenses, a factor giving new salience to the acquisition of cruise missiles.

Some governments (Iran and Pakistan) are turning toward land-attack cruise missiles (LACMs) in order to deal with the prospect of increasingly effective missile defenses, while others (Taiwan, South Korea, Japan, and India) are drawn to LACMs as precision delivery systems capable of supporting preemptive strike doctrines. China seems to be driven by the need to penetrate Taiwanese missile defenses while doing so preemptively. Terrorist interest in unmanned air vehicles is also worthy of examination.

MIDDLE EAST

Until recently, Israel has dominated development and acquisition of cruise missiles and UAVs in the region. Due to their precision qualities, they form a critical component of Israel's long-standing preemptive military strategy. Israel is a major developer of reconnaissance drones and has also developed the air-launched Popeye LACM, an advanced version of which is suspected of having been adapted for launch from Israel's German-furnished Dolphin-class submarines to a range of 1,500 km, carrying a small nuclear warhead. Although the latter possibility is just that, there is little doubt that the Popeye-class missiles could be readily upgraded to achieve ranges much greater than the reported 250 km.[1] Israel originally developed the Popeye as a short-range (less than 100 km) standoff missile powered by a solid-propellant rocket motor. It morphed into several variants and spread widely, including to the air forces of the United States, Australia, South Korea, Turkey, and India, among others.[2] Range extension seems inevitable—after ordering its 100-km-range version of the Popeye, called AGM-142 Raptor/Have Nap, from Israel, India sent out a request for information for a missile with twice the range, in spite of encountering test problems with the shorter-range variant.[3]

Besides being a major developer of advanced LACMs, Israel has turned to UAVs to perform counterforce missions against enemy missile launchers. Deployed systems include those used so effectively against Hezbollah's longer-range missile threats during the summer 2006 war in Lebanon. Israel has also investigated using UAVs to carry interceptors in order to attack missiles during their boost phase (within 90 seconds after launch). Clearly Israel's interest in and deployment of LACMs and UAVs has extended well beyond the delivery of nuclear weapons for deterrence purposes. Not surprisingly, given Israel's history, preemption and the precise delivery of conventional weapons figure heavily into the utility of these weapons.

Israel's cruise missile export behavior, particularly with respect to China, has incurred the occasional consternation of its principal ally, the United States. During the mid- to late 1990s, it was reported that Israel collaborated with China on developing a cruise missile similar to Israel's Delilah, an air-launched turbojet-propelled missile capable of reaching targets out to 400 km with extreme accuracy.[4] During the same period, Israel also transferred the Harpy UAV, a fire-and-forget weapon capable of attacking and destroying enemy radars out to a range of 500 km.[5] In 2005, the controversy over the Harpy transfer arose again following Israel's agreement to furnish China with spare parts to support that UAV.[6] Although precise details are uncertain, the concern here is the possible reexporting of controlled U.S. technologies that might be employed against another U.S. partner, Taiwan, or used by China against the United States in a conflict in which Washington came to Taiwan's aid.

Israel's vulnerability to Iraqi missile attacks during the 1991 Gulf War as well as Iran's and Syria's ballistic missile programs fostered the development of Israel's Arrow missile defense system. As Arrow and Patriot deployments have proceeded, Iran has become noticeably more interested in both LACMs and UAVs. Tehran has acquired cruise missile systems and technology from China to support its new anti-ship cruise missile (ASCM) program called Nur, which is essentially the Chinese C-802 cruise missile produced locally in Iran.[7] As already noted, Iran seems bent on converting surplus HY-2 ASCMs into LACMs, and some analysts have speculated that the new Raad cruise missile, with a range of 350 km, derives from the HY-2 and will eventually come in two forms, anti-ship and land-attack variants.[8]

What must concern Israeli, European, American, and Japanese defense planners are Iran's intentions with respect to the six Russian Kh-55 strategic-range LACMs acquired illegally from Ukraine in 2001. Even though the transfer may have also included a ground support system for testing, initializing, and programming the missiles, such a small number of LACMs was probably acquired primarily for purposes of examination and reverse engineering. If the latter, the laborious process would literally entail taking the missile and all of its subcomponents apart to create a set of engineering blueprints in order to understand how the system works in each and every regard, and then recreating the copied object or designing and replicating one with similar performance features. The process was employed with notable success during and shortly after World War II—e.g., when the Soviet Union reverse-engineered recovered American B-29 bombers to produce the Tupolev Tu-4 bomber. After the war, with the help of German scientists and engineers, both American and Soviet engineers copied German V-1 and V-2 missile designs in the development of military and space systems. China would have little trouble with reverse engineering, but Iran would probably have to count on North Korean or Chinese assistance to extract lasting benefit from the newly acquired half-dozen Kh-55s. That said, according to Israeli engineer and missile specialist Uzi Rubin,

> it is reasonable to assume that the theft of the Kh-55s will serve for the development of an indigenous version of a strategic cruise missile, perhaps through a joint program of the three participants [Rubin assumes North Korean complicity] in the theft. The eventual surfacing of an Iranian strategic cruise missile can therefore be anticipated with some degree of confidence.[9]

Iran also seems determined to supply Israel's neighbors with cruise missiles and UAVs, including armed ones. According to Jerusalem's Channel 2 television, the Syrian navy expects to receive a significant number of Iranian missile boats equipped with C-802 ASCMs—Chinese cruise missiles copied and manufactured in Iran, one of which succeeded in damaging an Israeli naval vessel during the 2006 war in Lebanon.[10] Syria has long sought Russia's Iskander-E ballistic missile system, which Moscow now plans to embellish with a new LACM, the R-500. Were Russia to agree at some point to furnish Syria with such a potent mix of ballistic and cruise missiles, such a combination of high- and low-angle missile threats could severely tax Israel's emerging missile defense system. A critical variable would, of course, be the volume of missiles Syria was capable of delivering to overwhelm more costly missile defenses.

Elsewhere in the region, new LACMs figure importantly into the defense plans of Saudi Arabia and the United Arab Emirates (UAE). The Saudis no doubt would prefer to see new British Prime Minister Gordon Brown look favorably on BAE Systems' wish to package the Storm Shadow LACM, clearly a Missile Technology Control Regime (MTCR) Category I transfer, with upgrades to their Tornado strike aircraft. The UAE, for its part, has already begun or will soon start to receive the first of 250 Anglo-French Black Shaheen LACMs in the aftermath of the highly controversial decision by London and Paris to transfer this stealthy cruise missile despite Washington's protests. But the UAE's appetite for even a broader array of cruise missiles appears evident from preliminary technical consultations with Russia's Novator Design Bureau, conducted in mid-2006. These discussions concerned as much as a $300 million purchase of Club cruise missiles, entailing a mix of ASCMs and LACMs, and perhaps even anti-submarine torpedoes for the UAE's small navy, which now includes not only coastal patrol and missile boats but also blue-water corvettes.[11]

According to the Iraq Survey Group's final report, Iraq began its MiG-21 conversion into a remotely piloted vehicle in late 1990, but the project ended in 1991 probably due to the war. Iraq then turned to the Czech L-29 trainer aircraft, apparently for the same mission of delivering chemical or biological agents.[12] It appears that Libya, too, had plans to obtain a long-range cruise missile with a range over 1,400 km, probably by converting surplus MiG-21s. The program's goal was to be able to strike targets in southern Europe and the Middle East with a payload of 500 kg. But being less advanced technologically than Iraq, Libya instead turned to a network of Serbian firms to get help with the project. The U.S. government reportedly intervened with Belgrade in late 2002 to bring a stop to the project, which had been in existence for several years.[13] If in fact Libya had intended to turn a surplus military aircraft such as the MiG-21 into a crude long-range delivery system, it would not be surprising to see other countries attempt similar feats. The technologies are at hand to do so; the critical barrier remains effectively integrating these component technologies to achieve success.

SOUTH ASIA

The barely stable balance of forces between India and Pakistan could be upset by the substantial addition of cruise missiles and UAVs to growing deployments of ballistic missile systems. Cruise missiles for attacking land targets would be useful to both India and Pakistan in serving basic nuclear deterrence requirements. LACM deployments on survivable submarines or mobile platforms obviously support an assured means of surviving counterforce attacks, assuming, of course, such missiles can penetrate missile defenses. But in this regard only Pakistan needs to worry about such an assured penetration capability because India alone is pursuing the acquisition of ballistic missile defenses. In that light, Pakistan's acquisition of LACMs will impose on India the additional requirement of defending against low-flying and difficult-to-detect cruise missiles, lest India's substantial investment in missile defenses prove effective against only one of two classes of missiles. Offensively speaking, however, India would not only benefit from the improved survivability afforded by LACMs but also from their capacity to undertake precise and effective attacks without requiring WMD payloads. This flexibility would help Indian strategists counter Pakistan's first-strike, early-use nuclear doctrine.

India has banked heavily on a joint venture with Russia to produce the BrahMos cruise missile, a multi-role missile capable of performing either anti-ship or land-attack missions. Named after the Brahmaputra and Moscow rivers, the BrahMos joint venture was registered in December 1995 and formally constituted in an intergovernmental agreement in February 1998, which outlined a plan for India's Defense Research and Development Organization (DRDO) and Russia's NPO Mashinostroenia to design, develop, produce, and sell the missile. India's ownership share is 50.5 percent; Russia's is 49.5 percent. BrahMos is the offspring of the Russian 3M-55 Onyx ASCM, developed by NPO Mashinostroenia in the early to mid-1980s but truncated by the Soviet Union's collapse. The missile is designed as a

3,000-kg supersonic ASCM, with a two-stage solid-rocket booster and liquid ramjet engine propelling the missile, carrying a 200-kg conventional payload, to a speed of between Mach 2.5 to 2.8.[14] Nominally, under the agreement Russia is to focus primarily on the propulsion system while India will handle guidance, onboard electronics, and fire control subsystems. But in fact, Russia's radar design bureau manufactures the active radar seeker for the ASCM version of BrahMos.[15]

Like most joint ventures, BrahMos has experienced some rough patches. For one, there has been considerable disharmony over which countries will get the missile. At present, the joint venture can produce roughly 100 missiles a year, and of the 1,000 missiles produced over the next ten years, it intends to earmark half for export. The missile's range is intentionally kept under 300 km to make its exportation compliant with Moscow's obligations under the MTCR. Russia's export sensitivity has far less to do with export control restrictions than with competition with several other Russian ASCMs, including those in the Novator Design Bureau's Club family of cruise missiles and the Raduga Design Bureau's 3M-80 Sunburn and its air-launched cousin, Moskit. In late 2006, for example, a Russian newswire released a report that accused BrahMos Aerospace of disparaging the export versions of its primary Russian competitors. Both Rosoboronexport and BrahMos were competing heavily for a prospective sale of cruise missiles to Malaysia.[16] Russia, too, according to Indian observers, has used the issue of intellectual property rights, especially pertaining to the source code needed to integrate BrahMos to foreign delivery platforms, as a form of leverage to encourage India to look favorably on Russian aircraft offered to meet the Indian air force's requirement for a multi-role medium-range combat aircraft—a contract worth $5 billion. Rosoboronexport's view is that the BrahMos joint venture is a one-way street favoring the Indian side, with little in it for Russia.[17] Such matters seemed to have been settled well enough to encourage Indian boosters to expect a robust export market for BrahMos among a growing list of interested countries, including Malaysia, South Africa, Kuwait, Chile, and Indonesia. In commemorating the induction of BrahMos into an Indian army unit on June 21, 2007, President Abdul Kalam said, "Today we have an order book worth two US billion dollars and serious business interest exists for an order of an equal amount."[18] No breakout of foreign and domestic orders was disclosed, however, although the Malaysian deputy defense minister formally announced on July 4, 2007 that Malaysia planned to procure a number of long-range cruise missiles while taking account of "sensitivities of neighboring countries."[19]

Some Indian commentators are frustrated by the Indian government's slow pace of incorporating BrahMos into army and air force units, by BrahMos Aerospace's seemingly exclusive focus on exports, and by Russia's reluctance to equip India's navy with the missile.[20] That said, BrahMos Aerospace moved out smartly beginning in 2001 to conduct nine missile tests over three years of the naval ASCM version of the missile. That initial success led to the creation of the so-called multi-role supersonic cruise missile, an adaptation of the missile to air- and ground-launched modes together with a capability to attack targets on land. The Indian navy was the first service to include BrahMos on its surface ships via an inaugural contract with BrahMos

Aerospace in late 2004. The navy's Rajput-class destroyers will have eight BrahMos missiles on board capable of either maritime strike or land attack. The first of those missiles reportedly were already deployed on at least one destroyer as of October 2007.[21] The navy's Project 15A destroyers will carry 16 BrahMos missiles fired from a vertical launch system (VLS), while the Talwar-class frigates will have 8 VLS, though the number of BrahMos missiles carried on these vessels is uncertain. Plans also call for the modular VLS unit to be fitted on board diesel-electric submarines, which should broaden the appeal of the missile for export.

The Indian air force's version of BrahMos commenced in 2005 and is expected to become operational sometime in 2009. To adapt to air launching, a lighter missile of roughly 2,500 kg will have a smaller rocket booster and additional control fins for launch stability. The missile will be mounted to the Russian Su-30 Flanker aircraft on the centerline of the aircraft's belly. The air force version will carry a 300-kg warhead, 100 kg heavier than the navy's, and the exclusive mission will be to attack fixed, high-value land targets. At first, it appeared that the BrahMos LACM would have limitations in prosecuting land attacks due to its dependence on an active radar seeker. Launched over water and flying low, the BrahMos employs an inertial guidance system and the active radar seeker: the former to get the missile near its intended target, the latter to seek out a high-contrast, large metal object (namely, a ship at sea). LACMs must navigate more variegated terrain before they reach their intended targets. If the land target is not a high radar-contrast target, then the LACM's accuracy suffers. The results of India's initial tests of BrahMos against land targets were improved in part by relying on satellite navigational updates provided by the Global Positioning System (GPS) and the Global Navigation Satellite System (GLONASS). Indian officials also indicated that the radar seeker underwent both software and hardware changes to improve its performance against land targets. As the Indian army became interested in BrahMos, too, for highly precise attacks against land targets, BrahMos Aerospace turned to an unspecified multi-mode seeker to improve terminal accuracy against lower-contrast land targets.[22]

The Indian army originally planned to induct the first BrahMos regiment, comprised of three batteries each having four mobile autonomous launchers, each launcher having three missiles, for a total of 36 per regiment (plus re-fire missiles), in 2008 or 2009. After Pakistan's surprise launch of its Babur LACM in August 2005, however, Indian officials apparently found the army's deployment schedule too dilatory and decided instead to muster a special Brahmos missile regiment, consisting of one mobile command post and two launchers, capable of firing six missiles, in June 2007. Now it appears that the army will eventually deploy three full regiments of the BrahMos LACM even thought it only planned one at the start.[23] If that proves to be the case, the army would eventually be capable of firing 108 missiles within 30 seconds. Operationally, each regiment would cover a frontage of between 500 and 600 km, but a single mobile autonomous launcher would still be able to operate outside of the other regimental batteries to engage targets elsewhere.[24]

BrahMos Aerospace, not unexpectedly, is exuberant about the future prospects of having a BrahMos cruise missile launched from ships, submarines, mobile ground units, and aircraft. On the occasion of the missile's induction into the army, the CEO of BrahMos Aerospace, Sivathanu Pillai boasted that "BrahMos will be a war winner and will play a crucial role in future warfare."[25] If produced and deployed in even larger numbers than currently planned, one defense writer predicts that the BrahMos land-attack version "could tilt the conventional arms balance between India and Pakistan."[26] And BrahMos is not the only LACM that could figure into India's future defense plans. In early May 2007, Russia handed over to the Indian navy an upgraded Kilo-class submarine equipped with the Club family of cruise missiles, likely including the 3M-14E LACM, capable of destroying land targets up to a range of 200–300 km.[27]

Pakistan's test of its Babur LACM in August 2005 and increasing evidence that Islamabad wishes to extend Babur's range to perhaps as much as 1,000 km have moved some Indian defense writers and editorialists to call on the Indian defense establishment to extend the range of their LACMs comparably, if not more.[28] The Indian government may well need encouragement in this regard, but it appears that the Indian army, for one, has had a long-term requirement for a LACM capable of delivering a nuclear payload to ranges in excess of 1,500 km.[29] India's missile-oriented president, A. P. J. Abdul Kalam, has promoted a Mark II BrahMos missile capable, within a decade, of hypersonic speeds (5 to 10 times the speed of sound), a range of more than 1,000 km, and even potential reusability, akin (if not in performance then at least conceptually) to America's Hypersonic Cruise Missile program.[30] But such goals appear highly optimistic in light of the enormously complex technical challenges of dealing with extreme temperature effects on materials and scaling up from simple models to a full system capable of carrying large payloads.[31] A more down-to-earth approach seems evident in New Delhi's reported attempt, in September 2006, to sign an agreement with France on the transfer of technology for production of French cruise missiles in India. News and editorial accounts in the Indian press suggest that the deal, which fell apart due to "last minutes hitches," involved a cruise missile with a reported range of 1,200 to 1,500 km, though accounts noted that both sides were guarded about the range.[32] The reasons for such circumspection surely must have entailed France's obligations as a member of the MTCR, which also may explain why the deal hit a snag.

About seven months later, however, revelations hit the Indian press about a secret and purportedly indigenous LACM program, called Sagarika, which aimed to develop a nearly 1,000-km-range cruise missile launchable from aircraft and submarines. After the Agni-3 test in April 2007, M. Natarajan, head of DRDO, hinted that the Sagarika—that is, "a strategic system I cannot talk about"—was successfully tested during the same timeframe.[33] Despite a press report that India still faced a major hurdle in designing a small enough nuclear warhead for the dual-capable LACM and sought to acquire or produce higher performance turbofan engines, the DRDO made a surprising announcement in early July 2007 that the Indian navy, after three successful Sagarika tests, had accepted the LACM for induction, most likely in its new Advanced Technology Vessel (submarine) in 2008.[34] But a DRDO scientist only confused the precise status of India's LACM ambitions when, three weeks after the supposed induction announcement of Sagarika, he announced a new LACM development program called Nirbhay (The Fearless). The director of DRDO's Advanced Systems Laboratory in Hyderabad described a missile having the same range (1,000 km) as Sagarika and characteristics similar to the U.S. Tomahawk but clearly not yet operational. Instead, Nirbhay's design was set and a technology demonstrator was planned for 2009.[35]

The pace of new LACM announcements picked up once again in the fall of 2007. The Indian defense ministry confirmed that India and Israel had teamed up to convert India's Lakshya pilotless vehicle into a LACM, with a goal of achieving a range of up to 600 km carrying a 350-kg payload. The team members reportedly had chosen a Russian propulsion system, the TRDD 50 MT, manufactured by NPO Saturn, for the Lakshya's engine, but Indian officials were uncertain whether the engine deal would pass muster with regard to the MTCR.[36] Although it is unsure precisely which programs will emerge from India's multiple and ambiguous LACM developments, the one thing sure is that New Delhi has no intention of allowing Islamabad to exceed India's missile ambitions.

Unless one is convinced, as many are, that China largely provided Pakistan with support for its Babur LACM, then Pakistan's cruise missile developments are even more opaque than India's, Sagarika and Nirbhay included. In 2002, Pakistan first showed evidence that it could develop a small turbojet-powered aerial target, called the Nishan-Mk 2TJ, purportedly produced by the commercial arm of Pakistan's National Development Complex (NDC). It included a small turbojet engine that propelled a target vehicle at a speed of 370 km per hour but had a range of only 35 km.[37] In theory, the Nishan development demonstrated the potential, albeit a slim one, to transition over time to a longer-range LACM. Following Babur's maiden test in 2005, Pakistani press accounts proudly boasted that Pakistan had single-handedly achieved a LACM whereas India had to resort to using "fast-track technology for its cruise missile . . . borrowed from Russia."[38] That Pakistan achieved such a transition in three years and was immediately prepared to commence serial production of the Babur and proceed from its initial ground-launched version to submarine-, ship-, and eventually air-launched missiles, entirely on its own, defies reason.

Pakistan's Babur LACM may well deserve to be hailed a product of "technical blowback." Of the several dozen Tomahawks that the United States launched against al-Qaeda training camps in Afghanistan in August 1998, reportedly six went awry and landed in Pakistan. Pakistan later acknowledged they had recovered two.[39] Pakistani sources told *Jane's Defence Weekly* that Pakistan commenced its own cruise missile program in 1998 based in part on the reverse engineering of the recovered Tomahawks.[40] Some degree of Chinese assistance seems fairly certain if, as reported, Pakistan handed over the two unexploded Tomahawks to Beijing for its own evaluation. For its own part, China has struggled mightily with developing small, efficient engines and has turned to Russia for the specialized skills needed to assist its own development programs.[41] Pakistan has not only depended extensively on Chinese and North Korean assistance in virtually all of its ballistic missile programs, but it has also repeatedly sought help from outside sources for far simpler military equipment than LACMs. There is little evidence that Pakistan possesses the necessary aeronautical, electrical, mechanical, and computer engineering skills needed to produce all of the critical component parts of such a missile program. More important, what separates the industrial from the developing world is the capacity to integrate technology components into complex systems that achieve repeatable results under often taxing operational environments. In this respect, Pakistan—and even far more advanced countries—comes up significantly short. Thus, the only real question here is the precise nature and extent of China's assistance.[42]

While Chinese pedigree seems reasonable to assume for Babur, Pakistan's test on August 25, 2007 of yet another new LACM, called Raad (not to be confused with Iran's LACM of the same name), only muddies the water further. Launched from a Mirage III aircraft, the LACM has a declared range of 350 km and will be capable of carrying a variety of different warheads, nuclear included. According to *Aviation Week & Space Technology,* the missile reportedly possesses stealth design materials and, unlike its multi-launch mode cousin, Babur, Raad appears destined for duty exclusively as an air-launched LACM. The missile has an air intake for its turbojet engine that juts out, while the Babur's is flush with its airframe. Most notably, Raad's tail configuration may suggest a South African connection, though the Pakistani weapons acquired from that country are not known to include LACMs.[43]

Some Indian observers fear that Pakistan's new cruise missile capabilities are of strategic importance. Less than a year after Babur's arrival, a respected Indian defense correspondent, Vishal Thapar, interviewed the Indian navy's Chief Admiral Arun Prakash, who characterized Pakistan's surprising cruise missile acquisition as a destabilizing event, particularly given its nuclear capability. Thapar summed up Babur's arrival on the scene as follows: "The worry is that the next arms race between India and Pakistan will be . . . cruise missiles. With Islamabad already declaring its intention to nuclear-tip the Babur, the prospects are ominous. Unlike ballistic missiles, the terrain-hugging cruise missiles are difficult to detect and are also deadly accurate. This is bad news for nuclear deterrence in the sub-continent."[44]

NORTHEAST ASIA

Missile contagion is most evident and potentially destabilizing in Northeast Asia. China's long-term quest to produce and deploy advanced LACMs is finally beginning to have consequences. It reflects the high priority Beijing has assigned to the Second Artillery of the People's Liberation Army (PLA). China has steadfastly increased the threat to Taiwan by adding 100 or more new ballistic missiles each year to Second Artillery missile regiments facing Taiwan. But as Professor Bernard D. Cole of the U.S. National Defense University has observed, "While the ballistic missiles Beijing keeps adding to in Fujian Province receive most of the media attention, China is also rapidly developing cruise missiles that will be at least as difficult for Taiwan's air defenses to counter."[45] At a time when Taiwanese experts speculate about when in the future the Chinese-Taiwan military balance will swing in Beijing's favor, Professor Cole declared in March 2007 that "the balance of military capability between Taiwan's military and the PLA has already shifted in the latter's favor."[46]

Precisely when, if at all, China first deployed LACMs remains a mystery. In its latest report, issued in March 2006, the U.S. Air Force's National Air and Space Intelligence Center, the most authoritative government source of information on ballistic and cruise missiles, cryptically listed two Chinese LACMs, the air-launched YJ-63 and a "new cruise missile" of undetermined range, operational capability, and launch mode. Indeed, NASIC even listed the YJ-63's operational status as undetermined.[47] Jane's, a highly respected compiler of open-source military developments, reported in 2000 that China was "racing ahead" with several LACM programs, although it was admitted that these developments were "not confirmed officially."[48] According to Jane's, China build its LACM capacity using expertise gained from its HY-1, -2, -3, and -4 ASCMs, which were, of course, derived from the Russian Styx ASCM. With this knowledge in hand, China started a LACM program, called the X-600, in 1977 and tested a small turbofan engine in 1985, which culminated in deploying a 600-km-range LACM called Hong Niao-1 (HN-1) in 1992. Similar in appearance to the Russian Kh-55 LACM, the HN-1 supposedly had all the necessary ingredients —mid-course inertial guidance aided by GPS updates, a radar altimeter, and a terminal terrain comparison television system to improve the missile's accuracy—to suggest a highly accurate, shorter-range version of an American or Russian LACM. Jane's figured that China had received and exploited one or more of the several American Tomahawk LACMs that were fired, but failed short of their target, during the 1990s. As the HN-1 became operational, the Chinese managed to develop, or perhaps acquire, a new engine that permitted them to deploy the HN-2 in 1996, with a range of between 1,500 and 2,000 km. By 2000, Jane's reported that the Chinese were attempting a further upgrade, the HN-3, with its range increased to 2,500 km.[49]

Jane's reported in October 2004 that China conducted a test of a new ground-launched LACM, called Dong Hai-10 (DH-10), to a range of 1,500 km. No mention was made of the HN-series of LACMs. Compared with the HN-1, the DH-10's features differ only with respect to the reputed addition of a TERCOM mapping system and digital scene-matching area correlation (DSMAC) terminal-homing system to improve the missile's accuracy to a circular error probability (CEP) of 10 m. The 2004 Jane's report described the DH-10 as a second-generation LACM but then curiously referred to another new but "first-generation" LACM, the YJ-63, which NASIC authoritatively listed in its 2006 report.[50] Again, the YJ-63 appears to have been derived from the Chinese C-601, the air-launched cousin of the HY-2 Silkworm (or Seersucker), with a range of around 500 km and a payload of 500 kg. Although most Taiwanese accounts of China's LACMs include the HN-series LACMs—pejoratively referred to as the "Russian copy series"—along with the new DH-10 (dubbed the HN-2000), it seems safe to say that China has two LACMs, the ground-launched DH-10 and the air-launched YJ-63.[51] On the basis of NASIC's last report in 2006, it also seems reasonable to assume that China has deployed at least 100 or more LACMs. In early 2007,

Taiwan's defense ministry announced that China had 980 ballistic and cruise missiles positioned to strike Taiwan, of which "over 100 cruise missiles are presently deployed."[52]

China's initially slow progress in LACM deployment in the 1990s could be explained by difficult accessibility to U.S.-controlled GPS signals in wartime, the then-problematic nature of Russia's GLONASS system, and the lack of a suitable and highly efficient turbofan engine to allow LACMs to reach ranges much beyond 1,000 km. Over time these problems have been ameliorated—by improvements in GLONASS performance as Russia's oil revenues increased; by China's investment in its own satellite positioning system, Beidou; prospectively by China's joining of the European Union's Galileo satellite positioning system in 2003; and finally, by technological benefits from China's illegal acquisition and exploitation of Russia's six Kh-55 3,000-km-range LACM in 2000, most notably the Kh-55's highly efficient turbofan engine, the R-95-300.

China is also likely to improve its penetration capabilities significantly through the application of radar and infrared reduction treatment to its LACMs, which can, for example, reduce a missile's radar signature by one and a half orders of magnitude.[53] The Beijing Institute of Aviation Materials has reportedly developed paint-based radar-absorbing materials, neoprene tile radar-absorbing coatings, and form-based radar-absorbing coatings, among others.[54] China's growing arsenal of UAVs, including those provided by Israel, also offer the PLA options to help shut down Taiwan's early warning and missile defense radars. Anti-radiation drones or UAVs like Israel's Harpy, which was sold to China, have standoff ranges of 400 km or more, and together with the enormous challenges associated with defending simultaneously against ballistic and cruise missiles, they could make Taiwan's investment in high-cost missile defenses highly problematic.

While China may have had reasons for delaying the emergence of its LACM arsenal, it has not been dilatory in thinking and writing about the doctrinal and tactical implications of employing ballistic and cruise missiles jointly. Referring to LACMs as "trump card" weapons, China's analyses have focused on the correct selection of missiles and warheads against the full array of potential targets. Generally, because ballistic missile accuracy does not match the precision accuracy of LACMs, ballistic missiles are assigned against area targets, such as airfield runways and taxiways, while LACMs are assigned command-and-control targets, airfield hangars, and logistics facilities. Much attention is devoted to saturation or "tidal wave" attacks, notably emphasizing the intensity of fire within a narrow timeframe and second-wave attacks to solidify initial success.[55] As China analyst Mark A. Stokes learned in the 1990s, some Chinese believe that, due to LACMs' low cost of development, deployment, and maintenance, their use maintains a 9:1 advantage over the cost of defending against them.[56] This may explain a report from the PLA's weekly *Military Digest* in May 2007 that it is transforming more than 1,000 retired Jian-5 fighters into cruise missiles, the cost of which, according to a Taiwanese analyst, would be around $100,000 for each conversion.[57] Rumor or not, the story does hint at China's growing appreciation of the advantages of offense over defense. Debate about and articulation of new doctrinal and tactical concepts is the first step toward combining and exploiting the synergistic effects of the undoubtedly growing Chinese ballistic and cruise missile arsenals. Now China's challenge is to put concepts into practice in realistic exercises to demonstrate that, in the event of war, it can indeed reliably execute such truly joint operations.

Under recurring pressure from the United States to forego long-range ballistic missiles, Taiwan has fallen prey to the intrinsic appeal—and comparative cost advantages—of offensive over defensive choices. China's relentless buildup of ballistic missiles, and latterly, LACMs, facing Taiwan has driven home the logic of the PLA's axiom about the 9:1 cost ratio advantage of offense over defense. Indeed, in the aftermath of China's 2004 test of its DH-10 LACM, a Taiwanese defense official told the *Financial Times* that "relying on purely defensive systems to protect ourselves from China means we will have to outspend them 10 to 1 . . . . That is impossible in the long run."[58] The reality of China's emerging LACM buildup compounds Taiwan's burden. Even were Taiwan's legislature to approve the $18 billion "defensive" arms package (including 3 Patriot PAC-3 missile batteries and 384 interceptors, 12 P-3C patrol aircraft, and 8 diesel-electric submarines), approved by President Bush in 2001 but held up because of legislative concerns about its daunting size, Taiwan would have to stretch out its PAC-3 deployments to 2019.[59] Even more important, Patriot batteries alone—whether Taiwan's existing PAC-2 batteries providing some protection for Taipei or new and improved PAC-3 batteries—cannot deal with China's LACM threat. The threat posed by China's LACMs would require additional investments in airborne sensors and improved command and control to detect and intercept low-flying LACMs. Thus, a seemingly powerful consensus has emerged that Taiwan should seek both defensive and offensive options to cope with China's missile threat.

According to a Taiwanese press report, the United States forced Taiwan, in 1981, to give up a nascent development program, called Tien Ma (Sky Horse), intended to produce a 1,000-km-range ballistic missile.[60] Washington did not, however, interfere with Taiwan's efforts to develop both the Hsiung Feng-2 (HF-2) ASCM and Tien Kung-2 air defense interceptors, both of which could be converted to offensive delivery systems. Beginning in 2003, Taiwanese government sources leaked stories to the press about a medium-range missile of unspecified type secretly under development at the military's Chung-Shan Institute of Science and Technology (CSIST) that would have a range to reach Shanghai.[61] But it was not until after Taiwan conducted its first test of the HF-2E LACM in early 2005 that it became clearer that CSIST had been working diligently on a truly long-range LACM that was not simply a conversion of the short-range HF-2 ASCM or the longer-range HF-3 supersonic ASCM. But still there remained no official acknowledgement of a Taiwanese LACM. Concerned about these developments, Washington reportedly sent a general to Taipei in August 2006 to learn more. Further leaks to the Taiwanese press indicated that Taiwanese officials were keen to highlight the deterrent value of their unofficial and apparently emerging missile capabilities. They suggested that the HF-2E was similar in size to the U.S. Tomahawk and possessed a range of 600 km, although the objective range sought was 1,000 km so as to cover high-value targets such as Shanghai, and potentially 2,000 km, so that even Beijing was within range. According to mainland press accounts, the subsonic HF-2E is 6.25 m long, a half-meter wide, carries a 400 to 450-kg warhead to an intended range of 1,000 km or more, and weighs a total of 1,600 kg.[62] Also secretly under development, according to such stories, was an offensive ballistic missile derived from Taiwan's nascent missile defense program.[63] As a means of giving notice of the existence and purpose of its emerging offensive missile programs, Taiwan used its most important annual military exercise, Hankuang, or Han Glory 23 (denoting the twenty-third exercise in the series), which started on April 15, 2007 with a five-day computer war game set in the year 2012, followed by a live field training exercise. The Han Glory series of exercises is predicated on Taiwan's defense against an attack by China and typically features one or more exercise goals, which since 1997 have all been cast in a joint-warfare context. With a delegation of Americans present, including retired U.S. Pacific Command Admiral Dennis Blair, Taiwan revealed in the simulated portion of Han Glory 23 a new kind of countermeasure against China's missile threat called the "Tactical Shore-based Missile for Fire Suppression" (TSMFS) system. Initial press reports described TSMFS in oblique terms without reference to cruise or ballistic missiles, while senior military authorities emphasized the system's "passive" and counterforce nature. The shore-based missile system was designed to attack Chinese missile batteries and airfields, not civilian targets, and to do so only after China initiated hostilities, which showed that Taiwanese officials wanted to downplay any previously intimated threats against Shanghai and the Three Gorges Dam. One press account reported that the simulation had Taiwan launching 100 LACMs and surface-to-surface missiles after China's attack, all targeted against PLA airfields to delay the takeoff of aircraft and help Taiwan secure air supremacy against the invasion.[64] Han Glory 23 did not include simulated U.S. involvement in the conflict, but Taiwanese officials were quick to state that U.S. representatives present at the exercise "were satisfied with the result as a whole."[65] Another report suggested even stronger, if tacit, U.S. endorsement.[66] Within days of Han Glory's conclusion, Taiwan's minister of national defense, Lee Jye, without disclosing specifics on Taiwan's TSMFS, suggested to lawmakers that Taiwan's new missile developments would not incur U.S. objections because "the U.S. believes that we could not win a war [with China] without [the missiles]." He then admitted that the United States had yet to actually approve the program.[67]

American approbation of TSMFS was not forthcoming. Instead, Stephen Young, who represents U.S. interests in Taiwan as director of the American Institute there, was quoted in the *South China Morning Post* on May 4, 2007, as saying, "the U.S. view is that the focus should be on defensive weapons, not on offensive weapons." In the same report, Young cited Dennis Wilder, a special assistant to President Bush on the National Security Council, as saying in late April 2007 that offensive weapons on the mainland or Taiwan were destabilizing. Finally, Young chided Taiwan about its stalled arms budget, including, among other new "defensive" weapons, Patriot PAC-3 missile batteries.[68]

At least some Taiwanese observers argue that the objective in revealing the TSMFS in the 2007 Han Glory exercise was to demonstrate to U.S. observers that Taiwan was well into full-scale development of both LACMs and ballistic missiles. Some Taiwanese officials reportedly believed that their straightforwardness about the maturity of these programs would cause the United States to acquiesce to Taiwanese offensive systems as a near-fait accompli and to be additionally inclined to supply Taiwan with needed technologies to support further LACM development.[69] Supporters of such forthrightness believed that there was ample evidence from the past to count on eventual American support. For example, America's Harpoon ASCM wasn't offered to Taiwan until CSIST developed and Taiwan deployed the HF-2 ASCM. Most notably, Taiwan's HF-2E LACM requires more advanced engine technology to reach its objective range goal of 1,000 km or perhaps more. Both mainland and Taiwanese press reports have also persistently mentioned guidance and navigation problems with the HF-2E, though some sources argue this has already been solved.[70] In Taipei's eyes, at least, the revelation of TSMFS thus served to show Washington that Taiwan's missile ambitions had purely tactical, counterforce intentions behind them, and that Washington should not be concerned that these systems served strategic objectives—foremost, threatening mainland civilian population centers or major civilian infrastructure targets.

Whether such thinking is purely wishful or not, Washington's signals to Taiwan—and the mainland—are not always consistent, not least due to turf battles among bureaucratic players in Washington.[71] For example, while the State Department reacts sharply when Taiwanese officials even hint about attacks on mainland civilian targets, the secretary of defense's congressionally mandated "Annual Report on the Military Power of the People's Republic of China" for 2004 paints an entirely different picture. The report listed Taiwan's "strike capabilities against the mainland," including the fact that its leaders have cited a "need for ballistic and land-attack cruise missiles," as the first of several of "Taiwan's strengths in countering PLA courses of action." The Pentagon's report went on to state, "proponents of strikes against the mainland apparently hope that merely presenting credible threats to China's urban population or high-value targets, such as the Three Gorges Dam, will deter Chinese military coercion." The Pentagon's authors saw these strengths as "asymmetric capabilities that Taiwan possesses or is acquiring [that] could deter a Chinese attack by making it unacceptably costly."[72] No matter whether or not the secretary of defense was officially backing such a Taiwanese strategy, and by implication, encouraging Taipei's offensive missile ambitions, viewers in Beijing read it that way. Referring to the 2004 report to Congress, one Chinese assessment of Taiwan's missile programs naturally interpreted the reference to counter-value attacks as the Pentagon's endorsement of such a strategy.[73] Regardless of the meaning of Washington's signals, however, Taiwan seems to be headed toward increasingly open acquisition of both cruise and ballistic missiles.

Missile ambitions are also alive and well in South Korea. They seem to flow from a wish to send a strong deterrent message not only to their brethren in the north, but also to Beijing and Tokyo. Kept under control for decades by persistent U.S. pressure to forestall an Asian arms race, these ambitions were unleashed in a deal struck in 2001 that at once permitted South Korea to join the MTCR and allowed Seoul a generally free hand with LACMs, provided it did not exceed the MTCR's range (300 km) and payload (500 kg) thresholds for ballistic missiles. That free hand with LACMs was supposed to have permitted Seoul latitude to pursue a cruise missile with a range of 500 km as long as the payload remained under 500 kg. But it now appears that Seoul's interpretation is decidedly more liberal. South Korea has embarked on what appear to be four LACM programs, with ranges falling between 500 and 1,500 km—ample enough, as one South Korea press account noted, to target not only Pyongyang but China and Japan as well.[74]

North Korea's demonstrative testing of seven ballistic missiles on July 5, 2006 furnished more than sufficient reason for Seoul to disclose the existence of its LACM programs. Within two days of Pyongyang's missile tests, Seoul's defense minister announced that South Korea had "tested cruise missiles probably more than ten times over the last three years," and that the United States was aware of these developments.[75] Two months later details about a new LACM, called Cheonryong, became known through press disclosures by South Korean military authorities. They included the missile's high accuracy (3-m CEP), range (500 km but with an objective of 1,000 km), and strategic use (attacking North Korean missile bases and national command authorities in the early stages of conflict). A new South Korean missile command would take responsibility for these LACMs and their use along with other South Korea attack capabilities (including ballistic missiles, artillery, and UAVs).[76] Rapidly on the heels of these revelations came a report, in late October 2006, that the government had succeeded in launching a 1,000-km-range LACM, which reportedly flew repeated circular routes 40 km removed from the target and then hit it within 5 m of its location. According to a military official, "an improvement of the maximum range to 1,500 km is also being carried out."[77] With details unfolding rapidly, the South Korean government apparently saw fit to disclose—albeit unofficially—even more about what appeared to be several programs under development. A day after the alleged test, it was reported that four LACM programs existed, three of which were still under development, while one was already being deployed. The four LACMs included the 500+-km-range Cheonryong, which was slated for future deployment on both submarines and ships; a 500+-km-range Bora-mae air-launched LACM; a ground-launched 1,000-km-range Hyunmoo-3, which was being deployed at an undisclosed base; and the 1,500-km-range Hyunmoo-3A, also intended for ground launching. The apparent reason for belated disclosure of multiple LACM programs, particularly those with ranges capable of striking Beijing and Tokyo, had to do with the government's concern that these missiles could raise tensions with China and Japan, both apparently now or soon to be within reach. But after Pyongyang's July multiple missile tests and October's nuclear test, some government officials pressured the South Korean defense ministry to disclose more details of their cruise missile developments.[78]

South Korea's newfound capacity to produce advanced weapon systems has bolstered Seoul's interest in becoming a global market leader in arms sales.[79] The government launched the Defense Acquisition Program Administration in 2006 to handle both its own procurement as well as sales of military equipment. The new organization has focused particularly on promoting military sales, which have already included supersonic trainer jets, self-propelled howitzers, advanced fighting vehicles, and other small arms to customers such as Turkey and Indonesia. It has showcased such advanced weapons as the Haeseong ASCM, which are replacing U.S.-furnished Harpoon ASCMs on South Korean naval vessels. Like its fellow MTCR members Russia and Ukraine, South Korea may find reason to market its own LACMs in an MTCR-compliant version once the LACM programs come to fruition.

North Korea's LACM developments are obscure. Pyongyang frequently manages to irritate Japanese government officials when it launches one of its Chinese HY-2 short-range LACMs into the Sea of Japan. According to missile specialist Joseph S. Bermudez, Jr., North Korea has long worked with some success to extend the range of its Chinese HY-2s to between 160 and 200 km, drawing Iran's interest and that of other parties.[80] While Iraq sought to transform this missile into a LACM and China is known to have used this ASCM as a test-bed for LACM development, there is no evidence thus far that North Korea has chosen to do so. More worrisome is the extent to which Iran may have shared with North Korea the fruits of its illegal acquisition, from Ukraine, of Russia's Kh-55 strategic-range LACM—or indeed whether Pyongyang may have acquired the actual item itself from Iran.

Perhaps the most surprising of all offensive missile developments in Northeast Asia is Japan's interest in long-range cruise missiles. Japanese military officials appear attuned to the merits of cheaper offensive answers to the growing missile threat they face. In October 2004, a Japan Defense Agency panel report indicated that Japan required a preemptive strike capability against certain foreign threats, such as ballistic missile launch installations.[81] Japan's then-prime minister, Junichiro Koizumi, rejected such a notion as inconsistent with Japan's "defense only" policy. Yet the high cost of missile defenses and growing recognition that these defenses might be overwhelmed by a combination of ballistic and cruise missiles may explain why Japan felt it necessary, in spite of Koizumi's public reassurances, to include a plan to study a 300-km-range ballistic missile in the fiscal 2005–2009 defense buildup program. Under pressure from its coalition partner, New Komeito, the ruling Liberal Democratic Party decided to drop the ballistic missile study plan from the budget request.[82] Still, by early 2005 it had become apparent that Japanese defense officials had decided not to abandon missile options but instead to focus their study on non-ballistic systems, most notably a LACM.[83]

This was not the first time that Japan had begun to investigate acquiring LACMs. In the spring of 2003, Japanese Defense Minister Shigeru Ishiba ordered a feasibility study on introducing Tomahawk LACMs to destroy enemy missile bases. Not wanting to provoke Japan's neighbors in the region, the chief cabinet secretary immediately announced that Ishiba's requested study would not be given to the cabinet.[84] During this period, prominent news accounts of the high cost of missile defense underscored Japan's offense-defense dilemma. Each Patriot PAC-3 missile costs an estimated $4.75 million, while each Standard Missile-3 (SM-3) interceptor, launched from U.S.-built Aegis ships, runs four times that amount. At these prices, Japan's defense budget will accommodate the purchase of only 12 to 13 PAC-3 and 9 SM-3 interceptors each year.[85] With Chinese and North Korean ballistic missile arsenals already large and growing, and with LACMs increasingly in the picture, economic and strategic logic seems to be compelling Japan to consider cheaper offensive options—despite its post-World War II constitutional constraints against offensive military options.

Part Two

Proliferation Instrumentalities

Knowledge

Founded in the 1930s to teach students at the Massachusetts Institute of Technology how to develop scientific instrumentation for making precise measurements of angular and linear motion, the Charles Stark Draper Laboratory in Cambridge, Massachusetts became world famous for developing the most accurate guidance, navigation, and control systems for intercontinental ballistic missiles during the 1960s. By 1977, the laboratory's annual report uncannily described the continuing importance of hands-on engineering, which its directors feared was no longer as fashionable in the rapidly emerging information age.

> We are concerned over a trend, a national one, that assumes that manual and mechanical skills are no longer necessary in a world populated by computers, which are impersonal, omniscient, and infallible. A result of this sort of thinking is that the people who are skilled at making things that work are considered expendable . . . . No computer ever made a piece of working hardware. No software ever made a measurement, ground a fitting, sealed a vacuum, cast a bearing, wound a plate . . . . The letdown in standards has not yet become a problem in this laboratory; but if the pool of the highly skilled dries up, we would be seriously affected, working as we do in areas where craftsmanship is a principal ingredient.[1]

Much the same argument could be made today about the quality of systems engineering, sometimes also referred to as systems integration. Systems engineering skills have become increasingly essential as engineering projects have become so complex. The systems engineer molds all the component parts of a project together to produce a system that operates in accord with design requirements. Nowhere are these skills more critical than in developing complex military systems. In the aftermath of the Soviet Union's launch of Sputnik in 1957, such skills proved central to the success of the U.S. space program and the development of highly accurate ballistic missiles. The very same skill set became equally essential to building ocean-spanning commercial aircraft and their high-performance military counterparts. Such specialized skills have spread to western Europe and east Asia. Yet some industry specialists have argued that the end of the Cold War and the consequent restructuring of the defense industry, which essentially consolidated 15 prime systems integration contractors into 5, have disproportionately affected the core of highly skilled American systems engineers. Knowing they were readily employable, the best ones took early retirements rather than put up with seemingly endless reorganizations that repeatedly disrupted their local laboratory or engineering environments.[2] This precious skill set has not been replicated at the level of competence reflected in Cold War-era military systems.

Of course, some military systems are less complex than others. Virtually every treatment of missile proliferation that compares ballistic and cruise missiles mentions that because of the relative simplicity of cruise missiles, they are easier to build than ballistic missiles. While this is true in principle, it is not true that land-attack cruise missiles (LACMs) are in practice simple to develop in a brief period of time. Even simpler military systems, such as the Joint Direct Attack Munition (JDAM), are relatively complex. Despite the fact that the JDAM is not really a stand-alone weapon system at all, but merely a "bolt-on" adjunct to an unguided bomb, the development program took roughly six years of research, development, and testing before it became operational. The JDAM contains two subsystems consisting of a tail control system and Global Positioning System (GPS)-aided inertial navigation system (INS); the former to provide aerodynamic stability during the bomb's flight, the latter to autonomously guide the bomb to its intended target.[3]

More complex systems, like LACMs, take considerably longer to develop, and often encounter extraordinary delays due to seemingly simple technical problems. The U.S. Air Force's new stealthy LACM, called the Joint Air-to-Surface Standoff Missile (JASSM), is remarkably similar to the Franco-British Storm Shadow, now operational with French and British military units. Started in 1995 to replace another joint LACM program that had collapsed under budgetary and technical problems after nine years, JASSM too has suffered from poor management and technical problems. In July 2007, after spending $5.8 billion on the program, a Pentagon review board decided to spend another $68 million and give Lockheed Martin, the missile's prime contractor, until the spring of 2008 to rectify the reliability problems related to the missile's navigation and guidance system.[4] More often than not, such reliability issues can be traced to poor-quality parts, subsystem assembly difficulties, and weaknesses in systems engineering skills.

SPECIALIZED KNOWLEDGE AND MATERIALS

A home-based New Zealand engineer by the name of Bruce Simpson triggered emphatically disproportionate attention to his engineering know-how when, in April 2003, claiming that he had been provoked by U.S. military experts who had challenged his claim that he could easily build a "do-it-yourself cruise missile" for under $5,000, he decided to do so—and to expose precisely how he would do it over the internet. Simpson's premise was simple: until the mid-1980s, building LACMs required restricted-access GPS and highly sophisticated terrain- and scene-mapping technologies, but since that time, due to rapid commercialization, much of the technology underlying LACMs has become publicly available. Thus, argued Simpson, "building a low-cost, autonomous, self-guided, air-breathing missile with a significant payload is now well within the reach of almost any person or small group of persons with the necessary knowledge and skills."[5]

Simpson created a construction diary consisting of 15 project milestones—from procurement of component technologies (largely through eBay) through flight testing to deployment. After he completed each phase, he posted an unrestricted and documented record of engineering steps and practices to his web site, while reserving an even more explicit record of his engineering activities to a paid subscription section of the web site. Mr. Simpson's demonstrative plans drew not only a claimed 400,000 hits on his web site but also e-mails from people in Pakistan, China, Iran, and Lebanon "wanting to buy his know-how." Others were keenly interested in Mr. Simpson's progress. Particularly in the aftermath of al-Qaeda's September 11, 2001 attacks on the World Trade Center and the Pentagon, there was palpable concern in government circles that exposing such know-how would potentially increase the risks of terrorist and rogue-state attacks. Within six months of the start of Simpson's provocative endeavor, the New Zealand government effectively shut down the project when it forced Simpson into bankruptcy over his failure to pay back taxes. Whether or not the U.S. government put pressure on Wellington to do so is publicly unknown, though that is surmised to have been the case.[6]

The Simpson case demonstrates that knowledge comes in more than one flavor. Scholars in the field of science and technology studies have argued for years that true technical knowledge is rarely just the product of explicit phenomena, such as easily acquirable materials, drawings or blueprints, formulas, or even engineering notes, all of which can be transmitted or purchased via the internet. Scientific practitioners adhering to the scientific method are required to transform such explicit knowledge into results—replicating an experiment, reverse-engineering or copying a recovered weapon system, or taking all the independent component parts of any complex system and successfully integrating them into a reliable working product. For this to happen, however, what is termed "tacit knowledge"—the kind of knowledge that one might equate to explaining to a young child how to ride a bicycle—is also indispensable. Tacit knowledge cannot be written down; rather, it is acquired through an often lengthy process of apprenticeship. As such it is a local phenomenon, the product of a unique social and intellectual environment composed of highly skilled senior and junior colleagues, who pass this specialized knowledge around from one individual to another. Accordingly, unlike explicit knowledge, tacit knowledge is not widely diffused.[7] In all probability, Mr. Simpson employed both explicit and tacit knowledge in his cruise missile project. The explicit component consisted of readily acquirable commercial technologies needed to build the missile and written instructions on how to accomplish the task. The tacit element was embedded in his "firm belief that building a . . . missile . . . is now well within the reach of almost any person or small group of persons *with the necessary knowledge and skills*" (emphasis added).[8] Simpson exposed all the explicit knowledge he could over his web site, but it is not at all clear that even he possessed the necessary tacit know-how to deal even with the simple task he had set out to accomplish.

To illustrate how crucial the distinction between explicit and tacit knowledge is in the Simpson case, it is important first to note that although his task was admittedly a simple one, it still required two relatively complex integration tasks. The overall goal was to construct and successfully test a small LACM having a limited range of 160 km, a limited payload of 10 kg, and an accuracy of roughly 100 m. Such a small missile armed with a conventional explosive represents a nuisance rather than a significant terrorist threat, yet even a 10-kg payload is sufficient to cause substantial unwanted effects were the missile to be carrying a biological agent. Cruise missiles are ideally suited to do so because of their aerodynamically stable flight features, which promote optimal agent aerosolization as the payload is disseminated along a line of contamination. But the requirements of developing a suitable agent such as anthrax, preferably in a dry form, and installing a suitable dissemination device on the cruise missile add additional layers of complexity to the overall task.[9]

More fundamentally, Simpson's seemingly simple cruise missile design, like all LACMs, had to provide for a suitable propulsion system and allow for autonomous flight with sufficient accuracy by means of a flight control system. Mr. Simpson was apparently no slouch with regard to engineering and systems integration. According to his web site, he has "considerable experience in electronics and software design, particularly in the areas of RF [radio frequency] telemetry/control and real-time systems development/implementation."[10] Moreover, Simpson claims to have developed a "Generation-3 X-Jet" prototype propulsion system, a more sophisticated version of his pulse-jet engine that he proposed as the means to propel his garage-built LACM. The German V-1 cruise missile employed a pulse-jet engine during World War II. But Simpson's web site does not include the abridged set of instructions for building his simple pulse-jet engine. Instead, it states ominously that the engine is capable of several pounds of thrust, "if built with thin enough tubing."[11] He then encourages the interested enthusiast to purchase—for $32—his "full step-by-step set of comprehensive instructions" that are contained on a CD-ROM including video "showing the entire construction sequence with plenty of tips and advice."[12]

Simpson does include limited details of his approach to designing and building a flight control system and notes that such a task was enormously complex up until recently, when infrared flight-stabilization systems were introduced to the model airplane and helicopter market. But he still is challenged enough by details of programming the flight control computer to caution that he planned to test the system on a much slower and smaller model airplane before doing so on the missile itself. He stops short of divulging too much about his approach by noting that he "will not be releasing full details of the flight control software to anyone except government or military departments from 'friendly' countries."[13] Without noting precisely where and why Simpson might have come up short on this critical task, it suffices to say that his confident technical approach belies the difficulty of accomplishing the task without more experienced engineering skills and a much more rigorous flight test program.[14] Although Simpson had access to all of the materials needed to build a small missile, it is not clear that he possessed all the specialized skills required to integrate subcomponents into a successful product. Furthermore, it should not be assumed that Simpson's skills in building a pulse-jet engine can readily be transferred, absorbed, and successfully replicated by means of a $32 investment and several hours of time given over to a CD-ROM.

KNOWLEDGE AND NUCLEAR AND BIOLOGICAL WEAPONS

The distinction between explicit and tacit knowledge tellingly manifests itself in the nuclear and biological weapons fields as well. The conventional wisdom holds that access to nuclear materials is the most daunting task and that the fabrication challenge has become relatively simple because scientific knowledge has become universally available via the internet and globalization. To be sure, more than just explicit knowledge of how to produce highly enriched uranium is involved in the process of acquiring sufficient materials for a nuclear bomb program. In its first nuclear attempt starting in the late 1980s, Iraq managed to buy rather than make from scratch much of the equipment associated with its materials program, but nonetheless it never quite mastered the skill set needed to operate its centrifuges and electromagnetic separation plant efficiently.[15] The Manhattan Project commenced under the assumption that the greatest hurdle facing its scientists was not designing and fabricating the bomb but producing sufficient quantities of plutonium and highly enriched uranium. Once that mountain was scaled, the challenge was presumed to be comparatively simple.[16] Plans at Los Alamos Laboratory, site of the project, called for a facility roughly the size of a large university's physics department. But once the Manhattan Project's scientists and engineers began dealing with what they expected would be simple design and engineering tasks (for example, manufacturing large castings of homogeneous materials and explosive lenses, and fabrication of fissile materials into bomb cores), they found they had greatly underestimated staff requirements, which ballooned to several thousand. As Donald MacKenzie has noted, "Technological skill turned out to be just as important as knowing nuclear physics."[17]

The limits of operating on explicit knowledge alone were on display in the Soviet nuclear weapons program, which depended in part on technical information pilfered from the Manhattan Project beginning as early as 1941. One of the two spies within the Manhattan Project, Klaus Fuchs, provided the Soviets with a sketch, measurements, and an explicit description of the plutonium implosion device that had been developed, tested at the Trinity site, and used later over Nagasaki, Japan. With the proven American know-how in hand, the Soviets decided to drop their own fission design effort and "copy" the American design. Despite Stalin's massive mobilization of physicists and engineers, having access to detailed, explicit design and manufacturing knowledge did not cut the time needed to copy the Americans' bomb design. In fact, it took the Soviets slightly longer to accomplish the task. This is largely because they were compelled to replicate virtually all of the American calculations and experimental work, while learning quickly that the burden they faced was more an engineering rather than a nuclear physics task.[18] Indeed, no matter how quickly explicit design information about the bomb spread thereafter, all subsequent nuclear weapons programs have taken longer to accomplish than did the original program.

Assumptions surrounding the development of biological weapons also severely underestimate the importance of tacit knowledge skills, which may be even more critical in the biological than physical sciences. In late July 2006, the *Washington Post* featured a front-page article titled "Custom-built Pathogens Raise Bioterror Fears."[19] The focus of the article's attention was on a 2002 poliovirus experiment conducted at the State University of New York at Stony Brook, the results of which were published in the journal *Science*.[20] It represented the first successful artificial synthesis of the poliovirus and immediately raised fears in Congress and the media about the potential application of synthetic genomics to the development of tailored biological weapons. Not surprisingly, the *Washington Post* article conveyed the impression that the poliovirus experiment and others like it mean that terrorists or criminals now have all the basic ingredients at hand to develop custom-built pathogens. The virologists at the State University of New York Stony Brook did indeed create a synthetic poliovirus using genetic information acquired over the internet, oligonucleotides ordered from a commercial source, and widely available laboratory equipment common to laboratory settings. But a closer analysis of the experiment, conducted by Cornell University's Professor Kathleen Vogel, showed that its success depended critically on mastery of an array of seemingly easy techniques, which, upon closer examination, involved specialized laboratory smarts that tended to be unique to local circumstances. Scientific papers and laboratory protocols may suffice to advance a laboratory's discoveries in the open literature, but they never include the detailed minutiae that more often than not requires many months to years of trial and error discovery to master.[21]

When the details of the 2002 poliovirus experiment were examined by Professor Vogel, she discovered that among the most difficult procedures was the making of cell-free cytoplasmic extracts needed for subsequent steps. Even a highly skilled technician who possessed 15 years of experience at Stony Brook found it trying to make the extract. As one senior participant observed about the extract-making procedure, "What makes it difficult is that it is highly irreproducible . . . . And we don't really understand why . . . . We were very happy that finally one other lab, maybe two years after the original paper was published, was able to reproduce our results."[22] The Stony Brook laboratory experienced difficulty with using so-called "standard laboratory equipment" (for example, a glass homogenizer used to break cells open to release cytoplasmic extract). Due to slight variations in equipment manufacturing, each laboratory is compelled to derive, through often elaborate trial and error, precisely the technique needed to effectively use such equipment. Even the most mundane of variables, such as the composition of water, proved critical to the success of the poliovirus experiment. One Belgian graduate student who spent some time at the Stony Brook laboratory and successfully made a couple of extracts was never able to replicate the process upon returning to Belgium, probably due to the variability of pH and minerals, as they are unique to each local circumstance.[23]

The importance of local circumstance also figured heavily into another biological weapons example. The Soviet Union not only successfully developed weaponized anthrax but also deployed the agent in certain of their intercontinental-range ballistic missile warheads—despite being a signatory to the Biological and Toxin Weapons Convention. The primary anthrax development, production, and weaponization facility was located in Stepnogorsk, Kazakhstan. Early on, the Kirov biological weapons facility in Russia sent Stepnogorsk between 400 to 600 pages of protocols describing the development and production of an earlier anthrax weapon. In addition, Stepnogorsk received samples from Kirov of this anthrax strain for local evaluation before beginning the process of replicating it. Despite the availability of this explicit knowledge and samples, Stepnogorsk bioweaponeers failed to produce the weapon after two years of struggling with the effort. In order to kick-start the Stepnogorsk program, Moscow ordered that Kirov and Sverdlovsk bioweapons facilities transfer 65 senior bioweaponeers to Stepnogorsk to adapt the anthrax protocols to that facility's infrastructure and environment. Even so, it took three additional years to successfully adapt Kirov's anthrax formula to Stepnogorsk's environment. It seems likely that the delays hinged on the need to reinvent tacit local knowledge by trial and error, as well as on unforeseen technical problems associated with scaling up production from a laboratory sample to much larger quantities of anthrax.[24]

SPECIAL KNOW-HOW IN BUILDING CRUISE MISSILES

The widely held perception that American Tomahawk cruise missiles represent the state of the art in advanced weaponry is largely based on the mistaken impression that the post-Cold War revolution in information technology has enabled Tomahawk's seemingly extraordinary performance as a highly precise weapon system. But the truth is that the Tomahawk cruise missile, even its latest manifestation, the Block IV Tactical Tomahawk, is fundamentally based on 1960s technology.[25] Although incremental improvements have been made to the missile's turbofan engines and guidance and navigation components, they still essentially are technologies invented in the 1960s.[26] What is truly novel about the Tomahawk is the enormous effort, over the course of the missile's development and then during its repeated use in multiple contingencies, that has gone into system diagnostics. Literally each and every Tomahawk event is analyzed to determine precisely what accounted for the missile's performance, no matter whether the missile crashed after take-off or hit precisely where it was programmed to land. Missile programs like North Korea's benefit their governments politically even when missile tests fail. But technically, missile developers only learn from their errors when they have the capacity to collect relevant data that provides hints about what might have caused system failure. The same holds true for missile successes. Such diagnostic sophistication is not only derived from advanced telemetry packages that furnish crucial flight and performance information but also from highly skilled systems integration specialists who possess tacit know-how accumulated over years of evaluating the complex components of missile performance. Tomahawk's ubiquitous appearance in multiple contingencies since the early 1990s has facilitated the creation of an enormous knowledge base that lends itself to steady improvement in Tomahawk performance.

Specialized know-how is not only essential to optimizing the performance of highly sophisticated LACMs but also to building even seemingly simple ones. Transforming a first-generation anti-ship cruise missile (ASCM) into a LACM represents perhaps the most straightforward path. Some analysts have suggested the possibility that a terrorist group, such as al-Qaeda, might entertain this possibility.[27] Indeed, according to two former National Security Council staff members, al-Qaeda is believed to possess 15 freighters, raising concern that terrorists could launch a cruise missile from just outside U.S. waters.[28] Both Pentagon and Missile Defense Agency officials have reportedly become concerned enough about just such a threat to cause the U.S. Air Force, in 2006, to issue a "request for information" from defense contractors about how to fill various capability gaps that exist in defending against it.[29] According to a 2007 study by the George C. Marshall Institute, "conversion of the Silkworm [Chinese HY-2 first-generation missile] from an ASCM to a LACM is accomplished with 'relative ease' and its range extended from 90 miles [145 km] to more than 310 miles [500 km]."[30] Fortunately, there is substantial reason to conclude that converting the Silkworm is very likely beyond the scope of most terrorist groups, including al-Qaeda. In the study I directed of such a conversion in 1997, the research team appreciated that any analytical assessment of the conversion task would differ in kind from actually undertaking all of the mechanical and electrical engineering steps along the path to completion. In that sense, the task we undertook dealt primarily with explicit knowledge. Not surprisingly, we found the process of locating sources of component technologies easy. Somewhat more difficult was the task of developing the written instructions for how to integrate component technologies into a fully working system. That task called ideally for the expertise of an experienced aeronautical engineer. Conceivably, however, it might have been achieved with lesser-skilled personnel, were an actual conversion team willing to accept more risk along the way. Such risk would emanate from potential flight stability problems that accrue when adjustments are made to the missile's internal configuration to accommodate a new engine, a new guidance and navigation system, and a larger fuel tank. A more experienced engineer could simulate the flight stability of the remodeled system beforehand to identify potential problems and adjust accordingly.

Because of the exclusive dependence on explicit knowledge of the task, the study team devoted extensive time considering the specific skill sets needed to undertake the conversion steps, subsequent test program, the creation of a serial production capability, and the integration of the missile into the acquiring nation's force structure.[31] Naturally, a terrorist group need not worry about the latter two steps but still would have to execute all the work needed to emplace the missile on a freighter in a suitable launch box and to erect and launch it successfully. While Donald Rumsfeld, chairman of the eponymous commission on the ballistic missile threat to the United States, believed that the overall conversion task would take not more than a year for Iraq or Iran to execute, our study team arrived at a far more conservative assessment. We judged that a country like Iraq or Iran would require between 6 and 10 years, which could be cut in half depending on the extent and nature of foreign assistance. Unless a terrorist group could call upon extensive outside technical assistance, converting an HY-2 into a LACM does not seem like a plausible threat.

The Iraq Survey Group's interviews with Iraqi engineers who were engaged in first extending the range of the HY-2 and then starting an attempt to convert it into a LACM (called Project Jinin) provide valuable evidence about the stiff challenges discussed here, as has Iraq's experience with converting manned aircraft into unmanned aerial vehicles (UAVs).[32] Iraq spent most of its time and effort on finding an appropriate propulsion system for extending the range of the HY-2 from 100 to 150 km. The program appears to have commenced sometime before July 1996, when Iraq formally disclosed to United Nations (UN) inspectors the existence of the Al Faw 150/200, which was declared an attempt to extend the range of the HY-2. The Al Faw 150/200 program was placed under a secret Special Projects Office that had direct links to Saddam Hussein's presidential office, increasing prospects for continuing financial support. The plan called for Iraqi engineers to make changes to the existing HY-2 engine (a liquid-rocket engine) using cannibalized components from spare C-601 and C-611 ASCMs. To achieve the desired 50 percent improvement in range, engineers experimented with adjusting engine fuel pumps to optimize fuel-oxidizer mixture ratios. Despite the program's apparent high priority, it wasn't until August 1999 that the missile was first tested. According to a senior Iraqi official, the missile ultimately achieved a range of 168 km, forcing engineers to make further engine adjustments to keep the missile under the UN's 150-km-range restriction.

Interestingly, the Iraq Survey Group report refers to the extended-range HY-2 missile as a LACM even though Iraq's exclusive priority at the time was given over to range extension, not land-attack navigation and guidance. Clearly, the HY-2's existing radar guidance system would have been inadequate to guide the missile—especially flying a low flight profile—over more variegated terrain. The Survey Group reported that Iraq's goal for the program was to furnish greater standoff capability against ships, but a senior Iraqi official indicated to Survey Group investigators that the extended-range HY-2 was deployed and targeted against Kuwait during the 2003 war.[33] In any event, compared with the task of modifying the engine to achieve additional range, engineers seemed unconcerned about acquiring a more sophisticated means of navigation and guidance. Only after some initial success with range extension did they lay plans for meeting this challenge, and then only clumsily. They figured that they could scavenge or adapt guidance components from the C-611 ASCM, or, that failing, turn to an outside source for assistance. The Survey Group report is unclear if any attempts were made to modify the HY-2's ASCM guidance system by the time Iraq began the Jinin program in June 2002. Overall, however, the Iraqi government's maladroit approach suggested that Iraq cared much less about achieving accuracy than reaching its goal of a 150-km range. Thus, only one of the five modified HY-2 cruise missiles used during the 2003 war came close (within 600 m) to its intended military target.[34]

Iraq's several years of research and development on extending the HY-2's range provided a useful head start on the Jinin project, which Iraq intended to be a three-to five-year development effort to achieve a 1,000-km-range LACM. The chief barrier in such an effort is finding and installing an appropriate turbojet engine that can produce enough thrust to propel the missile the desired distance. Only one of the Chinese HY-series ASCMs, the HY-4, comes with a turbojet engine. In the 1997 study I directed, we examined how far the HY-4's turbojet engine (WP-11) could propel the missile if certain modifications were made to the missile's airframe. The structural modifications included producing bulkheads or partitions between compartments and riveting shaped aluminum plates to increase the airframe's length by about a meter or so. By replacing the missile's original bulky autopilot and avionics with a combined GPS/inertial reference system, an accuracy of substantially less than 100-m circular error probability (CEP) could be achieved and space freed up for additional fuel. Modeling of the new design's flight stability showed that stable flight could be realized in spite of the various structural modifications and a substantial increase in fuel and overall missile weight. Carrying a 500-kg payload, the missile was theoretically capable of achieving around 700-km range, and with reduction of the payload to around 200 kg, a range of 1,000 km was achievable. With a more efficient turbofan engine, such as the AlliedSignal turbofan engines the United States sold to China in 1987, the U.S. intelligence community found that China could extend the range of their HY-series ASCMs to about 600 km carrying a 450-kg warhead, presumably without increasing the missile's length or replacing the bulky autopilot for additional fuel.[35]

The Iraqis, however, did not benefit from access to turbojet or turbofan engines, or possibly didn't think they were needed. Instead, they examined using Russian TV-2 turboshaft engines removed from surplus Mi-8 helicopters. Iraqi engineers admitted that converting the turboshaft's torque to thrust would prove to be a difficult challenge, but they felt with enough time and financing, it was achievable.[36] The TV-2 engine test-bed produced only 450 instead of the desired 600 pounds of thrust, causing Iraqi propulsion engineers to turn to the TV-3 from the Mi-17 helicopter, but that test-bed was shut down in December 2002 in anticipation of UN inspectors returning to Iraq. Information derived from interviews with participating Iraqi engineers differs as to whether or not the nearly six months of work on the TV-2 engine evaluation included a test of an operating engine. One way or the other, little was accomplished save for learning that the team had to find another engine to convert.

None of the evidence found in the Iraq Survey Group's interviews of Iraqi cruise missile engineers suggests that the Jinin conversion project, or for that matter, even the HY-2 range extension, could be achieved with "relative ease," particularly if the task were to be undertaken by a terrorist group. The sheer magnitude of Iraq's planning for the Jinin project suggests the overall complexity of the effort. The project was broken down into four phases. The first phase consisted of computer simulations to test concepts for maintaining structural integrity and stability during engine integration and estimative work on converting engine torque to thrust on alternative engines. Phase two entailed testing and installing the engines. The third phase involved building and flight-testing a prototype, while phase four would be devoted to guidance, navigation, and control. The fourth phase would await successful incorporation of the engine and adequate flight testing before commencement. Five different research, development, and production organizations were earmarked to work on the Jinin project: one on airframes and warheads; one for guidance, control, and aerodynamics; another devoted to the launcher; a fourth to engines; and the fifth handling final assembly.

With only six months of work before shutting down in December 2002, the Jinin effort did not have nearly enough time to demonstrate clearly whether or not the Iraqis would achieve their goal within the three- to five-year timeframe suggested. But given that propulsion engineers had only reached the modeling phase, without an apparent test of an operating engine meeting the program objective of 600 pounds of thrust, it appears doubtful that even five years of development and production work would have been sufficient to meet the program's objectives. Work on two prior conversion programs, largely conducted by the very same development organization, Ibn-Firnas, suggests that past flight control and stability problems were likely to crop up.

In late 1990, Iraq unsuccessfully experimented with modifying MiG-21 fighters to become remotely piloted vehicles (RPVs) for one-way missions delivering chemical or biological payloads.[37] The operational plan was for the converted MiG-21 to take off via remote control, apparently from the ground. A piloted aircraft would take over control as the RPV reached a given altitude, after which the RPV would be flown to the target area via its air controller and then, using its own autopilot, it would dive into the intended target. Despite turning to a foreign control system supplier (in Germany), the Iraqis failed to overcome flight control and stability problems, which also continued to vex Iraqi engineers with their next attempt at remote-control flight with the Czech L-29 trainer aircraft.

Dubbed Al Bay'ah, the conversion of the L-29 trainer into an RPV commenced in 1995. Control of the flight vehicle was to have taken place by means of a ground-control van borrowed from an Italian Mirach-100 UAV system. After some problems were solved in taxi testing, the initial flight test, in which the air vehicle stayed in the airfield traffic pattern, proved successful. But once tests began to determine how far the vehicle could fly under the ground controller's video and command signals, the vehicle could only remain under control for 60 to 70 km before losing signal and crashing. Engineers thought they could rectify the problem by installing the auto stabilizer system from the Chinese C-611 ASCM, but the instrument proved insufficient due to excessive instrument drift. Ibn-Firnas conducted another 26 flight tests of the L-29 between 1999 and 2001 trying to improve vehicle flight control, yet none of these tests were truly unmanned ones, controlled from the ground; a pilot was always present in the L-29's cockpit. When an unmanned flight crashed in 2001, Ibn-Firnas gave up and recommended program termination, which occurred promptly. Thus, after roughly six years, the Al Bay'ah conversion program was aborted due largely to persistent control problems. Perhaps influenced by control failures with the Al Bay'ah program, Ibn-Firnas engineers a year later expressed concern about control and stability problems with the Jinin project due to rearranging internal missile components.[38] Ibn-Firnas engineers proved much more successful with developing small reconnaissance UAVs capable of carrying payloads of about 20 kg while flying autonomously to a range of around 500 km. Larger UAVs, with a program goal of carrying a 30-kg payload, were less successful.[39]

From the documentary record of the Iraq Survey Group, Iraq's struggle with both cruise missile programs and manned aircraft conversion to RPVs stemmed largely from inadequacies in specialized know-how, not a shortage of component technology. Assumptions made by supposedly skilled engineers frequently took engineering teams down the wrong, or less ideal, path toward achieving success. Test diagnostics appeared weak to nonexistent, and overall, systems engineering know-how—with few exceptions—repeatedly came up short. But as for access to component technology, Iraq assumed that sanctions would not forestall its acquisition of whatever was needed. In one case, when GPS components were required, the Iraqi ambassador to Russia purchased the equipment from Russian technicians who worked for the Russian government but who also moonlighted from their homes for financial benefit.[40] Whether they worked with Ukrainian companies for gyroscopes and servo-mechanisms or entities in the Federal Republic of Yugoslavia for a navigation system for the Jinin project, the covert procurement program supporting Iraq's delivery systems rarely failed to deliver.

PROBLEMS IN ASSESSING FOREIGN MISSILE PROGRAMS

When it was released on July 15, 1998, the Rumsfeld Commission's assessment of the ballistic missile threat to the United States challenged the traditional intelligence community methodology for assessing foreign missile programs. The Commission predicated its assessment on the assumption that post-Cold War missile programs (namely, those of North Korea, Iran, and Iraq) were not patterned after U.S. or Soviet programs. These newer programs require neither the accuracy, safety, or reliability that U.S. and Soviet programs demanded, nor the numbers essential to meet more demanding strategic targeting requirements. Equally important, these newer aspirants to long-range ballistic missile programs can readily acquire foreign technical assistance. Both key assumptions, if true, would trim the amount of time needed to place a nation in the position to threaten the U.S. homeland with weapons of mass destruction. The Commission's bottom line conclusion: "A nation with a well-developed, Scud-based ballistic missile infrastructure would be able to achieve first flight of a long-range missile, up to and including intercontinental ballistic missile (ICBM) range (greater than 5,500 km), within about five years of deciding to do so."[41] Tellingly, North Korea, arguably the most advanced of the three states mentioned in the Rumsfeld Commission report, probably first acquired Scud missiles between 1979 and 1981 and initially began to produce and flight-test them by 1984.[42] Almost 25 years after successfully flight-testing a Scud, North Korea still remains short of achieving a range of 5,500 km with a ballistic missile.

Various nonproliferation and counterproliferation mechanisms may have contributed modestly to slowing North Korea's progress, yet there are undoubtedly other reasons that explain why aspiring states struggle. For one, senior advisory commissions and other government-executed or -sponsored assessments of security-related issues appear to rely all too heavily on the particular technology at hand rather than the specialized knowledge, skills, and diagnostic practices needed to achieve success.

Particularly when a missile program is shrouded in ambiguity because of the limits of intelligence collection or analysis, the tendency is to focus on the threatening missile's technology components rather than the quality and capacity of laboratory practices or systems engineering routines or the social context within which this type of tacit knowledge flourishes. Such a tendency to underestimate the critical importance of specialized know-how was the case when Chairman Rumsfeld argued that Iraq or Iran would be able to convert a short-range HY-2 ASCM into one with 7 to 10 times the range and with a modern land-attack navigation system enabling very low flight profiles and high terminal accuracy in roughly one year's time, not the 6- to 10-year (or half that time with ample outside help) estimate I set forth in my presentation in June 1998 to the Commission.[43]

A predilection to undervalue the importance of tacit knowledge skills also manifests itself, but in a decidedly different way, with the use of "red teams" that play the role of adversaries in the design of countermeasures to U.S. systems.[44] The ones I have observed or learned about through interviews consisted of a small group of young officers or civilians possessing recent engineering degrees. They are given no access to classified information but rather must design and sometimes build a threat system based only on what they can find and order over the internet or through commercial sources. They are generally also restricted to using only tools and electronic equipment readily available through the commercial marketplace. To constrain the team to operate within the limitations that might exist within the threat nations simulated in the experiment, a monitor from the intelligence community is asked to make certain that the experiment remains representative of the capabilities and technologies known or assumed to be available in particular threatening countries.

Although such red team experimentation may appear evenhanded in conception, monitors can introduce practices that end up poisoning red team objectives. The most pronounced problem stems from the peculiar role played by an oversight team of professional engineers, generally from major aerospace defense companies, who have frequently provided hints to the red team members on technical shortcuts that might be considered to reach desired technical outcomes. This type of information might consist of suggesting a particular vendor to acquire a commercially available fully integrated subsystem that otherwise might involve purchasing separate components and integrating them into a complete subsystem. The observer team might also establish the social context within which the red team activity occurred. During technical program reviews, it often seemed as though the oversight engineers, not the far less experienced team of young engineers, were in charge of the program. Rarely if ever was there an intelligence community "umpire" available to control such inadvertent tainting of the process. In a real sense, the highly experienced engineers inadvertently exaggerated the true skill levels of the simulated countries by supplying specialized know-how that would not be available to comparatively inexperienced foreign engineers.

Red teams need not misrepresent the true capabilities of states or terrorist groups. In another case I was asked to participate on a senior advisory panel evaluating the work of a contractor who was asked to examine the extent to which a hypothetical terrorist group could produce certain quantities of biological agents. We broke down into two groups: the larger group of about ten current or former government officials, academics, or industry executives with years of experience in some way related to the biological sciences, which provided general oversight of the project; and a smaller group of two acting as a red team and charged with evaluating and challenging the assumptions underlying the contractor's rather dire representation of surrogate adversary capabilities, rather than acting as the surrogate threat itself.

The chairman of the red team understood from the outset that with the exception of one member of the senior advisory panel, no other individual possessed the necessary skill set to appreciate the unique challenges of producing and weaponizing biological agents. In other words, the panel members' experience largely came from an explicit understanding of the processes and procedures for producing viable biological weapons. To lend credibility to the red team's task, the chairman insisted to the study's sponsor that a third member be included on the red team, specifically someone from the biopharmaceutical industry with heavy experience in research, development, and manufacturing. Such an individual was added to the senior advisory panel and, in the end, contributed substantially to qualifying the results of the contractor's final report. For the most part, these qualifications focused on the types of tacit knowledge skills that scientists found so critical to the Stony Brook poliovirus experiment conducted successfully in 2002, which were not fairly considered in the contractor's final results. In other words, while the protocols and formulae for producing biological agents seem straightforward, the overall process is laden with uncertainty. The final product of the overall effort was fairly modified to correct these shortcomings and the senior advisory group's membership reached a consensus on a fair wording reflecting the importance of such skills to a successful outcome.

SOURCES OF SPECIALIZED KNOWLEDGE

On June 30, 1999, a fight broke out between the captain of the North Korean freighter *Kuwolsan,* supported by his crew, and Indian customs officials in the Indian port of Kandla in northwestern India.[45] Having been forewarned about the freighter's suspicious cargo, customs officials sought to inspect its bay. Once they fought off and secured the North Korean crew at gunpoint, they were not surprised to discover that the *Kuwolsan* did not contain water refinement equipment, as the ship's manifest indicated, but they were shocked to learn the ship's actual contents: an entire assembly line for Scud B and Scud C missiles. According to U.S. intelligence, the assembly line was headed for Libya. As Joby Warrick of the *Washington Post* later reported, it was as if the contents had been transported directly from a North Korean missile factory. In addition to sheet metal for missile frames and guidance systems, one cargo bay also included missile subassembly components, machine tools for a fabrication facility, performance instrumentation for a full missile system, and calibration equipment. Another bay held missile nose cones, metal piping stacked high, heavy-duty presses for milling high-grade steel, and a plate-bending machine for rolling thick metal sheets. Much of the material found included foreign-made parts and machines bearings markings from China and Japan. A committee of Indian missile experts concluded that the cargo of the *Kuwolsan* embodied a missile-making capability, albeit not everything needed for a full missile production facility.[46]

Notwithstanding the wealth of technical components in the North Korean shipment, full-blown missile production, particularly in light of Libya's weak technical base, depended on the provision of specialized skills embodied in specially trained engineers and technicians. Accordingly, the *Kuwolsan* carried tangible evidence that those possessing such skills, if not on board, were sure to follow or already present in Libya: cookbooks in Korean, Korean spices, pickles, and acupuncture sets. Besides food to sustain long work hours and ancient techniques for restoring health and well-being, engineers and technician also need sources of explicit knowledge, and these too were in ample evidence aboard the *Kuwolsan*: boxes of engineering drawings, blueprints, notebooks, textbooks, and technical reports. Russian and Chinese scientific terms were transposed into a uniquely Korean jargon.[47]

Specialized know-how, both explicit and tacit, is unequally manifested in development programs of various states. Clearly, North Korea's capacities in this regard are less sophisticated and to some degree dependent on those of, say, Russia and China. As discussed in Chapter 3, missile specialist Uzi Rubin believes that Russian fingerprints are apparent in North Korea's expertise in storable-liquid propulsion for the BM-25/Musudan, a 3,500-km-range ballistic missile based on the Soviet-era SS-N-6 submarine-launched ballistic missile. Mastery of the production process associated with storable-liquid propulsion, as well as transforming the missile from a submarine-launched to a ground-launched system, demands not only special materials, tools, and facilities but also specialized integration skills. Rubin deduces that North Korean and Russian missile engineers collaborated face-to-face on a frequent basis as part of a "structured technology transfer process," in order for North Korea to have achieved such a breakthrough in ballistic missile capability.[48] Press reports support the likelihood that North Korea solicited Russian missile specialists in April 1991, including Yurly Bessarabov, one of the principal designers of the SS-N-6 missile, and that a plan was made and initially supported, allegedly by high officials in Moscow, to help North Korea establish a scientific base for missile production. Later on, after South Korea allegedly offered Moscow $1 billion in aid not to accommodate the North's missile ambitions, Moscow decided against supporting the plan and instead implemented restrictions on such technology transfers to North Korea. But that did not stop the flow of Russian specialists to North Korea, particularly those from the Makayev Design Bureau, where the SS-N-6 was concocted. Reportedly, 200 clean passports were obtained illegally by the sister of one of the first Russian scientists to accept work in Pyongyang. In October 1992, police detained 36 Russian scientists and members of their families at Sheremetyevo-2 Airport. At least 20 of the group were engineers from the Makayev Design Bureau who, upon questioning, said they were headed to North Korea to work on a space launcher program called "Zyb." Zyb was the previously classified code name for the Soviet SS-N-6 ballistic missile before it was declared operational.[49]

In the Middle East, Iran may not possess the level of specialized skill that either Russia or China could provide, but it can and does employ its vast energy reserves as a magnet to draw upon Russian and Chinese skills for assistance in its cruise missile ambitions. This has most notably been the case with respect to China. Although confirmed details are lacking with regard to the provision of specialized know-how to Iran, China, or its entities, have certainly furnished both complete systems and dual-use missile-related items. Chinese companies have been implicated in selling Iran the HY-1, HY-2, HY-4, C-601, C-801, and C-802 ASCMs.[50] Iran, in turn, has emulated Chinese use of the HY-2, or perhaps more logically, the HY-4, as a test-bed for longer-range cruise missiles. The HY-4 is the only missile in the HY-series that conveniently is equipped with a turbojet engine—the WP-11, a reverse-engineered Chinese version of the U.S. Teledyne-Ryan J69-T-41A that powered the Vietnam-era Firebee reconnaissance drone. That may explain how Iran's new ASCM, called the Raad, has achieved a range of 350 km, and why it might soon be deployed as a LACM. On the other hand, in 2006 Iran was reported to have made attempts to acquire engine components for longer-range cruise missiles from German and Swiss sources by employing cover firms registered in Dubai's free-trade zone.[51]

Even more important is if, when, and how Iran will transform the half-dozen illegally acquired Russian Kh-55 LACMs it reportedly paid Ukrainian and Russian sources $49.5 million for in 2001.[52] Rubin believes that the missiles were primarily for examination and reverse-engineering purposes, not to be made operational, and that eventually Iran will possess a strategic-range LACM patterned after the Kh-55, provided it gets technical support from China and possibly North Korea.

The former head of the National Council of Resistance of Iran (NCRI), Alireza Jafarzadeh, argued in an August 26, 2005 press briefing in Washington that two of the Kh-55s were delivered to the Parchin military complex in Tehran for reverse engineering. Another two missiles were transferred to a so-called "Cruise Center," a research division of Iran's defense ministry, which includes engineers trained in China, France, Germany, North Korea, and Russia. In his press briefing Jafarzadeh said that over the past four years experts from the Cruise Center "have been able to rebuild the pieces of these missiles" and that "the Iranian regime has gained knowledge and access to this missile's technology," so that they were nearly ready to reproduce the missile. But Jafarzadeh also improbably claimed that the remainder of the Kh-55s were transferred to the Islamic Revolutionary Guard Corps (IRGC) and placed in secret locations and were now "a portion of IRGC's missile capability."[53] The latter claim begs several questions, the most notable being how Iran would launch the few Kh-55s in its possession since the items, as designed, are air-launched missiles suitable for integration on large Russian bombers, not the kind of tactical aircraft Iran possesses. Although they could be outfitted with booster rockets for ground launching, it seems doubtful that Iran would expend resources on such a meager force of conventional missiles. And because the NCRI is naturally inclined to present the current regime in Iran in the worst possible light, its claims should be judged accordingly.[54] On the other hand, the Iranian deal to obtain the missiles also included a Kh-55-associated ground-targeting system, called the

KNO-120, along with service support provided by means of several visits to Iran by Ukrainian technical specialists between 2001 and 2003.[55] It seems safe to assume that Iran does indeed seek to acquire a strategic-range LACM, as well as that the extent of specialized know-how it acquires will determine how quickly the objective is achieved.

Pakistan makes no bones about its dependence on China for specialized know-how in such fields as civilian rocket science and space technology and defensive military systems. For example, in early 2007, Pakistan's foreign minister visited one of China's sensitive space technology centers in connection with Chinese assistance to Islamabad in developing a satellite launch capability, which also could assist Pakistan's increasingly long-range ballistic missile ambitions.[56] And just as India has turned to Israel to tap into its specialized know-how on advanced airborne warning and control systems, Pakistan and China in November 2006 agreed to long-term collaboration and co-development in aircraft manufacturing, including an airborne warning system.[57] The irony here is that in the 1990s China had turned to Israel for the very same AWACS-like system that India is now obtaining from Tel Aviv, called the PHALCON, but under strong pressure from the Bill Clinton administration, Israel's Ehud Barak cancelled the deal in July 2000. But such diplomatic leverage is most effectively employed when the international transactions are publicly known. The transfer of both specialized know-how and technology from China to Pakistan and from Israel to India is likely to occur behind the scenes. Unlike more formalized Sino-Pak space and military collaborations, China has obvious reasons, most prominently its nominal adherence to the guidelines of the Missile Technology Control Regime (MTCR) to keep LACM support to Pakistan as opaque as possible.

Indian commentators are naturally prone to boast of India's truly indigenous military programs, including the BrahMos supersonic cruise missile, the mysterious Sagarika LACM inducted into the Indian navy, and the newest addition, the subsonic Tomahawk-type LACM Nirbhay, in order to draw a palpable contrast with Pakistan's dependence on China for providing the Babur LACM and many of Islamabad's ballistic missile systems.[58] Yet, the substance of Indian specialized know-how in the cruise missile area is limited. BrahMos, a co-development program with Russia, is heavily derived from NPO Mashinostroenia's Yakhont ASCM, with India's contribution being the inertial navigation system. And even in this regard, India received Israeli assistance in mastering INS technology and has turned to European countries for guidance technology.[59] Had India been completely satisfied with its indigenous capacity to produce LACMs, it need not have sought—unsuccessfully it appears—French assistance in September 2006, which reportedly would have included both complete missile systems and the transfer of technology from the European consortium MBDA Missile Systems. India's main shortcomings are in turbofan engines and in the solid-rocket booster technology needed to permit ground-launched LACMs to achieve a smooth transition from launch to the cruise phase whereupon the missile is propelled by the engine. When India embarked on pursuing a turbofan-powered LACM early in this decade, one Indian expert from

New Delhi's Institute of Defense Studies and Analysis said that while India requires such a missile, an "indigenous project may take a long time to fructify."[60]

One need only review a handful of India's major weapons systems to appreciate just how dependent India remains on foreign assistance. After more than two decades of development and testing, the Akash surface-to-air missile system has incurred the disenchantment of the Indian air force. According to an Indian air force expert who witnessed Akash tests, "Out of 20 test trials . . . the majority of them ended in a failure."[61] A similar fate has lead to the demise of another of India's air defense systems, the short-range Trishul, which was scrapped in 2006 after 23 years of indeterminate trials. The main battle tank, Arjun, remains stuck in trials that have lasted 16 years.[62]

Launched in 1983 to replace the Soviet-era MiG-21, the Tejas light combat aircraft has suffered innumerable systems integration problems associated with three prototypes and two demonstrators, which made over 570 flights between January 2001 and the end of 2006. Changes continue to be made in man-machine interfaces and avionics and flight controls, while a new spate of future tests, including 600 more flights, is planned to concentrate on integrating missiles and sensor systems with the aircraft. The radar for the Tejas has experienced recurring software and signal processing problems, forcing the Defense Research and Development Organization (DRDO) to seek foreign assistance. That may be the only way to correct flaws in the DRDO's Kaveri engine, designed to replace the General Electric engine that currently powers the Tejas. In simulation altitude tests held in Russia in 2004, the Kaveri suffered from problems in internal aerodynamics, combustion, and structural integrity. The first flight test of the Kaveri was postponed from 2007 to an unspecified future date.[63] Frustrated by these repeated failures and cost escalation in defense programs, India's Parliamentary Standing Committee on Defense began pressuring the Indian defense ministry in late 2006 to implement a formal and independent means of monitoring DRDO programs to foster greater accountability and performance.[64]

Given the DRDO's underperformance in virtually every indigenously executed major weapons program, it remains unclear how India will satisfy its long-standing quest to deploy a turbojet- or, more likely, turbofan-powered LACM. If the attempted technology deal with France in 2006 is permanently off, and if Russia, too, decides to abide carefully to the provisions of the MTCR, then the most plausible source of foreign assistance would seem to be Israel.[65] Though Tel Aviv is an adherent to the MTCR's guidelines, it, like some full regime members, has liberally interpreted them when doing so suited its own security or economic interests. And with the United States and India forging a strategic partnership over the last several years, including an unprecedented civilian nuclear energy deal in 2006 and an expanding level of cooperation in spaceflight, satellite technology, and missile defense, Israel may view technology support to India's cruise missile programs as a reasonably safe bet.

There is little question that China has needed to look for significant outside sources of know-how in fashioning its military-technical approach to LACM development. One of the chief legacies of Mao's Great Leap Forward and Cultural

Revolution—besides the virtual loss of a generation of scientists and engineers—was an abiding recognition that China's future depended heavily on reconstituting and expanding its scientific and engineering talent. By 1986, Premier Zhao Ziyang acknowledged, "The biggest obstacle to the accomplishment of the four modernizations [Deng Xiaoping's reforms circa 1975] . . . lies in talented personnel"[66] According to specialists, China's defense industry still faces significant barriers to turning out even modestly successful, no less first-rate, weapons systems.[67] The obstacles include political interference, an obsolescent procurement system, difficulties with technology absorption, poor innovation, and the military's low priority. Producing a major naval or aircraft system, if it manages to make it past the prototype or demonstrator stage, takes at least 15 years.[68] But as China specialist Larry Wortzel has wisely noted, despite these admitted weaknesses, Chinese defense enterprises have succeeded in generating first-rate systems, such as the short-range missiles that are now deployed against Taiwan. Wortzel has also argued that future assessments of Chinese military-technical development need to include more attention to case studies reflecting the importance of systems engineering and production skills.[69]

China's long-term quest is to build a wholly indigenous defense industrial base that would benefit greatly from joint ventures in the civilian sector, an ever-growing body of intellectual capital derived from students studying abroad in the best engineering universities, and extensive military and civilian efforts at industrial espionage. Russia and, to a lesser extent, Israel, Ukraine, and Belarus have satisfied near-term requirements for weapon systems, technology, and specialized know-how. After the end of the Cold War, Russia and China's needs converged. China sought the most advanced technology it could acquire. Russian defense industries, faced with disappearing state subsidies, found a convenient lifeline in foreign military sales. With Moscow's governance over such matters questionable at best, China made deals, including licensed production of the Su-27 fighter, that would never have occurred in former times.[70]

Amid virtual chaos in the Russian defense sector, China reportedly obtained Russian consent to recruit a cruise missile research and development team.[71] Other unconfirmed sources in Taiwan also believe that China successfully recruited between 1,500 and 2,000 laid-off scientists and engineers and located them at a factory, named Xinxin, in Shanghai, where they work with Chinese missile specialists on intermediate-range cruise missiles, or "imitated versions of the Kh-55."[72] It remains doubtful that Russia provided China with either the Kh-55 or its turbofan engine during this period. Had it done so, there would not have been compelling reasons for China to have illegally procured six Kh-55 LACMs in 2000. But it does appear plausible that Russian personnel did furnish China with scientific and engineering know-how that advanced their LACM ambitions in the early to mid-1990s. However, the mysterious disappearance or downgrading of the Hong Niao (HN) series of LACMs, including a so-called HN-2 with a reputed range of 1,500 to 2,000 km, and its apparent replacement by a LACM first tested in October 2004, called the Dong Hai-10, with a range of 1,500 km, suggests the Chinese may have encountered problems with the HN-series LACMs, most likely with developing a small, highly efficient turbofan engine like the Kh-55's. Minus details about the nature and quality of the working relationship between Russian and Chinese engineers and technicians, including information about the social context within which tacit knowledge skills are honed, it is impossible to draw any conclusions about the lasting impact of Russian support during the 1990s to China's LACM program. If in fact a large cohort of skilled Russian technicians practiced in Shanghai during the 1990s, it is not clear that they or another group are still active in China today.

On the other hand, China's multi-prong strategy to indigenously produce military engines for both aircraft and LACMs remains squarely in place. With the liberalization of export controls on dual-use products and technologies that occurred at the end of the Cold War, China is continuing efforts to acquire production processes for U.S. jet engines. In 1996, for example, Pratt and Whitney Canada, a subsidiary of U.S.-based United Technologies, established a joint venture with China's Chengdu Engine Company to manufacture aviation parts. Chengdu not only manufactures components used in Boeing aircraft but also components for the PLA Air Force's WP-13 turbojet engine that powers the F-8 fighter.[73] This is one among many U.S.-Chinese joint ventures in areas where China could conceivably gain valuable production processing knowledge by working with top-notch U.S. engine manufacturers. Other prominent examples include a 2003 joint venture between General Electric and Shanyang Liming Aero Engine Corporation to co-produce the CF034-10A jet engine for one of China's regional jets and the much more direct acquisition of Russian know-how to assist China's development of the WS-10A turbofan engine for China's J-10 and J-11 version of the co-produced Su-27. Reportedly, China's new turbofan engine, which was first flight-tested in 2002, outperforms the Russian AL-31 engine that powers the Su-27.[74] The challenge now is to manufacture an efficient but sufficiently small turbofan engine, like the Kh-55's R-95-300.

Besides exploiting Russian expertise, diverting commercial engines to military use, and incrementally gaining specialized manufacturing know-how from joint ventures, China has purloined technology when targets of opportunity have become available. A notable success is the acquisition of six Russian Kh-55 LACMs from Ukrainian and Russian sources in 2000. Reverse engineering, even with its shortcomings with respect to a complex system like a turbofan engine, should have proven valuable already. China's acquisition and subsequent exploitation of recovered Tomahawks kindly furnished by Pakistan has probably also helped, with perhaps some reciprocal benefit flowing back to Islamabad in the form of the Babur LACM, or at least components thereof. And then there are failures, as when Ko-Suen "Bill" Moo, a Taiwanese national who worked for American defense contractor Lockheed Martin in Taiwan, was caught in 2005 by U.S. Customs agents in a sting operation attempting illegally to export military items to China. Moo and a French national, who was also indicted but remains at large, were charged by federal prosecutors with attempting to purchase an F-16 jet engine, cruise missiles, and air-to-air missiles for China. Moo provided an undercover customs agent with documents showing specific Chinese interest in acquiring the AGM-129 LACM, which is capable of carrying a nuclear warhead to a range of 3,700 km. Developed in the 1980s to penetrate thick Soviet

air defenses, the AGM-129 is a highly advanced stealthy cruise missile that was originally slated to remain in the U.S. nuclear inventory until 2020 but is being retired
early as part of U.S. nuclear reductions required under the Moscow Treaty of 2002.
Moo had deposited $3.9 million in a Swiss bank account to purchase the weapons
and, in a final meeting with customs agents to discuss exporting the F-16 engine to
an airport in China, Moo wired $140,000 for shipping fees to a Miami bank
account. Moo pleaded guilty in May 2006 to acting as a covert agent for the Chinese
government. In Taiwan, where Moo along with three high-ranking Taiwanese generals was considered a member of the air force's "Gang of Four," his indictment and
guilty plea created significant consternation over what Moo may have provided to
his handlers in Beijing that might adversely affect Taiwanese security.[75]

Taiwan, for its part, has not hidden its desire to see the United States not only
endorse its LACM ambitions but also furnish Taiwan with technologies and specialized know-how that would enable longer-range and more sophisticated attack means.
As discussed in Chapter 5, George W. Bush administration officials have expressed
mild opposition to Taiwan's emerging offensive options but seemingly with the same
purposeful ambiguity that has generally characterized the U.S.-Taiwan security relationship. A more assertive U.S. position may well have been delivered behind closed
doors, but some observers have wondered aloud whether the U.S. public stance
should be made in stronger language, if only to avoid the misperception that the
United States is assisting or at least approving of Taiwan's HF-2E LACM program.[76]
Publicly, the United States is critical of both China and Taiwan for developing destabilizing offensive options. This stance, however, could encourage single-minded proponents of Taiwan's offensive programs to believe that Washington actually supports
Taiwan's offensive missile programs as long as they are presented in tactical, defensive
terms, or merely as a "countermeasure" against China's overwhelming offensive missile buildup. Because some Taiwanese officials reportedly believe that the United
States would be inclined to provide Taiwan with the technical support they need—
in particular, to achieve greater striking range for the HF-2E LACM—and cite past
episodes of such U.S. support, it seems conceivable that such technical support could
be forthcoming. According to an industry source, early this decade a U.S. firm provided Taiwan's Chung-Shan Institute of Science and Technology with mission planning assistance for what seems, in retrospect, to have become the HF-2E LACM,
though only after obtaining an export license stipulating that the technology could
not apply to a missile with more than a range of 300 km.[77] While the precise technical details of this transaction are not known, there is reason to believe that embedded
within the technology provided to Taiwan was a reserve of knowledge about LACM
planning and utility generated by a country that has employed this weapon over
2,500 times since 1991—and diagnosed each use with determined scientific rigor.
Finally, in light of the inherent modularity of cruise missiles, it is inconceivable that
the U.S. could confine the applicability of any technology supplied to Taiwan to a
LACM having a range of 300 km or less.

South Korea and Japan alike have ample industrial and technological prowess to
develop their own LACM programs. Israel and France both succeeded in developing

their own LACMs, though they are believed to have unsuccessfully sought U.S. LACM help, or complete Tomahawk missiles, in the 1990s. Both nations wanted not merely to save time and money but also to tap into the huge reservoir of knowledge the United States has accumulated over the Tomahawk's long history of development and use in combat. South Korean press reports wax that Seoul's new LACMs are similar to the Tomahawk, which probably reflects aspiration rather than either actual technical performance or formal U.S. technology transfers of Tomahawk technology—although such transfers cannot be confidently ruled out, given reported U.S. assistance to Taiwan. Japan has manifested an interest in LACMs for a preemptive denial role. While its hankering for the stealthy American F-22 fighter has produced considerable negative feedback in some U.S. defense circles owing to congressional concern over foreign sale of stealth fighters, selling Japan Tomahawks may be less objectionable. At the same time, such a sale would almost inevitably stimulate regional tension and further LACM proliferation.

Narrative

Writing in 1981, less than two years before President Reagan's surprise launch of what became the Strategic Defense Initiative missile defense program, pejoratively dubbed "Star Wars" by its detractors, and nearly a decade before Tomahawks became militarily fashionable in the first Gulf War, Richard Burt wrote that "the widespread deployment of cruise missiles by the United States or other industrial powers is unlikely to lead to their proliferation in the third world." His explanation for reaching this conclusion was two-fold. First, the technical barriers to cruise missile development were simply too high for third-world powers to surmount. Second, and more important, many such nations already possessed sufficient means—advanced aircraft—to execute ground-attack missions, nuclear or conventional.[1] Burt may be excused for failing to anticipate the full pace and scope of ballistic missile proliferation in the 1980s and the fact that the Cold War's end substantially increased regional tensions, as well as U.S. willingness to intervene in third-world conflicts. The capacity of ballistic missiles to produce a feeling of defenselessness, regardless of their inaccuracy, still made them enormously appealing, and the need for specialized knowledge skills possessed by a handful of countries—notably the United States, Russia, and China—inhibits cruise missile development. Nevertheless, there are other factors that are highly likely to spread cruise missiles at an even faster pace.

From a purely American perspective, land-attack cruise missiles (LACMs) were initially attractive because they were unaffected by the arms control constraints associated with the 1972 Strategic Arms Limitation Treaty (SALT) and, more important, were relatively inexpensive and thus potentially deployable in large numbers.[2] Concern about growing Soviet quantitative conventional warfare advantages, notwithstanding U.S. technological superiority, had also fostered a welcoming environment for LACMs with civilian officials and strategists, though less so within the military services. Moreover, as Richard Betts has observed, LACMs also possessed certain qualitative advantages over ballistic missiles. Besides their accuracy and potential effectiveness as conventional delivery systems, especially as compared with ballistic missiles, LACMs were technologically simpler than advanced aircraft systems, which meant that they could readily be adapted to rapidly changing defensive threat environments.[3]

Operationally, LACMs appeared to trump ballistic missiles in accuracy (by at least a factor of ten), cost (cheaper by a factor of two or more), ease of operations and maintenance, greater mobility for ground-launched versions (making them less susceptible to counterforce strikes), aerodynamic stability, and effectiveness in delivery of biological agents (by at least a factor of ten in terms of lethal area covered). To be sure, ballistic missiles offer their owners longer potential range—particularly if one believes the Rumsfeld Commission finding that a nation possessing a Scud missile infrastructure could, within five years, flight-test an ICBM-range ballistic missile. Yet, as the late Albert Wohlstetter noted, LACMs can be brought within range of their targets and then launched from freighters, submarines, surface ships, and aircraft, and they do not need to be stabilized at these launch points to achieve their desired accuracy.[4] Building on these operational advantages, the circumstances of the 2003 war in Iraq have begun to diminish the relative appeal of ballistic missiles, which their speed of delivery and relatively reliable arrival had previously assured. In particular, the successful performance of U.S. missile defenses against ballistic missiles compared with their abject failure against LACMs during the 2003 invasion of Iraq has burnished the narrative appeal of LACMs.

MISSILE DEFENSES DURING THE 2003 WAR IN IRAQ[5]

Strategists immediately seized upon the U.S. military's 21-day march to Baghdad as a vindication of U.S. Secretary of Defense Donald Rumsfeld's determination to transform the U.S. military into a tightly integrated force capable of quickly and decisively defeating any conceivable adversary.[6] American air, sea, and land forces demonstrated an extraordinary capacity to deliver offensive military power in a highly orchestrated way. The promise of Network Centric Warfare—the Pentagon's appellation for a robustly networked joint force capable of sharing and acting upon a comprehensive common picture of operational activities—became evident when offensive firepower was brought to bear throughout the theater of war.

Yet the Rumsfeld-led transformation was not nearly as impressive on the defensive side of American military performance. The war's greatly anticipated engagement between Iraqi ballistic missiles and America's upgraded Patriot missile defenses did go decidedly in America's favor: all nine of Iraq's most threatening ballistic missile launches were successfully intercepted and destroyed. But American and Kuwaiti missile defenses and warning systems failed to detect or intercept all five Iraqi low-flying cruise missiles, and there is no evidence that Patriot missile batteries were involved in one way or the other.[7] One of the cruise missiles came perilously close to a U.S. Marine encampment on the war's first day. Furthermore, at least two Iraqi ultralight aircraft—which were feared capable of carrying chemical or biological agents—were detected only after flying over thousands of U.S. troops, as well as equipment and command facilities, prior to the division's advance on Baghdad.[8] Iraq's use of low-flying cruise missiles and slow-flying air vehicles also contributed to the Patriot's unfortunate series of friendly-fire incidents, two of which led to the loss of two aircraft and the deaths of three crew members. In a practical sense, the United States fielded only half a missile defense system, capable of handling but one dimension of the missile threat.

With every new war, of course, missile defenses are called on to perform missions that appear to be ahead of what the technology can provide.[9] But the shortcomings of cruise missile defense and steps needed to rectify them have been known for over a decade. The Pentagon's own Defense Science Board conducted at least two detailed reviews and offered recommendations for improvements during the 1990s, while Congress fashioned the "Cruise Missile Defense Initiative" in its National Defense Authorization Act of Fiscal Year 1996. A call for greatly improved cruise missile defenses to respond to an earlier-than-expected emergence of the cruise missile threat also made it into the Pentagon's Defense Planning Guidance in 1998.[10] And in a report issued prior to the 2003 war in Iraq, the Senate Armed Services Committee stated that the Pentagon's "longstanding" combat identification and friendly-force tracking weaknesses, which surely contributed to the Patriot's friendly-fire incidents, were not being rectified "in the most expeditious manner."[11] Accordingly, the poor performance of missile defenses against the first cruise missiles ever fired in combat against American or allied forces, including the related problem of friendly-fire casualties, should not have come as a surprise.

Unfortunately, America's adversaries will inevitably draw important lessons from the performance of U.S. missile defenses against Iraq. The chief of staff of the 32nd Army Air and Missile Defense Command told the *New York Times,* "This was a glimpse of future threats. It is a poor man's air force. A thinking enemy will use uncommon means such as cruise missiles and unmanned aerial vehicles on multiple fronts."[12] Officials should anticipate accelerated proliferation for at least two reasons. First, countries wishing to deter U.S. military interventions were unlikely to invest heavily in LACMs until American missile defenses performed decisively better against ballistic missiles than they did during the 1991 Gulf War. Patriot's success against Iraq's ballistic missiles in 2003 coupled with problems coping with LACMs increases the incentive for the potential adversaries of the United States to acquire LACMs. Second, adversaries are likely to see the operational advantages of combining ballistic and cruise missile launches to maximize the probability of penetrating even the best American or allied missile defenses. Converting small airplanes or unmanned aerial vehicles (UAVs) into weapons-carrying "missiles" offers a particularly attractive "poor man's" option. When these, in large numbers, are combined with more expensive and sophisticated ballistic and cruise missiles, they could have a distinct advantage over even thick, layered defenses.

SCORING BALLISTIC MISSILE DEFENSE

The Iraq War demonstrated positive returns on a $3 billion program to upgrade the Patriot since its abysmal performance during the 1991 Gulf War, when the U.S. Army rushed a modified version into combat. The 1991 version's major limitation came from a proximity fuse that failed to detonate the fragmentation warhead close enough to destroy the missile warhead. Even when it did hit the intended target, it merely knocked the missile off course—and potentially toward urban centers or troop concentrations. A U.S. Government Accountability Office report estimated that only 9 percent of the PAC-2 interceptors actually hit their targets during the 1991 Gulf War, while Israeli authorities reported that Patriot succeeded intercepting no more than 1 of the 39 Iraqi Scuds launched at Israel.[13] This time around, upgraded PAC-2 missiles, together with roughly 50 of the latest Patriot (PAC-3) interceptors, were deployed. According to the official U.S. Army report issued after the war, Iraq launched 19 ballistic missiles at coalition targets in Kuwait and Iraq, only nine of which threatened potential targets. Patriot missile defense batteries successfully intercepted all nine. Ten other nonthreatening missiles, most of which may have been hastily aimed because the Iraqis feared coalition counterfire, were allowed to land harmlessly in the desert or in Gulf waters.[14]

Patriot batteries were deployed in Kuwait, Qatar, Bahrain, Saudi Arabia, Israel, and Turkey, the last under North Atlantic Treaty Organization (NATO) control. Instead of remaining in fixed positions throughout the war, some Kuwaiti-based batteries moved with coalition ground forces toward Baghdad to furnish local-area protection. And rather than depending on just the space-based Defense Support Program for warning information on launch detections, Patriot units were furnished with early warning information from two dedicated sources: an Aegis cruiser equipped with a SPY phased array radar deployed in the Persian Gulf and a regionally deployed Cobra Judy ship-based radar system normally used to monitor missile tests.[15]

America's decade-long investment in upgrading Patriot's performance also led to overall communications and command-and-control improvements that yielded a seven-fold increase in the area each Patriot battery can protect. Of course, area protection is obtained only to the extent that Patriot's missile interceptors actually perform as expected. In Operation Iraqi Freedom, some missile defense batteries carried as many as three different interceptors—all deployed since the 1991 Gulf War. According to an army official, the Patriot's radar evaluates the incoming target's characteristics and automatically selects the best interceptor to engage it.[16] The first and most prominently used interceptor was the PAC-2 Guidance-Enhanced Missile (GEM). Designed to rectify the intercept limitations of the PAC-2, the PAC-2 GEM features an altered fragmentation pattern in its high-explosive warhead together with modified electronics that enhance the probability of an explosive impact near the target missile's nose cone. A second set of improvements came with the introduction of the PAC-2 GEM-Plus, which includes an upgraded fuse and a missile sensor that improves the chances of detecting and engaging smaller targets, presumably including cruise missiles. The third and most operationally tenuous of Patriot's upgrades was the entirely new PAC-3. Still in operational testing in early 2003, it appears that the entire inventory of 50 PAC-3 interceptors was rushed into the region. The PAC-3 features controversial hit-to-kill technology, whereby the interceptor destroys the target missile, including any chemical or biological agents, directly by kinetic impact rather than proximately with a high-explosive warhead. Because the PAC-3 is considerably smaller than the PAC-2 (roughly a quarter to a third of the PAC-2's weight), each Patriot launch canister can carry four PAC-3 interceptors compared with one PAC-2 GEM or GEM-Plus. Yet PAC-3's improved capabilities carry a hefty price tag: each four-missile canister costs $12–14 million, or close to $3.4 million per missile, compared with the original PAC-2's unit cost of $700,000.[17]

Beyond cost is the question of whether the PAC-3 had been tested realistically enough to warrant confidence about its prospective performance in battle. The PAC-3 performed well (in fact, missing only one target) during a developmental sequence of 11 tests, but this was only against ballistic missiles or target drones flying predictable trajectories. In the most recent operational testing before the war, when a higher degree of battlefield realism was introduced, only three of seven targets were destroyed. Most importantly, none of the PAC-3's tests featured a ballistic missile target similar to the ones that proved difficult to intercept in the 1991 Gulf War—in order to extend their range, the Iraqis had clumsily modified Soviet-furnished Scud missiles in the late 1980s. When they were launched in 1991, these longer-range Scuds encountered severe aerodynamic stresses which caused many of them to break up or flutter wildly, making them difficult to engage.[18]

During the war with Iraq, Patriot units were not tested against faster and more challenging Scud variants, as in 1991. American and British intelligence presume that about 25 of these variants existed in Iraq's possession. Instead, Iraq used al-Samoud-2 and Ababil-100 ballistic missiles, which, given their range of 150 km at most, are slower and easier to intercept. That said, a senior U.S. Army official noted that shorter-range missiles leave less time for defenders to respond to launches.[19] Moreover, al-Samoud and Ababil missiles are much more accurate than Scuds. Even armed with only high-explosive warheads, they represented a much greater threat to coalition forces than Iraq's inaccurate longer-range Scuds did during the 1991 war. For example, according to the army's post-event analysis, a Patriot missile intercepted an Ababil-100 only three kilometers before it would have struck the coalition's main command center at Camp Doha in Kuwait.[20]

More often than not, Patriot batteries employed the PAC-2 GEM interceptor to engage Iraqi ballistic missiles. Using PAC-2 GEMs, Kuwaiti-manned batteries were credited with shooting down two of the nine intercepted missiles. American-manned batteries successfully engaged the other seven Iraqi missiles—five with PAC-2 GEM interceptors and two with the new PAC-3 hit-to-kill interceptors.[21] All missile batteries practiced the standard targeting doctrine of sequentially expending two missiles per target—occasionally more—in order to increase the probability of intercept. According to army analysis, however, most intercepts came from the first missile fired.[22] To avoid inflated claims of success such as those that followed the 1991 Gulf War, army officials this time based their reports on electronic tapes of missile engagements and examinations of the remains of intercepted missiles found in the desert.[23]

While Patriot batteries performed well in their principal task, there was an extraordinarily high number of false alarms, despite the availability of both space-based and offshore ballistic missile warning radars. Because military officials had to assume that Iraqi missiles might be carrying chemical or biological payloads, they erred on the side of caution, forcing alerted ground units to don chemical suits and gas masks in temperatures that exceeded 100 degrees Fahrenheit. The repeated false alarms had such a debilitating effect on military performance that it led U.S. and British ground commanders, worried about the pace of the ground advance toward Baghdad, to request that such alerts occur only when a positive indication of a missile launch was obtained. But in light of the risks of just one chemically armed missile getting through, senior military officials continued to apply a risk-averse warning policy.[24] Without greatly improved broad-area detection and tracking of cruise missiles and UAVs, the false-alarm rate will have even more deleterious effects in the future. Cruise missile launch signatures, unlike those of ballistic missiles, are too faint for confident launch detection by space-based and even most airborne sensors. Given that cruise missiles are more effective than ballistic missiles in delivering chemical and biological payloads at least by a factor of ten, military decisionmakers in the future are likely to be even more risk-averse.

SUCCESS IS RELATIVE

Patriot missile defense batteries performed dimly against Iraq's improvised use of transformed Chinese anti-ship cruise missiles (ASCMs) and low-flying ultralight aircraft. In all, the Iraqis fired five Chinese-made HY-2 cruise missiles, each of which can carry a payload of 500 kg to a range of 150 km, flying a terrain-hugging profile to avoid radar detection. Iraq had modified a number of HY-2 ASCMs to permit them to fly over land to 150 km.[25] In spite of the primitive nature of the cruise missile threat—notably, the large radar cross-section of the HY-2—the Iraqis nearly achieved tactical success when, on the first day of the war (March 20), one HY-2 came undetected within one kilometer of striking Camp Commando, the U.S. Marine Corps headquarters in Kuwait.[26] Another did hit just outside a large Kuwaiti shopping mall later in the war, causing some damage and two casualties, while two more landed near the Iraq-Kuwait border and the remaining one struck an area where a coalition military unit had recently been deployed. All of Iraq's cruise missile launches emanated from the Al Faw peninsula.

Although army officials were quick to point out that every Iraqi ballistic missile that threatened coalition objectives was successfully destroyed, they only hinted why Patriot radars and other warning systems failed to detect any of the five Iraqi cruise missiles. An industry official claimed that no Patriot assets were assigned in the area in Kuwait in which the shopping mall was located, and that if there had been radars and interceptors in the area they could have engaged such low-flying threats.[27] But according to the official army history, because the cruise missile strike on the Kuwaiti shopping mall had caused panic among the civilian population and concern about protecting the coalition's rear area, military forces were sent into the Al Faw peninsula to prevent further missiles from being launched from the area. And Kuwait deployed an unknown number of short-range air defense batteries and established a missile engagement zone sufficient, they believed, to detect and interdict any future cruise missile threats headed toward Kuwait.[28] These batteries held their positions for the remainder of the war. Furthermore, the British placed the HMS *York* destroyer, equipped with air surveillance and target-tracking radars and air defense guns and missile interceptors, in the shallow waters of Kuwait City and tasked the vessel to intercept any further launches of Iraqi cruise missiles.[29] Notwithstanding all of these varied protective countermeasures against further cruise missile launches, counterforce and missile defense alike, Iraq fired three more cruise missiles three days later from the Al Faw peninsula, and not one was detected or intercepted. The brigade in charge of air and missile defense immediately ordered a Patriot battalion to execute cruise missile simulation tests to examine better ways of intercepting future cruise missile attacks "due to their low flight elevations."[30] Fortunately, no additional cruise missiles were launched at coalition targets. Specific details for some of these threats and responses are shown in Table 1.

In theory, the Patriot system is capable of engaging low-flying cruise missiles, but in practice the Patriot's ground-based radar probably would not detect low-flying missiles unless it was furnished with advanced warning information provided by airborne radar. Many ground-based radars supporting today's air defense missiles reduce the amount of ground clutter by tilting the search beam back about three degrees, effectively lifting it above the ground. This raises the chances that a low-flying cruise missile will go undetected. Moreover, whereas airborne radar systems (like the U.S. Air Force's Airborne Warning and Control System [AWACS]) can see several hundreds of kilometers, the earth's curvature means that the Patriot's ground-based radar, in trying to detect a cruise missile flying at a 50-m altitude, might first see it only when it has closed to within 35 km or less. This would leave roughly two and a half minutes to react to an incoming missile threat. Thus, William Schneider, chairman of the Pentagon's advisory Defense Science Board, called for integrating an airborne sensor like AWACS with Patriot to improve chances of intercepting low-flying cruise missiles.[31]

The two Iraqi ultralight aircraft that potentially imperiled thousands of soldiers and hundreds of millions of dollars' worth of military equipment at a large U.S. Army forward encampment south of Baghdad were also cause for dire concern. A day after the incident, U.S. Central Command officials were still telling reporters that the Iraqis were incapable of flying aircraft because their airfields were being kept closed and carefully monitored.[32] Ultralights and other kit-built aircraft, of course, do not need airfields to take off and land. Moreover, highly sophisticated surveillance aircraft like AWACS and the U.S. Air Force Joint Surveillance and Target Attack Radar System (JSTARS) are unable to detect them because their radars screen out slow-flying targets on or near the ground to ensure that their data processing and display systems are not overburdened.[33]

It remains unclear whether a Patriot battery was covering the army encampment, though it seems possible since missile defense units were deployed in Iraq in part to furnish protection for such assets. On-site reporting indicates that anti-aircraft units, consisting of Linebacker systems (Bradley fighting vehicles armed with Stinger anti-aircraft missiles) and Avenger systems (Humvees mounted with Stingers), received a mid-afternoon report on the ultralights and oriented their fire units to prepare to engage the small aircraft. Unit members visually spotted the ultralights flying at

Table 1   Threat and Response 2003 Iraq War

Date	Threat(s)—Real or Mistaken	Apparent Targets	Response
20 March, 0718Z	1 cruise missile— Seersucker	Marine Camp Commando	No detection indicated, nor missile interception attempted
20 March, 0924Z	1 unknown missile	TAA Thunder	Missile was detected by USS *Higgins* and intercepted after launch of three PAC-2 GEM missiles
20 March, 1030Z	1 ballistic missile— Ababil-100	Camp Commando and Camp Doha	Missile was detected by Air and Missile Defense Workstation (AMDWS) and intercepted after two PAC-3 missiles were fired
20 March, 2100– 2200Z	2 ballistic missiles— Ababil-100, al-Samoud		Missiles were not intercepted, fell into Persian Gulf
20 March, 2320Z	1 ballistic missile— Ababil-100	Camp Udari	Missile was intercepted after one GEM and one PAC-2 missile were fired
21 March, 1001Z	1 ballistic missile— Ababil-100	TAA Fox, Al Jahra	Missile was detected by AMDWS and intercepted after Kuwaiti Patriot battery fired two GEM missiles
23 March, 1547Z	Friendly fire— British Tornado GR-4	Somewhere in northern Kuwait	U.S. Patriot PAC-2 battery misidentified friendly aircraft as a missile threat and destroyed the aircraft, killing two pilots
23 March	1 ballistic missile— al-Samoud	Camp New Jersey	Missile was intercepted after U.S. Patriot battery fired one PAC-2 and one GEM missile
24 March, 1035Z	1 ballistic missile— al-Samoud	Camp Virginia and Camp New Jersey	Missile was intercepted after three GEM-Plus missiles were fired
24 March, 1342Z	1 ballistic missile— Ababil-100	Camp Doha	Missile was not intercepted, fell into Kuwaiti desert
25 March, 1248Z	1 ballistic missile— Ababil-100	Camp Commando	Missile was intercepted by Kuwaiti Patriot battery
26 March, 1250Z	Friendly fire—U.S. F-16 CJ	Patriot battery forward-deployed to protect 3rd Infantry Division	Mistaking the F-16 for a missile threat, the Patriot's radar "painted" the F-16, which in turn fired on the radar, damaging it. The Patriot battery, reportedly, was operating on automatic

26 March, **1658Z**	1 ballistic missile— Ababil-100		Missile blew up shortly after launch without causing damage
27 March, **0831Z**	1 ballistic missile— Ababil-100	Coalition Forces Land Component Command Headquarters	Missile was intercepted by U.S. and Kuwaiti batteries after four GEM missiles were fired
27 March, **2056Z**	1 ballistic missile— Ababil-100 or FROG-7	Northern Iraq	Missile was not intercepted, landed in the desert
28 March, **2250Z**	1 cruise missile— Seersucker	Struck shopping mall outside Kuwait City	Press reports indicate no detection and no interception
28 March	2 manned ultralights	U.S. Army forward encampment south of Baghdad	No detection until two penetrating aircraft were directly over encampment. Tracked by Avengers, but no interception attempted due to delay in execution authority
29 March, **1500Z**	1 ballistic missile— FROG-7	Northern Kuwait	Missile was not intercepted, fell into desert
1 April, **0603Z**	1 ballistic missile— al-Samoud	Forces in LSA Bushmaster	A U.S. Patriot battery intercepted the threatening missile with a PAC-3 interceptor
1 April	1 unknown missile		Missile was not intercepted
1 April	3 cruise missiles— Seersucker		Missiles were not intercepted, landed near Iraq-Kuwait border
2 April	Friendly fire—U.S. F/A-18C	Near Karbala	A U.S. Patriot battery misidentified the F/A-18 as a threatening missile and destroyed the aircraft, killing its pilot
3 April	3 ballistic missiles— FROG-7		Missiles were not intercepted, landed in An Najaf

Sources: [1] 32nd Army Air and Missile Defense Command (AAMDC), "Operation Iraqi Freedom Theater Air and Missile Defense History," September 2003. Available from web site of the Center for
Defense Information at http://www.cdi.org/PDFs/OIF_history.pdf. [2] Michael R. Gordon, "A Poor
Man's Air Force," *New York Times,* June 19, 2003, A1. [3] Sean D. Naylor, "Iraqi Ultralights Spotted
over U.S. Troops," *Army Times,* March 29, 2003.

about 270 m above the ground, roughly at the speed of a helicopter. But the Iraqi aircraft had departed the area by the time U.S. Central Command authorities had
approved firing on such targets, as required by local rules of engagement. An enormously cluttered friendly air environment probably accounts for the lengthy decision

process, especially in light of two friendly-fire incidents—on March 23 and 26—that had marred an otherwise outstanding performance by army air defenders against ballistic missile threats.[34]

UNINTENDED CONSEQUENCES

During the 1991 Gulf War, Patriot batteries had a relatively easy task. Coalition air forces had rapidly eliminated the Iraqi air force and no cruise missile, small airplane, or UAV threats existed. Thus, coalition defenders could afford to establish highly restrictive rules of engagement. Basically, they shut down Patriot batteries against everything but ballistic missiles with steep trajectories. This prevented friendly-fire accidents. But because a cruise missile and UAV threat had materialized by the time of the second Gulf War, such restrictive protocols no longer would suffice.[35] According to the chief of staff's overview for the official army history of air defense operations in 2003, the cruise missile threat, however ineffective from the standpoint of direct loss of life, altered air defense planning. "From an air and missile defense perspective," says the overview, "continued [Iraqi cruise missile] attacks may have forced us to change our tactics."[36] As a consequence, an American Patriot unit inadvertently shot down a British Tornado fighter three days into the war, killing two crew members. The next day, to avoid the same fate, a U.S. Air Force F-16 destroyed a Patriot ground-based radar after it had mistakenly "painted" the friendly aircraft, thus priming it for engagement. In spite of subsequent efforts to tailor Patriot rules of engagement, yet another friendly aircraft, a U.S. Navy F/A-18, was shot down and its pilot killed on April 2.

In press briefings on the heels of the first friendly-fire incident, senior military officials chose language that intimated the dilemma they faced in having to deal with both high-angle and low-flying missile threats. The senior air component representative to the ground headquarters in Iraq, Maj. Gen. Dan Leaf, noted that after the British Tornado was inadvertently shot down, a decision was taken to alter Patriot's rules of engagement to make them "more restrictive in certain modes." Still, Leaf stated that they had to remain sufficiently permissive to permit Patriot to deal with both ballistic and cruise missile threats.[37]

Press interviews with industry and military officials and reports on the formal post-war investigations focused specifically on the responsible Patriot batteries and friendly aircraft and on possible flaws in positive electronic means and procedural tactics (such as using protected engagement zones for returning friendly aircraft) associated with combat identification. Indeed, a malfunctioning electronic identification warning beacon on the British Tornado, the Patriot crew's decision to place its radar on automatic owing to heavy local fire, and heavy electronic interference due to the positioning of two Patriot radars too close to each other, have been cited as possible explanations for the respective friendly-fire incidents.[38] Yet, while the formal investigation was still underway, the U.S. Army's Center for Lessons Learned noted in its own evaluation that positive electronic means of identifying airborne objects have "low reliability." In fact, based on military exercises conducted in 1993, a

1996 National Research Council study reported that "attempts to coordinate air and [surface-to-air missile] intercepts in the same airspace led to unacceptably high level of [simulated] fratricide."[39]

Regardless of whether combat identification measures (such as acoustic signatures of friendly aircraft or identification-friend-or-foe transponders) or protected engagement zones are used, the levels of friendly-fire incidents have been disconcertingly high in simulated war games, often producing friendly aircraft attrition rates of 10–20 percent or more.[40] In its concluding observations on the 2003 war, the official army history of air and missile defense operations notes two challenges that help explain the reasons behind the friendly-fire incidents. One is termed the challenge of cluttered cyberspace—that is, the multitude of electronic emitters operating in close proximity to each other, increasing the chances of operator error.[41] The other is the challenge presented by LACMs. Simply put, it is "the ability of these older cruise missiles to penetrate friendly fire and reach their targets [that] should serve as a warning to joint and army leaders that the emerging cruise missile threat must be addressed."[42] Certainly establishing communications between airborne and ship-based sensors and Patriot batteries would be a step in the right direction. But problems will remain severe in the early stages of any future conflict when only minimal surveillance and battle management and control systems are likely to be in place and coordination among service air fleets and coalition partners is unlikely to have jelled. As the cruise missile and UAV threat grows, so will fratricide and missile defense challenges.

A NEW NARRATIVE BEGINS TO TAKE HOLD

The Patriot's general inability on its own to detect and intercept five Iraqi cruise missiles in 2003 had far less momentous consequences than its single failure to track and intercept an incoming Scud which hit an army barracks, killing 28 American soldiers at the Dhahran air base in Saudi Arabia in 1991. The official army history of the 2003 air and missile war solemnly observes, "In the twelve years since Operation Desert Storm, we have remembered the loss of our soldiers from the last launch on the last day of the war against Dhahran, Saudi Arabia. We vowed not to let this happen again and *no lives or equipment were lost in OIF* [Operation Iraqi Freedom]*from a TBM*[tactical ballistic missile]" (emphasis in original). Admittedly, as the history notes, "the cost of that success came at a price with the loss of two friendly aircraft [including three lives, one should add] to Patriot fires."[43] It was Iraq's surprising use of cruise missiles that gave rise to these unfortunate incidents. Given the substantially greater accuracy of LACMs, marines based at Camp Commando on March 20, 2003 were fortunate not to have suffered the same fate as the soldiers who died at Dhahran on February 25, 1991.

The lives lost at Dhahran and Patriot's overall dismal performance maintained the powerful narrative appeal that R. V. Jones had first assigned to ballistic missiles shortly after World War II, when he referred to their psychological capacity to foster a profound sense of defenselessness. But the army's investment of billions of dollars to prevent a repeat of Dhahran in 2003 helped change the narrative. No matter how insignificant a picture the official history painted of Iraq's use of cruise missiles and ultralights in 2003, in the end army officials actually perceived them as important. They warned that "a concerted effort along the lines of the post DESERT STORM Patriot effort must be made by the joint force to defeat the cruise missile threat."[44]

In the Middle East, where Iran's ambitions to pursue LACMs are evident if not terribly overt, the narrative appeal took hold about a year after the announced conclusion of "major military operations" in Iraq. On June 10, 2004 the Middle East Newsline, an online news service by independent journalists in the region, cast Iranian cruise missiles as "meant to defeat U.S.-origin missile defense systems," adding that the United States had offered to sell PAC-3 missile defenses to Gulf Cooperation Council states, while Kuwait and Saudi Arabia had already expressed interest in the system.[45] News of Iran's acquisition of 6 to 12 Russian Kh-55 strategic LACMs prompted a similar report from IsraCast, a multimedia broadcast network in Jerusalem in March 2005. It noted that it was "extremely difficult" to defend against cruise missiles, in spite of their subsonic speed, largely because they flew so low and they produced very small radar signatures. To illustrate, IsraCast drew attention to the contrast between Patriot's 100 percent success against ballistic missiles in the 2003 war in Iraq and its utter failure to intercept cruise missiles. This failure was seen as even more egregious due to the high level of defense preparedness of American forces in Kuwait. To discourage dismissing Iran's Kh-55s on account of their small quantity, the reporter highlighted their virtue "as a first strike surprise weapon." Were they to be fitted with a biological payload or a crude radiological device (dirty bomb), they could constitute "the perfect mass terror weapon."[46] However exaggerated the scenario, the difficulty of defending against cruise missiles enhanced their narrative appeal.

A similar, if more grounded, characterization of the Kh-55 acquisition by Iran appeared on the GlobalSecurity.org web site in February 2006. After reporting the details of Iran's illegal acquisition of the KH-55s from Ukraine, the story noted that despite Israel's significant investment in the Arrow missile defense system, that country's capabilities for handling low-flying cruise missiles "are less developed." The commentary went on to describe how a cruise missile's capacity to fly extremely low and to avoid detection by terrain masking suggested that the only solution may lie with an airborne radar like AWACS linked to fighters with air-to-air missiles for intercept. Even here, the challenge is difficult. "Trying to intercept cruise missiles over land is a difficult challenge for the defending side," the report concluded.[47]

More vociferously than any other country, Pakistan has articulated a new cruise missile narrative built around a LACM's ability to penetrate missile defenses. The very timing of Pakistan's inaugural Babur test in August 2005 seemed intended to send a blunt message to India, which had reportedly just received—in July 2005—U.S. approval to pursue the acquisition of Israel's Arrow missile defense system as part of the U.S.-India civilian nuclear deal.[48] Six months earlier, in February, a team of Pentagon technical specialists had visited New Delhi to brief their Indian counterparts on the PAC-2 missile defense system, even though India had expressed even keener interest in the more advanced PAC-3 hit-to-kill interceptor. Thus, Pakistan's President Musharraf set a narrative hook that has been reinforced with every Babur test. In the inaugural launch in August 2005, the president declared on Pakistani television, "The biggest value of this system is [that] it is not detectable. It cannot be intercepted."[49] Conservative Islamic newspapers in Pakistan immediately jumped on the bandwagon. "No radar can detect this missile and its movement nor can any defense system intercept it," intoned a *Nawa-e Waqt* editorial.[50] The Foreign Broadcast Information Service, in its own analysis of Pakistani press reaction to Babur's first test, reported that the moderate *Daily Times* "said development of cruise missile technology would not only enhance Pakistan's strike capability but would also serve to neutralize any anti-ballistic missile system that India is interested in acquiring."[51]

Ahmed Ijaz Malik, a researcher at the Islamabad Policy Research Institute, wrote an article in the Institute's Winter 2005 journal issue that noted Patriot's poor performance against Iraqi cruise missiles in the 2003 war. Titled "North Korea: Brinksmanship to Nuclear Threshold," the article steered clear of discussing South Asian missile developments and instead focused on North Korea's missile and nuclear ambitions set in the context of diplomatic and military measures for countering Pyongyang's brinksmanship. Even though Malik observed that North Korea was armed with ballistic, not cruise missiles, his article spent considerable effort pointing out Patriot's weaknesses, emphasizing that Iraq's cruise missiles "got through Patriot's radar unnoticed" and that upgraded Patriots were unable to handle a cluttered air environment "with objects of much smaller radar cross-section" than those used in the first Gulf War.[52]

This theme persisted after Babur's second and third operational tests during 2007. Reporting on the March 2007 test, the Associated Press of Pakistan called attention not only to Babur's capability to deliver both nuclear and conventional payloads with "pin-point" accuracy but also to its ability to remain "undetected by the radar system."[53] Even the Kuwait News Agency picked up the motif when it reported on Babur's second test by calling the system a "radar avoiding cruise missile with 700 km range."[54] By July 2007, after Babur's third test, Agence France-Presse, the global news agency, repeated the Pakistani government's preferred image of its new LACM: "The Babur, which has near stealth capabilities, is a low flying, terrain hugging missile with high maneuverability, pinpoint accuracy and radar avoidance features."[55]

The Pakistani characterization seemed intended as Islamabad's answer to India's Vedic mantras, chants meant to ward off danger or eliminate enemies. But even Indian commentators have begun to parrot the new LACM narrative. To be sure, Indian commentaries, including marketing materials, promoting the BrahMos cruise missile published prior to the 2003 Iraq War frequently mentioned the missile's low radar signature and supersonic velocity. But not until recently, after Pakistan's surprise testing of the subsonic Babur LACM, has the Indian account featured BrahMos's capability to penetrate missile defenses. When the ground-launched LACM version of BrahMos was introduced into the Indian army in June 2007, for example, the *Indian Express* boasted about the BrahMos being "almost impossible to intercept as it crosses 2.8 Mach during flight."[56] Immediately following the 2003 Iraq War, even as Indian defense experts praised the successful testing of BrahMos, some also began to sing the praises of subsonic LACMs like Tomahawk for their greater range capability and capacity to survive in spite of their slow speed. For example, in November 2003 one expert, in referring to Tomahawk, noted that "radar detection is difficult because of the missile's small radar cross-section and low altitude flight. Similarly, infrared detection is difficult because the turbofan engine emits little heat."[57]

The broader strategic implications of Pakistan's addition of LACMs to its arsenal, matched with India's capacity to thwart missile defenses, began to manifest themselves in India within a few months after Babur's first test in August 2005. In an April 2006 television interview with India's Naval Chief Admiral Arun Prakash, who argued that "a cruise missile would destabilize the deterrent," CNN-IBN defense correspondent Vishal Thapar characterized Islamabad's new LACM in much the same way as official Pakistani statements do after each test. Thapar said, "Unlike ballistic missiles, the terrain-hugging cruise missiles are difficult to detect and are also deadly accurate," concluding that such a development would not serve stability well in the region.[58] When India's attempt to fashion a cruise missile technology deal with France fell apart in October 2006, *The Tribune* held forth on the importance of India's acquisition of cruise missiles having substantially longer ranges than the Brah-Mos. It obliquely referred to the collapsed deal as having sought a French LACM with 1,200–1,500-km range, while noting that "a cruise missile can fly low and fast to escape radar detection. Pakistan has a cruise missile called 'Babur'."[59] The consequences of LACMs' new narrative appeal for South Asian offense-defense calculations was captured succinctly in January 2007 in *Asia Times*. According to Siddharth Srivastava, "Pakistan's bid to acquire cruise missiles, as well as accumulate ballistic missiles, is an attempt to balance India's declared intentions to incorporate the anti-ballistic missile defense (BMD) system from Israel (Arrow) and the U.S. (Patriot). The BMD system can be effectively checked by cruise missiles."[60] Not surprisingly, LACMs' new sexiness became a featured element with the July 2007 announcement that India was pursuing the Nirbhay, a 1,000-km-range LACM. Quoting Avinash Chander, the director of the Hyderabad laboratory leading the Nirbhay project, *The Telegraph* reported, "We have BrahMos, which is a supersonic cruise missile and the need was felt for a subsonic cruise missile that will be capable of being launched from multiple platforms in land, air, and sea." The reporter for *The Telegraph* added, as if the script was prepared in Islamabad rather than Hyderabad, "Nirbhay will be a terrain-hugging missile capable of avoiding detection by ground-based radar."[61]

The emergence of narrative changes in LACMs' appeal is subtler in regard to China's LACM programs. China's focus is less on rhetoric and more on system deployments and the development of related doctrine and tactics. But China's buildup of cruise missiles on top of ballistic ones is evidence enough that Chinese planners fully appreciate how LACMs challenge regional missile and air defenses. To date, they have emphasized the value of saturation attacks in achieving prompt and lasting effects that can be further exploited after the initial period of war. Particularly telling is China's belief that cruise missiles possess an overwhelming cost advantage compared with the price of defending against them.[62] In light of the considerable thought that Chinese strategists have devoted to LACM utility, especially with respect to how LACMs interact with ballistic missile use, they appear to have concluded that there is little reason to make boastful statements—particularly ones that would only exacerbate already tense circumstances prevailing in the region—about how their LACMs are certain to penetrate regional missile and air defenses.

Taiwan's decidedly inferior capabilities vis-à-vis China, on the other hand, have produced more provocative language. Three months after the conclusion of the 2003 Iraq War's invasion phase, a Taiwanese military columnist wrote about Chinese plans to complicate Taiwan's defensive systems by deploying LACMs within two years. "Different from the 'M series of missiles' well known to we Taiwanese, the cruise missile is a weapon more difficult to intercept than the ballistic missile," the columnist observed.[63] In April 2005, as China reportedly began to deploy its new LACMs, a Taiwanese national security official told *Liberty Times* that China's new cruise missiles were designed to "bypass Taiwan's current missile defense capabilities."[64] Of course, such a position considered in the context of Taiwan's concern about the high costs of missile defense supports its own desire to develop the HF-2E LACM.

South Korea did not have especially strong reasons to insinuate assured penetration into its parsimonious characterization of the new Cheonryong LACM program. North Korea's missile and air defenses are respectively nonexistent and patently below par. Yet, when leaks to South Korea's press outlets began in September 2006, they included statements attributed to unnamed ministry of defense officials about Cheonryong's capacity to "fly at an altitude of only 50 to 100 meters, making it a difficult target for air defenses."[65] After South Korea tested its new LACM the following month, another press report distinguished the South's new missiles from those of the North, while also implying an assured penetration advantage for Seoul's new missile. "Different from a ballistic missile, which soars up before flying to the target, a cruise missile is hard to intercept because it flies at a lower altitude: about 100 meters from the ground," the reporter intoned.[66]

The new formulation of LACMs' appeal has crept into Japanese thinking as well, growing out of the Japanese government's concern that cruise missile technology emanating from the illegal transfer of Kh-55 strategic cruise missiles from Ukraine to China and Iran may end up in North Korea's hands, courtesy of Iran. In June 2005, *Sankei Shimbun* reported that Japan had formally asked the Ukrainian and Iranian governments to look into the matter, while demanding that Tehran refrain from sharing the fruits of its acquisition with Pyongyang. Tokyo's concern, as reported in *Sankei Shimbun,* was due to the challenge of detecting and intercepting LACMs. "Because they are capable of flying at low altitudes, it is difficult to detect them by radar," reported *Sankei Shimbun.* More to the point, an unnamed Japanese government official was quoted as saying, "if [North Korea] succeeds in gaining cruise missile technology, we cannot respond with a [missile defense] system based on ground-to-air missiles or the next-generation sea-based [missile defense] system to be installed on Aegis vessels that the government is making preparations to deploy."[67] Yet, North Korea is not the only regional cruise missile threat drawing Tokyo's attention. In late January 2008, *Yomiuri Shimbun* reported that the Japanese defense ministry now recognized that its current ballistic missile defense initiatives would not suffice to defend against LACMs and that Japan planned to commence its own cruise missile defense programs to cope with the anticipated rise in regional LACM threats. China's growing LACM arsenal was particularly noted.[68]

Not least because Russia shares center stage with the United States in the development of highly sophisticated LACMs, Moscow officials fully appreciate the defense penetration potential of cruise missiles. But only recently has such appreciation substantially figured into their public posture. Stung by the effects of U.S. plans to deploy ground-based missile defense radars in Poland and the Czech Republic, Moscow responded in May 2007 by threatening offensive countermeasures designed to penetrate any conceivable American defensive system, including the new RS-24 ICBM with multiple warheads believed capable of taking evasive maneuvers in the terminal phase. Boasts from Russia about penetrating U.S. missile defenses were nothing new. The RS-12M, or Topol-M (SS-27) ICBM, also featured anti-missile maneuvering to penetrate American defense systems. What was new was the surprise addition of the R-500 LACM, or the Iskander-K. This appears to be a cruise missile launchable from the Iskander transporter-erector-launcher, which until the inaugural May 2007 test of the R-500 was thought to be exclusively a ballistic missile system. All along, the Iskander's 280 to 480-km-range ballistic missile was expected to possess a reentry vehicle capable of evasive maneuvers to confuse missile defenses, but the addition of the R-500 LACM further complicates the missile defense challenge. After the May 2007 test, Moscow's *Izvestiya* proclaimed in regard to the R-500 LACM: "neither the National Defense system (it has not been designed for this principle) nor even the most modern American Patriot surface-to-air missile systems are capable of noticing, still less intercepting such a target."[69]

As U.S. Army air and missile defense officials effectively admitted after the 2003 Gulf War, the lessons from Iraq should be taken as a rare glimpse of future threats. That a corresponding new narrative hinging on the virtues of cruise missiles has now been so frequently repeated should come as no great surprise. What does remain uncertain, however, is whether states most affected by cruise missile threats will heed the Iraq War's serendipitous warning.

Norms

In May 2005, along the Sutlej River near the Pakistan border, various formations of the Indian army, comprising about 25,000 troops and elements of a Panther division and an armored brigade, conducted a military exercise code named "Power of Thunder." With tactical offensive support from the Indian air force, the exercise was designed to test the Indian military's new operational doctrine, called "Cold Start." Lasting 10 days, the battle scenario began with a preemptive offensive by the "blue force" (that is, India) consisting of a lightning ground incursion into enemy territory supported by long-range precision strikes from the army and air force.[1] Such long-range conventional strikes will increasingly come from BrahMos and Nirbhay cruise missiles, which offer Indian military strategists a seemingly appealing option between a long offensive force buildup over several months, as in India's large-scale military mobilization vis-à-vis Pakistan in the aftermath of a December 2001 terrorist attack on India's parliament, and doing nothing at all.

India's newfound interest in preemption is by no means an exceptional phenomenon. Since the September 11, 2001 terrorist attacks on American targets, a consensus supporting a preemption doctrine has fitfully emerged around the globe. Responding to the events of 9/11 together with threats emanating from so-called rogue states in possession of nuclear, chemical, or biological weapons, and believing that such terrorist and state threats are no longer susceptible to traditional deterrence concepts, the United States turned a long-standing military option into a formal doctrine in the National Security Strategy released in September 2002.[2] To be sure, the George W. Bush administration linked the new preemption doctrine to the notion of "anticipatory self-defense," recognized in Article 51 of the United Nations Charter and normally tied to attacking in the face of an imminent threat. Yet the new document's language, together with confusing articulations by senior administration officials, obfuscated the doctrine's intent, leaving the impression that even long-developing threats, not just imminent ones, might warrant a first strike.[3] Thus, preemption tacitly grew to include prevention. The preemption doctrine became operational in America's 2003 invasion of Iraq, and its ramifications were immediate. India's Foreign Minister Yashwant Sinha declared that India possessed "a much better case to go for preemptive action against Pakistan than the [United States] has in Iraq."[4] Despite the implication that one might draw, that the United States believes preemptive doctrine is unique to its superpower status, other states besides India have also begun to consider it fashionable to adopt preemptive doctrines.

Cruise missiles, predominantly land-attack cruise missiles (LACMs), figure prominently into the growing propensity of nations to adopt preemptive policies. LACMs are seen as capable not only of precise and surprise delivery of conventional payloads but of nuclear and biological ones as well. Thus, when Indian planners face the dilemma of long force buildups vis-à-vis Pakistan and the choice of relevant intermediate options between acquiescence and diplomacy, long-range precision strikes offer them the theoretical hope of waging a limited conventional war, albeit under the threat of nuclear escalation. The appeal of cruise missiles lies in their presumed discriminateness. As Lawrence Freedman has written, "Cruise missiles . . . are to some extent the paradigmatic weapon of the RMA [Revolution in Military Affairs], as delivery systems that can be launched from a variety of platforms and strike in a precise manner and with low collateral damage."[5] In an era when one believes that traditional forms of deterrence, particularly threats of nuclear retaliation, have far less credibility than they did during the Cold War, military strategies formulated around the notion of denying one's enemy its military objectives via precision conventional weapons have begun to prevail. Generally speaking, then, cruise missiles have come to be seen in a more favorable light than ballistic missiles, and this makes efforts to control their spread increasingly problematic. LACMs are regarded as weapons of great discrimination, not mass destruction.

This normative differentiation was reflected in the formulation of the Hague Code of Conduct against Ballistic Missile Proliferation, adopted in November 2002 as a broad, if inherently weak, standard against ballistic missile proliferation. The Hague Code's formulators were the member states of the Missile Technology Control Regime (MTCR), a regime of partner states that from its creation has sought to control the spread of both ballistic and cruise missiles (and unmanned aerial vehicles [UAVs]). Just why the Hague Code's formulators effectively assigned cruise missiles second-class treatment by excluding them from the Code can only be guessed, as the MTCR membership is decidedly circumspect with respect to disclosing its deliberations. Yet, the evidence strongly suggests that the United States did not support the inclusion of cruise missiles in the Hague Code and remains steadfastly disinclined to support their inclusion in the future.[6] In this stance, the United States apparently stands apart from most of its fellow signatories to the Hague Code of Conduct. At an international conference in Vienna on May 30, 2007, just prior to the fifth regular meeting of the subscribing states to the Hague Code and with many of that meeting's delegates in attendance, all speakers agreed that missile proliferation was a growing problem and one that was not just related to ballistic missiles but also to cruise missiles, and most speakers agreed that the Hague Code should be extended to include cruise missiles. But the conference participants did not include any of the U.S. government's delegates who would attend the fifth meeting of the Code on the following day.[7]

Given the elevation of preemption from military option to strategic doctrine and the post-Cold War emergence of a denial strategy, largely dependent on precision conventional capabilities, as a replacement for nuclear deterrence, the normative differentiation between ballistic and cruise missiles is unlikely to change soon without the leadership of the United States. The weak normative treatment of missile systems generally and cruise missiles specifically only reinforces these factors. Furthermore, they allow states to mimic U.S. preemption doctrines.

PREEMPTION AND ITS UNINTENDED CONSEQUENCES

The rationale for the Bush administration's new preemption doctrine squarely rested on the presumed demise of classical deterrence doctrine, which had been the foundation of U.S. national security strategy for over 40 years. But apocalyptic terrorists bent on martyrdom and rogue states seeking WMD were thought to require something quite different from nuclear deterrence and containment. More important, the Bush administration's new national security strategy perceived "an overlap between states that sponsor terror and those that pursue WMD," a nexus that demanded, in their view, a preemptive strategy, with Iraq chosen as the strategy's test case.[8]

Those who crafted the 2002 National Security Strategy of preemption intended it to have consequences, but not the ones that seem to have occurred. According to Under Secretary of State John Bolton, "the outcome in Iraq we hope will cause other states in the region and indeed around the world to look at the consequences of pursuing WMD and draw the appropriate lesson that such pursuits are not in their long-term national interest."[9] The strategy may have worked with Libya, whose willingness to dismantle its WMD holdings appears to have been influenced by Washington's willingness to coercively impose regime change on Iraq.[10] But it appears to have backfired in the cases of North Korea and Iran. Pyongyang and Tehran appear to have drawn the lesson that accelerating their pursuit of WMD was in their best interests, given that the unanticipated Iraqi insurgency that arose after Saddam Hussein's ouster had effectively tied down American military forces and limited U.S. military options vis-à-vis other states.

Other countries, like India, have simply begun to mimic the U.S. preemption strategy to fit their own needs. It is not just formal U.S. preemption strategy that is being copied but also several subsidiary components that relate to the diminished ability of nuclear deterrence alone to cope with new post–Cold war challenges. These concerns came to a head in the publication of the Bush administration's Nuclear Posture Review (NPR) in late December 2001.[11] The waning credibility of nuclear threats played a feature role in the new posture, but in a radically new way. The 2001 NPR in effect grafted the notion of global conventional strike to a substantially reduced nuclear force and accompanying nuclear stockpile, along with having active and passive defenses and a revitalized defense infrastructure, to create the "New Triad."[12]

Rather than resting on the threat of nuclear retaliation, the NPR's authors turned to what is essentially a denial strategy that hinges on developing credible war-fighting options to deprive adversaries of the capacity to do America and its allies and friends harm—especially by employing nuclear, biological, or chemical weapons.[13] Because post–Cold War threats are more diverse, the NPR's authors argued that they demand a better integration of a full range of offensive and defensive weapons (including both conventional and nuclear) and the respective doctrines governing their military utility. By calling for such integration, however, the NPR wrongly conflated both nuclear and conventional weapons as if they were equally useful weapons of war. Like past efforts of other U.S. presidents to make nuclear weapons just like any others, the Bush administration's attempt produced a firestorm of controversy, which focused most intensely on the potential development of new types of nuclear weapons designed to destroy underground bunkers.[14] Lost in the noise of the nuclear debate were questions related to an emerging strategy of denial relying on conventional precision strike systems and greatly improved (or so it was hoped) missile defenses.

Of course, the turn toward a denial strategy originated in the early to mid-1970s when the Department of Defense made substantial investments in precision guidance and long-range strike weapons, including the Tomahawk LACM. Although only 5 percent of the weapons employed in the 1991 Gulf War were precision guided, they demonstrated at least an order of magnitude greater effectiveness than unguided air-delivered ("dumb") bombs, thereby showing truly revolutionary promise.[15] Just before stepping down from his post as the Bill Clinton administration's first secretary of defense, Les Aspin announced in late 1993, as part of that administration's controversial counterproliferation initiative, denial objectives that remain equally prominent today. They included capabilities to locate, identify, and attack hardened targets and WMD-armed mobile missiles, and to shoot down enemy missiles that survived counterforce attacks.[16] The 2001 NPR specially called out high-value hardened underground targets, mobile or relocatable targets, and defeating chemical and biological targets as the most difficult denial challenges, and missile defenses were prominently included as a fundamental part of the New Triad. Those WMD-armed missiles that managed to avoid counterforce attacks had to be intercepted by improved missile defenses if a denial strategy was to have any prospect of achieving the NPR's stipulated requirements—assuring allies, dissuading adversaries from pursuing WMD programs, deterring them from employing such weapons, and, if all else failed, denying them the capacity to strike the United States, its allies, and friends.

After the United States' otherwise superlative performance against Iraq in the 1991 Gulf War, two glaring military weaknesses stood out: the inability of coalition air forces (overwhelmingly, U.S. forces) to find and destroy Iraq's mobile missile launchers and the poor performance of missile defenses.[17] Although losing the "Scud hunt" had little direct military impact—except for accounting for 15 percent of the coalition's air sorties—Iraq's continued missile attacks nearly proved disastrous politically when Israel considered (but ultimately decided against) entering the war to take on the counterforce battle itself. Such an action could have split the coalition at a decisive point in the war. By early 1994, the U.S. Joint Chiefs of Staff formulated and approved a new joint doctrine for theater missile defense that featured four necessary pillars to achieve success against ballistic and cruise missiles.[18] They included attack operations (counterforce), active defenses (against launched missiles), passive defenses, and command and control. While all were seen as necessary, joint doctrine specified attack operations as the preferred method for countering enemy missiles, defining success to be the destruction of WMD payloads on enemy territory before countermeasures (like decoys) could be employed to complicate missile defense performance. Some modest improvement was demonstrated during Operation Allied Shield in Kosovo, but of course Serbia did not possess mobile long-range missiles and U.S. and North Atlantic Treaty Organization (NATO) air forces experienced difficulty identifying and striking Serbian targets that were well camouflaged or operating under thick cloud cover.

The Pentagon's new joint doctrine for theater missile defense, with its pronounced promotion of offense, rapidly found its way into the respective doctrinal publications of each military service. For example, in a 1996 pamphlet entitled "Army Theater Missile Defense Primer," the distinction between defense and offense is simplistically drawn:

> During the Cold War, America's Army was on the defense. Even though our doctrine emphasized offensive spirit and the necessity to seize and maintain the initiative, the Army's mission was to defend [NATO's] Central Region from a massive attack by the Soviet Union and Warsaw Pact . . . . On the other hand, Soviet commanders were on the offensive. Their primary organizational objectives were to establish [command and control] that allowed rapid, deep maneuver to establish land dominance and to achieve quick victory.[19]

An accompanying illustration comparing the U.S./NATO approach, as governed by the "Spirit of the Defense," with the Soviet/Warsaw Pact's "Spirit of the Offense" reflects the U.S. Army's desire during the 1990s to usurp control of joint theater operations from the U.S. Air Force, a battle that was waged throughout that decade but ultimately lost to the air force. The important point here is the U.S. emulation of the Soviet approach to war. The army pamphlet trumpets the virtue of seizing the initiative, maneuvering rapidly, and fighting at extended ranges, concluding that "the Soviets had it right!"[20] China too has shown a pronounced preference for offense in its posture vis-à-vis Taiwan.

Given the post-Cold War prominence in U.S. military doctrine of a decidedly preemptive style of offensive warfare linked to an improving global missile defense capability, it should come as no great surprise that foreign armies too have begun to adopt such an emphasis. Thousands of foreign military officers attend U.S. military institutions of learning each year where they absorb the very same curriculum as American officers. Since its founding in 1909, the Naval Postgraduate School in Monterey, California alone has graduated 45,000 foreign officers and defense officials, including the commander of Turkish naval forces, the chief of staff of Israel's air force, and King Abdullah of Jordan. About 15 percent of the 1,000 students attending the National Defense University in Washington, D.C. each year are foreign officers or civilian officials. Beijing has now opened up its premier and formerly opaque military educational institution, the PLA National Defense University, to foreign military officers. According to a 2004 white paper on China's national defense, officers from 44 nations participated in a special International Symposium Course, while over the two years preceding publication of the paper, 1,245 military personnel from 91 countries matriculated in Chinese military colleges and universities.[21] Such military-to-military arrangements are an indispensable means of cementing long-standing relationships among the host country and allied and friendly nations. Yet the seemingly innocuous promotion of preemptive tactics in the "spirit of the offense" as the preferred way of warfare through such intergovernmental programs can have destabilizing unintended consequences.

America's movement towards an offensively oriented denial strategy does not involve merely doctrinal change. Virtually continuous combat operations since the terrorist attacks of 2001 have led to notable progress in attacking fleeting targets, including mobile missiles. Initial combat against Taliban forces in Afghanistan demonstrated the imaginative fusion of target identification on the ground by special operations forces controllers linked to precision air strikes from above. Nearly instantaneous relay of the target's positional information to strike aircraft greatly reduced the amount of time between identifying a target and attacking it. By the time of the Iraq invasion in 2003, American forces were much better prepared to find and attack mobile missiles. In his book on the war and its aftermath, *Washington Post* reporter Tom Ricks tells the story of how, in the midst of a huge three-day sandstorm and rainstorm that stalled the U.S. military advance on Baghdad, the U.S. Air Force nonetheless managed to find, attack, and destroy an Iraqi missile launcher and its related support vehicles located off the road, hidden deeply under trees, at night, in one of Baghdad's northern suburbs. An Iraqi Republican Guard captain later reported that the missile troops were so demoralized by the attack's effectiveness that they fled the area without returning to their unit. Word spread that a spy must have reported on the unit's location because no satellite or aircraft could so precisely isolate the target, given its cover and the adverse weather.[22]

Conceptual and organizational changes have as much to do with progress in attack operations as with new reconnaissance and surveillance capacity, notably that realized by UAVs for dedicated reconnaissance missions. Conceptually, until recently the U.S. Air Force saw no need to differentiate finding and attacking mobile missiles (and terrorists) from finding and attacking any target that moved. But the air force now believes that such highly fleeting targets constitute a critically important and distinctively different combat goal, meriting special joint treatment.[23] With special operations forces and perhaps other support on the ground seamlessly integrated with attack forces in the air, shortening the attack cycle against fleeting targets is possible. The average time needed to execute a time-sensitive targeting strike has fallen from 2 hours in 2002 to 10 minutes in 2004.[24] The air force goal is now to achieve what their former Chief of Staff Gen. John Jumper called "time of flight" time-sensitive targeting, or hitting the target in the amount of time it takes to deliver the weapon—less than a minute for a manned or unmanned weapons platform loitering nearby. While Israel, in its recent war in Lebanon, struggled to find and attack Hezbollah's ubiquitous short-range Katyusha rockets, which can be put in place and launched by one man in just moments, Israeli air and ground forces effectively flooded the skies with UAVs networked together to provide loitering aircraft with precise targeting coordinates of detected medium- and long-range Hezbollah rocket launchers. As a result, Israel managed to destroy between 80 and 90 percent of Hezbollah's longer-range launchers (around 125), all within a timeframe of 45 to 60 seconds between detection and attack.[25]

If U.S. conventional denial capabilities are demonstrably robust today, they are destined to become even more potent over the next two decades. While improvements will further diminish the salience of nuclear alternatives, such as those the Bush administration has striven but failed to study after launching the 2001 NPR, the fact that such offensive capability is now married to a more formalized preemption doctrine could have undesirable results. Conventional options have already begun to replace nuclear ones as U.S. military planners integrate conventional and nuclear strike planning consistent with the 2001 NPR and 2002 preemption doctrine. The U.S. Strategic Command (STRATCOM), which as the Strategic Air Command had been responsible for planning and delivering nuclear attacks during the Cold War, has turned the offensive leg of the New Triad into a strike force, called Global Strike, which includes an increasingly large conventional component.[26] STRATCOM's operational plan for dealing with WMD threats like those posed by Iran and North Korea reportedly rejects a large-scale multi-service campaign in favor of decisive conventional and cyber attacks complemented by special operations forces on the ground to locate and secure targets, if needed. Such preemptive strike plans differ from traditional American war scenarios sculpted by regional commands and based on responses to regional invasions, such as Iraq's occupation of Kuwait in 1990. Current global strike plans give the U.S. president the option to attack within hours of a decision to do so.[27]

The U.S. Air Force contribution to STRATCOM's new global strike mission includes today's B-52, B-1, and B-2 bombers loaded with conventional precision strike munitions, and plans call for a new long-range bomber by 2018. The U.S. Navy has converted 4 of its 18 Trident submarines to carry 154 Tomahawk LACMs, with options to trade off a few cruise missiles for special operations minisubs or small UAVs for reconnaissance missions. The Pentagon also sought to spend $503 million to outfit a small number of Trident D-5 nuclear missiles on the remaining 14 Ohio-class submarines with conventional warheads (either many small-diameter bombs or fewer bunker-buster warheads) to achieve a prompt (within one hour of a decision to launch) global strike option.[28] Even more robust global strike forces could emerge from current research and development programs involving small expendable rocket boosters launching highly maneuverable conventionally armed aerospace vehicles with intercontinental ranges and reusable hypersonic cruise missiles that can carry huge payloads over intercontinental distances within two hours.[29]

But while clear opportunities for diminishing America's dependence on nuclear weapons appear promising, the precision conventional road ahead is not without its own bumps. The most immediate challenge is designing a safe path to virtually exclusive reliance on robust conventional forces, particularly ones tied to a preemptive strike doctrine. Two immediate problems stand out. The first has to do with the inherent difficulty of distinguishing a conventionally armed long-range ballistic missile from a nuclear-armed one. The 2001 NPR's intentional conflation of nuclear and conventional strike planning as part of the New Triad only exacerbates this problem. Russia, which possesses an early warning system, has already raised this concern. In response, both the House and Senate have reacted with caution to the Pentagon's $503 million request to arm some of the navy's Trident missiles with conventional warheads. They have asked the Bush administration to provide details on how to ensure that use of such a missile would not result in an inadvertent or accidental retaliatory nuclear response.[30] One obvious way to allay these concerns is to provide advance notification on missile flight trajectories for all ballistic missile launches. Russia and the United States agreed to such a joint warning concept in September 1998, which was subsequently made more formal in June 2000 when Presidents Clinton and Putin agreed to establish a Joint Data Exchange Center in Moscow. Legal and tax issues have prevented the center from becoming operational thus far, although President Putin has reenergized the issue in his response to the U.S. decision to deploy missile defenses in central Europe. In any case, the only true means of eliminating ambiguity over whether a missile is nuclear or conventional is to move to an exclusively and verifiably conventional missile force. Doing so is by no means an inconceivable prospect given trends in precision conventional weapons and past success in verifying even more complex strategic nuclear agreements. In the meantime, the current legislative pause offers an opportunity to explore the pros and cons of turning never-used intercontinental ballistic missiles (ICBMs) into usable conventional ones, particularly at a time when international norms—notably the 2002 Hague Code of Conduct—against their acquisition are in an early, formative stage.[31]

If counterforce represents the American military's preference, missile defenses are still considered essential to build confidence in a denial strategy—especially insofar as it involves projecting American forces abroad. But effective attack operations or counterforce strikes against mobile missiles will reduce the in-flight threat missile defenses must face. And passive defenses, too, such as vaccines for biological attacks, can reduce the effectiveness of missiles that survive attack operations and manage to penetrate missile defenses. How current and possible future adversaries perceive the effectiveness of U.S. missile defenses (either separately or in combination with counterforce and passive defenses) is difficult to assess. Yet, with the exception of widely perceived LACM penetration effectiveness, there is little evidence that foreign audiences share missile defense critics' belief that current or future ballistic missile defenses will not perform as promised.[32] Indeed, even the critics realize that many of the reasons for poor missile defense performance turn less on the impossibility of the mission than on the intense political pressures to maintain politically mandated development and deployment schedules. This so-called "rush to failure" was self-evident to supporters of missile defense late in the Clinton administration and persists today.[33]

The Bush administration has pursued missile defenses much more aggressively than its predecessor did. Arguing that the 1972 Anti-Ballistic Missile (ABM) Treaty prevented the United States from testing and deploying a limited missile defense of U.S. territory, it formally withdrew from the treaty and deployed the first layer of global missile defense, to consist of 20 ground-based interceptors employing exoatmospheric kill vehicles (as of mid-2007 there were 44), 3 Aegis-class cruisers/destroyers armed with Standard SM-3 interceptors (about 130 in mid-2007), and an unspecified number of Patriot PAC-3 interceptors deployed both at home and overseas. Various early warning systems and command, control, and communications systems support these interceptors. The appellation "global" replaced "theater" and "national" missile defenses, conceptually merging the two into one broad notion of missile defense. Effectively, it seemed, the Bush administration was proposing an umbrella of protection for the United States, its allies, and its friends. Simultaneously, the Departments of Defense and State sent political and technical teams around the globe to brief allied and friendly states about the merits of and need for their own investments in missile defense. The administration's abrogation of the ABM Treaty came two weeks before the release of its nuclear posture review and launching of the New Triad.

Advocates of ballistic missile defense in the United States appreciate the risks of pursuing a strategy of early deployment, which entails product improvements (or so-called "blocks") introduced every two years. They argue that it would be negligent to deny the nation some capability against emerging threats, however problematic in the case of the ground-based system for mid-course interception of ICBMs. Frequently cited is Israel's early deployment of the Arrow missile defense system, which is thought to be providing some degree of protection while Israel pursues fuller missile defenses. Moreover, the highly successful Aegis SM-3 program is touted as furnishing substantial capability now against short- to medium-range ballistic missile threats. Potentially, the SM-3 could provide a future platform for boost-phase intercept (which involves engaging an enemy ballistic missile very shortly after it is launched). This will depend on making progress toward developing a new high-acceleration booster coupled with a boost-kill vehicle for SM-3 by the end of this decade.[34] As additional blocks of capability are added over time, a truly layered if still imperfect global missile defense system will begin to take shape.

The chief limitation of current and prospective U.S. missile defenses became clear in 2003 during combat operations in Iraq. For U.S. officials, the events finally drove home the fact that current missile defenses have little or no value against low-flying cruise missiles unless they undergo significant improvements in airborne sensors (for both wide-area surveillance and the provision of fire-control information for targeting) that are linked effectively to airborne and ground-based missile interceptors. Fighters equipped with advanced detection and tracking radars and air-to-air missiles possess a modest capability to deal with low-volume LACM attacks. But huge gaps remain for effective defense against LACMs in both regional and homeland settings. Indeed, a 2006 Pentagon assessment of the overall U.S. capability to defend the American homeland against LACMs identified ten capability gaps that may not be filled until 2015.[35]

From a foreign perspective, the chief problem with such an ad hoc approach to building a global missile defense system is fear of the unknown. During the summer of 2007, Russian concerns about Poland and the Czech Republic becoming sites for parts of the ground-based interceptor system became manifest. Under the U.S. proposal, Poland would have 10 interceptors deployed at one site while the Czech Republic would have 1 radar installed on its territory. Although such an insubstantial deployment would hardly threaten Russia's many hundreds of ICBMs or thousands of warheads, Russia's concern presumably centers more broadly on the overall direction of U.S.-led global missile defenses. During the Cold War, arms control was predicated on the importance of transparency—on making both sides of any competition aware, within the limits of security, of what the other side was doing. If not entirely dismissive, the Bush administration has been less than forthcoming in making its future intentions with regard to missile defense fully transparent. To be sure, administration figures have attempted to reassure Russia and China that they have no reason to fear American global missile defenses, which are meant only to protect American interests from comparatively small missile attacks from rogue states, not strategic threats from Russia or China. But Russia reportedly fears that future American ground- and space-based sensors might provide the basis for a "break out" option in which the United States could rapidly expand a putatively "limited" missile defense system into one that degraded Russia's strategic nuclear deterrent—in particular, the second-strike deterrent—as well as China's substantially smaller offensive arsenal.[36] American and Russian specialists alike have already raised fears about the growing disparity between U.S. and Russian strategic offensive and defensive forces.[37]

Lest anyone assume that acquiring an effective denial strategy is a readily achievable task, it is worthwhile examining how other nations, singly or in collaboration with others, might thwart U.S. plans, even while they are ostensible participants in existing multilateral arms control regimes.[38] In regard to missile defense effectiveness, suppose Russia decided to skirt inadequate or nonexistent rules governing the spread of countermeasure technology that would complicate defenses against both ballistic and cruise missiles. Or, what if both Russia and China decided to exploit weaker norms relating to the spread of LACMs much more aggressively than at present, in order to enable Syria, Iran, and North Korea to obtain sophisticated ground-launched LACMs? The latter would make the counterforce challenge more difficult. Prelaunch detection of LACMs is far more problematic than with ballistic missiles. Because LACM launchers are significantly smaller than ballistic missile launchers, airborne tracking will become more difficult. One government-sponsored study suggested that the proportion of civilian and military vehicles with essentially the same characteristics as missile launchers will more than double as smaller LACM launchers are deployed. As this "look-alike" population grows, airborne sensors will be hard-pressed to distinguish real targets from false ones, which could have both military and political consequences.[39] Thus, the real U.S. challenge is not just integrating more effective global missile defenses and counterforce capabilities into an effective denial strategy but also simultaneously developing an overarching strategic vision that is responsive to the concerns of Russia, China, and other major powers or at least maintains stable relations with them.

As noted, the U.S. elevation of preemption from a military option to the level of doctrine or national strategy carries with it the undesirable element of emulation. Whether a nation interprets preemption as the United States has (as an act of preventive war intended to preclude a possible future conflict) or in its classical sense (seeing signs of an imminent attack, a nation strikes first)—given the inherent tendency of such a policy to generate instability, the near-perfect intelligence required for defensible implementation of such a policy, and the prevalence of tense regional military competitions—U.S. preemption doctrine could have serious unintended consequences.[40] Most worrisome is the prospect that such copycatting will not only foster a disposition toward lowering the threshold of war but also result in too little attention to nonmilitary solutions.

THE UNINTENDED CONSEQUENCES OF NONPROLIFERATION NORM-BUILDING

Missiles capable of delivering nuclear, biological, and chemical payloads remain decidedly outside any kind of effective normative nonproliferation framework.[41] But it is not for want of trying. The initial step taken was to create a cartel, or an informal association, of member states wishing to restrict the spread of complete missile systems and related technologies from nonmember states. Created in 1987, the MTCR consisted of the original Group of Seven (G7) industrial states (the United States, Canada, France, Germany, Italy, Japan, and the United Kingdom). Since then it has grown to 34 member states, and there are several nonmember countries that broadly adhere to the regime's guidelines. By the late 1990s, the MTCR had become the only multilateral mechanism designed to deal with both ballistic and cruise missile systems and related technologies.

MTCR member states adhere not only to a common set of export guidelines but also to an extensive list of controlled items or technologies. Yet the MTCR is not involved in export license decisions, which remain the sovereign responsibility of each member and are made in accordance with national export control legislation. New members are expected, however, to adjust their national export controls to make them consistent with the regime's guidelines and list of controlled technologies. Member states also participate in significant outreach activities to promote the regime's objectives. Despite routine criticism of the MTCR as an ineffective tool for stemming the spread of missiles, especially from strong supporters of missile defenses, the truth is that the regime's supply-side controls have been successful thus far in confining the spread of ballistic missiles to those with ranges of medium-range ballistic missile (MRBM) systems. Only recently have the signs of significant cruise missile proliferation begun to suggest that this class of unmanned delivery systems could eventually join ballistic missiles to create truly worrisome regional instability in the Middle East, South Asia, and Northeast Asia.

Sensibly, it seemed at the time, as cruise missiles looked to become a more significant proliferation factor, the 34-nation MTCR felt compelled, beginning in 1998, to address the obvious shortcomings of employing only supply-side solutions to missile proliferation: the absence of a comprehensive and broadly agreed norm defining what kind of missile activities were undesirable. Rather than establishing a rigid standard of right or wrong, as regimes dealing with landmines and nuclear, biological, and chemical weapons have done, the MTCR states attempted to create an instrument that would, in the Canadian view, "draw the line between acceptable and unacceptable activities."[42] This would differentiate the MTCR's initiative from WMD treaties by focusing narrowly on defining "rules of the road" instead of attempting to create a legal treaty regime with norms enforceable through legal procedures and verification mechanisms.

The year 1998 represented the nadir of any consensus about the danger of cruise missile proliferation and thus offered a particularly unfavorable context in which to inaugurate norm building via the MTCR. The proximate reason then had to do with the decisions taken by Paris and London to contract with the United Arab Emirates for the sale of the Black Shaheen LACM, a Category I missile subject to the MTCR's "strong presumption of denial" provision. Washington, of course, protested vigorously but without changing any French or British minds on the matter. But it is important to note that during the 1990s no MTCR member state, the United States included, had taken a strong stand on cruise missile proliferation, in spite of the equal treatment presumably given to ballistic and cruise missiles. In a 1995 monograph, *Controlling the Spread of Land-Attack Cruise Missiles,* K. Scott McMahon and I found that while a consensus against missile proliferation in general had yet to be firmly established, there appeared to be far more uniform attitudes—even among MTCR members—about restricting ballistic rather than cruise missiles or UAVs, which was consistent with the export activities of MTCR member governments.[43]

The second-class status that cruise missiles held during the 1990s was also reflected in official policy pronouncements of senior government officials. During the first term of the Clinton administration, for example, when the most-senior officials, including the president, addressed the administration's missile nonproliferation priorities during major foreign policy speeches, congressional testimony, and other policy proclamations, cruise missiles went unmentioned as a missile proliferation problem. Rather, the focus was on the proliferation of ballistic missiles and space launch vehicles. Of course, the ballistic missile threat in 1995 was far more mature than the LACM threat, but the time to staunch the spread of any system is before rather than after the contagion has begun. In the years preceding the formulation of what became the Hague Code of Conduct (and, indeed, even today), LACMs and UAVs were seen more as important weapon systems for the emerging Revolution in Military Affairs, which emphasized precision delivery of conventional weapons, and less as mass-destruction delivery systems that would proliferate like ballistic missiles into the arsenals of rogue states. Thus, commercial interests in selling them rather than national security interests in controlling their spread created the conditions for treating cruise missiles as either a lesser-included case that would somehow be handled adequately through the MTCR's control of ballistic missile proliferation or simply be forgotten altogether.[44]

Within this virtually exclusive preoccupation with ballistic missiles, the MTCR norm-building initiative gathered sufficient momentum by 2000 to issue a public statement on its progress after its annual plenary meeting in Helsinki, Finland. The MTCR partners, the statement said, "continued their deliberations started in the previous Plenary in 1999 on a set of principles, commitments, confidence-building measures and incentives that could constitute a code of conduct against missile proliferation."[45] Noticeably, the press statement cast the prospective norm as a "code of conduct against missile proliferation," not ballistic missile proliferation, which at the time would have appeared normal given the fact that the MTCR's guidelines in theory applied equally as well to ballistic and cruise missiles. Whether or not early drafts of the code included the same delivery systems that the MTCR now covers is not publicly known, but by September 2001, during its plenary session in Ottawa, the MTCR member states reached consensus on a draft code text that dealt only with ballistic missiles. Given the code's origin in the MTCR, it was not at all surprising to see that this first stab at norm building for missiles dealt with behavior, not possession. Thus, the widest consensus, not only within the MTCR membership but in the broader international community as well, turned on the notion that unbridled ballistic missile proliferation was not in the best interests of peace and regional stability. In addition, the code contained various general measures in regard to adhering to space treaties; exercising maximum possible restraint with respect to development, testing, and deployment of ballistic missiles; exercising care in supporting space-launch programs (as a basis for ballistic missile development); and generally not contributing to, supporting, or assisting any ballistic missile program in a country that might be developing WMD programs. Finally, various transparency measures and reporting requirements were included to enhance the prospects for increased confidence regionally and globally.[46]

At the Ottawa meeting, MTCR members decided to move the norm-building process out from under the MTCR's opaque umbrella to a more transparent setting open to all states. The European Union (EU) took up this process of universalizing the draft code, with the French government hosting the first international meeting in Paris in February 2002 and Spain hosting the next in Madrid the following June. After some additional revisions to the code's text, the EU decided that a sufficient number of states were ready to endorse it and scheduled a launching meeting in The Hague, Netherlands in November 2002. Ninety-three states initially subscribed to what became known as the Hague Code of Conduct against Ballistic Missile Proliferation; today that number is 124. In deciding to leave cruise missiles out the Hague Code's nascent normative treatment of missile systems capable of delivering nuclear, biological, or chemical weapons, the international community inadvertently sent the message that cruise missile acquisition might well be viewed as acceptable behavior. Put another way, the Hague Code implied that while curbing the spread of ballistic missiles is in the best interests of peace and regional stability, the unbridled spread of cruise missiles somehow has less pernicious consequences.

REGIONAL EVIDENCE OF UNINTENDED CONSEQUENCES

A compelling immediate need seemed to precipitate the Bush administration's 2002 articulation of the doctrine of preemption. In that sense, any unintended consequences may well have been foreseen by the doctrine's authors but simply accepted as the cost of doing necessary business. It may well be that the preemption doctrine will eventually be softened and its more dire consequences thus avoided. On the other hand, leaving cruise missiles out of the international community's initial attempt at a normative formulation for missile proliferation was patently short-sighted, particularly in light of subsequent LACM developments in three regional settings.

Middle East

That Israel might wish to piggyback on America's newfound interest in preemption in order to more readily justify its historic preference for it should have come as no surprise. The prospect of Iran obtaining a deliverable nuclear weapon only gave added urgency to the matter. Particular insight into just how Israel may have further emboldened its preemption predilections is furnished in the work of the "Project Daniel" study group, consisting of six Israeli and American academics and former senior Israeli government officials, which fashioned a report entitled "Israel's Strategic Future: The Final Report of Project Daniel" and delivered it to Israel's Prime Minister Ariel Sharon a few months prior to the U.S.-led invasion of Iraq in 2003. Project Daniel's chairman, Professor Louis René Beres of Purdue University, wrote a lengthy overview of the study group's recommendations for the Spring 2007 issue of the journal *Parameters,* published by the U.S. Army War College.[47] In it Beres focused heavily on how Project Daniel linked the concept of "anticipatory self-defense" to not only the September 2002 White House document "The National Security Strategy of the United States," which articulated preemption doctrine, but also to various preemption scenarios of particular importance to Israel's security. Not surprisingly, too, Project Daniel focused on how to improve strategic cooperation between the United States and Israel, "with particular reference to maintaining Israel's 'qualitative edge' and associated issues of necessary funding."[48]

As noted, U.S. preemption doctrine, or more accurately, prevention doctrine, figured heavily in Project Daniel's recommendations. Beres writes, "Considering the US strategy on expansion of preemption, the Project Daniel group suggested to Prime Minister Sharon that such policy could pertain as well to certain nuclear or biological threats against Israel. The group suggested that this policy be codified as doctrine, and that such responsive actions be conventional in nature."[49] Conventional-only preemptive actions should be executed "exclusively by . . . high-precision weapons."[50] Beres draws particular attention to the need for Israel to be "empowered with a 'Long Arm' to meet its preemption objectives." Such a "Long Arm" capability would include a stealthy long-range fighter aircraft supported by air refueling, long-range UAVs, and survivable high-precision weapons (presumably

LACMs), among other capabilities. Saddam Hussein also employed the term "Long Arm" to emblemize his failed attempt to develop long-range LACMs and other UAVs. The only difference was that Saddam Hussein sensibly predicated his "Long Arm" policy on the belief that Iraqi fighter aircraft could play no part due to their inability to survive crippling counterforce strikes. Invoking the virtues of preemption, Israel, on the other hand, has sought and keenly still seeks new counterforce attack means, if not to replace, then to improve the prospects of active defense protection furnished by missile defenses. These counterforce attack systems include rumored Israeli efforts to develop UAVs capable of finding and destroying enemy mobile missile launchers, presumably before or after launch, as well as the so-called "boost-phase launcher intercept" concept (successfully employed during the summer of 2006 in Lebanon) entailing the use of UAVs to detect the launch of a missile and then promptly destroy it before the launcher can be reused.[51]

Project Daniel took a dim view on employing nuclear weapons preemptively but did not rule out the prospect as entirely unreasonable. Here, too, emulation of U.S. nuclear preemptive doctrine provided a comfortable cushion on which to support Project Daniel's thinking on the subject. Of course, the study group's preference was to regard Israel's new doctrine of preemption using conventional attack means as preventing adversarial Arab states or Iran from acquiring nuclear or biological weapons. But should the doctrine fail, Project Daniel recommended that Israel openly declare its nuclear deterrent's existence framed around a policy of secure, second-strike, counter-value attacks against select enemy population centers. While avowing a second-strike strategy, Beres notes that even though it would be unlikely if not impossible for Israel to preempt an enemy using nuclear means, circumstances are conceivable where such a strike would be "rational and also acceptable under international law," though improbable in execution. The basis for such rationality and acceptability under international law, according to Beres, derives from U.S. adoption, in March 2005, of Joint Publication 3-12, "Doctrine for Joint Nuclear Operations." This highly controversial publication, which changed doctrine to accommodate requests for preemptive nuclear use under a wider range of conditions, created a firestorm of protest after its contents were disclosed in September 2005, leading to the publication's cancellation by the Pentagon.[52] Yet, when the White House formulated its 2006 National Security Strategy, the document continued to endorse the original 2002 doctrine of preemption, including the role that nuclear weapons would play in preemptive strikes.[53]

Feeling under the kind of extreme pressure that must derive from being placed on a preemption hit list by the Bush administration, Iran has probably accelerated its quest to obtain nuclear weapons in the hopes of having a more potent source of deterrence than its conventional military forces provide. Iran is compelled to find a means of successfully penetrating regional missile defenses. Of course, Iran's first requirement is to avoid any significant impact that Israeli counterforce attacks might have on Iranian ballistic and cruise missile launchers. Given the advantage accruing from Iran's ample strategic depth and launcher mobility, that impact can largely be avoided. But Israel and America's improved ballistic missile defenses make assured penetration by Iran's ballistic missiles at least open to some question. This doubt has inspired Iranian interest in acquiring LACMs and UAVs. According to U.S. officials, Iran sees cruise missiles as working hand in hand with its ballistic missile force, supporting the latter in the sense that U.S. and Israeli missile defenses would have more difficulty defending against both systems rather than just ballistic missiles alone, as the 2003 war in Iraq showed.[54]

Senior leaders of Iran's Islamic Revolutionary Guard Corps (IRGC) have studied closely U.S. military actions in Afghanistan and Iraq to draw lessons for restructuring the IRGC primarily to cope with U.S. rather than neighboring threats. Not surprisingly, the conclusion is that the best defense against preemption is rapid deployment of asymmetrical forces together with increasing reliance on missiles and real-time intelligence activity. Accordingly, the newly appointed chief of the IRGC, Mohammad Ali Ja'fari, who spent two years at the IRGC Strategy Center preparing for the restructuring, reportedly intends to incorporate the lessons he learned from the 1980–88 war with Iraq about the use of surprise attacks into a new IRGC structure emphasizing lighter combat units and missile use. Ja'fari believes Iranian-backed missile attacks by Hezbollah played a critically important role in the war with Israel in southern Lebanon.[55]

Weak missile nonproliferation norms figure only indirectly in the case of Iran. The challenge for Israeli and U.S. defense planners is to ascertain when Iran's apparently nascent LACM arsenal will emerge to represent a significant threat. Iranian officials have chosen a decidedly different way compared with, say, Pakistan, to deal with disclosing progress or announcing tests of LACM systems. This may well reflect the comparatively slow progress being made in LACMs, but Iranian officials may alternatively see some virtue in keeping their LACM programs under wraps. As noted before, monitoring the development of foreign LACM programs, even with the most sophisticated means of technical intelligence collection, is problematic. LACMs can be easily hidden within military or civilian aircraft programs or in underground facilities, and their testing is highly difficult to detect due to the absence of telltale infrared signatures from any large rocket boosters, which aren't needed to launch a LACM. If Iran's primary purpose in pursuing LACMs is to make Israeli and American missile and air defenses less effective, then an opaque, nonprovocative strategy makes more sense. Pakistan's LACM certainly surprised India, and Islamabad could have kept the program quiet even longer, but it chose instead to emphasize to India that its interest in Arrow and Patriot missile defenses would have little or no impact on Pakistan's newfound capacity to penetrate even future Indian missile defenses.

Chinese fingerprints are all over Pakistan's Babur, and they may well be present too in Iran's LACM programs, with respect to the transformation of anti-ship cruise missiles (ASCMs) into LACMs and reverse-engineering assistance on the Kh-55, which both countries obtained illegally from Ukraine. Washington waived sanctions on Chinese entities involved in missile-related exports to Pakistan and Iran in November 2000 in exchange for China's agreement not to export nuclear-capable ballistic missiles. Cruise missiles did not figure into the November 2000 quid pro quo, and Beijing's convenient interpretation of its adherence to the MTCR's guidelines remains in place, perhaps providing enough space to assist Pakistan and Iran in their cruise missile ambitions.

South Asia

Indian Foreign Minister Sinha's prompt assertion of New Delhi's right to preempt Pakistan in the aftermath of the U.S. invasion of Iraq in 2003 involved an element of grandstanding. Nonetheless, Washington reacted quickly to New Delhi's copycatting provocation with the following State Department pronouncement: "Indian officials have recently speculated that U.S. preemptive action in Iraq could be seen as a justification of similar action by India against Pakistan over Kashmir. Any attempts to draw parallels between the Iraq and Kashmir situations are wrong and are overwhelmed by the difference between them."[56] Yet, from the Indian perspective, the advantages of preemptive action figure prominently into more than provocative public statements from its foreign ministry. Indian national security planners were deeply influenced by the lessons they drew from Operation Parakram, India's military response to the terrorist attack on the Indian Parliament in New Delhi on December 13, 2001. The immediate consequence of Operation Parakram was to bring the subcontinent to the edge of war, but this time with two nuclear-armed adversaries facing off along the Line of Control in Kashmir.[57]

Parakram was a prime example of coercive diplomacy, entailing a huge Indian military mobilization and deployment of roughly 400,000 troops designed to pressure Pakistan to meet a set of stated objectives related to curtailing future terrorist attacks and eliminating terrorist networks. Pakistan conducted its own countermobilization, including raising the alert level of its missile force. India's military mobilization took several weeks to execute and troops remained at high alert levels for ten months. Only after U.S. diplomatic intervention did the standoff between two nuclear powers come to an end. Frustrated by the Indian military's slow buildup and the consequent loss of surprise, Indian strategists set out following Parakram to grapple with alternative approaches. Significantly, the Indian demobilization occurred within a month after the U.S. launch of its 2002 doctrine of preemption. By April 2004, the Indian military had developed its "Cold Start" strategy involving lightning strikes from fully integrated and highly mobile battle groups supported by long-range precision strikes from Indian army and air force strike elements. The design of this new strategy aimed to achieve a fait accompli rapidly with a capacity to strike and withdraw before Pakistan could respond. "Cold Start" reflected the frustration of Indian military planners that nuclear threats had diminished the scope for credible military action—an essential ingredient in coercive diplomacy. Yet the risks of nuclear escalation remain palpably self-evident.

There seems little doubt that the U.S. articulation of its 2002 preemption doctrine helped legitimize India's "Cold Start" strategy. The subsequent equipping of army units with the land-attack version of the BrahMos cruise missile and plans to deploy BrahMos on Indian aircraft by 2009 offer Indian military planners precisely the kind of deep-strike weapon that suits preemptive action. India's mimicking of U.S.

military doctrine and tactics has also increased substantially since the cementing of a new strategic partnership in early 2006.[58] For example, the Indian air force "hopes to become 'an expeditionary force' on the lines of U.S. air force, with a capability to rapidly deploy and operate across the globe."[59]

Weak international norms related to LACMs have affected India's behavior with regard to the utility of confidence-building measures (CBMs) and attempted access to foreign cruise missile technology. Regarding CBMs, although India has not subscribed to the Hague Code of Conduct against Ballistic Missile Proliferation, which does urge subscribers to implement ballistic missile launch notifications, New Delhi has cooperatively pursued a missile launch notification agreement with Islamabad as a priority CBM. From the outset of negotiations, Pakistan sought to include cruise missile launches in any future agreement. India balked, not least because prior to reaching tentative agreement in August 2005 only India had tested cruise missiles. But with Pakistan's surprise launch of its own LACM coming barely a week after the tentative accord was reached, New Delhi must have begun to reconsider the shortsightedness of keeping cruise missiles out of the agreement. By April 2006, after Pakistan had successfully conducted its second flight test of Babur, India signaled its interest in bringing cruise missiles into the joint notification accord.[60] To date, however, cruise missiles remain outside the agreement, intensifying concerns about the destabilizing impact of a cruise missile arms race in South Asia.

Weak nonproliferation norms with respect to cruise missiles have certainly influenced Indian attempts to acquire critical component technologies (notably, turbojet or turbofan engines) and seemingly even complete cruise missile systems. The impact of Pakistan's surprise test of a LACM in 2005 prompted calls in the Indian press for India to extend the range of BrahMos at least to that of Pakistan's Babur, and much farther if possible. Such an extension would require access to restricted technologies from Russia, Indian's co-development partner in the BrahMos program. The assumption in the Indian press was that obtaining cruise missile technologies was feasible because the BrahMos cruise missile, unlike India's ballistic missile programs, was "not under the global scanner."[61] Thus far, there is no evidence that Russia is aiding India in an extended-range program, but Indian officials, including A. P. J. Abdul Kalam, have publicly spoken of a BrahMos follow-on capable, within a decade, of 1,000-km range at hypersonic speeds. Even more provocative was India's failed attempt in 2006 to flout existing MTCR guidelines by approaching the European missile giant, France-based MBDA Missile Systems, in hopes of obtaining a technology transfer arrangement and also complete cruise missile systems.[62] The Indian press reported that the deal fell apart in last minute negotiations, but a more likely explanation is that after respective French and Indian defense organizations reached agreement the deal was nixed by the French government in light of obvious MTCR restrictions.[63]

Pakistan has reacted strongly against India's fascination with preemption. The most detailed commentary appeared immediately in the aftermath of the May 2005 Indian exercise "Power of Thunder" and was written by S. M. Hali for the Pakistani newspaper *The Nation*.[64] Hali equated India's "Cold Start" strategy to a mere conceptual doctrine, implying that India's interest in blitzkrieg-style campaigns bears no relationship to true military capability. Indeed, in mimicking the U.S. style of warfare beginning in 1991 through Afghanistan and the invasion of Iraq in 2003, Hali believes that India has clearly learned the wrong lessons—a phenomenon that Hali argued occurred once before, with dangerous consequences. Under a former Indian army chief of staff in the early 1980s, India practiced the concept of massing strike formations and employing them for deep penetrations into enemy territory to seize strategic targets. This concept centered on armored and mechanized columns and culminated with the infamous Exercise Brass Tacks during the tenure of Gen. K. Sundarji, from 1986 to 1987. By holding the Brass Tacks exercise of November 1986 provocatively close to Pakistan's border, India ensured Pakistani counter-deployments. Brass Tacks nearly morphed into an armed conflict with Pakistan. By early 1987, fear of war's outbreak led to Pakistan's President Zia-ul-Haq traveling to India to attend a cricket match and meet with Indian officials, which calmed military tension. Because both sides recognized the stakes involved, they also reached agreement on a crisis hot line.

Two decades after Exercise Brass Tacks, regional tension is no less palpable and missile arsenals, ballistic and cruise missile alike, have grown substantially, as each side ponders how best to exploit the unique features that missiles offer to help achieve military objectives. Both sides seek to exploit cruise missile accuracy by arming them with a variety of tailored conventional warheads. Yet India and Pakistan share the need to make their LACMs capable of delivering nuclear warheads to satisfy nuclear deterrence requirements. Pakistan, at present more so than India, also sees LACMs as the most assured means of penetrating future Indian missile defenses. And India, more than Pakistan, is intent on employing LACMs in support of an emerging quick-strike conventional strategy. These developments underscore the need for both sides to agree on including all missiles, ballistic and cruise, in their 2005 missile test notification CBM. Even India now admits that it was a mistake to have left cruise missiles out of the original agreement. As each side has upped the ante with surprise cruise missile tests since August 2005 (Pakistan's Babur and Raad and India's Sagarika and Nirbhay), the probability of a destabilizing missile arms race on the subcontinent has increased.[65]

Northeast Asia

The preponderance of evidence suggests that China espouses a military strategy of actively endeavoring to catch the enemy unprepared. Such a preemptive outlook has its origins less in Chinese fascination with repeated displays of U.S. military operations since the fall of the Soviet Union than adhering to that Soviet military doctrine and strategy that originated primarily under Marshal Nikolai Ogarkov in the 1980s. On the other hand, after the iron curtain fell even the U.S. Army, in its doctrinal literature, bowed to the virtues of the "spirit of the offense" once practiced by their primary communist foe. LACMs figure heavily in the U.S. application of military force to achieve preemptive aims and have gained prominence in China's offensive planning. In a recent analysis in *Jane's Defence Weekly* Timothy Hu argued that the PLA's missile forces will allow China to gain military ascendancy over Taiwan by 2010. Should war occur, Hu indicated that China would execute a "decapitation strategy that would neutralize Taiwan's civilian and military command-and-control apparatuses and vital infrastructure and communication facilities."[66] While LACMs would play a companion role alongside ballistic missiles, their higher accuracy makes them ideally suited for such a decapitation strategy. Hu also argues that China could conceivably contemplate sending land-, air-, and sea-launched cruise missiles against U.S. bases in Guam and Okinawa.[67] Clearly, LACMs will increasingly represent the weapon of choice for such preemptive action.

As China has pursued LACMs to meet its own preemptively oriented military strategy, it has also used its tendentiously weak interpretation of MTCR guidelines as cover for assisting close allies to acquire LACMs of their own. China has backed away from the kind of brazen support it once provided Pakistan to satisfy that country's ambitions to acquire solid-fuel missile programs. Sanctions and negotiations with Washington to more clearly define the nature of China's adherence to the MTCR may have played a role in diminishing such support. But clear holes remain as to cruise missiles and the technologies critical to their development. Until a more satisfactory agreement is struck defining the nature of China's adherence to the MTCR or China is permitted to join the MTCR as a full partner, Beijing is likely to continue its selective interpretation of guidelines as well as its ambiguous relationship to the MTCR, in order to aid friendly nations. And even though China has yet to subscribe to the Hague Code of Conduct, the fact that the international community has seen fit to leave cruise missiles out of the Code only reinforces Beijing's convenient definition of MTCR adherence.

Taiwan has received mixed signals from U.S. officials about whether operationalizing an offensive missile option was acceptable behavior and how Washington might view any use of such an offensive system. While U.S. State Department and National Security Council officials have tended toward dissuading Taiwan from pursuing its HF-2E LACM program, U.S. defense officials have acted otherwise. After Taiwan tested its HF-2E in February 2007, a Taiwanese military officer told the U.S. trade newspaper *Defense News* that the State Department had been pressuring Taipei to terminate the program for over a year.[68] But in the same account, an unnamed U.S. defense official saw some virtue in Taiwan's pursuit of LACMs: the ultimate goal was achieving deterrence against China. The official said, "Taiwan wants to hold China at risk. I do not know if the missiles are intended for counter-value or counter-force. In either case, the objective is the same: to make China think before they resort to using force against Taiwan." But because Taiwan was unlikely to produce enough LACMs to have a true military effect on any cross-strait conflict, the U.S. defense official thought that their chief value was as a morale booster. Whether by coincidence or design, these observations are uncannily consistent with the Pentagon's 2004 report to Congress that saw deterrent strength in Taiwan's pursuit of an asymmetric strategy of offensive missile attacks against Chinese urban population centers or high-value targets like the Three Gorges Dam.[69]

In an insightful white paper prepared by an adviser to Taiwan's Ministry of Foreign Affairs, Dr. Holmes Liao makes it clear that Taiwan has paid close attention to U.S. Army doctrinal literature on the value of attack operations as well as counter-value operations in complementing missile defense.[70] Written nominally to assess the implications of China's LACM threat to Taiwan, Liao first addresses active missile defense operations by noting the comparative difficulties of detecting and intercepting LACMs flying low and having small radar cross-sections. After reviewing the various challenges associated with missile defenses, Liao turns to passive defense measures consistent with prescribed U.S. Army doctrine. But the most enlightening aspect of Liao's paper is his discussion of attack operations—Pentagon parlance for counterforce strikes. Because U.S. Field Manual 100-12 argues for a complementary mix of attack operations and passive and active defenses, tied together by command, control, and intelligence means, Liao sees reasons for Taiwan to place greater emphasis on long-range strike assets and special operations forces, while admitting that such a doctrinal turn would shift Taiwan's traditionally defensive thinking to an offensively oriented strategy more heavily dependent on near real-time reconnaissance and long-range precision strike assets. Liao looks at possible reconnaissance options, including commercial space satellite imagery, but finds greater utility in UAVs linked to long-range precision strike systems, which would be ideally suited to engage in counterforce strike against Chinese logistics and command-and-control centers.

Liao's assessment concludes with an appraisal of offensive missiles employed in counter-value strikes against Chinese industrial and economic centers (Shanghai and Hong Kong are singled out). The main limitation, Liao notes, is that then-existing weapons in Taiwan's possession were largely "defensive . . . lacking range, lethality, and precision."[71] Without a more robust offensive conventional strike force, China won't be deterred. Liao's solution: Taiwan should develop long-range precision-strike LACMs. Compared with ballistic missiles, Liao argues, LACMs without terrain contour-matching (TERCOM) cost 30 percent of a ballistic missile and those with TERCOM cost 70 percent, making them a cost-effective solution. Unmentioned by Liao, but certainly understood by others, is the decided cost advantage of offensive missiles compared with missile interceptors (a 10 to 1 advantage for the offense, according to one Taiwanese government official).[72] Liao then examines the technological challenges for Taiwan of producing its own LACMs and finds that Taiwan's engineering talents are capable of handing the LACM guidance system. (While mission planning for TERCOM and digital scene-matching area correlation [DSMAC] is a stiff challenge, it appears to have been met with U.S. mission planning assistance.) The biggest difficulty facing Taiwan, Liao notes, is developing a fuel-efficient engine with a high thrust-to-weight ratio similar to the U.S. Tomahawk and Franco-British Storm Shadow engines. Liao ends by returning to his central premise, while alluding to U.S. military doctrine: "If offensive operation is a critical pillar of missile defense, Taiwan will have to put emphasis on the yet-to-be-defined doctrine and come up with 'creative means' to overcome the technological obstacle [engine technology]."[73] Surely at the time Liao wrote his white paper in late 2003 he must have known about Taiwan's HF-2E LACM, then under development at the Chung-Shan Institute of Science and Technology. Taiwan's first LACM test took place in early 2005.

South Korea's four new LACM programs have their origin in the weak normative basis upon which Washington attempted to constrain Seoul ballistic missile ambitions. The agreement between Washington and Seoul that permitted Seoul to join the MTCR in 2001 constrained ballistic missiles to 300-km range and 500-kg payload but gave Seoul essentially the freedom to deploy LACMs with a range of 500 km conditional on the payload remaining under 500 kg. But Seoul has apparently chosen to interpret the agreement as having no maximum range threshold for cruise missiles.[74] Thus, Seoul is developing four new LACMs with ranges between 500 and 1500 km. Ironically, the U.S. objective was to avoid precipitating an Asian arms race in ballistic missiles, but the unintended consequence has been to fuel one in LACMs instead.

Within days of disclosing the existence of the new LACM programs in October 2006, South Korea's Joint Chiefs of Staff launched a new three-stage "nuclear defense" plan that included a preemptive strike option featuring South Korea's new LACMs. The plan consisted of "extended deterrence," whereby South Korea would depend on U.S. nuclear and advanced conventional weapons to deter Pyongyang; "surgical strike," or preemptive use of South Korea's precision-strike weapons, including its new long-range LACMs, when an attack by the North appeared imminent; and finally, "damage control," in particular, dealing with the consequences of nuclear weapon strikes. Press coverage of the new strategy repeated details of the South's multiple LACM programs, including its 1,500-km range missile now under development.[75]

Although the proximate reason for Seoul's new attention to preemptive strike options is surely related to the high likelihood that North Korea has nuclear weapons, signs that South Korea is looking beyond the North Korean threat are beginning to emerge. The ranges of South Korea's new LACMs exceed what would be required to handle North Korean targets by as much as a factor of three. In publicly disclosing the new LACMs, Seoul was careful not to provoke anxieties in the region but probably intended that the press draw the conclusion that the ranges were sufficient not only to deal with North Korea but also Tokyo and Beijing. In March 2007 South Korean Defense Minister Kim Jang-soo reportedly told visiting Central Intelligence Agency Director Michael Hayden that Seoul felt "squeezed" between the growing military ambitions of China and Japan.[76] Instead of focusing on circumstances in North Korea, the South Korean message to the United States was clear: you need to constrain the arms race between China and Japan before it is too late. In the meantime, South Korea's turn toward long-range precision-strike LACMs and a preemptive strike doctrine represents a precautionary though worrisome step as the Northeast Asian missile arms racing is showing strong signs of contagion.

Japan's interest in preemptive attack options superficially appears to be directly related to North Korea's renewal of ballistic missile tests in July 2006.[77] The fact that Pyongyang decided to conduct it first nuclear test four months later must have only bolstered the logic of such an option from the standpoint of senior Japanese military officials. Less than two weeks after the North Korean missile tests, the *Yomiuri Shimbun* newspaper's staff reporter Hidemichi Katsumata wrote a surprisingly explicit story about the thinking within the Japanese Self-Defense Force (SDF), covering the reasons for their interest in a preemptive strike option as well as what specific military capabilities the SDF would need to produce such a capability.[78] According to Katsumata, Japanese SDF officers have been highly impressed with the success achieved by the U.S. military (especially its air force) in tactical preemptive operations since the 1991 Gulf War. These examples could serve as a model for Japan's own preemptive strike doctrine.

In the last several years, Japanese policymakers have begun to struggle with how Japan could best manage its emergence as a "normal" power.[79] Thus, retired Japanese military officers have undertaken a debate, largely in military journals, about the need for Japan to move from its current policy of "defensive defense" toward the adoption of "offensive defense" capabilities, principally employing LACMs and advanced aircraft. The most forceful and detailed advocate of this position is retired Vice Admiral Hideaki Kaneda. In a February 2007 article in the naval monthly *Sekai no Kansen,* Kaneda first noted the unpredictable nature of the North Korean missile threat, then turned his attention to China's growing missile arsenal and South Korea's and Taiwan's cruise missile developments. He then focused on the merits of a Japanese denial capability, involving LACMs (including submarine-launched Tomahawks) and other precision weapons, for undertaking direct attacks on missile launchers and related command-and-control facilities "before a missile is launched to neutralize or render it harmless."[80] Of course, a denial strategy is fundamental to the U.S. military's approach to missile defense. In arguing for Japan to possess LACMs for such counterforce attacks, the former head of the Japan Defense Agency, General Fukushiro Nukaga, in a speech in Washington, D.C. on May 1, 2007, said, "[ballistic missile defense or BMD] is very reliable . . . but we need to consider whether BMD is infallible in the case of repeated attacks by multiple ballistic missiles."[81] General Nukaga might have added LACMs to the list of expected enemy missile threats.

While Japan seems headed toward joining a growing list of countries practicing preemptive strike doctrines, including all four regional powers in Northeast Asia, Tokyo's choice of LACMs over ballistic missiles appears connected at least in part to the weakness of international norms pertaining to cruise missiles. In a trip to Japan in early 2005, I had the opportunity to interview several Japanese defense officials. They all anticipated fewer adverse reactions, both inside and outside Japan, to acquiring LACMs rather than ballistic missiles.

Part Three

Policy Responses

Nonproliferation and Defense Policy Responses

Writing in 2001 at a time when the contagion discussed in this book had yet to become manifest, I argued that if cruise missile proliferation were to proceed unimpeded and become widespread, it might combine with the further spread of ballistic missiles to furnish multidimensional offense a decided advantage over layered missile defenses—no matter how much was invested in such defenses.[1] In Roberta Wohlstetter's classic study of intelligence failure and decisionmakers being caught unawares by Japan's surprise attack on Pearl Harbor in December 1941, she argued that the United States was unable to distinguish signals of Japanese plans from the noise of other information that was "pregnant with conflicting meanings."[2] The signals of missile contagion in the Middle East, South Asia, and Northeast Asia are hardly indistinct.

When signs of missile contagion were more obscure than they are now, I proposed a two-pronged hedging strategy consisting of a mix of nonproliferation policy improvements together with a modestly funded but well coordinated set of technology development programs to support the deployment of highly effective defenses against the cruise missile threat, were signs of its emergence to become evident.[3] If I were asked to issue a report card judging the quality of nonproliferation and defense policy responses to missile proliferation since 2001, the grades would not be passing ones. In the case of nonproliferation policy, the Missile Technology Control Regime (MTCR) membership established a most unfortunate normative precedent by leaving cruise missiles and unmanned aerial vehicles (UAVs) out of what became the Hague Code of Conduct against Ballistic Missile Proliferation in 2002. That same year, however, at its plenary meeting in Warsaw, Poland, the MTCR membership began the difficult challenge of improving the regime's guidelines and equipment and technology annex addressing cruise missile and UAV proliferation issues.

As for defense policy, the long-standing unevenness in missile defense spending that has effectively relegated the cruise missile threat to the status of a lesser-included case has continued over the last seven years. Prior to and even after the September 11, 2001 terrorist attacks, the Rumsfeld-led Pentagon voiced support for elevating the importance of cruise missile defenses, but little came from these rhetorical flourishes.[4] At the same time, the improved performance of U.S. missile defenses against shorter-range ballistic missiles, together with remaining gaps in defending against cruise missiles, has fostered the unintended consequence of promoting interest in land-attack cruise missiles (LACMs) and UAVs. This consequence is displayed most powerfully in a swiftly spreading narrative message about the diffi-culty of defending against this growing class of delivery systems. Perversely, one out-come of the George W. Bush administration's global sales program has been increased interest by several states in acquiring LACMs and UAVs, not only because of the difficulty-of-defense narrative but also because cruise missiles offer a much cheaper alternative to ballistic missile defenses.

Sadly, unintended cruise missile proliferation is having precisely the opposite effect of what the founders of the MTCR expected. Richard Speier, one of the MTCR's principal architects in the mid-1980s, in 2000 argued cogently that the MTCR and missile defenses were not in fact antithetical pursuits but complementary ones.[5] From the outset of the regime, Speier noted, this complementarity was reflected in the MTCR's goal of targeting missile research, development, and produc-tion, while missile defenses focused on targeting the missile once it was launched. Ideally, Speier calculated, effective missile defenses raised the cost of offensive mis-siles by compelling nations to seek more effective offensive missiles, larger invento-ries, and countermeasures (at least for long-range missiles traveling in space). In the same way, Speier saw the MTCR raising the cost of offensive missiles, stretching the development time, lowering the missile's reliability, and reducing missile sophis-tication—making the job of missile defense easier to achieve. This ideal approxima-tion of how nonproliferation and defense policy might complement each other has proven valid at least in the area of short- to medium-range ballistic missile defense, which has improved markedly in the last decade. But the complementarity is effec-tive only if the same relationship applies equally to *both* cruise and ballistic missiles.

Given the unevenness of ballistic and cruise missile defenses, the broadly perceived difficulty of defending against LACMs and UAVs has combined with the high cost of missile defenses to precipitate not only cruise missile proliferation but also their use as counterforce strike weapons against adversary missile systems. Aiding and abetting the process are the unintended effects of the Bush administration's overzealous response to the events of September 11, 2001, in particular its national strategy of preemption, which has afforded states a convenient way to justify their newly acquired missile arsenals. Given their high accuracy and perceived utility as weapons that can readily be employed short of the use of WMD, LACMs have increasingly become a featured component of conventionally oriented preemptive strike doctrines in all three regional settings examined in this book. The copycatting behavior can also be traced to a growing fascination with an offensively oriented U.S. denial strat-egy and its related doctrinal components, including the importance of counterforce or attack operations in defending against missile threats. For doing so little to improve U.S. cruise missile defenses and for inadvertently fostering the spread of LACMs, defense policies over the last seven years deserve failing grades.

REPAIRING NONPROLIFERATION POLICY

It is not too late to repair faulty or shortsighted policies. But whereas in 2001 it seemed appropriate to hedge against the emergence of the cruise missile threat, today there is no choice but to act promptly to stop an accelerating missile contagion. Effective nonproliferation policy is the first line of defense, with the goal being to elevate, at long last, cruise missiles and UAVs to the equal status with ballistic missiles that the MTCR's guidelines explicitly stipulate.

When the MTCR was formulated in the mid-1980s its authors found that delineating controls on cruise missiles and UAVs was a more challenging proposition than identifying which ballistic missile technologies to control.[6] Still, a consensus was reached to make a "presumption to deny" the export of certain cruise missile and UAV systems capable of delivering at least a 500-kg payload to 300 km or more. In 1993, the regime members agreed to include certain complete missile systems not covered in Category I—that is, those capable of a range of 300 km or more, regardless of payload weight—in Category II, which previously dealt only with dual-use items or subsystems, components, machinery, and technologies. These so-called Item 19 delivery systems were added out of concern that chemical and particularly biological weapons did not need a payload of anything like 500 kg to achieve mass-destruction effects. This new level of scrutiny was primarily aimed at cruise missiles, which are particularly adept at delivering such agents. Moreover, because missiles captured under Item 19 were also subject to the regime's range-payload tradeoffs, even some short-range anti-ship cruise missiles (ASCMs) might be covered if they could be modified through payload reductions to reach a range of at least 300 km. By the late 1990s, however, while a theoretical consensus existed in regard to controlling cruise missiles, putting it into practice proved more difficult and disruptive.

However much the regime struggled with and succeeded in reaching a modest consensus about cruise missiles and UAVs, actions taken by MTCR members between 1998 and 2002 cemented status of cruise missiles and UAVs as a neglected lesser-included case. The first was the decision taken in 1998 by French and British leaders to sell the stealthy Black Shaheen cruise missile to the United Arab Emirates (UAE), U.S. protestations notwithstanding. Making the transaction even more profoundly disturbing was the missile's advanced characteristics. Not only was the missile subject to the regime's strong presumption of denial due to its combination of range and payload, but it also possessed an extraordinarily low radar cross-section and stealthy aerodynamic design, giving it the same characteristics possessed by ballistic missiles (if not at present, then at the MTCR's creation in 1987) that inspired the MTCR in the first place—that is, difficulty of defense, short warning, and shock effect. This came at a time when regime members had examined but failed to gain a consensus on tighter controls on stealthy cruise missiles. Of even greater concern was the precedent such a sale might have on other MTCR members or adherents, such as Russia or China, respectively.

Although U.S. objections to the Black Shaheen transaction may have suggested a firm U.S. position with respect to equal treatment of ballistic and cruise missile transfers, U.S. behavior after the Black Shaheen decision was ambiguous. In its long, drawn-out negotiations with Seoul prior to South Korea's joining the MTCR in March 2001, Washington strongly urged a cap of 300-km range and 500 kg on

Seoul's future ballistic missile programs but allowed South Korea the option of pursuing LACM development to what it thought would be a maximum range of 500 km, as long as the payload was under 500 kg.[7] Here again, Washington's differentiation between cruise and ballistic missiles conveyed the impression that the consequences of cruise missile proliferation were not terribly important compared with the spread of ballistic missiles. Ironically, during missile negotiations with Seoul in 1999, Washington steadfastly insisted that Seoul not pursue missiles beyond 300-km range, arguing that 500-km systems provided little additional military utility especially in light of the financial cost and the risk of fueling a missile competition with Pyongyang as well as fomenting suspicion with China, Japan, and Russia.[8] Such differentiation reappeared when, reportedly in 2002, the State Department approved a license permitting a U.S. firm to furnish Taiwan's Chung-Shan Institute of Science and Technology, the technical organization responsible for Taiwan's HF-2E LACM, with mission planning technology critical to the missile's successful development. Five years later, of course, Washington would find it necessary to send a general officer to Taiwan to restrain that country's growing LACM ambitions, now provocatively married to a preemptive strike doctrine. Furthermore, there is no evidence that the United States supported the inclusion of cruise missiles in what became the Hague Code of Conduct in 2002. Informal differentiation had become the normative standard.

Accordingly, the MTCR plenary that convened in Warsaw in September 2002 began to address several shortcomings in its treatment of cruise missiles and UAVs. The unfortunate Black Shaheen sale in 1998 underscored the critical need to create a uniform set of ground rules for determining the true range of cruise missiles. The regime's rules were originally written with ballistic missiles primarily in mind, and they involved a straightforward calculation of a ballistic missile's maximum range trajectory from its point of launch to the target. Much greater variability exists in defining a cruise missile's range; such missiles can be launched from the ground or from an airborne platform. Moreover, gas-turbine engines used in LACMs achieve greater ranges when they fly at higher altitudes. Cruise missile manufacturers frequently quote a cruise missile's range using a low flight profile to avoid detection. But cruise missiles need not fly their entire distance using such a low profile. They can be launched at or reach a range-maximizing altitude and then drop to a terrain-hugging profile when they become more susceptible to detection. Flying a range-maximizing profile, a cruise missile's range can be extended by a factor of three over a low flight profile. At the Warsaw plenary, regime members eliminated this confusion by establishing a new definition of range for cruise missiles and UAVs built around the range-maximizing principle. The new language specified that "the most fuel-efficient flight profile" would be used to determine the range of a cruise missile or UAV and maximum capability would be assessed "based on the design characteristics of the missile when fully loaded with fuel."[9] Yet, a regime statement weakened the improved definitions by stating that the determination of range is the sole responsibility of the exporting government.[10]

The 2002 Warsaw plenary also called for efforts to limit the risk of controlled items and their technologies falling in the hands of terrorist groups and individuals. Terrorist use of large commercial airliners on September 11, 2001 came as a complete shock to American planners. As one of the air force generals in charge of continental air defense observed after the attacks, "This was something we had never seen before, something we had never even thought of."[11] To be sure, the terrorist attacks of 9/11 engendered a whole rash of reforms to cope with a repeat of just such an attack. But these reforms dealt largely with commercial aircraft security rather than private aviation. Even though small converted aircraft cannot begin to approach the carrying capacity of a jumbo jet's 60 tons of fuel, the mere fact that gasoline, when mixed with air, releases 15 times as much energy as an equal weight of TNT means that even relatively small aircraft can do significant damage to certain civilian and industrial targets.[12] Such platforms, too, stand as effective means of delivering biological weapons.

The hardest part of transforming a kit or small private aircraft into a weapons-carrying autonomous attack system is developing and integrating a fully autonomous flight management system into the aircraft.[13] Certainly, states are capable of such transformations, but it is quite doubtful that a terrorist group, on its own, could develop and integrate autonomous flight controls into such aircraft. However, a handful of small U.S. aerospace companies—which spun off in the mid-1990s from larger defense-oriented systems integration firms—started to sell fully integrated flight instrument or navigation systems to enable manned aircraft to be transformed into UAVs. Moreover, these new firms offered not just the fully integrated navigation systems but also support services to help write the aerodynamic equations needed for autonomous flight and the support essential to properly integrate the navigation subsystem into the aircraft. When the Warsaw plenary met in late 2002, these integrated flight systems were not covered by the MTCR's technology annex. An armed UAV in the hands of a terrorist suggests that launches could take place from hidden locations in close proximity to intended targets. Kit-built airplanes, for example, do not need a hardstand to take off, only a grassy field much shorter than a football field. Detecting such low- and slow-flying planes is also dubious due to the fact that sophisticated airborne sensors eliminate slow-moving targets near the ground to prevent their data processing and display systems from being overtaxed. In short, if the primary technological barrier standing in the way of building such an autonomous delivery means is represented by integrated flight instrument packages, then it appeared in 2002 to make great sense to bring them under some form of review before they are sold.

In 2003 both the MTCR and its companion Wassenaar Arrangement—which strives to achieve transparency and greater responsibility in transfers of conventional arms and dual-use goods and technologies, including UAVs—began to examine ways of limiting the risk of terrorist access to UAVs. The Wassenaar group considered a U.S. "antiterrorism" proposal addressing terrorist use of kit airplanes and other civil aircraft as makeshift and lethal UAVs. But as written the proposal proved to be too conceptual and not sufficiently detailed with respect to the desired technology to be controlled. After a congressional hearing in March 2004 drew attention to this shortcoming, the proposal was reconstituted and finally gained the necessary 33-nation consensus to be incorporated as an amendment to the Wassenaar Agreement's control lists in December 2005.[14] A month prior to that, the MTCR reached consensus on changes to its technology annex that effectively added new controls on complete UAVs equipped with aerosol dispensers.[15]

The year 2006 saw even more export control progress on several fronts within the MTCR. The regime's members agreed to changes providing for more effective oversight of technologies that constitute the two key components of LACMs: propulsion and guidance and control. The first change broadened coverage of engines to include those usable in rockets and UAVs (including cruise missiles) capable of 300 km regardless of payload (Category II systems). Previously, only Category I systems were controlled. On integrated navigation systems, the MTCR in 2002 had incorporated new language specifying in detail what comprised such a system but had limited its application only to Category I missiles (capable of delivering at least 500 kg to a range of at least 300 km). In 2006, member states broadened such coverage to include Category II systems as well, which more effectively covers the type of UAVs terrorists might attempt to acquire. Finally, new language was added to control certain heading sensors that could be integrated with other flight control and navigation systems.[16]

The import of these seemingly arcane adjustments was, in fact, substantial. Creating a coordinated list of controlled technologies representing potentially the most dangerous items from a proliferation point of view is a critical component of effective, if not foolproof, nonproliferation policy. The items then are subjected to a case-by-case review before being exported to make as certain as possible that they do not inadvertently support a discouraged weapons project. Indeed, in 2003 the MTCR also added "catch-all controls," which cover both missiles and technologies that may be destined for a WMD-delivery system but not explicitly captured under the MTCR.[17]

The MTCR has adapted well to the rapidly changing pace of technologies that are bound to improve cruise missiles and UAVs over the next two decades. In 2003 the Pentagon's Defense Technology Support Agency put together an interdisciplinary team of technology experts to identify emerging technologies that could radically transform the future of delivery systems, including cruise missiles and UAVs. Microminiature guidance and navigation controls, as well as possible breakthroughs in hypersonic technologies, featured heavily into the panel's initial consideration.[18] But however valuable such continuous assessments might be, it remains critical to address nearer-term technologies or subsystems that remain currently outside of the MTCR's purview.

Arguably, the LACM threat could grow dramatically worse if countries incorporate stealthy features or, worse, add certain highly tailored countermeasures to already stealthy cruise missiles. Under such circumstances, nations could acquire a mix of cheaper LACMs and combine them with higher-cost but virtually impossible-to-detect LACMs with very low radar observability and terminal countermeasures, greatly complicating and increasing the already high cost of defense.

Adding ballistic missiles to the threat mix only stretches the defense closer to the breaking point. This concern is nothing new. Calls for tighter controls on stealthy cruise missiles are long-standing and thus far unmet. MTCR members have not succeeded in reaching a consensus on just how low a radar cross-section should trigger regulatory control. Category I systems are already subject to the highest level of control, so the question remains whether or not to cover stealthy Category II missiles. Although this is highly advisable, an even more effective measure would be the addition of language covering specially designed countermeasure equipment, such as towed decoys and terrain-bounce jammers. The latter two devices could become commonplace as the observability of LACMs shrinks through improved aerodynamic design and the addition of stealthy materials. This is so because as the observability of LACMs shrinks, the value of adding endgame countermeasures increases.[19]

There is reason to believe that endgame countermeasures for LACMs can be controlled under the MTCR.[20] Equipment that can be legitimately exported as part of a manned aircraft is not subject to control under the MTCR. But endgame countermeasures, such as towed decoys and terrain-bounce jammers, must be specially designed to work with the particular LACM they are to protect, so as to achieve the intended mimicking of the radar signature. The time to address this critical area is before stealthy LACMs become a more prominent proliferation threat.

DO NO HARM

Just as important as closing gaps in export control coverage is the need to prevent erosion of existing controls. From the start, the Bush administration seemed intent on liberalizing standards covering both missile defense interceptors and large UAVs. With regard to missile interceptors, ever since President Bush signed the December 2002 National Security Presidential Directive/NSPD-23, specifying national policy on ballistic missile defense, the White House has pressured both the State Department and the Pentagon to "promote international missile defense cooperation, including bilateral and alliance structures . . . [and to] eliminate unnecessary impediments to such cooperation."[21] As one senior Bush administration official put it, "the MTCR is not, should not be, and is not intended to be a restraint on missile defense. It is intended to restrict trade in ballistic missile technology."[22] Many pro-missile defense advocates view the MTCR as a hindrance to sharing such missile interceptors with friends and allies, but the truth is that the MTCR has rarely stood as the primary reason for preventing missile defense interceptors from being exported.[23] Various classified export controls affecting highly sensitive "black box" technologies have been a long-standing impediment to technology transfer, even with America's closest allies. For very good reasons, the MTCR does treat so-called "defensive" missile interceptors as potential "offensive" delivery systems when their propulsion systems make them the equivalent of Category I offensive missiles. The Soviet-era SA-2 air defense interceptor has seen stalwart service as the basis for offensive missile programs in at least China, India, Iran, Iraq, and Serbia. There is an ample supply of U.S. missile defense interceptors (Patriot and the Terminal

High-Altitude Area Defense system, or THAAD) that clearly could be exported without sacrificing the MTCR's goal of arresting the spread of mass-destruction delivery systems. The singular controversy surrounds India's long-standing interest in Israel's Arrow ballistic missile defense system, which was jointly developed with the United States and includes a missile interceptor that is clearly subject to the MTCR's strong presumption of denial. Prior to the signing of the U.S.-India nuclear deal in July 2005, Washington had resisted authorizing Israel to sell the Arrow system to India, but the *Washington Post* reported that as part of the deal Washington gave India a free hand to purchase the Arrow system.[24] By making Arrow an extraordinary exception to the U.S. policy of preventing Israel from exporting missile technology to India, or worse, implicitly removing missile defense interceptors altogether from MTCR consideration, that deal could open the floodgates to other even less sensitive MTCR members and regime adherents to selectively repudiate the regime's most important range-payload provision.

As for liberalizing standards related to large UAV transfers, early in 2002 the Bush administration established a confidential interim policy governing the export of UAVs that otherwise merited Category I treatment.[25] Increasingly in demand to furnish reconnaissance and surveillance in support of precision delivery of conventional weapons, large UAVs (the Predator, for example) were seen as promoting force discrimination, not mass destruction. On the other hand, in the wrong hands, these seemingly benign UAVs can be readily converted into systems capable of delivering WMD to significant distances. The danger of loosening any Category I controls— the heart of the MTCR since its creation 20 years ago—is in creating a slippery slope by which systems such as space-launch vehicles, including their hardware, technology, and production facilities, lead to long-range ballistic missile capabilities.[26]

There are preferable options to changing long-standing constraints on Category I UAVs. Current rules, as evidenced by the rare exception of the Black Shaheen sale to the UAE, permit some flexibility for dealing with exceptional circumstances without changing the rules entirely. Alternatively, another option is to develop the UAV industry along the lines of the space-launch business, involving the provision of "services" without the transfer of hardware beyond the jurisdiction or control of the state considering a sale.[27] Comparable examples exist in the area of commercial overhead imagery. The Israeli air force is now purchasing "visint [visual intelligence] by the hour" from a civilian firm.[28] And after losing a weather-monitoring satellite in 2002, the U.S. Air Force supporting the U.S. Pacific Command requested the assistance of an Australian firm to fly weather-monitoring UAVs.[29] In short, there appear to be ample alternatives to fundamentally weakening the MTCR by way of permanently loosening controls over Category I UAVs.[30]

INTANGIBLE TECHNOLOGY TRANSFERS

The ways and means of acquiring a ballistic or cruise missile system have become much more complex since the creation of the MTCR in 1987. What was once little more than the Soviet Union's provision of Scud ballistic missiles and Styx ASCMs to its client states has morphed into a network of many components, including multiple front companies, intermediaries, transshipment means, and diversionary routing of subsystems and materials, all often supported by money-laundering transactions. But another important change has occurred since 1987: the increasingly central role of specialized knowledge. The MTCR has leaned toward defining this know-how or "black art" as being composed of controlled technology that is not passed from supplier to recipient in any physical manner but rather through intangible means, including the internet, fax machines, or direct interaction between specialists.[31] The latter phenomenon, however, captured in direct, face-to-face engagements between highly skilled and novice engineers, is the context within which tacit knowledge skills are learned. Such knowledge is not highly diffused but rather accumulated within a local setting consisting of small groups of people.[32]

The Libya-bound North Korean freighter *Kuwolsan* was carefully outfitted with creature comforts, not to create an appropriate working environment in some Libyan engineering laboratory for skilled North Korean engineers to turn their Libyan brethren into equally skilled missile designers—rather, those comforts were aboard the *Kuwolsan* to enhance the working environment for the Korean engineers, probably working largely alone, at least until they could extend a turnkey production capability to Libya. These circumstances underscore the importance of fashioning local circumstances in ways that promote the development of an appropriate social context within which the master-novice relationship can mature over time. Language barriers, cultural idiosyncrasies, and, perhaps most importantly, the length of time during which the process of tacit knowledge transfer occurs, are the key variables involved in successful knowledge transfer. Common language, values, and culture become important ingredients in what is essentially a learn-by-doing process. Given a suitable amount of time and a comfortable working environment within which to scale language barriers and attenuate cultural impediments, chances of critical specialized knowledge transfer are greatly improved. India and Russia's co-development work on the BrahMos cruise missile program and China's reported recruitment of large numbers of laid-off Russian missile specialists to work in a special facility in Shanghai with Chinese engineers in the early 1990s come to mind as offering good prospects for successful transfer of "black art" skills.

The transfer of explicit knowledge via the internet or fax machines is virtually impossible to detect unless intelligence services are tipped off in advance to suspicious activity. On the other hand, the nature of tacit knowledge transfer as well as the physical and social circumstances under which such transfer takes place suggest that a fairly specific set of observables probably exist to detect evidence of illicit activities. There is reason to believe that the pool of highly skilled missile specialists is not unmanageably large. Repeated defense industry restructurings in the United States since 1991 have contributed to an acute shortage of highly skilled systems engineers remaining in today's defense industry. Russia's key design bureaus specializing in cruise missile development may be more flush with financial support today than they were when circumstances apparently led many to retreat to Shanghai to train China's engineers in the 1990s. But the names of key individuals are knowable, and conceivably the Russian government and perhaps other governments too ought to be able to monitor such activities to stanch their flow.

If Russia wished to constrain the illicit transfer of tacit knowledge skills, current evidence suggests that adequate controls are in place. After retirement, Russian defense industry specialists are subject to a five-year travel restriction, requiring notification and government approval for foreign travel. What's more, Russia's Federal Security Service, which replaced the Soviet-era KGB, practices an assumption-of-guilt attitude toward many Russian defense industry specialists who maintain any contact with foreign nationals.[33] The Russian case of detecting 200 illegally obtained passports for Makayev Design Bureau scientists, engineers, and their families, and the detention of 36 of them at a Moscow airport before their departure for Pyongyang in 1992 demonstrates that such substantial activities can be detected and stopped. Moreover, the Russian government has in the past advised scientists and engineers at enterprises suspected of aiding Iranian and North Korean missile programs that if they were subjected to U.S. sanctions for their activities, the government would take additional measures to penalize such behavior.[34] The critical point is that detecting substantial tacit knowledge transfers is in fact conceivable and therefore risky for the perpetrator. The MTCR should heighten awareness of the importance of monitoring tacit knowledge transfers and highlight opportunities for intelligence-sharing and collaboration among key member states.

Other new nonproliferation tools could also combine with heightened MTCR awareness to improve prospects of monitoring and intervening in intangible technology transfers. The Proliferation Security Initiative (PSI), created in May 2003, has already proven its value in several ways. First, it has greatly enhanced cooperation among a growing list of partner states in regard to intelligence collection and analysis, diplomacy, and operational techniques for enhancing the capability of participants to detain, inspect, and seize suspicious cargo. Although security constraints prevent disclosure of successful interdictions, in May 2005 Secretary of State Condoleezza Rice announced, "in the last nine months alone, the United States and 10 of our PSI partners had cooperated on 11 successful efforts." At the same time, Denmark's ambassador to the United States, Ulrik Federspiel, observed that "the shipment of missiles has fallen significantly in the lifetime of PSI."[35]

Seemingly marginal initiatives, such as the United Nations Security Council Resolution (UNSCR) 1540, which was adopted in 2004 to address the risk that nonstate actors could acquire WMD and their means of delivery, and the State Department's Export Control and Related Border Security (EXBS) program, could play a more prominent and effective role in enhancing awareness of intangible technology transfers were they given more focused attention and resources to improve export control systems. UNSCR 1540 requires all states to implement national legislation to prevent WMD proliferation, but thus far its implementation has been ineffective. The resolution's ambitious set of legal requirements for all states could so spread United Nations (UN) resources as to lose focus on a narrower set of key states that are more relevant actors from the standpoint of WMD and delivery system proliferation. More effective implementation strategies have been suggested, but it remains to be seen if UN authorities can muster the fortitude to refocus this important new mechanism for fighting proliferation challenges.[36] By contrast, the State Department's EXBS program is focused on 40 countries, many located along primary WMD weapons-trafficking routes. It promotes training and proliferation awareness programs and offers customs and border control agencies modern detection technology. Certainly EXBS could focus more useful attention on the subject of intangible technology transfers; however, at present, the entire program has funding of only $42 million a year spread across all 40 countries.[37]

Last but not least is the matter of new MTCR members. Beginning in the early 1990s the MTCR became preoccupied with expanding its membership from the original 7 founding states to 34 nations as of this writing. Such growth has certainly enhanced the regime's representational value and nominally broadened the applicability of international norms, although the regime's decision to leave cruise missiles out of the Hague Code of Conduct has unintentionally fostered, rather than constrained, the spread of LACMs. The true effectiveness of any export control regime depends on a number of important factors, but ideally, full supplier participation and supplier consensus on the technologies to control are the two most important ones.[38] The MTCR is criticized both for including states that matter little as threats to proliferate missile-relevant items and for not including the world's foremost proliferators.[39] Arguably, should China become the chief global dispenser of not only LACMs but also the specialized know-how central to their further development, an intensification of the emerging missile contagion is a certainty, and it will be all the worse if Pakistan, North Korea, Iran, and Syria were to become secondary proliferators of LACMs. China's membership status as well as its specific point of view on what technologies should be controlled stands as perhaps the MTCR's greatest challenge today.

China's prospective membership in the MTCR first became an issue after Beijing applied for entry in July 2004. Having failed to reach a consensus on Beijing's application in the October 2004 MTCR plenary in Seoul, the issue came up again at the 2005 plenary in Madrid, but the regime's members were not even willing to consider the matter. According to U.S. and British officials, the membership largely remained concerned about inconsistencies in China's implementation record vis-à-vis MTCR standards.[40] Besides having a design of one of its nuclear warheads and nuclear test information transferred to Pakistan via the A. Q. Khan illicit network, Beijing has continued its missile-related activities with Iran in spite of repeated U.S. sanctions. The apparent Chinese parentage of Pakistan's Babur LACM does not engender confidence in Beijing's nonproliferation performance. Beijing's poor enforcement record is also reason to be concerned about its admission to the MTCR.

The scale of China's export control challenge is enormous, not least because of the country's immense land, sea, and air borders and the cumbersome and inherently conflictual nature of the system's bureaucratic components. In addition to generating the political will to act decisively, China will have to invest substantial financial resources to acquire highly trained personnel and new technology needed to bring the nation up to even minimum essential standards. This is unlikely to happen until Beijing appreciates the fact that its long-term economic interests are intricately linked to its nonproliferation performance. Instead of stonewalling against China's entry into the MTCR, the regime's membership should work more closely with China in ways that might foster increased transparency and improved enforcement.[41] Extending the capacities of the State Department's EXBS program to Beijing, especially in the area of export control and nonproliferation training, represents one of several possible courses of action worthy of implementation.[42]

On balance, it would be better to have China operating from within the MTCR than as a mere adherent. Even though China was a target country for years, Beijing was permitted to join the Nuclear Suppliers Group (NSG) in 2004. Critics used most of the very same concerns about Beijing's poor proliferation track record and weak enforcement mechanisms to argue against Beijing's NSG accession, but Bush administration officials countered by stating that China had made enough improvements to warrant membership.[43] Formal accession to the MTCR would mark not only China's involvement in a key security institution it doubted for many years but also, more broadly, its increasingly close engagement in international economic and political institutions. Continuing to block China's accession to the MTCR could backfire by encouraging Beijing to increase its iconoclastic behavior regarding missile sales. That would make it easier, not harder, for China to subvert U.S. security interests from the comfort of Beijing's imprecise and occasionally self-serving adherent relationship with the MTCR today.

REPAIRING MISSILE NONPROLIFERATION NORMS

Patience is surely a virtue in regard to repairing missile nonproliferation norms. Ironically, since the creation of the Hague Code of Conduct against Ballistic Missile Proliferation, realities on the ground, in all three regional settings examined in this book, suggest that the Code not only failed to address half the missile threat but that it arguably left out the most worrisome proliferation problem. While ballistic missile proliferation has gained some vertical momentum (increased missile ranges), its horizontal path has been reasonably contained. Cruise missiles, on the other hand, show signs of both vertical and horizontal momentum. New LACM programs are spreading contagiously across the Middle East, South Asia, and Northeast Asia. Not surprisingly, this normative shortcoming is matched by the U.S. approach to defending against missile threats. The United States fielded only half a missile defense system during the 2003 invasion of Iraq, a system capable of handling ballistic but not cruise missiles. Similarly, the international community formulated a 50 percent solution to norm construction for missiles. But there is an important difference between the two half-solutions. The matter of poor missile defense performance against LACMs is an example of the "lesser-included case" fallacy, which Albert Wohlstetter once described as akin to assuming "that the dog that could deal with the cat could easily handle the kitten."[44] Although the algebra works in the missile defense case, where Patriot possesses a nominal capability to intercept both ballistic and cruise missiles, norm construction has simply failed altogether to address the spread of cruise missiles.

Recognizing the importance of broadening the Hague Code's normative treatment to include cruise missiles is a growing phenomenon. After forming in late 2003, a 14-member independent Weapons of Mass Destruction Commission, chaired by Dr. Hans Blix, deliberated for over two years to develop "realistic proposals aimed at the greatest possible reduction of the dangers of weapons of mass destruction." The commissioners included retired flag and general officers from China and India, several internationally prominent diplomats, heads of international think tanks, and former Secretary of Defense William J. Perry. The scope of the WMD Commission's investigation included nuclear, biological, chemical, and radiological weapons and means of delivery.[45] On WMD-delivery systems, the WMD Commissioners unanimously recommended the following: "States subscribing to the Hague Code of Conduct should extend its scope to include cruise missiles and unmanned aerial vehicles."[46] The Commission also recommended the creation of a multilateral data exchange on missile launches from early warning systems, while encouraging more transparency measures and the formulation of launch notification agreements. Given the rapid buildup of LACMs in regional settings like South Asia and long-standing mistrust over historical legacies in Northeast Asia, not to mention rampant missile racing on both sides of the Taiwan straits, there is much value in most of what the Commission recommended. At the very least, both India and Pakistan should fold their new LACMs into their 2005 agreement on ballistic missile launch notification before they are deployed widely.

States subscribing to the Hague Code should keep in mind that the currently weak normative status of cruise missiles and UAVs, even within the MTCR, only solidifies the belief that LACMs and armed UAVs—weapons of great discrimination and extraordinarily high accuracy—somehow do not share the same characteristics that precipitated interest in the Code's original formulation. Missile proliferation specialist Mark Smith has written that, in the attempt to establish norms on missiles, states should not exaggerate the link between missiles and WMD as the foundation for control. Smith has suggested instead that we focus on the unique characteristics that distinguish missiles (meaning ballistic missiles) from other delivery systems. These would include, in Smith's view, range, speed, and low susceptibility to missile defenses, which combine to furnish strategic advantage. Improved accuracy would only add to ballistic missiles' strategic advantage.

But a closer look at each of Smith's unique characteristics, which purportedly distinguish ballistic missiles from other means of delivery and make them worthy of normative treatment, suggests that LACMs' characteristics compare favorably with those of their ballistic cousins. LACM range is currently ample and growing in each of the three regional settings examined here and more than adequate to achieve strategic effects. Although the United States is on track to develop an intercontinental-range cruise missile possessing perhaps Mach 6 speed, adversary LACMs will be limited to perhaps 3,000 km for the foreseeable future. Nevertheless, cruise missiles can readily achieve strategic range by means of their multiple launch possibilities.

Ballistic missiles exploit their speed to achieve shock effect, but because they are subject to launch detection, effective missile defenses can compensate for speed of delivery. On the other hand, it is much more difficult to detect a LACM's launch, and, because of its ability to fly low and alter its flight path into a target unpredictably, or to incorporate stealth materials to reduce its observability to radar, a LACM can readily achieve equivalent or better shock effect, if not total surprise, no matter its speed. That said, the speed of LACMs will inevitably grow as scramjet technology improves. Today's Mach 2.8 BrahMos may achieve double that speed in two decades.

As for low susceptibility to missile defenses, the 2003 war in Iraq showed that while missile defenses performed admirably against ballistic missiles, they failed altogether against a small number of crude LACMs. The perceived effectiveness of cruise missiles has thus begun to resonate broadly as a compelling incentive to acquire LACMs.

In fact, due to their high accuracy, LACMs' appeal as a tool of increasing discrimination has fostered the illusion that they are entirely different from ballistic missiles, which are so inaccurate delivering conventional payloads that they are only good for mass-destruction purposes. But, taking a longer-term view, the truth is that ballistic missiles' accuracy is improving enough to make them useful as conventional leveraging systems to enhance the effectiveness of air forces, particularly when used against opposing air forces situated on vulnerable airfields. China's missile threat to Taiwan's air force is the contemporary example. Moreover, U.S. attempts to arm Trident D-5 ballistic missiles with conventional payloads attests to the prospects of using ballistic missiles in more discriminating ways. And lest we forget, while LACMs today are well suited as weapons of discrimination, they are also fully capable of delivering mass-destruction payloads significantly better than ballistic missiles. Pakistan's decision to arm its Babur LACM with a nuclear warhead illustrates the point.

Several more characteristics might be added to Mark Smith's list, but I will mention only one: cost. The cost advantages that LACMs have over ballistic missiles not only give them added appeal but also make the prospect of effective defense increasingly more problematic. Importantly, too, ballistic and cruise missiles leverage each other's effectiveness by necessitating dual-mode missile defenses. Witness Iran's view that its new LACMs will support the effectiveness of their Shihab ballistic missiles.

By these measures, the absence of cruise missiles in the Hague Code underscores its palpably limited scope. If there is anything that the subscribing states to the Code agree upon, it is that the unconstrained proliferation of missiles undermines regional and international stability. If LACMs and UAVs run free, missile defenses against ballistic missiles will perform less effectively. Broadening the scope of the Hague Code is a modest step toward dealing with the new direction that missile proliferation has taken. Seemingly simple perceptual differences in the way ballistic and cruise missiles are normatively treated can motivate behavior that promotes LACM growth. Broadening the Code's scope to include cruise missiles and UAVs could send an important signal that curbing the spread of both ballistic and cruise missiles is a cause that merits the international community's attention.[47]

DEPLOYING EFFECTIVE CRUISE MISSILE DEFENSES

Compared with ballistic missile defense, cruise missile defense has second-class status. In 1995, the U.S. Congress fashioned the "Cruise Missile Defense Initiative" in its National Defense Authorization Act of Fiscal Year 1996. The act directed the Pentagon to strengthen defenses against existing and near-term threats, while urging the creation of a well coordinated technology development program to support future deployment against advanced cruise missile threats (that is, ones with lower radar cross-sections).[48] The Cruise Missile Defense Initiative may have been the brainchild of Congress, but the need for greatly improved defenses against cruise missiles emanated from two Defense Science Board summer studies that had drawn attention to existing weaknesses in air defenses against low-flying cruise missiles.[49] Little progress was achieved during the remaining years of the Bill Clinton administration, other than some spurts in funding and the creation of a new bureaucratic organization. Called the Joint Theater Air and Missile Defense Organization (JTAMDO), it tended to be seen as either a threat to service prerogatives on theater air and missile defense or a waste of Joint Staff resources altogether.[50]

Just short of the first anniversary of the September 11, 2001 terrorist attacks on New York and Washington, a front-page story in the *Washington Post* suggested that the Bush administration might well take action to address long-standing shortcomings in cruise missile defenses.[51] Reportedly, Secretary of Defense Rumsfeld had sent a classified memo to the White House warning about the spread of cruise missiles and the need for a government-wide effort to defend against them. Rumsfeld's concern grew out of anticipation rather than any specific threat warning from the intelligence community. Such anticipation was based on the recognition that all the underlying technologies needed to support LACM development were commercially available. Such countries as Iraq, Iran, and North Korea or nonstate actors like al-Qaeda could employ such technology to readily convert aircraft or ASCMs into crude but effective LACMs, or "poor man's" cruise missiles, capable of delivering biological or chemical agents. This specific concern prefigured the administration's subsequent attempt in 2003 to make changes in the Wassenaar Arrangement to control the technology that would permit rapid and easy conversion of an airplane into a UAV.[52]

The *Washington Post* story did include a brief synopsis of existing shortcomings in defending against LACMs, including the absence of a single integrated air picture (meaning radar data that could be fused into one view of the threat), air fratricide difficulties, and little linkage between airborne radar platforms and ground-based interceptors. All of these potential problems would materialize seven months later when Iraq employed converted ASCMs as LACMs, causing three friendly-fire incidents and loss of lives.

Perhaps the most salient observation made in the *Washington Post* story came from Lt. Gen. Joseph Cosumano, head of the U.S. Army's Space and Missile Defense Command. According to the *Post* story, Cosumano had complained in a speech "about the absence of a single Pentagon agency to coordinate development of cruise missile defenses the way the Missile Defense Agency (MDA) oversees work on anti-ballistic missile systems." In effect, Cosumano had implied that while "we ought to balance our capabilities" to deal with both ballistic and cruise missiles, the real problem was less a technological fix than one of centralized organizational control over individual service programs. This particular challenge goes to the heart of why existing cruise missile defenses will remain inadequate in the face of a clearly growing threat.

Left to its own narrow interests, each service will tend toward pursuing what it alone perceives is critical to its way of warfare. Even though missile defense systems such as the U.S. Army's Patriot and the U.S. Navy's SM-3 perform double duty against ballistic and cruise missiles, their comparative advantages in shooting down ballistic missiles derives in part from historical legacy. The eventual success of defenses against both manned aircraft and unmanned cruise missiles (in the British case) during World War II led to huge investment in air defenses after the war—several hundred billion dollars by the United States alone.[53] Under Title 10 to the U.S. Code, each military service has the sole authority to train, man, and equip its forces, including its respective air defenses. Air defense systems that exist today support tactical forces of each of the separate military services deployed around the globe. They include the U.S. Air Force's E-3 Airborne Warning and Control System (AWACS), the U.S. Navy's E-2C Hawkeye airborne surveillance aircraft, the U.S. Army's Patriot air defense system, the U.S. Navy's Standard Missile deployed on Aegis ships, and an array of manned air-to-air interceptors deployed on air force and navy aircraft. Given service prerogative under Title 10, it is no surprise that the U.S. Navy tends to focus on scenarios involving defense in depth to protect its carrier task forces. The U.S. Air Force, on the other hand, concentrates on wide-area air defense of the homeland and operational regions, using counter-air assets against enemy aircraft on the ground and AWACS and interceptor aircraft (armed with air-to-air missiles) as an outer layer of defense. The U.S. Army is preoccupied with protecting its maneuver forces and bases on the ground from enemy manned and unmanned air threats. Along the historical path of supporting these respective ways of warfare, each of the services has developed, procured, and integrated equipment and procedures—encompassing command-and-control systems, data links, message formats, and doctrine—that are unique to that particular service. Accordingly, knitting them into a coherent whole is fraught with technical, procedural, and doctrinal friction.

The problems now being encountered with cruise missile defense are largely absent regarding ballistic missile defense.[54] This is because of the peculiar manner in which ballistic missile defense programs are acquired. Whereas each service establishes requirements for and manages the acquisition of its own air defense programs, ballistic missile defense acquisition operates under the highly centralized control of

MDA. Although this degree of control has always been substantial—especially from the standpoint of budgetary control—compared with normal Title 10 oversight of service programs, it was made even more so in January 2002, when Secretary of Defense Rumsfeld wrested control over the establishment of a program's operational requirements from the services and elevated it to the MDA. Rumsfeld also decided to transfer management of some ballistic missile defense programs from the services to MDA. The underlying logic for these decisions hinged on the fully integrated nature of the mission—the very same logic that underlies cruise missile defense. That is, to achieve any degree of effectiveness, the ballistic missile defense system, composed of so many disparate components, demands an extraordinary degree of integration among sensors and interceptors in order to identify, track, and engage ballistic missiles. The concept of Network Centric Warfare suggests that when more than one service operates pieces of this complex whole, the whole system is more effectively managed by one agency throughout development and acquisition.[55]

When Defense Secretary Rumsfeld sent his classified memo to the White House in the summer of 2002, it had been only six months or so since the last of service control over ballistic missile defense programs had been removed. This may explain why a Rumsfeld aide told *Washington Post* reporter Bradley Graham that instead of doing what Lt. Gen. Cosumano had suggested or spending more money on the problem, the Pentagon would try improving coordination among existing service programs —something tried without demonstrable success for several decades. For example, efforts begun formally in 1969 to achieve a single integrated air picture (SIAP)— the first step in netting service sensor data together into a common picture of the threat air environment—remain frustrated but all the more urgent today, given the advent of even more difficult-to-detect targets like cruise missiles. Since the 2002 *Washington Post* story on Rumsfeld's urgent call for improvements in cruise missile defenses, rumors have periodically arisen and then quickly disappeared that MDA would take over centralized control of service programs. Instead, according to a trade journal report in mid-2006, the U.S. Strategic Command is operating as "an unofficial coordinating body for large-area cruise missile defense."[56]

Leaving cruise missile defense to the disparate ways of each military service or to the fledgling attempts of civilian defense officials to compel "coordination" virtually guarantees an inefficient solution to defending against LACMs. Should the cruise missile contagion result in large numbers of cheap enemy LACMs over the next decade, such inefficiency will turn into abject impotence. A little bit of theory helps explain why current cruise missile defenses are so palpably weak.

Conceptually, the objective of air defense is to create as large a surveillance and engagement zone—called battlespace—as possible. The payoff for achieving large battlespace is enormous, particularly if the adversary is able to employ saturation attacks. Substantial battlespace permits the creation of a layered defense in depth, starting with counterforce attacks against the enemy's peacetime cruise missile bases or any aircraft armed with LACMs but still bedded down on air bases. But if aircraft scramble before such counter-air attacks or ground-launched LACM units are mobilized and moved to hide locations, then individual service shooters (e.g., Patriot,

Standard Missile, or air force fighters armed with air-to-air interceptors) take over the defensive fight.[57] Long-range detection of LACM launches, however, is valuable on its own: it provides warning of attack and implementation of passive defense measures, such as scrambling to protective shelters or donning chemical or biological defensive suits.

Long-range detection of LACMs is also essential to optimally execute a defense in depth. For example, an AWACS surveillance aircraft can detect an enemy aircraft with a seven square-meter radar cross-section (RCS), traveling at 800 km/hour, at a distance of 370 km, giving defenders about 28 minutes of time to plan multiple shots, possibly including both air-to-air and ground-based interceptors.[58] But if the AWACS aircraft were facing a LACM with an RCS of a tenth of a square meter (by no means stealthy), traveling also at 800 km/hour, detection occurs at 130 km and reaction time drops to only 10 minutes. A truly stealthy LACM traveling at the same speed could cut that time to less than 2 minutes.

Writing seven years ago in *Dealing with the Threat of Cruise Missiles,* I argued that then-existing weaknesses in sensor networking challenged the conventional wisdom that U.S. air defenses could cope rather well with first-generation LACMs.[59] Of course, two years later, in 2003, the conventional wisdom was sadly proven wrong during the invasion of Iraq—no LACMs detected and several friendly-fire incidents. I speculated counterfactually in 2001 about the consequences for American missile defense planning had Iraq operated in the 1991 war with both ballistic and cruise missiles. Dual-mode missile defense systems like Patriot would have had to operate simultaneously against both high-angle ballistic missiles and low-angle LACMs. In retrospect, the 1991 war against Iraq was the last war in which the U.S. military could operate using highly restrictive rules of engagement, which, by virtue of shutting down missile defenses against everything but ballistic missiles, greatly reduced the possibility of inadvertently shooting down friendly aircraft. Despite pleas from numerous Defense Science Board studies and think tanks between the first and second Gulf Wars, virtually no networking among service sensors existed in the 2003 war against Iraq. The U.S. Air Force's AWACS surveillance planes were incapable of communicating with the U.S. Army's ground-based Patriot units.[60]

Although the services have made some progress since the conclusion of combat operations against Iraq in 2003, just how well U.S. air and missile defenses would perform against LACMs by 2010 remains open to question. The critical question is the type and nature of the LACM threat U.S. cruise missile defenses would face. Modest improvements in connectivity and airborne sensors would permit such defenses to handle the kind of threat Iraq presented in 2003: a small number of first-generation LACMs arriving one at a time. But as a senior American military planner during the 1991 Gulf War observed before the 2003 invasion, "The U.S. is not going to get the luxury of one cruise missile arriving every five minutes. If I were the enemy, I'd fire [LACMs] in barrages. And I'd put dummies up front and at a little higher altitude to attract the defenses. I'll bet eighty percent would get though."[61] The notion that future LACM threats will evolve along these speculative lines is hardly far-fetched. Consider the attention Chinese military strategists pay to the value of "tidal wave" or saturation attacks with both ballistic and cruise missiles, the 9:1 cost advantage they attribute to using LACMs compared to defending against them, and reports that they are converting large numbers of retired fighters into UAVs. Casting China's apparent approach as the exception rather than the rule would be extremely shortsighted.

DESIRE VERSUS REALITY

A solution to the challenges of large-scale saturation attacks of LACMs would necessarily include the following component parts: first, a mechanism for fighting jointly, including with coalition partners or allies; second, the capacity to restore lost battlespace by means of improved sensors for detecting, identifying, tracking, and intercepting large numbers of low-observable LACMs with endgame countermeasures; and third, the development of lower-cost solutions to intercepting LACMs. The U.S. Air Force has improved attack operations against mobile missiles, most notably when such targets consist of ballistic missiles carried on large transporter-erector-launchers. Although air force stock in this regard has risen dramatically since 2001, as discussed in Chapter 8, detection challenges against smaller LACM launchers, both when they are operating in the field and when they are launched, will remain significant. Thus, substantial counterforce success against ground-mobile LACMs will remain out of reach over the next decade. Moreover, LACMs will also be launched from aircraft, ships, and submarines. This reality underscores the importance of improving air and missile defenses against cruise missiles.

Fighting jointly, including with allies and coalition partners, depends heavily on making SIAP work. This would entail the merging of disparate sources of sensor data sent via different service data links to arrive at a common view of the air picture. If SIAP were fully realized, it would afford users, including allies, the wherewithal to share multiple-aspect viewing of threats over a much broader geographic region than currently is the case, greatly reducing gaps in coverage and widening the window within which to provide timely cues to air and missile defense weapons. Conceivably, achieving SIAP implementation could accelerate the identification of friendly air vehicles as distinct from enemy cruise missiles, especially if improved sensors possessing the capacity to produce fire-control-quality information were available.

The connectivity and data sharing offered by SIAP implementation is one thing, but if the U.S. military is ever to field an effective defense against large numbers of LACMs, particularly ones with low observability, it will need to deploy new airborne surveillance radars and improve the performance of seekers on interceptors. The ideal sensor for identifying and tracking small, low-flying cruise missiles would possess agility and precision sufficient to pass fire-control-quality information to ground- and air-based interceptors on targets detected at ranges of several hundreds of kilometers. With that much battlespace created due to improvements in high-performance radars using active electronically scanned array (AESA) technology—such technology is part of the Multi-Platform Radar Technology Insertion Program (MP-RTIP)—it would be possible to implement new operational concepts that would radically alter the current decentralized, service-centric approach to air defense. For example, the Patriot missile defense battery's ground-based but horizon-limited radar guides each of its interceptors to a target. If a centralized platform, flying at an altitude of 11,000 m, could literally take over directing the ground-based interceptor by providing it with mid-course and terminal guidance updates (the interceptor could alternatively depend upon its own seeker in the terminal phase), the airborne platform's direction would permit Patriot interceptors to be used to their full potential range (100–150 km), unhampered by the 25–35-km limit imposed by their horizon-limited ground-based radars. Besides providing fire control for air-directed surface-to-air missiles (known as ADSAM) like the Patriot PAC-3, such an elevated platform could also furnish precision cues to fighters' air-to-air interceptors to increase their effective range as well (around 60 km).

Turning ADSAM from concept into practice would pay enormous dividends. The most valuable would be the significant increase in depth of fire for all weapon systems, which affords the defense multiple shot opportunities and greatly increased effectiveness against large onslaughts of cruise missiles. The possibility of fratricide would also be greatly reduced, owing to the high-quality fire-control information that AESA radars can furnish on targets detected, identified, and tracked over hundreds of kilometers. Cost also comes into play when considering the limited inventories of expensive interceptors like the Patriot's PAC-3. Operating under the ADSAM concept, a single battery of ground-based interceptors could (depending on the system) provide defense for 10,000 to 70,000 square kilometers of territory. For example, this would relax the requirement to bunch Patriot batteries around point targets (say, airfields) to provide 360-degree protection against cruise missiles. Less reliance on ground-based radars would also streamline deployment into regional campaigns, make more efficient use of already limited interceptor inventories, and provide force protection early in the war when defenses are least capable. While improved elevated sensors are needed to make the ADSAM concept real, in a high-threat environment so too are improved seekers on interceptors, in order to cope with high-clutter environments and increasingly stealthy cruise missiles employing endgame countermeasures.

Paying for such an idealized system of defending against cruise missiles has proven thus far to be one of several reasons why today's cruise missile defenses are so paltry. Of course, defending against ballistic missiles has absorbed up to $10 billion a year of the Pentagon's annual budget—though this is a measly sum according to missile defense supporters. As the cruise missile threat grows more potent, it will become increasingly clear that investment in defending against only half the missile threat makes little sense. Yet it will be very difficult to maintain cost effectiveness at the margin. A fairly conservative study, conducted by the Pentagon's Defense Advanced Research Projects Agency (DARPA), showed that effective defense against a salvo of 200 cruise missiles would require an investment of $475 million, or $4 million per kill. Of course, while the study assumed that the defense had the necessary ingredients to handle such salvo attacks, the consequence of such an attack would mean a dwindling of interceptor inventories and the compromising of other missions—notably, in the case of Patriot and the Standard Missile, defending against ballistic missiles.[62] While achieving cost effectiveness at the margin may be inconceivable in the long run, to make cruise missile defense possible against saturation attacks, the cost of interceptors must come down substantially.

The inadequacy of cruise missile defense today and its prospects out to 2010 do not engender much confidence at all that the United States will come even close to achieving a sufficient defense. While the quest to achieve a workable SIAP among the services has shown some progress, much remains to be done, particularly in regard to broadening SIAP applicability to allies and coalition partners. The SIAP task is now under the management of a Joint SIAP System Engineering Organization (JSSEO), which is a division under the assistant secretary of the army for acquisition, logistics, and technology. JSSEO formulates integrated technical approaches for data sharing, a process that costs an estimated $160 million through fiscal year 2009. But in the end, each service has to muster sufficient funding to integrate SIAP technology into its respective systems, a cost estimated at $600 million.[63] Sensitivity over sharing data protocols and encryption with allies and coalition partners is still a key hurdle to broadening the SIAP. Thus, although SIAP architecture and software development is moving steadily forward toward a 2009 implementation, extending SIAP capability fully to key allies appears more problematic. The benefits of such an extension outweigh the risks of sharing sensitive data. During the critical early stages of any contingency, when forces are just beginning to bed down, SIAP connectivity with key allies capable of participating in defending against large-volume LACM attacks could prove crucial to campaign success. Overall, achieving a fully implemented SIAP remains a troubled if ongoing endeavor that may be achievable only under the stronger management arm of a centralized authority such as MDA.

Achieving any substantial capacity to deal with large-volume LACM attacks was dealt a devastating blow with the cancellation in the 2008 budget of the U.S. Air Force's next-generation wide-area surveillance and battle management platform, called the Multi-Sensor Command and Control Aircraft (MC2A), or E-10 program. Intended originally to incorporate the functions of both the airborne and ground surveillance missions of the air force's AWACS and the Joint Surveillance and Target Attack Radar System (JSTARS) aircraft, the air force decided subsequently to develop separate platforms for airborne and ground tracking missions. The E-10's potential capacity to execute the ADSAM mission was truly transformative. Acting as an airborne means of detection, tracking, and command and control of the air defense battle, the E-10 could have provided ground- and air-based interceptors with fire-control-quality data on targets out to ranges approaching 500 km—more than a half-hour of battlespace time within which to optimize multiple intercept opportunities.[64] Importantly, too, fire-control-quality data would also furnish a fine-grain distinction between friendly aircraft and enemy cruise missiles. Combined with lower-cost interceptors, the E-10 offered the greatest prospect for coping with large-salvo, low-observable cruise missiles. None of the alternative solutions begin to approximate the cancelled program's large AESA radar antenna, measuring 4 by 21 feet. With the E-10's cancellation, some money was slated to employ a very scaled-down version of the radar in the Global Hawk UAV, but Northrop Grumman reportedly claims that the Global Hawk, with a 1.5 by 5-foot AESA radar, will focus on missions other than cruise missile defense due to the radar's limited size and performance against small LACMs. MP-RTIP funding has also been cut substantially, and even were that radar to make it into the JSTARS, its smaller size (2 by 21 feet) would effectively reduce its ability to detect and track low-flying cruise missiles.[65] AWACS, on the other hand, has undergone a radar system improvement program to increase its surveillance capacity against low-observable cruise missiles.

Absent the E-10, or any airborne platform with sufficient space to accommodate the 4 by 21–foot AESA radar, the air force has turned to relying on its prized but enormously expensive F-22 fighter for both overseas and homeland defense against cruise missiles. Indeed, the extraordinarily high cost of the F-22 compelled the air force hierarchy to focus intensely on the cruise missile defense mission as the F-22's top responsibility. There seems little doubt that the demise of the E-10 program resulted in part from its potentially high cost. It also did not help the E-10's cause to be part of a service that is run by fighter pilots inclined to protect its latest fighter, despite its unit cost of $361 million. It was also rumored that senior civilians within the Rumsfeld-led Pentagon preferred a space-based radar and UAV solution to a new expensive airborne platform.[66] To be sure, the F-22 possesses a fuel-efficient super-cruise capability that enables it to quickly come within range of an enemy cruise missile, whereupon its AESA radar can effectively track and allow the fighter's air-to-air missiles to engage the target. This scenario is more than adequate as long as the threat is limited to a small number of LACMs conveniently launched into an air defense zone occupied by F-22s. Facing multiple barrages of LACMs, however, the defense would fall apart quickly. Substantially increasing the number of F-22s would please the air force hierarchy, but operationally it would not compare favorably to simply pursuing the E-10 program instead.

The air force attitude toward defending against cruise missiles errs decidedly on the side of the kill vehicle (namely, the F-22) when it should be skewed towards expanding battlespace and enabling the integration of other service interceptors into what is fundamentally a network centric solution to cruise missile defense. By starting with the kill vehicle first—and a costly one at that—and leaving joint battle management and command-and-control integration behind, the nation will be less prepared to cope with the growing threat of cruise missiles.

In the meantime, the other services are striving to develop component pieces of what could eventually become a truly networked solution to cruise missile defense. There is a nearer-term, if substantially lesser-performing, alternative to the E-10 program, managed by the U.S. Army, called the Joint Land-Attack Cruise Missile Defense Elevated Netted Sensor System (JLENS). Started in 1995 and scheduled now for initial deployment in 2010, JLENS is an airborne sensor suite deployed with a surveillance and a fire-control radar situated on separate aerostat platforms, which are blimp-like balloons using lighter-than-air gas for buoyancy. JLENS will be able to link up with ground-based Patriot batteries and the navy's Aegis cruisers outfitted with Standard Missiles, furnishing these horizon-limited interceptors with precision cues on threatening LACMs out to perhaps half the distance (250 km) that the E-10 was designed to achieve. The army also has or plans to add a slew of other air defense systems that would protect maneuver forces in regional contingencies and have potential to furnish preferential defense of high-profile point targets, such as Olympic events or a Super Bowl venue. Around the corner, in 2013, the army intends to deploy a follow-on to Patriot, called the Medium Extended Air Defense System (MEADS), which will also be deployed by Italy and Germany. MEADS is slated to have true interoperability built in and may be equipped with a range double that of today's PAC-3 missile.

Exploiting battlespace most effectively would entail engaging cruise missiles when they are as far as possible from their intended targets. Not only does JLENS come up short by half in its effective range compared with the E-10, but its operating altitude of 3,000 to 4,500 m is less than the E-10's by a factor of roughly two and a half. Low-flying LACMs have the capacity to exploit terrain features—valleys, for example—to mask their detection. The possibility that an enemy LACM might effectively exploit such protection is much greater when faced with a sensor platform like JLENS than one operating two and a half times higher. Speed of entry into a quickly emerging regional campaign also favors an aircraft over an aerostat, which is not only slow moving but also limited by adverse weather, particularly high winds. "I don't get too excited about the platform, other than to say that aerostats nowadays are not like the Hindenburg," said Col. Kurt Heine, the army's program manager for JLENS in 2004.[67] Were JLENS successfully shot at with large-caliber ammunition, the aerostat's helium gas would allow the platform to sink gracefully and slowly enough (over several hours) so that the platform's expensive sensor might be recovered safely. Still, obvious questions remain about JLENS's vulnerability. The truth is that JLENS was never meant to be the primary means of furnishing precision surveillance and cues within a joint cruise missile defense network, but it was rather intended as a complement to more mobile, faster-reacting, weather-insensitive, fixed-wing aircraft like the now-cancelled E-10. The special appeal of JLENS as a complementary system is its ability to stay on station during lengthy pre-hostility periods for roughly one-tenth the cost of a fixed-wing aircraft.[68]

Conceptually, the U.S. Navy has practiced defense in depth (the navy's way of saying achieving significant battlespace) for decades as a means of protecting fleet operations at sea. The most important component of the navy's approach is the outer ring, fulfilled by the E-2C Hawkeye aircraft, the navy's propeller-drive counterpart to the air force AWACS. The Hawkeye operates about 150 km from the carrier battle group it protects, while it focuses on aircraft and ships that are up to twice that distance farther removed from the protected battle group. When not protecting a carrier battle group, the Hawkeye can quite readily support operations over the land. Indeed, two Hawkeye squadrons were commandeered to provide almost two-thirds of the overland coverage in northern Iraq in support of the 2003 invasion. Since the mid-1990s, defense experts have urged the navy to support the land battle in more prominent ways, and no way could be more instrumental than furnishing surveillance and fire support for airborne and ground-based interceptors of the other services. There are now positive indications that a new Hawkeye variant, the E-2D, slated for deployment in 2011, will incorporate a new radar with two and a half times more search volume and an improved capacity to detect LACMs over land.[69] Combined with the navy's F-18 and F-35, both of which possess AESA radars, the improved Hawkeye could in theory fill gaps in defensive coverage that air force and army components were unable to handle. That said, the Hawkeye's overall capacity to extend battlespace will not compare with what the E-10 offered, nor can the navy be counted on too heavily given that its primary responsibility is to operate over water, not land.

Service efforts to achieve cost effectiveness at the margin have been decidedly uneven. The army and DARPA have focused on developing affordable interceptors designed to cope with unsophisticated LACMs and UAVs, meaning air vehicles having larger radar cross-sections, which correspondingly reduces the costs of the interceptor's seeker. The army's Surface-Launched Advanced Medium-Range Air-to-Air Missile (SLAMRAAM) system employs the AIM-120 air-to-air missile from a mobile ground launcher tied to the Sentinel radar. The system already is in operation with the Norwegian and Spanish militaries and will become operational with the U.S. Army in 2008. While the $650,000 cost of each interceptor compares favorably with the several-million-dollar cost for each PAC-3 interceptor, it doesn't begin to approach the desired objective of producing interceptors for under $100,000 each. DARPA, on the other hand, is pushing the envelope in its quest to lower the cost of missile seekers, which overwhelmingly dominate (on average, 65 percent) an interceptor's cost. Its target goal is an interceptor costing $45,000, while the army's low-cost interceptor program seeks a missile with a unit cost of $100,000. Despite evidence that stealth materials and design are finding their way into missiles like Pakistan's Raad LACM, efforts to produce much lower-cost interceptors against unsophisticated LACMs and UAVs will remain critically essential, particularly in light of the U.S. Air Force's dependence on the astonishingly expensive F-22 fighter as its premier defender against cruise missiles.

DEFENDING THE HOMELAND

If defending against cruise missiles in overseas contingencies remains a challenging proposition, so too does homeland cruise missile defense, a controversial area for a number of reasons. The array of service platforms and missile interceptors just discussed could play roles in defending the homeland. Certainly turning to what already stands as a limited but potentially effective set of capabilities for protecting forces overseas makes good sense. But when one investigates the problem of homeland defense against cruise missiles more carefully, a cautious approach seems warranted.

All the weaknesses in defending against cruise missiles in regional campaigns are compounded by the sheer size of the homeland defense problem. The North American Air Defense Command (NORAD) routinely detects and tracks ballistic missile threat to North America from spaceborne assets. Doing the same for cruise missile launches would be ideal and make things at least straightforward. But, according to one conservative estimate, it will take at least another three decades before space-based sensors might become capable of reliably detecting and tracking low-flying cruise missiles.[70] Absent broad area coverage by spaceborne sensors, airborne sensors capable of monitoring nearly 20,000 km of U.S. coastline are required. The threat du jour derives from the thousands of commercial container ships in the international fleet and the fact that a standard 12-m shipping container can readily accommodate a converted Chinese Silkworm missile—which from just outside territorial waters could threaten virtually any important capital or large industrial area of the United States. Armed with a biological payload, the use of such a system could theoretically achieve devastating effects. Of course, the threat need not emanate only from the sea. Although the threat of converting small airplanes into UAVs has not garnered the attention that sea-launched LACMs have, it was compelling enough to cause the U.S. government to convince the memberships of both the Wassenaar Arrangement and the MTCR to tighten controls on integrated navigation and guidance systems that would ease the conversion of manned airplanes into unmanned ones. Small UAV threats could emanate from virtually any location with flat terrain for takeoff and within range of the intended target. Preferential defense of high-value targets would make the most sense against this class of threats.

Even assuming that Pentagon officials believe the threat warrants immediate action, their assessments of the LACM threat to the homeland do not yield much optimism for a near-term solution. In 2006, news reports indicated that the Department of Defense had found at least nine major "capability gaps" in providing a defense of the homeland against cruise missiles.[71] Worse, the gaps were unlikely to be solved until 2015. Naturally, multiple study groups were tasked once again with examining the best approaches to filling these gaps. In the late 1990s at least two major Pentagon reviews of homeland defense met to discuss the requirements for and probable costs of a comprehensive defense of the homeland, and generally the conclusions suggested that the cost would probably be at least $30–40 billion.[72] Needless to say, the gaps in the late 1990s were the same as those re-articulated in 2006: the need for a SIAP, inadequate wide-area surveillance, incapacity to deal with slow-moving air threats, little tracking and high-quality fire-control information, low combat identification, and an insufficient number of interceptors to cover the entire country.

Notwithstanding the Pentagon's sobering prognosis, one major defense contractor has sought to recast the problem in a more manageable light. In a briefing on Capitol Hill to congressional staff and media during the summer of 2007, a Lockheed Martin senior executive argued that the United States could deploy a cruise missile defense system that could protect the area from Washington, D.C. to Boston for "several billion dollars" within 14 months. His optimism may have emanated from the fact that the existing weapons (PAC-3 interceptors) or sensors under development (the High Altitude Airship) that would enable deployment within such a brief time were the contractor's own programs. But the overall system's success hinges critically—though by no means exclusively—on the performance of the High Altitude Airship operating at 21,000-m altitude and carrying sensors needed to furnish surveillance and fire control for ground-based interceptors. MDA, however, cut the airship program back sharply in 2007 and then decided to remove funding altogether in 2008. One of several technical issues concerning airships is their ability to remain on station during extremely high winds that are common at stratospheric altitudes.[73]

One way or the other, any solution to homeland defense against cruise missiles will not only be expensive but also hard to implement, not least due to the lack of centralized Pentagon control over the component pieces of the puzzle. The real question is the seriousness of the threat. Although LACMs are spreading significantly in all three regional contexts examined in this book, unless a terrorist group could call upon extensive outside technical assistance, the idea of converting a Chinese Silkworm ASCM into a LACM, much less successfully weaponizing and delivering a WMD payload, does not seem like a plausible enough threat to expend the billions of dollars needed to defend successfully against it. What does seem imperative, on the other hand, is a significant bolstering of programs aimed at providing early warning of threats emanating from container ships, including measures to improve Coast Guard inspections of suspect merchant ships and capabilities supporting the Proliferation Security Initiative. Armed with early warning information, U.S. forces can stop ships at sea, or fighters equipped with AESA radars can be launched to protect against such low-volume threats. The recapitalization of the military services' overworked equipment inventories will necessarily make very-low-probability, high-consequence threats—such as terrorist employment of ballistic or cruise missiles from sea— low-priority requirements. Cruise missile defenses needed for safely projecting force over great distances, however, will remain a high priority. But such programs will remain mired in narrow, service-centric optimization rather than supportive of the broader U.S. security strategies and interests unless centralized agency control is instituted.[74] In this light, repairing nonproliferation policies is all the more urgent.

AVERTING UNINTENDED CONSEQUENCES

Much of this book has been about the failure to anticipate and avert the unintended consequences of U.S. actions. Various U.S. policies—including the promotion of ballistic missile sales and the establishment of the preemption doctrine— have come together to help accelerate the missile contagion. Continuing along these lines will only worsen that contagion, particularly as America and its allies and friends struggle with challenges of defending effectively against cruise missiles. At the very least, the Pentagon will have to engage much more cooperatively than it might have anticipated in technical discussions with allies and friends about ways to deal eventually with LACM threats.

Promoting ballistic missile defenses without making definitively clear what these systems can and cannot accomplish against cruise missiles transfers the Pentagon's lopsidedly ballistic missile-oriented defense strategy to our close allies and friends. In some cases, this emphasis has created incentives for adversaries of these allies and friends to acquire LACMs. In other cases, driven by the high costs of defense, U.S. allies and friends have turned towards LACMs as a more affordable defense option. Some of these consequences are perhaps inevitable, but practicing a more systematic appraisal of the potential consequences of policies and actions makes good sense even if only to fine-tune those consequences to avoid unwanted regional instability.

Although it is unlikely to happen during the remainder of the Bush administration, Washington would do well to demote preemption from national doctrine back to one among many options.[75] But there is also the matter of inadvertently encouraging preemptive strike doctrines with allies and friends when their officers attend U.S. military institutions and are taught about the benefits of adopting counterforce, preemptively oriented strike doctrines to complement active missile defenses. Service school instruction on the counterforce pillar of missile defense should remind foreign students that it has taken over two decades of substantial technology investments and doctrinal debate for the U.S. military services to substantially improve offensive attack operations against mobile missiles. Indeed, nine years ago the U.S. Air Force was so frustrated with shortcomings in its attack capabilities against mobile missiles that it cancelled its program.[76] In military-to-military exchanges with allies and friends, the objective of regional stability would benefit from candid expressions of the difficulties of ever executing offensive attack operations against mobile missiles with any degree of effectiveness. Discussions also should occur about the potentially deleterious effects for regional stability of formally promoting a preemptive counterforce military strategy. In the context of a regional contingency with a close ally, offensive attack operations should be left exclusively to the U.S. military to execute, if necessary.

There is also a compelling need for U.S. policymakers to revert to practices that once encouraged cooperation between the United States and the Soviet Union. Then arms control theory was predicated on the importance of transparency, or making both sides of any competition aware—within the limits of security—of what the other side was doing. In considering how the United States might adjust its behavior to mitigate Russian and Chinese cruise missile transfers or related conveyance of specialized knowledge, nothing is more valuable than increased American transparency in regard to U.S. defense programs. Neither the 2001 Nuclear Posture Review (NPR) or the new U.S. emphasis on global missile defenses was launched with any degree of reassuring candor and openness in mind. According to the 2001 NPR, Russia no longer figures into American targeting plans as a primary threat. But nothing was said to allay concerns about the 2001 NPR's revolutionary turn toward depending on strategic strikes with conventionally armed ballistic missiles that once were armed with nuclear warheads. Nor did it appear that the Bush administration had gamed out in advance how such a policy change—reflecting as it did a growing American interest in ballistic missile use—would affect missile nonproliferation policies.[77] On global missile defenses, Russia and China were told not to fear limited American defenses. But the opaque nature of U.S. missile defense development—consisting of an open-end system architecture and periodic block deployments—engenders strategic uncertainty rather than stabilizing transparency.

The purest form of reassurance would resurrect formal arms control constraints, perhaps involving quantity limits on mid-course and upper-tier interceptors, or even constraints on ground- and space-based sensors. China is most animated over U.S. prospects for deploying weapons in space, including the positioning of space-based kill vehicles for mid-course intercept. Here the United States might alleviate international concerns, including China's, by agreeing to an international code of conduct to promote peaceful uses of outer space. Russian offers of cooperation in the missile defense area should be seriously entertained by the next U.S. administration. Joint missile defenses together with closer cooperation on early warning systems would foster stability instead of rancor in what otherwise may evolve into a permanent state of tension between the two nations. The next administration might also wish to expand informal outreach activities with Russian and Chinese military and diplomatic officials to inform them about the direction, scope, and pace of U.S. offensive and defensive military programs. Such initiatives might not entirely answer Russian and Chinese concerns, but they might partially lift the veil of secrecy now surrounding America's longer-term strategic direction. Greater transparency with regard to increasing U.S. reliance on conventionally armed global strike concepts and forces seems especially important.

The signs of a missile contagion documented in this book represent one of a host of challenges facing the next U.S. administration. Nothing could be more important to stanching the contagion than improving relations with Russia and China. In dealing with China, Robert Zoellick, who served as deputy secretary of state before assuming the World Bank presidency in 2007, wisely put it this way: "Picture the wide range of global challenges we face in the years ahead—terrorism and extremists exploiting Islam, the proliferation of weapons of mass destruction, poverty, disease— and ask whether it would be easier or harder to handle those problems if the United States and China were cooperating or at odds."[78] The same concern applies equally to Russia.

Appendix A

Selected Cruise Missile Programs

Country	System	Range (km)	Payload (kg)	Status	Origin	Export/Transfer
China	3M-14E	1,500		Acquired	Russia	
	Dong Hai-10 (DH-10)/HN-2000			In Development	China	
	Hong Niao-1 (HN-1)	600		Operational?	China/Russia	
	Hong Niao-2 (HN-2)	1,500–2,000		Operational?	China/Russia	
	Hong Niao-2 (HN-3)	2,500		In Development?	China/Russia	
	YJ-63	500	500	In Development	China	
France	Apache	140	520	In Service	France/United Kingdom	
	SCALP-EG	400–600		Operational	France/United Kingdom	
Germany	Taurus KEPD-350*	350	500	In Development	Germany/Sweden/France/United Kingdom	Spain
Greece	SCALP-EG/Storm Shadow			Acquired		
India	3M-14E	200–300		Acquired	Russia	
	Lakshya***	350	600	In Development	Israel	
	Nirbhay	1,000		In Development	India	
	PJ-10 BrahMos	290	300	In Development/In Service	Rusia/India	Possibly Malaysia, South Africa, Kuwait, Chile, and Indonesia
Iran	Sagarika	1,000?		In Development	India	
	Converted HY-2	300?	500?	Possible Development	China	
	Kh-55	3,000	410	Possible Development	Ukraine	
	Nur ASCM			Possible Development/Unknown	China	
	Raad	350		Possible Development	China	

178

Country	Missile	Number	Status	Origin	Destinations
Israel	Delilah Derivative (STAR-1)*	400	In Development	Israel	Possibly China
	Harpy	400+	Operational	Israel	China, Turkey, possibly India
Italy	Popeye Turbo	250+	In Service/For Export	Israel	Possibly India
	Storm Shadow*		In Service	France/United Kingdom	
North Korea	Kh-55		Unknown	Iran/Ukraine	
Pakistan	Babur/Hatf-7	700+	In Development	China	
	Raad/Hatf-8	350	In Development	China	
Russia	Iskander-K/R-500	500?	In Development	Russia	
	Kh-55	3,000	In Service	Russia	
	Kh-65E	280	For Export	Russia	
	Kh-555	5,000	In Service	Russia	
	3M-14E	300	In Service/For Export	Russia	China, India, possibly Indonesia
	PJ-10 BrahMos	290	In Development	Russia/India	Possibly Malaysia, South Africa, Kuwait, Chile, and Indonesia
Saudi Arabia	SS-N-21/Rk-55 Granat**	1,500+	In Service	Russia	
	Storm Shadow	300	Acquisition Pending	France/United Kingdom	
South Africa	Mupsow**	125+	Operational	South Africa	
	Torgos**	185+	Operational	South Africa	
South Korea	Boramae	500+	In Development	South Korea	
	Cheonryong	500+	In Development	South Korea	
	Hyunmoo-3	1,000	In Development	South Korea	
	Hyunmoo-3A	1,500	In Development	South Korea	
Spain	BGM-109 Tomahawk		Acquired	United States	
	Taurus KEPD-350		Acquired	Germany/Sweden	

Country	Missile			Status	Origin	Operators/Exported
Taiwan	Hsiung Feng-2E (HF-2E)	<1,000	400–450	In Development	Taiwan/United States?	
Ukraine	AS-15 Kent/Kh-55	3,000	410	Reported Sent to Russia or Destroyed	Russia	Iran, China, possibly North Korea
	Korshun	280	480	For Export/Unknown	Russia/Ukraine	
United Arab Emirates	Black Shaheen/Storm Shadow	300	500	Acquired	France/United Kingdom	
United Kingdom	BGM-109 Tomahawk*	1,600	320	In Service	United States	
	Storm Shadow	650	400*	In Service/For Export	France/United Kingdom	Saudi Arabia, Greece, Italy
United States	AGM-86 Conventional Air-Launched Cruise Missile	1,100+	680–1,360	In Service	United States	
	AGM-129 Advanced Cruise Missile	3,700	Nuclear Payload	In Service/Early Retirement Expected	United States	
	AGM-158 JASSM	370+	450	In Development	United States	Possibly Australia
	BGM-109 Tomahawk	2,500	450	In Service/For Export	United States	United Kingdom, Spain

Note on Sources: Unless otherwise noted, this table of selected land-attack cruise missile programs includes missiles documented in the book. Supplementary sources include: Andrew Feickert, "Missile Survey: Ballistic and Cruise Missiles of Selected Countries," Congressional Research Service, July 26, 2005 (indicated in table by *), http://www.fas.org/sgp/crs/weapons/RL30427.pdf; "Ballistic and Cruise Missile Threat," National Air and Space Intelligence Center, March 2006 (indicated in table by **); and Vivek Raghuvanshi, "Indian-made UAV To Become A Cruise Missile," *Defense News*, October 1, 2007 (indicated in table by ***), http://www.defensenews.com/story.php?F=3061901&C=airwar.

Appendix B

Selected Ballistic Missile Programs

Country	System	Range (km)	Payload (kg)	Status
China****	CSS-2 (DF-3/3A)	3,100	1,900**	In Service/Retirement
	CSS-3 (DF-4)	5,500	2,200*	In Service
	CSS-4 (DF-5/5A)	13,000	3,200*	In Service
	CSS-5 (DF-21/21A)	2,150	600*	In Service
	CSS-6 (DF-15/M-9)	600	500******	In Service
	CSS-7 (DF-11/M-11)	300	500******	In Service
	CSS-8 (M-7/Project 8610)	93**	190*	In Service
	CSS-N-3 (JL-1)	1,700+	600*	In Service
	DF-31	8,000	700******	In Development
	DF-31A	12,000	800******	In Development
	DF-41*	12,000	800	In Development
	JL-2	8,000	700*	In Development
India	Agni-1	700–1,200	1,000	In Development
	Agni-2	2,000	1,000	In Development
	Agni-3	3,500+	1,500***	In Development
	Prithvi-1	150	1,000	In Service
	Prithvi-2	250	500–750	In Production
	Prithvi-3/Dhanush	400	500	In Development
	Surya******	5,500+	2,000	In Development/Unknown
	BM-25/Musudan	3,500		In Development/Acquired from North Korea
Iran	CSS-6 (M-9)*	600	500	Possibly in Development
	CSS-7 (M-11) variant*	300	500	Possibly in Development
	CSS-8 (Tondar-69)*******	150	190	In Service/Acquired from China
	Fateh-110*******	200	600	In Development
	Iran 7000 (Scud-C variant)*	600/700	500	In Service

182

	System			
	Mushak-120 (Iran-130, Nazeat)*	130	500 or 190	In Service
	Mushak-160*	160	190	In Service
	Mushak-200*	200	500	In Development
	Shihab-3	1,300–2,000	750–1,200	In Development
	Shihab-4*	2,000–2,500 (or 4,000)	1,000	Possibly in Development
	Shihab-5*	10,000		Possibly in Development
	SS-1 Scud-B*	300	1,000	In Service
	Zelzal-1*	100–150		In Production
	Zelzal-2*	350–400		In Production
	Zelzal-3*	1,000–1,500		In Development
Israel	Jericho-1 (YA-1)	500	750*	In Service
	Jericho-2 (YA-3)	1,500	1,000*	In Service
	Jericho-3	4,800	500–1,000	In Service
North Korea	BM-25/Musudan	2,500–4,000	680******	In Development
	KN-02	100–120		In Development
	Nodong	1,300	1,000*	In Service
	Scud-B	300	1,000*	In Service
	Scud-C variant	500	700*	In Service
	Taepodong-1	2,200	1,000*******	Operational**
	Taepodong-2	3,500–6,000	1,000*******	In Development
Pakistan	Ghauri-2	1,500–2,300	700	In Development
	Ghauri-3	2,700–3,500		In Development
	Haft-1	80	500	Operational
	Haft-2	300	500	In Development
	Haft-3/Ghaznavi	280–400	500	In Service
	Haft-4/Shaheen-1	450	1,000	Operational
	Haft-5/Ghauri-1	1,300	500–750	In Development
	Haft-6	2,000–2,500	700	In Development
Russia***	Iskander-M			In Development
	R-24			In Development

Country	Missile			Status
	SS-18 Satan	9,000/11,000*	8,800*	In Service
	SS-19 Stiletto	10,000*	4,350*	In Service
	SS-25 Sickle	10,500*	1,000*	In Service
	SS-26/Iskander-E	280	480	Operational
	SS-27/Topol-M	10,500*	1,000	In Service/In Production
	SS-N-18 Stingray	6,500/8,000*	1,315*	All Removed from Subs
	SS-N-23 Skiff	8,300*	1,360*	In Service
	SS-NX-30 Bulava*******	10,000	1,000+	
Saudi Arabia	CSS-2 (DF-3)	2,400/2,800*	2,150*	Acquired from China/ Possibly Not Operational
South Korea******	ATACMS*	300	560	Operational
	NHK-1	180	560	In Service*
	NHK-2	300	500	In Service*
Syria******	Scud-B	300	1,000	In Service*
	Scud-C	500	600–770	In Service*
	Scud-D	700	500	In Development
	SS-21	120	480	In Service*
Taiwan	Ching Feng (Green Bee)	100+	400	In Service
	Tien Kung-1 (Sky Bow)			
	Tien Kung-2B			
	Tien Ma (Sky Horse)	600–1,000	500	Program Ended

Note on Sources: Unless otherwise noted, this table of selected ballistic missile programs includes missiles documented in the book. Supplementary sources include: Andrew Feickert, "Missile Survey: Ballistic and Cruise Missiles of Selected Countries," Congressional Research Service, July 26, 2005 (indicated in table by *), http://www.fas.org /sgp/crs/weapons/RL30427.pdf; "Ballistic and Cruise Missile Threat," National Air and Space Intelligence Center, March 2006 (indicated in table by **); Hans Kristensen, Nuclear Notebook: "India's Nuclear Forces, 2007" and "Pakistan's Nuclear Forces, 2007," *Bulletin of the Atomic Scientists*, July–August 2007 (indicated in table by ***); "Annual Report to Congress: Military Power of the People's Republic of China 2007," Washington, DC: Office of the Secretary of Defense, 2007 (indicated in table by ****), http:www.defenselink.mil/pubs/pdfs/070523-China-Military-Power-final.pdf; Pavel Podvig's estimates of "systems," listed in Strategic Russian Forces (as of January 2007) (indicated in table by *****), http://www.russianforces.org/; "Worldwide Ballistic Missile Inventories," Arms Control Association, September 2007 (indicated in table by ******), http://www.armscontrol.org/factsheets/missiles.asp.

Notes

PREFACE AND ACKNOWLEDGMENTS

1. Albert Wohlstetter, Foreword to K. Scott McMahon and Dennis M. Gormley, *Controlling the Spread of Land-Attack Cruise Missiles* (Marina del Rey, CA: American Institute for Strategic Cooperation, 1995).

2. Gregory F. Treverton, *Reshaping National Intelligence for an Age of Information* (New York: Cambridge University Press, 2003).

3. Kurt M. Campbell, Robert J. Einhorn, and Mitchell B. Reiss, eds., *The Nuclear Tipping Point: Why States Reconsider Their Nuclear Choices* (Washington, DC: The Brookings Institution, 2004).

CHAPTER 1

1. LACMs, one example of which is the U.S. Tomahawk cruise missile, are to be distinguished from widely proliferated anti-ship cruise missiles (ASCMs), 75,000 of which are now deployed by over 70 countries. LACMs generally have substantially longer ranges (300–3,000 km) than ASCMs and fly over land to their intended targets, while ASCMs are employed generally against ships at sea from comparatively shorter ranges (75–300 km). Unmanned air or aerial vehicles (UAVs) comprise a third category of unmanned systems that could assume missions involving delivery of weapons. Relegated, until recently, largely to reconnaissance and target-drone roles, UAVs such as the U.S. Predator have been adapted to deliver munitions, with some notable success attacking al-Qaeda targets in Afghanistan and Yemen. Armed UAVs such as Predator distinguish themselves from LACMs and ASCMs in that they can be reused. Finally, a fourth category consists of unmanned combat air vehicles (UCAVs), which are essentially high-performance aircraft flown by a ground operator (like Predator) that are capable of performing various lethal and nonlethal missions. Notably, unlike ballistic missiles, which for the most part operate outside the atmosphere, cruise missiles,

UAVs, and UCAVs are fitted with aerodynamic surfaces that furnish lift to keep them airborne, within the atmosphere, during their entire flight. See Dennis M. Gormley, "New Developments in Unmanned Air Vehicles and Land-Attack Cruise Missiles," in *SIPRI Yearbook 2003* (Oxford: Oxford University Press for SIPRI, 2003), 409–432.

2. "President Musharraf Compares Babur Missile with India's BrahMos," Islamabad PTV World (in English), August 11, 2005 (Foreign Broadcast Information Services [FBIS] transcribed text). The opening two paragraphs originally appeared in Dennis M. Gormley, "Cruise Control," *Bulletin of the Atomic Scientists* 62, no. 2 (March/April 2006): 26–33.

3. The other main hurdle is acquiring or building one's own propulsion system to achieve the desired range. See Dennis M. Gormley, *Dealing with the Threat of Cruise Missiles*, Adelphi Paper 339 (Oxford: Oxford University Press, 2001), 17–28.

4. For historical, technical, application, and policy details related to GPS technology, see Scott Pace et al., *The Global Positioning System: Assessing National Policies*, MR-614-OSTP (Santa Monica, CA: The RAND Corporation, 1995).

5. Joseph Cirincione, "The Declining Ballistic Missile Threat," Carnegie Endowment for International Peace, January 25, 2005, http://www.carnegieendowment.org/static/npp/Declining_Ballistic_Missile_Threat_2005.pdf.

6. W. Seth Carus, *Cruise Missile Proliferation in the 1990s* (Westport, CT: Praeger, 1992), 3.

7. K. Scott McMahon and Dennis M. Gormley, *Controlling the Spread of Land-Attack Cruise Missiles* (Marina del Ray, CA: American Institute for Strategic Cooperation, 1995), 26.

8. Making sense of epidemics, particularly social phenomena, was popularized most notably in Malcolm Gladwell, *The Tipping Point: How Little Things Can Make a Big Difference* (New York: Little, Brown and Co., 2000). For a popular science treatment, see Mark Buchanan, *Ubiquity: Why Catastrophes Happen* (New York: Three Rivers Press, 2001). As for its application to nuclear proliferation, see Kurt M. Campbell, Robert J. Einhorn, and Mitchell B. Reiss, eds., *The Nuclear Tipping Point: Why States Reconsider Their Nuclear Choices* (Washington, DC: The Brookings Institution, 2004).

9. *Report of the Defense Science Board Task Force on Nuclear Capabilities, Report Summary* (Washington, DC: Office of the Under Secretary of Defense for Acquisition, Technology, and Logistics, December 2006), http://www.fas.org/irp/agency/dod/dsb/nuclear.pdf.

10. For the classic treatment, see Michael Polanyi, *Personal Knowledge* (London: Routledge and Kegan Paul, 1958). As it applies to missile technology, see Donald MacKenzie, *Inventing Accuracy: A Historical Sociology of Nuclear Missile Guidance* (Cambridge, MA: MIT Press, 1990).

11. Donald MacKenzie, "Theories of Technology and the Abolition of Nuclear Weapons," in Donald MacKenzie and Judy Wajcman, eds., *The Social Shaping of Technology* (Philadelphia: Open University Press, 1999), 425–429.

12. See Donald MacKenzie and Graham Spinardi, "Tacit Knowledge, Weapons Design, and the Uninvention of Nuclear Weapons," *American Journal of Sociology* 101, no. 1 (July 1995): 44.

13. While the Rumsfeld Commission was formally tasked by Congress only to evaluate the threat of ballistic missiles to the United States, the Commission's final report did note that "cruise missiles have a number of characteristics which could be seen as increasingly valuable in fulfilling the aspirations of emerging ballistic missile states." Besides my and Dr. Gregory DeSantis's unclassified presentation, delivered on June 3, 1998, my separately delivered unclassified working paper, entitled "Transfer Pathways for Cruise Missiles," was also appended to

the Commission's full final report. For the Rumsfeld Commission's executive summary, see http://www.fas.org/irp/threat/bm-threat.htm.

14. *Comprehensive Report of the Special Advisor to the DCI on Iraq's WMD,* Vol. II (Washington, DC: Central Intelligence Agency, September 30, 2004), 39–41.

15. Ibid., 42–56.

16. "Focus on Iran," Geostrategy-Direct, October 18, 2005.

17. Gormley, *Dealing with the Threat of Cruise Missiles,* 9–10 (see Chap. 1, n. 3).

18. Ibid., 9. These advantages notwithstanding, possession of even a short-range ballistic missile puts a country on a path toward developing a much longer-range delivery system. Today's longest-range LACMs are limited to roughly a range of 3,000 km.

19. Dennis M. Gormley, "Missile Defence Myopia: Lessons from the Iraq War," *Survival* 45, no. 4 (Winter 2003–04): 61–86.

20. Michael R. Gordon, "A Poor Man's Air Force," *New York Times,* June 19, 2003, A1.

21. Dana Milbank and Dafna Linzer, "U.S., India May Share Nuclear Technology," *Washington Post,* July 19, 2005, A1. Such permission is required because of the significant presence of U.S. technology in the Arrow system.

22. "Pakistan Test Fires Nuclear-Capable Cruise Missile," Agence France-Presse (in English), March 22, 2007 (FBIS).

23. "Iran Seeks Cruise Missile to Support Shihab," *Middle East Newsline,* June 10, 2004.

24. For a useful treatment, see Dinshaw Mistry, *Containing Missile Proliferation* (Seattle, WA: University of Washington Press, 2003), 15–40.

25. Ariel E. Levite and Elizabeth Sherwood-Randall, "The Case for Discriminate Force," *Survival* 44, no. 4 (Winter 2002–03): 89–90.

26. Steve Andreasen and Dennis Gormley, "Edging Ever Closer to a Nuclear Death Row," *Minneapolis Star-Tribune,* March 29, 2006, 29.

27. S. M. Hali, "Exercise Vajra Shakti," *The Nation,* May 19, 2005.

28. "Preemptive Strike Ability Said Necessary for Japan," *Japan Times,* October 2, 2004.

29. Interviews with Japanese defense officials in Tokyo, March 2005.

30. Joint Publication 3–01.5, *Doctrine for Joint Theater Missile Defense* (Washington, DC: Government Printing Office, 1994).

31. Sources differ over the precise payload weight, with Korean news reports stating for the most part that regarding cruise missiles there is no restriction on range as long as the payload is under 500 kg.

32. "S. Korea's Cruise Missile Program Revealed," *Chosun Ilbo* (internet version, in English), October 25, 2006, http://english.chosun.com/w21data/html/news/200610/200610250007.html.

33. Chin Tae-ung, "Military Works on Nuclear Defense Plans," *The Korea Herald* (internet version, in English), October 28, 2006.

34. Instead of purchasing expensive American Patriot missile defenses, Seoul has turned to Germany to discuss buying a modest number of older, surplus Patriots. See Jin Dae-woong, "Korea, Germany Discuss Patriot Missile Deal," *The Korea Herald* (internet version, in English), March 13, 2007.

35. Wendell Minnick, "Taiwan Tests 'Brave Wind' Cruise Missile," *Defense News,* March 12, 2007, http://www.defensenews.com/story.php?F=2610742&C=asiapac.

36. Chang Li-the, "Taking a Look at Taiwan's Cruise Missile Requirements and Capabilities—A Report on the Successful Test-Firing of the Hsiung-Feng 2E,"*Defense Technology Monthly,* July 2005 (FBIS report in Chinese, October 3, 2005).

37.   Wu Ming-chieh, "Publicizing Cruise Missile Meant to Pressure United States into Exporting Technology," *Taipei Chung-Kuo Shih-Pao* (internet version, in Chinese), April 27, 2007 (FBIS translated text in English).

38.   I am grateful to Sharad Joshi, on whose PhD dissertation committee I served, for drawing my attention to Indian interest in preemptive strategy. See Sharad Joshi, *The Practice of Coercive Diplomacy in the Post 9/11 Period,* Unpublished PhD dissertation, Graduate School of Public and International Affairs, University of Pittsburgh, December 2006. Also see Walter C. Ladwig III, "A Cold Start for Hot Wars? The Indian Army's New Limited War Doctrine," *International Security* 32, no. 3 (Winter 2007/08): 158–190.

39.   "No Time to Lose," *New Delhi Force* (internet version, in English), March 9, 2005 (FBIS transcribed text).

40.   The asymmetric use of swarming tactics, consisting of large numbers of small fast patrol boats, complemented by large-volume cruise missile attacks from land and the air, was featured prominently in a 2002 U.S. war game in which such adversary tactics overwhelmed the U.S. Navy's capacity to deal with the attack, leading to its rapid defeat. The implicit threat of such tactics became evident in early January 2008 when Iranian speedboats harassed three U.S. Navy vessels in the Strait of Hormuz, but without incident. See Thom Shanker, "Iran Encounter Grimly Echoes '02 War Game," *New York Times,* January 12, 2008, A1.

41.   "NIE 95–19: Independent Panel Review of 'Emerging Missile Threats to North America During the Next 15 Years,' " December 1996, http://www.fas.org/news/usa/1997/02/msg00032b.htm.

42.   John Liang, "DoD Finds Cruise Missile Defense 'Gaps,' " *InsideDefense.com News-Stand,* August 17, 2006, http://www.military.com/features/0,15240,110199,00.html.

43.   James C. Mulvenon, et al., *Chinese Responses to U.S. Military Transformation and Implications for the Department of Defense* (Santa Monica, CA: The RAND Corporation, 2006), 50.

CHAPTER 2

1.   Steve Fetter, "Ballistic Missiles and Weapons of Mass Destruction," *International Security* 16, no. 4 (Summer 1991): 12.

2.   R. V. Jones, *Most Secret War: British Scientific Intelligence 1939–1945* (London: Hamish Hamilton, 1978), 455, as cited in Aaron Karp, *Ballistic Missile Proliferation: The Politics and Technics* (Oxford: Oxford University Press, 1996), 48.

3.   Karp, *Ballistic Missile Proliferation,* 41 (see Chap. 2, n. 2).

4.   Richard K. Betts, "Innovation, Assessment, and Decision," in Richard K. Betts, ed., *Cruise Missiles: Technology, Strategy, Politics* (Washington, DC: The Brookings Institution, 1981), 5.

5.   Karp, *Ballistic Missile Proliferation,* 45 (see Chap. 2, n. 2) reports that half of Tehran's population evacuated the city as a consequence of 1988's intense al-Hussein missile strikes. Other sources report a figure of one-third of the population. See K. S. Chun, *Thunder Over the Horizon* (Westport, CT: Praeger Security International, 2006), 121, and the GlobalSecurity.org web site, http://www.globalsecurity.org/military/world/war/iran-iraq.htm.

6.   GlobalSecurity.org web site (see Chap. 2, n. 5).

7.   W. Seth Carus, *Ballistic Missiles in the Third World: Threat and Response* (Westport, CT: Praeger, 1990), 4–5.

8. Karp, *Ballistic Missile Proliferation,* 36 (see Chap. 2, n. 2).

9. Dennis M. Gormley and K. Scott McMahon, "Who's Guarding the Back Door?" *Jane's International Defense Review* 29 (May 1996): 21–24.

10. Karp, *Ballistic Missile Proliferation,* 46 (see Chap. 2, n. 2).

11. K. Scott McMahon, *Pursuit of the Shield: The US Quest for Limited Ballistic Missile Defense* (Lanham, MD: University Press of America, 1997), 55–92, 297–306.

12. Andrea Stone, "Friend or Foe to Allied Troops," *USA Today,* April 14, 2003, http://www.usatoday.com/news/world/iraq/2003-04-14-patriot-missile_x.htm.

13. Only 1 of 39 Iraqi missiles fired at Israel was successfully intercepted. See my unsigned essay, "Defending Against Iraqi Missiles," *IISS Strategic Comments* 8, no. 8 (October 2002).

14. The reasons behind Patriot's immature status in August 1990 relate largely to the fact that during the Reagan administration's second term, the Patriot program came close to cancellation. Not only the White House but the services as well were less concerned with defending against short- and medium-range ballistic missiles than against Soviet intercontinental-range ones. In a Senate hearing in January 1986, my testimony drew attention to Patriot's immaturity to deal with emerging missile threats. See U.S. Congress, Senate Committee on Armed Services, *Soviet Military Developments and NATO Antitactical Ballistic Missile Defenses: Hearings Before the Committee on Armed Services,* S. HRG. 99–804, PR 4, 99th Congress, 2nd session, January 30, 1986.

15. "Defending Against Iraqi Missiles" (see Chap. 2, n. 13).

16. For an account of Patriot's performance, see Dennis M. Gormley, "Missile Defence Myopia: Lessons from the Iraq War" *Survival* 45, no. 4 (Winter 2003–04): 61–86.

17. These shortcomings are analyzed in Chapter 4 of Dennis M. Gormley, *Dealing with the Threat of Cruise Missiles,* Adelphi Paper 339 (Oxford: Oxford University Press, 2001).

18. Karp, *Ballistic Missile Proliferation,* 47 (see Chap. 2, n. 2).

19. Quoted in Hajo Holborn, "The Prussian-German School: Moltke and the Rise of the General Staff," in Peter Paret, ed., *Makers of Modern Strategy* (Princeton: Princeton University Press, 1986), 289.

20. N. V. Ogarkov, *Krasnaya Zvezda,* May 9, 1984 (BBC Monitoring Service translation [SU/7/639/C/10]).

21. Originally called the SAM-D (Surface-to-Air Missile, Development) when it was first conceived in 1964, the Patriot air defense system was developed to deal exclusively with aerodynamic, not ballistic missile, threats. In 1988, the system was upgraded to provide a limited capability (in diverting the direction of the incoming missile rather than destroying its warhead) against tactical ballistic missiles.

22. For an elaboration, see Dennis M. Gormley, *Double Zero and Soviet Military Strategy: Implications for Western Security* (London: Jane's Publishing Co., 1988).

23. Ibid., 62.

24. Based on information provided by Jane's Strategic Weapons Systems, the SS-23 missile's technical specifications can be found at http://www.aeronautics.ru/archive/wmd/ballistic/ballistic/ss23-01.htm. By comparison, U.S. terminal guidance systems for ballistic missiles such as Pershing II, which was also eliminated under the provisions of the 1987 INF Treaty, produced roughly the same CEP as the SS-23.

25. Robert P. Berman, *Soviet Air Power in Transition* (Washington, DC: The Brookings Institution, 1978), 31.

26. Central Intelligence Agency, National Foreign Assessment Center, *Estimated Soviet Defense Spending: Trends and Prospects* (Washington, DC: Government Printing Office, 1978), 3–4.

27. Lt. Col. D. J. Alberts, *Deterrence in the 1980s, Part II: The Role of Conventional Airpower,* Adelphi Paper 193 (London: International Institute for Strategic Studies, 1984), 18–19.

28. A. I. Eiseev, "On Certain Trends in Change in the Content and Nature of the Initial Period of War," *Voyenno-istoricheskiy Zhurnal* (November 1985): 15.

29. For the classic treatment, see Marshal V. D. Sokolovskiy, *Soviet Military Strategy,* Harriet Fast Scott, ed., 3rd ed. (New York: Crane, Russak, 1975).

30. B. T. Surikov, *Combat Employment of Ground Forces' Missiles* (Moscow: Voyenizdat, 1979), 160–161.

31. Gormley, *Double Zero and Soviet Military Strategy,* Chapter 2 (see Chap. 2, n. 22).

32. Roger Cliff, et al., *Entering the Dragon's Lair: Chinese Antiaccess Strategies and Their Implications for the United States* (Santa Monica, CA: The RAND Corporation, 2007), 28–29. Also of value regarding Chinese military doctrine is James C. Mulvenon and David M. Finkelstein, eds., *China's Revolution in Doctrinal Affairs: Emerging Trends in the Operational Art of the Chinese People's Liberation Army* (Alexandria, VA: CNA Corporation, 2005).

33. Mark A. Stokes, "The Chinese Joint Aerospace Campaign: Strategy, Doctrine, and Force Modernization," in Mulvenon and Finkelstein, eds., *China's Revolution in Doctrinal Affairs,* 256 (see Chap. 2, n. 32).

34. Paul Bracken, *Fire in the East: The Rise of Asian Military Power and the Second Nuclear Age* (New York: Harper Collins, 2000), 58.

35. It should also be noted that missile strikes against runway surfaces could also pin aircraft out, rather than down, meaning that aircraft may well escape their airfields but have no immediate runway surface to return to for ordnance refurbishment and logistical support.

36. Stokes, "The Chinese Joint Aerospace Campaign," 256 (see Chap. 2, n. 32, 33).

37. The Voroshilov General Staff Academy lectures were acquired by the U.S. intelligence community in the 1980s and subsequently declassified and released to specialists first and then the general public, when they were published by the National Defense University. They are now available through the Defense Technical Information Center. See, for example, http://stinet.dtic.mil/oai/oai?&verb=getRecord&metadataPrefix=html&identifier=ADA233504. The material cited here is taken from Phillip A. Petersen and John R. Clark, "Soviet Air and Antiair Operations," *Air University Review* (March–April 1985): 12.

38. Stokes, "The Chinese Joint Aerospace Campaign," 256 (see Chap. 2, n. 32, 33).

39. Ibid.

40. A. A. Sidorenko, *The Offensive* (Moscow: Voyenizdat, 1970), translated and published by the U.S. Air Force (Washington, DC: Government Printing Office, 1974), 22.

41. On the lessons derived from war games at Newport in the 1920s, see Barry Watts and Williamson Murray, "Military Innovation in Peacetime," in Williamson Murray and Allan R. Millett, eds., *Military Innovation in the Interwar Period* (Cambridge, UK: Cambridge University Press, 1998), 392. And for the classic naval treatment of the virtues of attacking effectively first, see Wayne P. Hughes, Jr., *Fleet Tactics: Theory and Practice* (Annapolis, MD: Naval Institute Press, 1986).

42. The Chinese estimate is based on information in *Annual Report to Congress: Military Power of the People's Republic of China 2007* (Washington, DC: Office of the Secretary of Defense, 2007), http:www.defenselink.mil/pubs/pdfs/070523-China-Military-Power-final.

pdf. For the rationale for Soviet launcher numbers, see Gormley, *Double Zero and Soviet Military Strategy,* Chapter 2 (see Chap. 2, n. 22).

43.   *Jane's All the World Air Forces,* Issue 25 (February 2007), 527–532.

44.   For a balanced appraisal of China's capacity to execute such a campaign in the future, see Cliff et al., *Entering the Dragon's Lair* (see Chap. 2, n. 32).

45.   Joseph Cirincione, "The Declining Ballistic Missile Threat, 2005," Carnegie Policy Outlook, February 2005, http://www.carnegieendowment.org/pdf/The_Declining_Ballistic_Missile_Threat_2005.pdf. At the time of publication, Cirincione was director for nonproliferation at the Carnegie Endowment for International Peace, in Washington, D.C.

46.   The Russian deployment figures were taken from the web site Russian Strategic Nuclear Forces, compiled by Pavel Podvig of Stanford University's Center for International Security and Cooperation, http://russianforces.org/missiles/. U.S. deployment figures were derived from "U.S. Nuclear Forces, 2007," *Bulletin of the Atomic Scientists* 63, no. 1 (January/February 2007), 79–82.

47.   "Iran Bought Missiles From North Korea: Press," *Defense News,* December 16, 2005, http://dfn.dnmediagroup.com/story.php?F=1415703&C=mideast and Ze'ev Schiff, "New Iranian Missiles Put Europe in Firing Range," *Tel Aviv Ha'aretz* (internet version, in English), April 27, 2006.

48.   Sharad Joshi and Peter Crail, "India Successfully Tests Agni-III: A Stepping Stone to an ICBM?" *WMD Insights* (May 2007), http://cns.miis.edu/pubs/other/wmdi0705b.htm.

49.   Cirincione, "The Declining Ballistic Missile Threat, 2005," 6–7, 11 (see Chap. 2, n. 45).

50.   "Executive Summary of the Report of the Commission to Assess the Ballistic Missile Threat to the United States," July 15, 1998, http://www.fas.org/irp/threat/bm-threat.htm.

51.   "Executive Summary of the Report of the Commission to Assess the Ballistic Missile Threat to the United States." The Rumsfeld Commission concluded that lightweight versions of the North Korean Taepodong-2 were capable of flying as far as 10,000 km, placing the western United States at risk. Of course, the notion of producing a small-diameter nuclear weapon for, say, a 200-kg warhead is still problematical today. For a recent, less bullish appraisal of North Korean capabilities, see "CNS Special Report on North Korean Ballistic Missile Capabilities," March 22, 2006, http://cns.miis.edu/pubs/week/pdf/060321.pdf.

52.   For a still-useful appraisal of the difficult challenges of ballistic missile staging and separation, see Karp, *Ballistic Missile Proliferation,* 132–137 (see Chap. 2, n. 2).

CHAPTER 3

1.   Janne Nolan, *Trappings of Power: Ballistic Missiles in the Third World* (Washington, DC: The Brookings Institution, 1991).

2.   According to GlobalSecurity.org, the Syrian chemical arsenal contains mustard gas, sarin, tabun, and VX. Besides several thousand aerial bombs, Syria, which has not signed the Chemical Weapons Convention (CWC), is thought to have produced between 50 and 100 warheads for its missile arsenal. See http://www.globalsecurity.org/wmd/world/syria/cw.htm. Iran, for its part, signed and ratified the CWC and declared and eliminated two chemical weapons production facilities, but it remains most uncertain that Iran has chosen to forgo its chemical arsenal, which is believed to contain both blister and nerve agents, including the highly persistent nerve agent VX. Iran used chemical agents in response to Iraq's use during their 1980–1988 war. See http://www.globalsecurity.org/wmd/world/iran/cw.htm.

3. *Ballistic and Cruise Missile Threat,* (Wright-Patterson Air Force Base, OH: National Air and Space Intelligence Center, March 2006), 4–6.

4. See Nuclear Threat Initiative's "Syria Profile, Missile Overview," http://www.nti.org/e_research/profiles/Syria/Missile/index.html.

5. See "Syrian Ballistic Missile Arsenal," April 16, 2003, http://www.defense-update.com/2003/04/syrian-ballistic-missile-arsenal.html.

6. Ibid.

7. See, for example, Aharon Levran, "The Military Balance in the Middle East," in Aharon Levran, ed., *The Middle East Military Balance: 1987–1988* (Boulder, CO: Westview Press, 1988), 224, as quoted in Nolan, *Trappings of Power,* 79 (see Chap. 3, n. 1). CEP estimates are my own.

8. See details at http://www.globalsecurity.org/military/world/syria/airforce.htm.

9. For details on the Arrow-2 missile, see http://www.israeli-weapons.com/weapons/missile_systems/surface_missiles/arrow/Arrow.html.

10. See my unsigned essay, "Defending against Iraqi Missiles," *IISS Strategic Comments* 8, no. 8 (October 2002) for a general description and assessment of Israel's missile defense capabilities.

11. Lee Kass, "Syria After Lebanon: The Growing Syrian Missile Threat," *Middle East Quarterly* 12, no. 4 (Fall 2005), http://www.meforum.org/article/755. For technical details on the SS-26, see http://www.fas.org/nuke/guide/russia/theater/ss-26.htm.

12. The MTCR takes into consideration the fact that a missile can achieve greater range by trading off warhead weight for extra range. The Iskander's announced payload is 480 kg—and like its export model, it is just under the regime's 300-km-range threshold. But the fact that there is a 480-km-range version casts suspicion on the export model's true range and payload capability—a matter Moscow would have to attend to if it decides to sell the missile. Also in light of the general consensus that Syria possesses chemical warheads for its missiles, Moscow would be obligated under the MTCR to obtain end-use assurances from Syria that the missile would not be used to deliver such a chemical payload—a dubious proposition indeed. For relevant details, see K. Scott McMahon and Dennis M. Gormley, *Controlling the Spread of Land-Attack Cruise Missiles* (Marina del Ray, CA: American Institute for Strategic Cooperation, 1995), 32–35.

13. According to Uzi Rubin, the SS-26's speed is 1,500 m per second, or roughly Mach 4.4. Quoted in Kass, "Syria after Lebanon" (see Chap. 3, n. 11).

14. See Barbara Opall-Rome, "Sensor to Shooter in 1 Minute," *Defense News,* October 2, 2006, 1. Opall-Rome reports "over 100" Hezbollah rocket launchers were destroyed. The figure, 125, is reported in No'am Ofir, "Look Not to the Skies: The IAF vs. Surface-to-Surface Rocket Launchers," *Strategic Assessment,* November 1–30, 2006, e-mail text published by the Jaffee Center for Strategic Studies, Tel Aviv, Israel, http://www.inss.org.il/.

15. Kass, "Syria after Lebanon" (see Chap. 3, n. 11).

16. "Syria Profile, Missile Overview" (see Chap. 3, n. 4).

17. The Wisconsin Project on Nuclear Arms Control reported in 2005 that Syria was expected to seek such items as machine tools, flow-forming machines, autoclaves, and measurement and control equipment, all key to solid-rocket motor production. See http://www.wisconsinproject.org/countries/syria/syria-missile-update2005.html. The Jericho-3's operational status was reportedly revealed by the Wisconsin Project. See list-serve e-mail

report, "Jericho III Missile Distance Capability Extended," produced by Joseph P. Durant, Riverside Research Institute—Boston Research Office, dated May 3, 2007.

18. See *The Wednesday Report: Canada's Aerospace & Defence Weekly,* http://www.thewednesdayreport.com/twr/syria/syria.htm.

19. Israel also has the 130-km-range Lance missile, supplied by the United States. See the Wisconsin Project's web site for details at http://www.wisconsinproject.org/countries/israel/IsraelMissile2005.html.

20. This range estimate is referred to at the GlobalSecurity.org web site, http://www.globalsecurity.org/wmd/world/israel/jericho-2.htm.

21. For one such view, see Louis René Beres, "Israel's Uncertain Strategic Future," *Parameters* 37, no. 1 (Spring 2007): 37–54, http://www.carlisle.army.mil/USAWC/Parameters/07spring/beres.pdf.

22. Uzi Rubin, *The Global Reach of Iran's Ballistic Missiles,* Memorandum 86 (Tel Aviv: Institute for National Security Studies, November 2006), 18–19.

23. "Iran's Ballistic Missiles: Upgrades Underway," *IISS Strategic Comments* 9, no. 9 (November 2003).

24. Rubin, *The Global Reach of Iran's Ballistic Missiles,* 7 (see Chap. 3, n. 22).

25. These conclusions are consistent with Rubin's (ibid., 46–47) and, with respect to Iran's quest for an ICBM, with the CIA's National Intelligence Estimate. See National Intelligence Council, "Foreign Missile Developments and the Ballistic Missile Threat to the United States through 2015," December 2001, 6.

26. "Iran's Ballistic Missile Program," Wisconsin Project on Nuclear Arms Control, August 2004, 2, http://www.iranwatch.org/wmd/wmd-iranmissileessay.htm.

27. Uzi Rubin detects signs of Soviet design technique in the extended-range Shihab-3: it is longer than the earlier version and has a redesigned reentry vehicle with a "baby-bottle-like shape." Rubin, *The Global Reach of Iran's Ballistic Missiles,* 19–20 (see Chap. 3, n. 22).

28. Andrew Feickert, "Iran's Ballistic Missile Capabilities," Congressional Research Service Report for Congress, RS21548 (August 23, 2004). For confirmation of the Musudan, see "N. Korea Believed to be Developing Intermediate-Range Missile From Early 2000s," *Yonhap News,* May 18, 2007, as cited in Daniel A. Pinkston, "North Korea Displays Ballistic Missiles During Military Parade, Some for First Time," *WMD Insights* (June 2007),http://www.wmdinsights.com/I16/I16_EA1_NKDisplays.htm.

29. "Iran's Ballistic Missile Program," 6 (see Chap. 3, n. 26).

30. Based on an analysis of the missile by Charles P. Vick, GlobalSecurity.org, http://www.globalsecurity.org/wmd/world/dprk/nd-b.htm.

31. Rubin, *The Global Reach of Iran's Ballistic Missiles,* 30 (see Chap. 3, n. 22).

32. Ibid., 32.

33. Charles P. Vick, "The Closely Related Collaborative Iranian, North Korean & Pakistani Strategic Space, Ballistic Missile and Nuclear Weapon Program," GlobalSecurity.org, May 23, 2006, http://globalsecurity.org/wmd/world/iran/missile-development.htm and "Taepo-dong 2 (TD2)," GlobalSecurity.org, July 1, 2006, http://www.globalsecurity.org/wmd/world/dprk/td-2.htm.

34. Iran's geography provides it with a variety of options for developing a safe and optimally positioned launch location to place satellites in an appropriate orbital inclination. There are also several satellite programs already underway, including one (Safrir 313) slated for eventual launch into low earth orbit. See Rubin, *The Global Reach of Iran's Ballistic Missiles,* 40–42 (see Chap. 3, n. 22).

35. Khalid Hilal and Jack Boureston, "Iran's Announcement of a Space Rocket Test: Fact or Fiction," *WMD Insights* (April 2007), http://cns.miis.edu/pubs/other/wmdi070404.htm.

36. "Iran's Ballistic Missile Programs," 6 (see Chap. 3, n. 26).

37. Ibid., 7.

38. "U.S. Congressmen Attack India's Relations with Iran, Link This to Nuclear Deal," *The Hindu,* May 6, 2007, http://www.hindu.com/2007/05/06/stories/2007050604280800.htm.

39. Richard Speier, "U.S. Space Aid to India: On a 'Glide Path' to ICBM Trouble," *Arms Control Today* 36, no. 2 (March 2006), http://www.armscontrol.org/act/2006_03/MARCH-IndiaFeature.asp.

40. Ibid.

41. These accomplishments are listed in Dr. Kalam's biography, which can be found at his personal web site, at http://www.abdulkalam.com/kalam/index.jsp.

42. India has expressed keen interest in Israeli airborne radars, unmanned reconnaissance drones, air-to-surface munitions, and, most notably, the Arrow ballistic missile defense system. See Harsh V. Pant, "India-Israel Partnership: Convergence and Constraints," *Middle East Review of International Affairs* 8, no. 4 (December 2004), http://meria.idc.ac.il/journal/2004/issue4/jv8no4a6.html.

43. Varun Sahni, "India and Missile Acquisition: Push and Pull Factors," *South Asian Survey* 11, no. 2 (2004), 292–293.

44. Sharad Joshi and Peter Crail, "India Successfully Tests Agni-III: A Stepping Stone to an ICBM?" *WMD Insights* (May 2007), http://cns.miis.edu/pubs/other/wmdi0705b.htm.

45. Quoted in Joseph Cirincione, Jon B. Wolfsthal, and Miriam Rajkumar, *Deadly Arsenals: Nuclear, Biological, and Chemical Threats* (Washington, DC: Carnegie Endowment for International Peace, 2005), 228.

46. Ibid., 228–229, and *Ballistic and Cruise Missile Threat,* 6 (see Chap. 3, n. 3).

47. "Production Sample of Prithvi Missile to be Test Fired by Indian Army," http://www.india-defence.com/reports/3132.

48. Bharat Rakshak, "Agni-I MRBM," http://www.bharat-rakshak.com/MISSILES/Agni-I.html.

49. Ibid.

50. Joshi and Crail, "India Successfully Tests Agni-III" (see Chap. 3, n. 44).

51. Cirincione, Wolfsthal, and Rajkumar, *Deadly Arsenals,* 252 (see Chap. 3, n. 45).

52. Ibid., 250–251 and "Pakistan's Nuclear Forces," *Bulletin of the Atomic Scientists* 63, no. 3 (May/June 2007), 71–73.

53. Cirincione, Wolfsthal, and Rajkumar, *Deadly Arsenals,* 251–252 (see Chap. 3, n. 45).

54. Dennis M. Gormley and Lawrence Scheinman, "Implications of Proposed India-U.S. Civil Nuclear Cooperation," Issue Brief, July 2005, http://www.nti.org/e_research/e3_67a.html.

55. Dana Milbank and Dafna Linzer, "U.S., India May Share Nuclear Technology," *Washington Post,* July 19, 2005, A1.

56. India Defence Consultants, "What's Hot?—Analysis of Recent Happenings," March 15, 2004, http://www.indiadefence.com/rice-visit.htm.

57. Ibid. Also see Gormley and Scheinman, "Implications of Proposed India-U.S. Civil Nuclear Cooperation" (see Chap. 3, n. 54).

58. See the Israeli.Weapons.com web site, http://www.israeli-weapons.com/weapons/missile_systems/surface_missiles/arrow/Arrow.html.

59. "Missile Defense: DRDO To Test Ballistic Missile Interceptor in June 2007," http://www.india-defence.com/reports/3156.

60. For the argument that economic growth and cooperation might stabilize regional tensions, see Denny Roy, "The Sources and Limits of Sino-Japanese Tensions," *Survival* 47, no. 2 (Summer 2005): 191–214.

61. These South Korean views are those of Jun Kyung-man, vice director of the Korea Institute for Defense Analyses, the Republic of Korea's premier state-run defense think tank. See Jung Sung-ki, "S. Korea in Nutcracker of Regional Arms Race," *The Korea Times* (internet version, in English), May 20, 2007.

62. Ibid.

63. Carl E. Behrens, "Space Launch Vehicles: Government Activities, Commercial Competition, and Satellite Exports," *CRS Issue Brief for Congress,* Congressional Research Service, March 20, 2006, http://www.fas.org/sgp/crs/space/IB93062.pdf.

64. Reiji Yoshida, "Missile Defense Plans Have Their Skeptics," *The Japan Times,* July 28, 2006, http://search.japantimes.co.jp/cgi-bin/nn20060728f1.html.

65. See "China's Missile Imports and Other Assistance from Russia," Nuclear Threat Initiative, "China Profiles," produced by the Monterey Institute's Center for Nonproliferation Studies, http://www.nti.org/db/China/imrus.htm.

66. Jim Mann, "Russia Boosting China's Arsenal," *Los Angeles Times,* November 30, 1992, as cited in ibid.

67. "China's Missile Imports and Other Assistance from Russia" (see Chap. 3, n. 65).

68. Jing-Dong Yuan, "Effective, Reliable, and Credible: China's Nuclear Modernization," *Nonproliferation Review* 14, no. 2 (July 2007), 291–292.

69. Ibid.

70. *Annual Report to Congress: Military Power of the People's Republic of China 2007* (Washington, DC: Office of the Secretary of Defense, 2007), 19, http:www.defenselink.mil/pubs/pdfs/070523-China-Military-Power-final.pdf.

71. Jing-Dong Yuan, "Effective, Reliable, and Credible," 292 (see Chap. 3, n. 68).

72. *Annual Report to Congress: Military Power of the People's Republic of China 2007,* 4 (see Chap. 3, n. 70).

73. Wu Ming-chieh, "Publicizing Cruise Missile Meant to Pressure United States into Exporting Technology," *Taipei Chung-Kuo Shih-Pao* (internet version, in Chinese), April 27, 2007.

74. Dinshaw Mistry, *Containing Missile Proliferation* (Seattle, WA: University of Washington Press, 2003), 97.

75. Ibid.

76. GlobalSecurity.org, http://www.globalsecurity.org/military/world/taiwan/skybow-1.htm.

77. Dinshaw Mistry, *Constraining Missile Proliferation,* 99 (see Chap. 3, n. 74).

78. Ibid.

79. This account relies on Dinshaw Mistry, *Constraining Missile Proliferation,* 90–97 (see Chap. 3, n. 74).

80. Ibid., 96. Mistry reports that the 2001 agreement between Seoul and Washington stipulated that the 500-km-range cruise missile could carry a 400-kg payload. However, more recent press reports stipulate that the payload must remain below 500 kg. See, for example, "South Korea Develops Own Cruise Missile, Media Say," *Associated Press,* September 22, 2006, http://www.taipeitimes.com/News/world/archives/2006/09/22/2003328727.

81.   The test missile only reached a distance of 40 km, but presumably based on U.S. intelligence forensics, the missile possessed enough capability to reach 300 km. See MissileThreat.com, http://www.missilethreat.com/missilesoftheworld/id.81/missile_detail.asp.

82.   "S. Korea's Cruise Missile Program Revealed," *Chosun Ilbo* (internet version, in English), October 25, 2006, http://english.chosun.com/w21data/html/news/200610/200610250007.html.

83.   "India Missiles: S. Korea Interested," *The Asian Age* (internet version, in English), May 31, 2007, http://www.asianage.com.

84.   See Daniel A. Pinkston, "South Korea, Russia Seek to Accelerate Development of South Korean Space Launch Vehicle," *WMD Insights* (May 2007), http://cns.miis.edu/pubs/other/wmdi0705c.htm.

85.   For the unclassified summary of the December 2001 National Intelligence Estimate "Foreign Missile Developments and the Ballistic Missile Threat Through 2015," see http://www.fas.org/spp/starwars/CIA-NIE.htm.

86.   Unless otherwise noted, details on North Korean missiles are drawn from "CNS Special Report on North Korean Ballistic Missile Capabilities," March 22, 2006, http://cns.miis.edu/pubs/week/pdf/060321.pdf.

CHAPTER 4

1.   At the very least, China, Taiwan, South Korea, and India began LACM programs in the 1990s.

2.   A United Nations Panel of Governmental Experts took a decidedly different view of missile proliferation in 2002. See United Nations General Assembly, *The Issue of Missiles in All Its Aspects: Report of the Secretary-General,* UN Document A/57/229, July 23, 2002. For an example of this different view of missile proliferation, see also Jurgen Scheffran, "Missiles in Conflict: The Issue of Missiles in All Its Complexity," *Disarmament Forum* 1 (2007): 11–22.

3.   M. L. Cummings, "The Double-Edged Sword of Secrecy in Military Weapon Development," *IEEE Technology and Society Magazine* (Winter 2003–2004): 4–12.

4.   On GPS and its impact on the spread of LACMs, see Dennis M. Gormley, *Dealing with the Threat of Cruise Missiles,* Adelphi Paper 339 (Oxford: Oxford University Press, 2001), 19–21.

5.   Early cruise missiles were so inaccurate due to the fact that inertial navigation systems accumulate errors as a function of the distance (time) they fly. Integrating a GPS receiver together with a cheap inertial navigation system allows it to correct accumulated errors and send correction signals to the cruise missile's flight management system, which adjust the missile's course to bring it precisely back on its intended preprogrammed course to the target. This low-cost solution essentially eliminates the need for TERCOM guidance altogether, although many industrial countries still use both TERCOM and GPS/INS solutions for reasons of redundancy.

6.   David J. Nicholls, *Cruise Missiles and Modern War: Strategic and Technical Implications,* Occasional Paper No. 13 (Maxwell Air Force Base, AL: Center for Strategy and Technology, Air War College, 2000), 10–12. Nicholls compared a $300,000 cruise missile with a $30 million aircraft. Seven years after his analysis, the cost of cruise missiles generally has

dropped while aircraft costs continue to escalate. The unit cost of the F-22 Raptor, according to a 2006 Government Accountability Office estimate, is $361 million (whereas the incremental cost of each additional F-22 would be around $120 million). Nicholls also included four JDAM weapons costing $20,000 each and assumed that the cost of aircraft support operations was twice its procurement cost. Cruise missile support was assumed to be 10 percent of the weapon's cost. For alternative views on the cost of each F-22 Raptor, see James W. Rawley, "F-22—Super Stealth, Super Fast, Super Costly," Media General News Service, http://originmedia.mgnetwork.com/breaking/f22raptor/.

7. Whereas a Scud missile might cost between $500,000 and $1 million and a Chinese M-9 close to $2 million, cruise missiles can be acquired for between $250,000 and $1 million. Gormley, *Dealing with the Threat of Cruise Missiles,* 53 (see Chap. 4, n. 4).

8. For an analysis of Tomahawk effectiveness, see *Operation Desert Storm: Evaluation of the Air Campaign* (Washington, DC: Government Accounting Office, June 1997), 139–143. Additional analyses after Operation Desert Storm found serious weaknesses in the military's capacity to assess battle damage, which only muddied the water further in regard to determining Tomahawk's true effectiveness.

9. See the Federation of American Scientists' web site at http://www.fas.org/man/dod-101/sys/smart/bgm-109.htm.

10. Defense Update, http://www.defense-update.com/products/s/storm-shadow.htm.

11. On the importance of air superiority and sorties flown, see Andrew Krepinevich, "Operation Iraqi Freedom: A First Blush Assessment," September 16, 2003, http://www.csbaonline.org/4Publications/PubLibrary/R.20030916.Operation_Iraqi_Fr/R.20030916.Operation_Iraqi_Fr.php.

12. Ibid.

13. Dennis M. Gormley, "Missile Defence Myopia: Lessons from the Iraq War," *Survival* 45, no. 4 (Winter 2003–04): 61–86.

14. David C. Isby, "Cruise Missiles Flew Half the Desert Fox Strike Missions," *Jane's Missiles and Rockets,* February 12, 1999.

15. "Statement of RADM Michael G. Mullen, U.S. Navy before the Seapower Subcommittee, Senate Armed Services Committee, on Surface Warfare Systems for the 21st Century," March 23, 2000, http://www.navy.mil/navydata/testimony/seapower/mullen0323.txt.

16. See http://en.wikipedia.org/wiki/BGM-109_Tomahawk.

17. Lee Willett, "TLAM and British Strategic Thought," *Undersea Warfare* 2, no. 3 (Spring 2000), http://www.navy.mil/navydata/cno/n87/usw/issue_7/tlam.html. Of course, Russian pressure on Milocevic arguably played an equally important role in compelling Serbia to come to terms with NATO's demands.

18. "Cruise missiles and smart bombs used in Afghanistan," *Jane's Missiles and Rockets,* November 1, 2001.

19. See http://www.navy.mil/navydata/testimony/seapower/mullen0323.txt.

20. Daniel Benjamin and Steven Simon, *The Age of Sacred Terror* (New York: Random House, 2001), 294. The time included presidential decisionmaking, spinning the missile's gyroscopes, and flight time to the target.

21. "BGM-109 Tomahawk," GlobalSecurity.org, http://www.globalsecurity.org/military/systems/munitions/bgm-109-var.htm.

22. Some may trade off a few LACMs for special operations minisubs or small UAVs for reconnaissance missions.

23. The first articulation of the Bush administration's strategy of preemption was formulated in September 2002. It was reaffirmed in March 2006. For the text of the 2006 strategy document, see http://www.whitehouse.gov/nsc/nss/2006/sectionV.html.

24. Andy Nativi, "Lockheed Martin Bets on New Concepts to Shore Up Weapons Business," *Aviation Week & Space Technology,* May 28, 2007, 46.

25. For more on the Global Strike Force concept and hypersonic cruise vehicles, see Dennis M. Gormley, "Conventional Force Integration in Global Strike," in James J. Wirtz and Jeffrey A. Larsen, eds., *Nuclear Transformation: The New U.S. Nuclear Doctrine* (New York: Palgrave, 2005), 53–68.

26. Gormley, *Dealing with the Threat of Cruise Missiles,* 93–94 (see Chap. 4, n. 4).

27. Bill Gertz, "Analysts Missed Chinese Buildup," *Washington Times,* June 9, 2005.

28. Daniel A. Pinkston, "South Korean Response to North Korean July Missile Exercise Includes Unveiling of New Cruise Missile," *WMD Insights* (October 4, 2006), http://cns.miis.edu/pubs/other/wmdi061004_pinkston.htm.

29. In 2001, China, France, Britain, Germany, Sweden, and South Africa had LACM programs under development, while only the United States, Russia, and Israel had completed LACM programs. Of these countries, all were MTCR member states except for China and Israel, who were adherents to the regime's missile guidelines.

30. In 2001 MBDA was created with the merger of Matra BAE Dynamics in the United Kingdom and France, Aerospatiale Missiles in France, the missile activities of Alenia Marconi Systems in the United Kingdom and Italy, and EADS/LKF in Germany. EADS and BAE Systems each hold a 37.5 percent ownership share, while Finmeccanica controls the remaining 25 percent.

31. Flight modeling of the Apache conducted at Pacific-Sierra Research in 1996 demonstrated that the missile could readily fly beyond 300 km carrying a 500-kg payload.

32. "Proliferation: How Paris Arms the UAE," *Intelligence Newsletter,* no. 398, January 2001, 6.

33. Douglas Barrie, "Downing Street Will Have to Sign Off on Releasing the Storm Shadow," *Aviation Week & Space Technology,* May 7, 2007, 41.

34. Ibid.

35. Gormley, *Dealing with the Threat of Cruise Missiles,* 37–39 (see Chap. 4, n. 4).

36. See GlobalSecurity.org web site, "Land-Attack Cruise Missiles (LACM), Hong Niao/Chang Feng," http://www.globalsecurity.org/wmd/world/china/lacm.htm.

37. See "Russia: Novator Design Bureau (OKB Novator)," at the Nuclear Threat Initiative web site, http://www.nti.org/db/nisprofs/russia/delivry/novator.htm.

38. Ryan Green, "Russia: Overview of Missiles Exported by Russia," Nuclear Threat Initiative web site, http://www.nti.org/db/nisprofs/russia/exports/general/expmsl.htm.

39. Richard Fisher, Jr., "China's New Strategic Cruise Missiles: From the Land, Sea and Air," International Assessment and Strategy Center, June 3, 2005, http://www.strategycenter.net/research/pubID.71/pub_detail.asp; and "Russia Hands Over Upgraded Indian Submarine for Sea Trials," New Delhi PTI News Agency (in English), May 9, 2007.

40. "Russia: Novator Offers Advanced Missile System to Indonesian Navy," Moscow Interfax (in English), November 23, 2006.

41. Mark Forbes, "Jitters as Indonesia Buys Russian Subs," *Sydney Morning Herald,*September 5, 2007, http://www.smh.com.au/news/world/jitters-as-indonesia-buys-russian-subs/2007/09/04/1188783237164.html.

42. Piotr Butowski, "Ukraine Unveils Its 'Korshun' Missile," *Air & Cosmos,* April 8, 2005, 24.

43. Ibid.

44. "Ukraine Investigates Alleged Illicit Weapons Sales to Iran and China," *NIS Export Control Observer* 24 (February 2005): 13–14. On the judgment of U.S. intelligence, see "Iran, China reportedly got Ukraine missiles," MSNBC, http://www.msnbc.msn.com/id/7229637/.

45. "Ukrainian President Plans Radical Customs Cleanup and Confirms Illicit Missile Transfer," *NIS Export Control Observer* 26 (April 2005): 12–13.

46. "Missile Designs' Leak Feared," *Washington Times,* June 27, 2005, 17.

47. "Weekly Reports Russian Air Force Adoption of New Long-Range Cruise Missile," *Voyenno-Promyshlenny Kuryer* (in Russian), June 8, 2005 (Foreign Broadcast Information Services [FBIS] translated text).

48. Ibid. The range claim of 5,000 km in Russian press sources seems inconsistent with going from a lighter nuclear payload to a heavier (500 kg) conventional warhead.

49. For an acerbic view on Russia's new preventive option, see Pavel Felgengauer, "Long-Range and Pointless," *Moscow Times* (internet version, in English), December 21, 2004, 11.

50. Nikolai Sokov, "Russia Tests a New Ground-Launched Cruise Missile and a New Strategic Missile on the Same Day," CNS Research Story, Monterey Institute's Center for Nonproliferation Studies, June 1, 2007, http://cns.miis.edu/pubs/week/070601.htm.

51. Ibid.

52. For an analysis of the INF Treaty's impact on Soviet-era missile planning, see Dennis M. Gormley, *Double Zero and Soviet Military Strategy: Implications for Western Security* (London: Jane's Publishing Co., 1988).

53. There will inevitably be some ambiguity associated with the true range of a ballistic missile, too. Keeping flight testing of the new Iskander-M under 500 km does not mean that the missile could not be used to ranges exceeding that distance. Frequently, new short-range ballistic missiles are flight-tested to about two-thirds of their intended longest range. In short, full-range testing is not essential to furnish confidence that a missile can reliably perform at a range beyond what is reflected in a flight test program.

54. Rajat Pandit, "Pak Missile Is Made in China," *The Times of India* (internet version, in English), August 12, 2005.

55. Prasun K. Sengupta, "Babur's Flight," *New Delhi Force* (internet version, in English), September 9, 2005.

56. Prasun K. Sengupta, "Dr. Khan's Second Wal-Mart," *Force,* Noida, India, April 2006, 9–11.

57. Gormley, *Dealing with the Threat of Cruise Missiles,* 82–83 (see Chap. 4, n. 4).

58. Quoted in Alex Wagner, "Washington to Sanction China, Pakistan for Missile Cooperation," *Arms Control Today* 31, no. 7 (September 2001), http://www.armscontrol.org/act/2001_09/chinasept01.asp.

59. Stephanie Lieggi, "China's New Export Controls," http://cns.miis.edu/research/china/chiexp/chiexp.htm.

60. Quoted in Phillip C. Saunders, "Preliminary Analysis of Chinese Missile Technology Export Control List," September 6, 2002, http://cns.miis.edu/research/china/pdfs/prc_msl.pdf. For a translated list of new Chinese control regulations, see "Chinese Export Controls and Jiang Zemin's Visit to the United States," at http://cns.miis.edu/research/china/chiexp/.

61.   Dennis M. Gormley, "Hedging Against the Cruise-Missile Threat," *Survival* 40, no. 1 (Spring 1998): 92–111. This conclusion was drawn from a study I directed at Pacific-Sierra Research Corporation between 1996 and 1997.

62.   CEP is an indication of missile accuracy, as defined by the radius of a circle within which half of the missiles are expected to fall. On the YJ-63, see Evan S. Medeiros, Roger Cliff, Keith Crane, and James C. Mulvenon, *A New Direction for China's Defense Industry* (Santa Monica, CA: The RAND Corporation, 2005), 94.

63.   Lothar Ibrugger, "Report of the NATO Parliamentary Assembly, Subcommittee on the Proliferation of Military Technology, Missile Defences and Weapons in Space," November 2004, http://natopa.ibicenter.net/default.asp?SHORTCUT=497.

64.   "2004 Report to Congress of the U.S.-China Economic and Security Review Commission," June 2004, http://www.uscc.gov and Bill Gertz, "China Breaks Vow on Halting Arms Transfers," *Washington Times,* August 23, 2004, 1.

65.   *Comprehensive Report of the Special Advisor to the DCI on Iraq's WMD,* Vol. II (Washington, DC: Central Intelligence Agency, September 30, 2004), 39–41.

66.   Ibid., 39.

67.   Ibid., 44. The Iraqi program was called Al Bay'ah, based on turning the L-29 trainer aircraft into a remotely piloted vehicle. The C-611 component was an auto stabilizer system, which was integrated into the project in an attempt to maintain the command link to the L-29 by improving the air vehicle's controllability, but this proved unsuccessful due to excessive instrument drift.

68.   Efforts to tighten controls on such dual-use items as propulsion systems and integrated flight instrument and navigation systems in the MTCR's technology annex will make it more difficult for such dual-use items to be obtained. This issue is addressed in more detail in Chapter 9.

69.   Riad Kahwaji and Barbara Opall-Rome, "Hizbollah: Iran's Battle Lab," *Defense News,* December 13, 2004, 1.

70.   For technical details and an insightful analysis, see Eugene Miasnikov, Center for Arms Control, Energy and Environmental Studies, Moscow, Russia, http://www.armscontrol.ru/UAV/mirsad1.htm.

71.   "Hezbollah Mirsad-1 UAV Penetrates Israeli Air Defenses," *Defense Industry Daily,* April 20, 2005, http://www.defenseindustrydaily.com/2005/04/hezbollah-mirsad1-uav-penetrates-israeli-air-defenses/index.php.

72.   Barbara Opall-Rome, "Israeli Missiles Down Armed Hizbollah UAVs," *Defense News,* October 2, 2006, http://defensenews.com/story.php?F=2138218&C=airwar.

73.   Ibid.

74.   Ibid.

CHAPTER 5

1.   On one possibility of extending the Popeye's range to 1,500 km see the Federation of American Scientists (FAS) web site, http://www.fas.org/nuke/guide/israel/missile/popeye-t.htm.

2.   For details see "AGM-142 Raptor, Popeye I Have Nap, and Popeye II Have Lite," Federation of American Scientists web site, http://www.fas.org/man/dod-101/sys/smart/agm-142.htm. On India's acquisition, see Rahul Bedi, "Israeli Missile Fails Again in Test-Firing," *Bangalore Deccan Herald* (internet version, in English), May 31, 2005.

3.   Bedi, "Israeli Missile Fails Again in Test-Firing" (see Chap. 5, n. 2).

4. Yitzhak Shichor, "Israel's Military Transfers to China and Taiwan," *Survival* 40, no. 2 (Spring 1998): 90, n. 39. Shichor otherwise argues that Israel's transfers have not been particularly destabilizing. For further technical details on Delilah, see http://www.israeli-weapons.com/weapons/missile_systems/air_missiles/delilah/Delilah.html.

5. For technical details on Harpy, see http://www.israeli-weapons.com/weapons/aircraft/uav/harpy/HARPY.html.

6. Ze'ev Schiff, "US Sanctions Still in Place, Despite Deal Over Security Exports," *Tel Aviv Ha'aretz* (internet version, in English), August 28, 2005.

7. For details on Iran's Nur ASCM, see CNS Missile Chronology, http://www.nti.org/e_research/profiles/Iran/Missile/1788_4967.html.

8. Uzi Rubin states that the Raad missile is for anti-ship missions and has a range of 350 km. See his "The Global Range of Iran's Ballistic Missile Program," *Jerusalem Issue Brief* 5, no. 26 (June 20, 2006), http://www.jcpa.org/brief/brief005-26.htm. On the other hand, Lothar Ibrugger, "Report of the NATO Parliamentary Assembly, Subcommittee on the Proliferation of Military Technology, Missile Defences and Weapons in Space," November 2004, http://natopa.ibicenter.net/default.asp?SHORTCUT=497, states that Raad will come in both anti-ship and land-attack variants.

9. Rubin, "The Global Range of Iran's Ballistic Missile Program," 28 (see Chap. 5, n. 8).

10. Jerusalem Channel 2 Television (in Hebrew), May 7, 2007 (Foreign Broadcast Information Services [FBIS] translated text).

11. "UAE to Decide on Purchase of Russian Club-M Systems in Late 2006," *Moscow Agentstvo Voyennykh Novostey* (internet, text in English), August 24, 2006.

12. Iraq declared to the United Nations that the MiG-21 conversion was intended to deliver chemical or biological weapons. At least one Iraqi official claimed that the L-29 conversion was meant to replace the failed MiG-21 project, including the latter's WMD-delivery mission. See *Comprehensive Report of the Special Advisor to the DCI on Iraq's WMD,* Vol. II (Washington, DC: Central Intelligence Agency, September 30, 2004), especially 45.

13. "US Reportedly Ties Libya Missiles to Serbia," *Boston Globe,* October 31, 2002, A15. According to this account, a Serbian military analyst speculated that the MiG-21 was the likely conversion vehicle for the project.

14. Douglas Barrie, "Indian Air Force Proceeds with Test Plans for a Supersonic Land-Attack Program," *Aviation Week & Space Technology,* February 27, 2006, 36.

15. Ibid.

16. *The Telegraph* (internet version, in English), January 7, 2007.

17. Bulbul Singh, "Russia Threatens to Retain BrahMos Source Code," *Battlespace* 7, no. 40 (October 10, 2005).

18. New Delhi PTI News Agency (in English), June 21, 2007.

19. Jon Grevatt, "Malaysia Plans to Buy Cruise Missiles, Confirms Deputy Defence Minister," *Jane's Defence Industry,* August 1, 2007.

20. See, for example, Pravin Sawhney, "A Babur for BrahMos," *New Delhi Force* (internet version, in English), April 1, 2007.

21. "BrahMos missile deployed on INS Rajput; eight more warships to follow," Domain-b.com, http://www.domain-b.com/industry/defence/20071006_brahmos.htm.

22. On the air force approach, see Barrie, "Indian Air Force Proceeds with Test Plans for a Supersonic Land-Attack Program," 36 (see Chap. 5, n. 14); on the army approach, see Pravin Sawhney, "Surging Ahead," *New Delhi Force* (internet version, in English), November 1, 2006.

23. New Delhi PTI News Agency (in English), June 21, 2007.

24. Sawhney, "Surging Ahead" (see Chap. 5, n. 22).

25. New Delhi PTI News Agency (in English), June 21, 2007.

26. Sawhney, "Surging Ahead" (see Chap. 5, n. 22).

27. New Delhi PTI News Agency (in English), May 13, 2007 and Chu Yun, "Russian Delivers 3M-14 Land Attack Cruise Missile to India," *Beijing Feihang Daodan* (in Chinese), March 1, 2006 (FBIS translated text).

28. See, for example, the editorial in *New Delhi Rashtriya Sahara* (in Hindi), March 24, 2007, 8 (FBIS translated text) and Sawhney, "A Babur for BrahMos" (see Chap. 5, n. 20).

29. *The Times of India* (in English), June 16, 2007.

30. On U.S. hypersonic programs, see Dennis M. Gormley, "Conventional Force Integration in Global Strike," in James J. Wirtz and Jeffrey A. Larsen, eds., *Nuclear Transformation: The New U.S. Nuclear Doctrine* (New York: Palgrave, 2005): 53–68.

31. The U.S. National Aeronautics and Space Agency (NASA) has had several successful test flights of its X-43 hypersonic aircraft, reaching Mach 7 and Mach 10 with a scramjet that uses hydrogen and oxygen—the use of which presents enormously difficult infrastructure challenges when applied to a cruise missile. The U.S. Navy, working with the Pentagon's Defense Advanced Research Projects Agency (DARPA), is employing a scramjet/ramjet hybrid that uses standard hydrocarbon fuels to develop a cruise missile capable, they hope, of over Mach 6. See *Military Aerospace Technology* (online edition), http://www.military-aerospace-technology.com/print_article.cfm?DocID=1914.

32. See New Delhi PTI News Agency (in English), September 5, 2006 and "Cruise Control: Missile Deal Can Boost Tech Capability," *The Tribune* (online edition), September 7, 2006, http://www.tribuneindia.com/2006/20060907/edit.htm#top.

33. Sandeep Unnithan, "The Secret New Missile," *India Today* (internet version, in English), April 30–May 6, 2007.

34. Ibid. On the induction announcement, see Vishal Thapar, "India Gets Submarine Missile Power" (television), CNN-IBN, July 7, 2007.

35. Sujan Dutta, "Fearless Tomahawk-Type Missile on Radar," *The Telegraph* (internet version, in English), July 20, 2007.

36. Vivek Raghuvanshi, "Indian UAV to Become a Cruise Missile," *Defense News,* October 1, 2007, http://www.defensenews.com/story.php?F=3061901&C=mideast.

37. Andrew Koch, "Pakistan's Aerial Target Could Spawn Cruise Missile," *Jane's Defence Weekly,* October 23, 2002.

38. Muhammad Saleh Zaafir, "Naval Version of Hataf-VII Soon," *The News* (internet version, in English), March 25, 2006.

39. On the six errant missiles, see Mark Williams, "The Missiles of August—Part II," *Technology Review,* August 29, 2006, http://www.technologyreview.com/read_article.aspx?id=17374. On Pakistan's acknowledgement of a recovery, see Robert Hewson and Andrew Koch, "Pakistan Tests Cruise Missile," *Jane's Defence Weekly,* August 17, 2005, 4.

40. Hewson and Koch, "Pakistan Tests Cruise Missile" (see Chap. 5, n. 39).

41. Duncan Lennox, "China's New Cruise Missile Programme 'Racing Ahead,'" *Jane's Defence Weekly,* January 12, 2000, 12.

42. China is not the only potential source of foreign assistance to Pakistan on the Babur LACM. Pakistan has reportedly worked with Ukrainian engineers for several years on advanced missile programs and has also acquired air-launched systems from South Africa, which produces and exports its own LACMs. Hewson and Koch, "Pakistan Tests Cruise Missile" (see Chap. 5, n. 39).

43. "LO Contagion Spreads; Search for Antidote Underway," *Aviation Week & Space Technology,* September 3, 2007, 32.

44. Vishal Thapar, "Pakistan Flaunts N-Missile, Catches India Unawares" (television report, in English), Noida CNN-IBN, April 5, 2006.

45. Bernard D. Cole, "China's Modernization and its Impact on the United States and the Asia-Pacific," Testimony before the U.S.-China Economic and Security Review Commission, March 29, 2007, 5.

46. Ibid., 2

47. *Ballistic and Cruise Missile Threat,* (Wright-Patterson Air Force Base, OH: National Air and Space Intelligence Center, March 2006), 26.

48. Duncan Lennox, "China's New Cruise Missile Programme 'Racing Ahead,'" 12 (see Chap. 5, n. 41).

49. Ibid.

50. Wendell Minnick, "China Tests New Land-Attack Cruise Missile," *Jane's Missiles and Rockets,* October 1, 2004.

51. *Lu-chun Shuang-yueh-k'an* (internet version, in Chinese), October 31, 2006 (FBIS translated text) and *Kuang Chiao Ching* (in Chinese), September 16, 2004 (FBIS translated text).

52. Taipei Central News Agency, January 23, 2007 and Bradley Perrett, "Almost 1,000 Chinese Missiles Ranged Against Taiwan," *Aviation Week & Space Technology,* January 29, 2007, 27.

53. Yihong Shang, "Beijing Develops New Radar Absorbing Materials," *Jane's Defence Weekly,* February 24, 1999, 3.

54. Wu Xincheng, "China Develops New Aviation Material," *Kanwa Defense Review* (internet version, in English), December 1, 2006.

55. "A Number of Issues in Joint Operations with Cruise Missiles and Operational and Tactical Missiles," *Kanwa Defense Review* (Hong Kong, in Chinese), October 1, 2005 (FBIS translated text).

56. Mark A. Stokes, *China's Strategic Modernization: Implications for the United States* (Carlisle, PA: Strategic Studies Institute, U.S. Army War College, 1999), 81.

57. Minnie Chan, "Old Jets Converted into Cruise Missiles Could Hit U.S. Ships," *South China Morning Post,* May 12, 2007.

58. Kathrin Hille, "Taiwan Speeds Up Race to Match Beijing Missiles," *Financial Times* (Asia edition), September 25, 2004, 3.

59. "Taiwan to Purchase and Deploy Six Patriot Batteries by 2019—But Are They Enough?" MissileThreat.com, March 3, 2004.

60. Lu Te-yun, "Military Deploys Special Missile," *Lien-Ho Pao* (internet version, in Chinese), October 16, 2006 (FBIS translated text).

61. See, for example, Brian Hsu, "Taiwan to Develop Missile to 'Hit Deep Inside China,'" *Taipei Times* (internet version, in English), October 10, 2003 and "Chungshan Institute of Science and Technology Provides Two Medium-Range Missile Development Plans for the Defense Ministry to Choose From," *Lien-ho Pao* (internet version, in Chinese), October 31, 2003 (FBIS translated text).

62. Erik Quam and Jing-Dong Yuan, "China Eyes Taiwanese Cruise Defensive Missile Developments with Concern," *WMD Insights* (November 2006), http://www.wmdinsights.org/I10/I10_EA2_ChinaEyesTaiwanese.htm.

63. Lu Te-yun, "Military Deploys Special Missile" (see Chap. 5, n. 60).

64. Wu Ming-chieh, "Han Kuang Military Exercise Discloses Advanced Weapons to Demonstrate to the United States," *Chung-Kuo Shih-Pao* (internet version, in Chinese), April 23, 2007 (FBIS translated text).

65. Herman Su, "Simulation Shows Taiwan Weak Against PRC Attack, MND Says," *Taiwan News* (internet version, in English), April 25, 2007.

66. Wu Ming-chieh, "Han Kuang Military Exercise Discloses Advanced Weapons to Demonstrate to the United States" (see Chap. 5, n. 64).

67. Herman Su, "MND Says Newer Missiles Able to Hit Bases in China," *Taiwan News* (internet version, in English), April 27, 2007, 2.

68. Lawrence Chung, "US Opposes Long-Range Missiles for Taiwan," *South China Post* (internet version, in English), May 4, 2007.

69. Wu Ming-chieh, "Han Kuang Military Exercise Discloses Advanced Weapons to Demonstrate to the United States" (see Chap. 5, n. 64).

70. For an assessment of the HF-2E by mainland analysts, see Zhou Yi, Cui Dongjie, et al., "Analysis of Development of Ballistic and Cruise Missiles in Taiwan," *Feihang Daodan* (in Chinese), May 2005, 22–24, 29 (FBIS translated text).

71. See "Turf Battles Characterize US' Taiwan Policy," *Taipei Times,* July 10, 2006.

72. *FY04 Report to Congress on PRC Military Power* (Washington, DC: Office of the Secretary of Defense, 2004), 53–54.

73. Zhou Yi, Cui Dongjie, et al., "Analysis of Development of Ballistic and Cruise Missiles in Taiwan" (see Chap. 5, n. 70).

74. "S. Korea's Cruise Missile Program Revealed," *Chosun Ilbo* (internet version, in English), October 25, 2006, http://english.chosun.com/w21data/html/news/200610/200610250007.html.

75. Daniel A. Pinkston, "South Korean Response to North Korean July Missile Exercise Includes Unveiling of New Cruise Missile," *WMD Insights* (October 2006), http://cns.miis.edu/pubs/other/wmdi061004_pinkston.htm.

76. Ibid. On use strategy see *JoongAng Ilbo* (internet version, in English), September 20, 2006.

77. "Korea Test Fires 1000 km Cruise Missile," *Dong-A Ilbo* (internet version, in English), October 24, 2006 and "ROK Successfully Develops Cruise Missile Capable of Hitting DPRK Strategic Targets," *Yonhap* (in English), October 24, 2006.

78. "S. Korea's Cruise Missile Program Revealed" (see Chap. 5, n. 74).

79. "South Korean Defense Industry Aims to Go Global," Korea Overseas Information Service, July 3, 2007.

80. Joseph S. Bermudez, Jr., "North Korea Tests Short-Range Missile," revised May 27, 2007.

81. "Preemptive Strike Ability Said Necessary for Japan," *The Japan Times,* October 2, 2004.

82. "Japan Drops Long-Range Missile Deployment Plan in Defense Program," *Jiji Press* (in English), December 7, 2004.

83. Interviews with Japanese defense officials in Tokyo, March 2005.

84. "Carrying a Big Stick Again?" *Aviation Week & Space Technology,* April 14, 2003.

85. Shigeru Handa, "Whom is Missile Defense For?" *Tokyo Shimbun* (internet version, in Japanese), December 24, 2004 (FBIS translated text).

CHAPTER 6

1. Quoted in Donald MacKenzie, *Inventing Accuracy: A Historical Sociology of Nuclear Missile Guidance* (Cambridge, MA: MIT Press, 1990), 239, n. 195.

2. Interviews with current and former industry executives in Los Angeles in December 2005 and Washington, D.C., in May and July 2007.

3. For technical details and program-related information, see http://www.fas.org/man/dod-101/sys/smart/jdam.htm.

4. Amy Butler, "Pentagon to Announce JASSM Decision in 2008," *Aviation Week & Space Technology,* July 20, 2007, http://www.aviationweek.com/aw/generic/story_generic.jsp?channel=aerospacedaily&id=news/JASSM072007.xml.

5. Bruce Simpson, "The Low Cost Cruise Missile: A Looming Threat?" http://aardvark.co.nz/pjet/cruise.shtml.

6. During Simpson's activities, the New Zealand government refused to respond to formal press inquiries, but an anonymous New Zealand defense official told the *New Zealand Herald* that Simpson's web site might be violating the MTCR, of which New Zealand is a member. See "DIY Missile Hits Target," Australian Broadcasting Corporation, NewsOnline, http://www.abc.net.au/news/indepth/featureitems/missile.htm.

7. Donald MacKenzie, "Theories of Technology and the Abolition of Nuclear Weapons," in Donald MacKenzie and Judy Wajcman, eds., *The Social Shaping of Technology* (Philadelphia: Open University Press, 1999), 425.

8. Simpson, "The Low Cost Cruise Missile: A Looming Threat?" (see Chap. 6, n. 5).

9. On the complexity of developing biological agents, see Milton Leitenberg, *Assessing the Biological Weapons and Bioterrorism Threat* (Carlisle, PA: Strategic Studies Institute, U.S. Army War College, 2005), http://www.strategicstudiesinstitute.army.mil/pubs/display.cfm?pubID=639.

10. "Who's Building This Thing? The Man Behind the Missile," http://www.interestingprojects.com/cruisemissile/bio.shtml.

11. "Another No-Weld Pulsejet Engine," http://www.aardvark.co.nz/pjet/noweld_pulsejet.shtml.

12. "The Enthusiast's Guide to Pulsejets: A Book Filled with Theory, Practice, and Advice," http://www.aardvark.co.nz/pjet/pulsejetbook.shtml.

13. "A DIY Cruise Missile: Phase 2: The Flight Control System," http://www.interestingprojects.com/cruisemissile/flightcontrol.shtml.

14. Before the New Zealand government shut down Simpson's project, I asked a highly knowledgeable engineer, experienced in aeronautical systems integration, to evaluate Simpson's technical approach to each task. Even with the limited information available, the conclusion was that Simpson's approach to flight control depended too heavily on assumptions relating to model airplanes rather than, albeit small, cruise missiles.

15. MacKenzie, "Theories of Technology and the Abolition of Nuclear Weapons," 428 (see Chap. 6, n. 7). For a good summary of Iraq's first nuclear program, see the Federation of American Scientists' web site story, "Iraqi Nuclear Weapons," http://www.fas.org/nuke/guide/iraq/nuke/program.htm.

16. This account is based on MacKenzie, "Theories of Technology and the Abolition of Nuclear Weapons," 419–442 (see Chap. 6, n. 7) and Donald MacKenzie and Graham Spinardi, "Tacit Knowledge, Weapons Design, and the Uninvention of Nuclear Weapons," *American Journal of Sociology* 101, no. 1 (July 1995): 44–99. For what the subject might mean for current and prospective nuclear weapons developments, see Dennis M. Gormley, "Silent

Retreat: The Future of U.S. Nuclear Weapons," *Nonproliferation Review* 14, no. 2 (July 2007): 183–206.

17. MacKenzie, "Theories of Technology and the Abolition of Nuclear Weapons," 427 (see Chap. 6, n. 7).

18. MacKenzie and Spinardi, "Tacit Knowledge," 69–70 (see Chap. 6, n. 16).

19. Joby Warrick, "Custom-Built Pathogens Raise Bioterror Fears," *Washington Post,* July 31, 2006, A1.

20. Jeronimo Cello, Aniko V. Paul, and Eckard Wimmer, "Chemical Synthesis of Poliovirus cDNA," *Science* 297 (August 9, 2002): 1016–1018, as cited in Kathleen M. Vogel, "Bio-securization: A Constructivist Approach to Assessing Bioterrorism Threats," Unpublished manuscript dated March 30, 2007, provided courtesy of the author.

21. Ibid. Also see Kathleen M. Vogel, "Framing Biosecurity," *Science and Public Policy* (forthcoming).

22. Vogel, "Bio-securization," (see Chap. 6, n. 20).

23. Ibid.

24. Interview with Dr. Sonia Ben Ouagrham and Dr. Kathleen Vogel, Arlington, VA, July 2007. Between 2000 and 2002, Drs. Ben Ouagrham and Vogel conducted extensive interviews with Soviet-era bioweaponeers involved in the Stepnogorsk anthrax program. See Sonia Ben Ouagrham and Kathleen M. Vogel, *Conversion at Stepnogorsk: What the Future Holds for Former Bioweapons Facilities,* Occasional Paper No. 28 (Ithaca: Cornell University Peace Studies Program, 2003).

25. This section benefited greatly from interviews, in May 2007 and July 2007, with a senior defense industry executive intimately familiar with the history of the Tomahawk program. Actually, the TERCOM principle was patented in 1958 and later became part of the supersonic low-altitude cruise missile, which was cancelled in 1963. See Ron Huisken, "The History of Cruise Missiles," in Richard K. Betts, ed., *Cruise Missiles: Technology, Strategy, Politics* (Washington, DC: The Brookings Institution, 1981), 88.

26. Much is made about the advent of GPS obviating the need for depending on terrain contour-matching and digital scene-matching guidance and navigation systems. While GPS was added to the Tomahawk Block III missile after the first Gulf War, it still remains an adjunct to the original TERCOM and DSMAC systems. Worried that the United States might deny access to GPS or jam the missile's receiver, China, among other new developers of LACMs, has striven to develop TERCOM-like mid-course and terminal sensors for improved and assured accuracy.

27. See, for example, Jeff Kueter and Howard Kleinberg, *The Cruise Missile Challenge: Designing a Defense Against Asymmetric Threats* (Washington, DC: The Marshall Institute, 2007), 25–26.

28. Daniel Benjamin and Steven Simon, "The Worse Defense," *New York Times,* February 20, 2003, A31.

29. John Liang, "DoD Finds Cruise Missile Defense 'Gaps,'" *InsideDefense.com News-Stand,* August 17, 2006, http://www.military.com/features/0,15240,110199,00.html

30. Kueter and Kleinberg, *The Cruise Missile Challenge,* 25 (see Chap. 6, n. 27). The authors base this judgment on two citations, including one of my own works, "UAVs and Cruise Missiles as Possible Terrorist Weapons," in James Clay Moltz, ed., *New Challenges in Missile Proliferation, Missile Defense, and Space Security,* Occasional Paper No. 12 (Monterey, CA: Monterey Institute's Center for Nonproliferation Studies, 2003), 3–10. To the contrary, I wrote in the cited work, on page 6, that "converting a surplus Silkworm for launch from a

freighter seems a considerable stretch for a terrorist group not possessing advanced mechanical and engineering experience."

31.   The effort entailed looking closely at where skill sets could be developed. Certainly, there are clear indicators of greater or lesser potential: a nation that possessed only rudimentary aeronautical experience, based entirely on its commercial airports, and no significant supporting industrial capabilities from which to draw needed engineering support, would have a low potential to handle cruise missile integration challenges. By contrast, a state with a well-respected technical university, an established automotive industry, emerging electronics and computer industries, and at least some aviation development and production industry, would be much better prepared to deal with the Silkworm conversion task. For more on where these skills may exist in the developing world, see Dennis M. Gormley, *Dealing with the Threat of Cruise Missiles,* Adelphi Paper 339 (Oxford: Oxford University Press, 2001), 25–28.

32.   *Comprehensive Report of the Special Advisor to the DCI on Iraq's WMD,* Vol. II (Washington, DC: Central Intelligence Agency, September 30, 2004), 37–46.

33.   Ibid., 39.

34.   Dennis M. Gormley, "Missile Defence Myopia: Lessons from the Iraq War," *Survival* 45, no. 4 (Winter 2003–04): 69.

35.   Jack Anderson and Michael Binstein, "Worrisome Engine Sales to China," *Washington Post,* May 9, 1994, C14.

36.   Iraqi engineers believed that the turboshaft conversion would be difficult because the engine's stators, or small stationary vanes that are typically attached to the casing of the engine, could not be removed because they were integral to the engine's ball bearing assembly. *Comprehensive Report of the Special Advisor to the DCI on Iraq's WMD,* Vol. II, 40 (see Chap. 6, n. 32).

37.   Ibid., 44.

38.   Ibid., 41.

39.   Ibid., 46–56.

40.   Ibid., 50.

41.   "Executive Summary of the Report of the Commission to Assess the Ballistic Missile Threat to the United States," July 15, 1998, http://www.fas.org/irp/threat/bm-threat.htm.

42.   For details, see the chart in the Nuclear Threat Initiative's "North Korea Profile," http://www.nti.org/e_research/profiles/NK/Missile/index.html.

43.   It is important to acknowledge that our estimate assumed that Iraq or Iran desired reasonably accurate (~100-m CEP) and reliable LACMs and that it would take some time, depending on the intended military utility of the LACMs, to incorporate them into the existing force structure. China, for example, currently spends a lot of time ironing out the tactical and doctrinal details of how conventionally armed ballistic and cruise missiles will be employed in modern combat, not just together but in a joint context with aircraft, ground, and other operational components. While Iraq (circa 1998) or contemporary Iran may not dwell on these nontechnological components as much as China does today, they still merit analytical attention from a threat perspective.

44.   For an overview and assessment of this practice, see "Defense Science Board Task Force on The Role and Status of DoD Red Teaming Activities," Office of the Under Secretary of Defense for Acquisition, Technology, and Logistics, Washington, D.C., September 2003, http://www.acq.osd.mil/dsb/reports/redteam.pdf.

45.   Joby Warrick, "On North Korean Freighter, a Hidden Missile Factory," *Washington Post,* August 14, 2003, A1.

46.   Ibid.

47. Ibid.

48. Uzi Rubin, *The Global Reach of Iran's Ballistic Missiles,* Memorandum 86 (Tel Aviv: Institute for National Security Studies, November 2006), 30–31.

49. For details from Russian and other press reports, see Charles P. Vick, "The Operational Shahab-4/No-dong Flight Tested in Iran for Iran & North Korea Confirmed," GlobalSecurity.org, http://www.globalsecurity.org/wmd/library/report/2006/cpvick-no-dong-b_2006.htm. Also see "Missile Chronology, December 1992," NTI web site, http://www.nti.org/e_research/profiles/NK/Missile/65_684.html.

50. "2004 Report to Congress of the U.S.-China Economic and Security Review Commission," June 2004, 144, http://www.nti.org/db/China/engdocs/USChina_Commission04annual_report.pdf.

51. "Report: Iran Has Conducted Four Missile Tests in 2006," BBC Worldwide Monitoring, February 15, 2006.

52. Bill Gertz, "Missiles Sold to China and Iran," *Washington Times,* April 6, 2005, http://www.iranfocus.com/modules/news/article.php?storyid=1807.

53. "Focus on Iran," Geostrategy-Direct, October 18, 2005.

54. For an assessment of the NCRI's source reliability, see "Resistance Group Claims Evidence of Iranian Bomb Ambitions," The Media Line, January 11, 2006, http://www.nci.org/06nci/01/02.htm.

55. "Ukraine Investigates Alleged Illicit Weapons Sales to Iran and China," *NIS Export Control Observer,* 24 (February 2005): 13–14, http://cns.miis.edu/pubs/nisexcon/pdfs/ob_0502e.pdf.

56. See http://www.thenews.com.pk/print1.asp?id=48458.

57. Hong Kong Agence France-Presse (in English), November 24, 2006.

58. See, for example, Ranjit Kumar, "Pakistan's Conceit Is Thanks to Others' Strength," *New Delhi Navbharat Times* (in Hindi), April 1, 2007, 11 (Foreign Broadcast Information Services [FBIS] translated).

59. "Fifth Brahmos Missile Test Successful," An Indian Defense Consultants Analysis with Inputs from Sayan Majumdar, New Delhi India Defense Consultants (internet, text in English), November 13, 2003.

60. "India Has Begun Cruise-Missile Project," http://forum.keypublishing.co.uk/archive/index.php?t-37966.html.

61. "Indian Air Force 'Not Impressed' With Akash Surface to Air Missile System," India-defence.com, http://www.india-defence.com/reports-3083.

62. "Indian Missile a 'Dud,' Air Force Doesn't Want It," http://www.hindustantimes.com/storypage/storypage.aspx?id=15b77d03-5681-44e5-abef-cc9265d37d69.

63. Ibid.

64. Amitav Ranjan and Shiv Aroor, "House Panel: Report Call for Independent and External Experts to Monitor Performance," *New Delhi Indian Express* (internet version, in English), December 28, 2006.

65. One notably unreliable Indian defense writer, Prasun K. Sengupta, has suggested that New Delhi and Tel Aviv have hidden a 1,200-km range LACM development program within a contract signed in January 2006 to develop a family of guided missiles. The hidden effort, he claims, includes both sea- and air-launched supersonic LACMs, and the air-launched missile is the long-mysterious Sagarika. See his "Flights of Fancy," *New Delhi Force* (internet version, in English), December 1–31, 2006. Of course, even were this claim true, which is highly

doubtful, it leaves open the question of where India might turn to acquire an engine to power a subsonic LACM, which it has long sought to do.

66. Quoted in Eric Arnett, "Military Technology: The Case of China," in *SIPRI Yearbook 1995: Armaments, Disarmament, and International Security* (Oxford: Oxford University Press, 1995), 366.

67. See, for example, Bates Gill, "China's Military-Technical Developments: The Record for Western Assessments, 1979–1999," in James C. Mulvenon and Andrew N. D. Yang, eds., *Seeking Truth From Facts: A Retrospective on Chinese Military Studies in the Post-Mao Era* (Santa Monica, CA: The RAND Corporation, 2001), 141–172.

68. On the PLA Navy, see Christopher D. Yung, *People's War at Sea: Chinese Naval Power in the Twenty-First Century* (Alexandria, VA: Center for Naval Analyses, 1996); on the PLA Air Force, see Kenneth W. Allen, Glenn Krumel, and Jonathan D. Pollack, *China's Air Force Enters the 21st Century* (Santa Monica, CA: The RAND Corporation, 1995).

69. Larry M. Wortzel, "Comments on 'China's Military-Technical Developments: The Record for Western Assessments, 1979–1999,'" in Mulvenon and Yang, eds., *Seeking Truth from Facts,* 173–180 (see Chap. 6, n. 67).

70. Stephen J. Blank, *The Dynamics of Russian Weapon Sales to China* (Carlisle, PA: Strategic Studies Institute, U.S. Army War College, 1997).

71. Blank indicates Chong-Pin Lin of the American Enterprise Institute, a Washington think tank, as the source of this information, which dates to August 1995. Chong-Pin Lin is a Taiwanese national currently believed to be President of the Foundation on International and Cross-Strait Studies and a professor at Tamkang University in Taiwan.

72. "Current Research and Development of Cruise Missiles in the PRC," *Taipei K'ung-chun Hsueh-shu Yueh-k'an* Issue no. 588 (internet version, in Chinese), February 27, 2006 (FBIS translated).

73. *U.S. National Security and Military/Commercial Concerns with the People's Republic of China,* Select Committee of the United States House of Representatives, 105th Congress, 2d Session, Report of the Select Committee on U.S. National Security, submitted by Mr. Cox of California, Chairman Report 105–85 (Washington, DC: Government Printing Office, January 3, 1999), Chapter 10.

74. "U.S.-China Jet Cooperation," Northeast Asia Report, Geostrategy-Direct, October 7, 2003.

75. "Taiwan National Charged with Plotting Illegal Export of Engines, Missiles to China," *International Export Control Observer* 5 (March 2006): 10–11, http://cns.miis.edu/pubs/observer/pdfs/ieco_0603e.pdf.

76. See, for example, Shirley A. Kan, *Taiwan: Major U.S. Arms Sales Since 1990,* RL30957 (Washington, DC: Congressional Research Service, July 12, 2007), 38–39.

77. Interview with industry executive, Alexandria, VA, June 2007.

CHAPTER 7

1. Richard Burt, "Local Conflicts in the Third World," in Richard K. Betts, ed., *Cruise Missiles: Technology, Strategy, Politics* (Washington, DC: The Brookings Institution, 1981), 226.

2. Betts, "Innovation, Assessment, and Decision," 5 (see Chap. 7, n. 1).

3. Ibid., 6.

4. Albert Wohlstetter, Foreword to K. Scott McMahon and Dennis M. Gormley, *Controlling the Spread of Land-Attack Cruise Missiles* (Marina del Ray, CA: American Institute for Strategic Cooperation, 1995), v–ix.

5. This accounting and analysis of the 2003 war appeared in a slightly different form in Dennis M. Gormley, "Missile Defence Myopia: Lessons from the Iraq War" *Survival* 45, no. 4 (Winter 2003–04): 61–86. The material has been updated in light of new historical data collected by the U.S. Army and other subsequent analyses.

6. See, for example, Max Boot, "The American Way of War," *Foreign Affairs* 82, no. 4 (July/August 2003): 41–58.

7. "Operation Iraqi Freedom Theater Air and Missile Defense History," 32nd Army Air and Missile Defense Command, Ft. Bliss, TX, September 2003, http://www.cdi.org/PDFs/OIF_history.pdf.

8. According to the U.S. Federal Aviation Administration, an ultralight aircraft is defined as a single occupancy-only aircraft, used for sport or recreational purposes only. No airworthiness certificate is required. Moreover, a powered vehicle cannot be operated when it has an empty weight of 254 pounds (115 kg) or more, a fuel capacity exceeding 5 U.S. gallons (19 liters), or an air speed of more than 55 knots at full power in level flight. Whereas sport paragliders possess a steerable parachute canopy, ultralights have a fixed, stable wing frame. The two Iraqi ultralights spotted over U.S. troops on March 28, 2003 possessed wings roughly 4.5–6 m in length. See Sean D. Naylor, "Iraqi Ultralights Spotted Over U.S. Troops," *Army Times,* March 29, 2003.

9. I am grateful to Michael Krepon for this point.

10. These executive- and legislative-branch initiatives are documented in Chapter 4 of Dennis M. Gormley, *Dealing with the Threat of Cruise Missiles,* Adelphi Paper 339 (Oxford: Oxford University Press, 2001). See also Dennis M. Gormley, "Cruise Missile Threat Quietly Rises," *Defense News,* March 27, 1995, 27; *Cruise Missile Defense: Progress Made But Significant Challenges Remain,* GAO/NSIAD-99–68 (Washington, DC: USGAO, March 1999); and Dennis M. Gormley, "Cruise Missile Threat Rises: U.S. Navy, Army Lag in Defense Preparations," *Defense News,* May 31, 1999, 15.

11. David Ruppe, "United States: Army Describes Patriot Friendly Fire Difficulties," *Global Security Newswire,* July 29, 2003, http://www.nti.org/d_newswire/issues/2003/7/29/12s.html.

12. Michael R. Gordon, "A Poor Man's Air Force," *New York Times,* June 19, 2003, A1.

13. Andrea Stone, "Friend or Foe to Allied Troops," *USA Today,* April 14, 2003, http://www.usatoday.com/news/world/iraq/2003-04-14-patriot-missile_x.htm.

14. "Operation Iraqi Freedom Theater Air and Missile Defense History" (see Chap. 7, n. 7).

15. Gordon, "A Poor Man's Air Force" (see Chap. 7, n. 12).

16. Elaine M. Grossman, "Most Intercepts of Iraqi Rockets Were by Older Patriot Missiles," *Inside the Pentagon,* April 24, 2003, 1.

17. Andy Murray, "Missile Test," *The Eagle-Tribune,* March 23, 2003. For further details on each Patriot interceptor, see the Federation of American Scientists' web site, http://www.fas.org/spp/starwars/program/patriot.htm.

18. Murray, "Missile Test" (see Chap. 7, n. 17).

19. The official was Lt. Gen. Joseph Cosumano, commander of the army's Space and Missile Defense Command, as cited in Robert Wall, "Dangerous Missile Mix Sparks Scrutiny," *Aviation Week & Space Technology,* July 7, 2003, 47–48.

20.   Gordon, "A Poor Man's Air Force" (see Chap. 7, n. 12).

21.   Grossman, "Most Intercepts of Iraqi Rockets Were by Older Patriot Missiles" (see Chap. 7, n. 16).

22.   Wall, "Dangerous Missile Mix Sparks Scrutiny" (see Chap. 7, n. 19).

23.   Bradley Graham, "Radar Probed in Patriot Incidents," *Washington Post,* May 8, 2003, A21.

24.   "U.S. Ground Forces in Iraq Wearied of Repeated False Missile Alarms," *Inside the Pentagon,* June 26, 2003, 21.

25.   The interim progress report of the Iraq Survey Group, known as the Kay Report for its head, Dr. David Kay, states that 10 converted HY-2 LACMs were delivered to the Iraqi military prior to the war's beginning. See http://www.cnn.com/2003/ALLPOLITICS/10/02/kay.report/.

26.   For the most detailed account of the attack on Camp Commando, see Lt. Col. Phil Tissue et al, "Attacking the Cruise Missile Threat," Paper prepared for Class #03–3, Joint Forces Staff College, September 8, 2003. There are differences between press accounts and the official U.S. Army history over precisely when Iraq launched the five HY-2 LACMs. The army history does not mention the HY-2 attack on Camp Commando of March 20, 2003, but Michael Gordon of the *New York Times* does. After the war, I interviewed a colleague who was at Camp Commando on March 20 who provided details of the attack, including just how close the missile came to achieving success and the missile's unique audio signature prior to hitting just outside the Marine encampment. Besides the attack on March 20, Michael Gordon reports that two more cruise missiles were fired on March 28 and two again on March 31. The army report mentions the March 28 cruise missile strike on the Kuwaiti shopping mall but then, on the following page, refers to the cruise missile attack on Kuwait City occurring on March 29. The army account states that on April 1, Iraq fired three cruise missiles. One way or the other, a total of five HY-2s appears to be the correct number. See Gordon, "A Poor Man's Air Force" (see Chap. 7, n. 12) and "Operation Iraqi Freedom Theater Air and Missile Defense History," 68, 71, and 73 (see Chap. 7, n. 7).

27.   Wall, "Dangerous Mix Sparks Scrutiny" (see Chap. 7, n. 19).

28.   The Kuwaiti batteries are outfitted with the Aspide air defense missile system, an Italian-made product.

29.   "Operation Iraqi Freedom Theater Air and Missile Defense History," 68 and 71 (see Chap. 7, n. 7).

30.   Ibid., 73.

31.   Wall, "Dangerous Mix Sparks Scrutiny" (see Chap. 7, n. 19).

32.   Naylor, "Iraqi Ultralights Spotted Over U.S. Troops" (see Chap. 7, n. 8) was the exclusive unofficial source of information for this incident. Naylor was embedded with the 3rd Infantry Division (Mechanized) at the time. His detailed article disappeared from the *Army Times* web site soon after its appearance. The army's official history furnished little detail and, of course, none of the rich detail gathered by Naylor from his on-site interview with operational and intelligence officers and enlisted personnel.

33.   Gormley, *Dealing with the Threat of Cruise Missiles,* 11 (see Chap. 7, n. 10).

34.   Army air defense and intelligence personnel were not completely surprised by the appearance of the Iraqi ultralights. In December 2002, months before the invasion, about six Iraqi ultralights were detected flying over U.S. military camps in Kuwait. For reasons unspecified, U.S. air defenses failed to engage the aircraft. Air defense officers were told that the Iraqis attempted to procure at least 100 ultralights from an overseas company, but only around

50 were delivered by the war's outbreak in March 2003. One army intelligence officer believed the Iraqis might use ultralights for either strategic reconnaissance or spreading chemical or biological agents—or suicide attacks with high explosives. Despite this intelligence, pre-war threat briefings advised air defense units to expect the Iraqis to use paragliders (which use a parachute canopy) rather than fixed-wing ultralights. On-site interviews by embedded Army Times reporter Sean Naylor indicate that air defenders and intelligence officers sighted two ultralights, with wingspans of 15 to 20 feet, not canopied paragliders. See Naylor, "Iraqi Ultralights Spotted Over U.S. Troops" (see Chap. 7, n. 8). Interestingly, the official army history only mentions one Iraqi paraglider as reported flying near one of their air defense units on March 28, the day of Naylor's on-site reporting. See "Operation Iraqi Freedom Theater Air and Missile Defense History," 67–68 (see Chap. 7, n. 7).

35.   Before the invasion of Iraq in 2003, senior Bush administration officials fostered the expectation that allied forces would face a threat from armed Iraqi UAVs, possibly carrying chemical or biological agents. Anonymous officials leaked information suggesting that President Bush was concerned about the Iraqis sneaking a small UAV into the United States for use against homeland targets. In the post-war search for Iraqi WMD, however, U.S. forces recovered abandoned Iraqi UAVs that appeared capable of performing only reconnaissance, not weapons-delivery, roles. The important point, however, is that prudent defense planning had to be predicated on the expectation that Patriot missile batteries might have to intercept both ballistic and UAV threats. See David Rogers, "Air Force Doubts Drone Threat: Report Says Bush Exaggerated Perils of Unmanned Iraqi Aircraft," *Wall Street Journal,* September 10, 2003.

36.   "Operation Iraqi Freedom Theater Air and Missile Defense History," 9 (see Chap. 7, n. 7).

37.   Elaine M. Grossman, "Patriot May Mistake Aircraft for Missile in Combat's Electronic Glut," *Inside the Pentagon,* April 24, 2003, 1.

38.   For various explanations regarding the Patriot friendly-fire incidents, see Pamela Hess, "The Pentagon's Fratricide Record," *United Press International,* April 24, 2003; Grossman, "Patriot May Mistake Aircraft for Missile in Combat's Electronic Glut" (see Chap. 7, n. 37); Ruppe, "United States: Army Describes Patriot Friendly Fire Difficulties" (see Chap. 7, n. 11); Stone, "Friend or Foe to Allied Troops" (see Chap. 7, n. 13); Graham, "Radar Probed in Patriot Incidents" (see Chap. 7, n. 23); Wall, "Dangerous Mix Sparks Scrutiny" (see Chap. 7, n. 19); Michael Smith, "US 'Clears' Crew Who Shot Down Tornado," *Daily Telegraph,* July 16, 2003.

39.   Hess, "The Pentagon's Fratricide Record" (see Chap. 7, n. 38).

40.   Interviews with former government officials in Washington, D.C. in December 2000 and January 2001.

41.   MIT Professor Theodore Postol elaborates the reasons behind the friendly-fire incidents with much greater specificity. He argues that when two or more Patriot radars are tracking the same aircraft, multiple signals from several radars are reflecting radar energy of the tracked aircraft, creating spurious missile trajectories that are analyzed by the Patriot radar's artificial intelligence software as a threatening missile. He also argues that Patriot operators were not adequately trained to cope with such a possibility, made worse due to Patriot's lack of connectivity to other sensor platforms such as AWACS, Aegis, and Cobra Judy, which would have enhanced situational awareness. See PowerPoint presentation by Theodore A. Postol, MIT Security Studies Program, April 20, 2004, http://www.globalsecurity.org/space/library/report/2004/patriot-shot-friendly_20apr2004_apps1-2.pdf.

42. "Operation Iraqi Freedom Theater Air and Missile Defense History," 94 (see Chap. 7, n. 7).

43. Ibid., 9.

44. Ibid.

45. "Iran Seeks Cruise Missile to Support Shihab," *Middle East Newsline,* June 10, 2004.

46. Iddo Genuth, "Ukraine's Sale of Cruise Missiles with a Nuclear Potential to Iran Also Pose Deadly Threat to Europe," IsraCast, March 21, 2005, http://www.IsraCast.com.

47. "X-55 Long Range Cruise Missile," GlobalSecurity.org web site, http://www.globalsecurity.org/wmd/world/iran/x-55.htm.

48. Dana Milbank and Dafna Linzer, "U.S., India May Share Nuclear Technology," *Washington Post,* July 19, 2005, A1.

49. "President Musharraf Compares Babur Missile with India's BrahMos," Islamabad PTV World (in English), August 11, 2005 (Foreign Broadcast Information Services [FBIS] transcribed text).

50. "Pakistan's Missile Program: Message of Courage and Valor for the Muslim World," *Nawa-e Waqt* (in Urdu), August 12, 2005 (FBIS translated).

51. "Pakistan-India: Musharraf, Indian Officials on Pakistani Cruise Missile Test," FBIS Analysis, September 15, 2005.

52. Ahmed Ijaz Malik, "North Korea: Brinksmanship to Nuclear Threshold," *IPRI Journal* 5, no. 1 (Winter 2005), http://ipripak.org/journal/winter2005/northkorea.shtml.

53. Islamabad Associated Press of Pakistan (in English), March 22, 2007.

54. "Pakistan 3rd Country of the World in Latest Missile Technology," Kuwait News Agency, March 24, 2007, http://www.kuna.net.kw/home/Story.aspx?Language=en&DSNO=964788.

55. Agence France-Presse in Hong Kong, July 26, 2007.

56. Manu Pubby, "Army to Get BrahMos on June 21," *Indian Express* (internet version, in English), June 16, 2007.

57. Sayan Majumdar, "Fifth BrahMos Missile Test Successful," New Delhi Defence Consultants (internet version, in English), November 13, 2003.

58. Vishal Thapar, "Pakistan Flaunts N-Missile, Catches India Unawares" (television report, in English), Noida CNN-IBN, April 5, 2006.

59. "Cruise Control: Missile Deal Can Boost Tech Capability," *The Tribune* (online edition), September 7, 2006, http://www.tribuneindia.com/2006/20060907/edit.htm#top.

60. Siddharth Srivastava, "India Sets Sights on Cruise Missile Market," *Asia Times,* January 30, 2007, http://www.atimes.com/atimes/South_Asia/IA30Df05.html.

61. Sujan Dutta, "Fearless Tomahawk-Type Missile on Radar," *The Telegraph* (internet version, in English), July 20, 2007.

62. Mark A. Stokes, *China's Strategic Modernization: Implications for the United States* (Carlisle, PA: Strategic Studies Institute, U.S. Army War College, 1999), 81.

63. Chen Tsung-yi, "Military Talk Column," *Hsin Tai Wan* (in Chinese), July 18, 2003 (FBIS translated). Belying the writer's understanding of just how difficult effectively defending against LACMs really is, he goes on to suggest that short-range air defense systems then in Taiwan's possession could be used to intercept cruise missiles. Although in theory, this is true, in practice, it depends on the density of the defense, the amount of airspace in which defense engagements occur, and several other factors. As Chinese strategists argue, the offensive side has a 9:1 cost advantage over the defense. See Chapter 8 for more details.

64. Rich Chang, "China to Deploy Cruise Missiles," *Taipei Times* (internet version, in English), April 24, 2005.

65. Kim Min-seok, "Seoul Has Longer-range Cruise Missile," *JoongAng Ilbo* (internet version, in English), September 21, 2006.

66. "Korea Test Fires 1000 km Cruise Missile," *Dong-A IIbo* (internet version, in English), October 24, 2006.

67. "Cruise Missile Technology May Have Leaked to DPRK From Iran; All Parts of Japan Fall Within Range," *Sankei Shimbun* (internet version, in Japanese), June 26, 2005 (FBIS translated).

68. "Government Set to Step Up Air Defense/Cruise Missile Attack Fears," *Yomiuri Shimbun,* January 27, 2008, http://www.yomiuri.co.jp/dy/national/20080127TDY01304.htm.

69. Dmitriy Litovkin, "West Takes Fright at Satan's Heir," *Izvestiya* (in Russian), May 31, 2007 (FBIS translated).

CHAPTER 8

1. This description is derived from S. M. Hali, "Exercise Vajra Shakti," *The Nation,* May 19, 2005.

2. The National Security Strategy of the United States of America, September 2002, http://www.whitehouse.gov/nsc/nss.pdf.

3. For a useful appraisal of the new doctrine, see William W. Keller and Gordon R. Mitchell, eds., *Hitting First: Preventive Force in U.S. Security Strategy* (Pittsburgh: University of Pittsburgh Press, 2006).

4. Quoted in Husain Haqqani, "Why India Cannot Afford a Pre-emptive Strike on Pakistan," Carnegie Endowment for International Peace, http://www.carnegieendowment. org/publications/index.cfm?fa=view&id=1239.

5. Lawrence Freedman, *The Revolution in Strategic Affairs,* Adelphi Paper 318 (Oxford: Oxford University Press, 1998), 70.

6. Interview with a non-U.S. diplomat who participated in MTCR's formulation of the Hague Code of Conduct, June 2003, Surrey, UK. This individual heavily insinuated that the United States disproved of the inclusion of cruise missiles in the Hague Code. Also see Vann Van Diepen, "Missile Nonproliferation: Accomplishments and Future Challenges," *International Export Control Observer* 5 (March 2006): 16–18. Van Diepen's comments here came as he was about to step down from his position as director, Office of Missile Threat Reduction, U.S. Department of State. In that position, Van Diepen served as head of the U.S. delegations to the MTCR and Hague Code of Conduct. Although Van Diepen did not state that the United States blackballed the inclusion of cruise missiles in the Hague Code, when asked, during his February 15, 2006 presentation at the Center for Nonproliferation Studies in Washington, D.C. if he thought that the United States might change its position in that regard, his answer was blunt: he was willing to bet his pension that the answer would be no.

7. For the report of the international conference, see "Challenges in Missile Non-Proliferation—Multilateral Approaches: The Hague Code of Conduct against Ballistic Missile Proliferation," May 30, 2007, http://www.iss-eu.org/activ/content/s2007e.html#5.

8. For a useful analysis of the flaws of such a strategy and some suggested alternative approaches, see Antony J. Blinken, "From Preemption to Engagement," *Survival* 45, no. 4 (Winter 2003–04): 33–60.

9. Quoted in ibid., 36–37.

10. See Moammar Gadhafi's interview with CNN, http://www.cnn.com/2003/WORLD/africa/12/22/gadhafi.interview/index.html. However, the Libyans commenced discussions with British and U.S. intelligence operatives before the invasion of Iraq.

11. For an analysis of current debates emanating from the 2001 NPR, see Dennis M. Gormley, "Silent Retreat: The Future of U.S. Nuclear Weapons," *Nonproliferation Review* 14, no. 2 (July 2007): 183–206.

12. The 2001 NPR remains a classified document but most of it has been posted on the GlobalSecurity.org web site, http://globalsecurity.org/wmd/library/policy/dod/npr.htm. The three legs of the old triad consisted of land-based, nuclear-armed ballistic missiles, submarine-launched ballistic missiles, and strategic aircraft.

13. The notion of conflating nuclear, biological, and chemical weapons into the common appellation "WMD" implies that they produce mass destruction effects that are broadly comparable. But the late physicist Wolfgang Panofsky argued cogently that the effects of chemical weapons are not too different from those produced by conventional weapons. And while the effects of biological weapons are potentially devastating, such agents are notoriously difficult to disseminate effectively, and protective measures or antidotes in many cases can greatly diminish their effects. Thus, Panofsky concluded, only nuclear weapons are deserving of treatment as truly mass casualty weapons. See Wolfgang K. H. Panofsky, "A Damaging Designation," *Bulletin of the Atomic Scientists* 63, no. 1 (January/February 2007): 37–39.

14. The 2001 NPR discussed the possibility of studying the feasibility of converting existing nuclear bombs into earth-penetrating ones adequate to contain collateral damage while destroying deeply buried facilities, or their contents. Both houses of the U.S. Congress have been steadfast in their aversion to sponsoring or even funding a study of such a weapon, however. Past nuclear controversies of a similar character include President Eisenhower's "New Look" policy, which attempted unsuccessfully to reduce the stigma associated with nuclear use, and President Carter's failed attempt to produce an enhanced radiation weapon, or "neutron bomb," presumably one that would greatly reduce collateral damage and thus become more plausibly "useful."

15. Thomas A. Keaney and Eliot A. Cohen, *Gulf War Air Power Survey: Summary Report* (Washington, DC: Government Printing Office, 1993), 243.

16. Les Aspin, "The Defense Department's New Nuclear Counterproliferation Initiative," Address to the National Academy of Sciences, Washington, D.C., December 7, 1993.

17. Special operations forces achieved the only recorded success. Clyde Walker, director of the Defense Intelligence Agency's Missile and Space Intelligence Center, acknowledged this accomplishment in his public remarks at the April 27, 2006 Cruise Missile and IED Conference, held in Arlington, VA.

18. Joint Publication 3–01.5, *Doctrine for Joint Theater Missile Defense* (Washington, DC: Government Printing Office, 1994).

19. U.S. Army Space and Strategic Defense Command, "Army Theater Missile Defense Primer," PAM 10–1, April 1, 1996, 1.

20. Ibid., 2.

21. See China's 2004 White paper, http://www.fas.org/nuke/guide/china/doctrine/natdef2004.html#10.

22. Thomas E. Ricks, *Fiasco: The American Military Adventure in Iraq* (New York: Penguin Press, 2006), 124–125. To be sure, the Iraqis managed to continue firing ballistic and cruise

missiles throughout the brief campaign, but not nearly at the same rate per day as during the first Gulf War in 1991.

23.   In military parlance, this means developing special tactics, techniques, training, and procedures to find and attack such targets. See Robert P. Haffa and Jasper Welch, "Command and Control Arrangement for the Attack of Time-Sensitive Targets," Northrop Grumman Analysis Center, November 2005, 34.

24.   Gen. Hal M. Hornburg, U.S. Air Force air combat commander, quoted in *Air Force,* November 2004, 72, as cited in ibid., 39. Much of this improvement inevitably relates to rules of engagement. For example, in Operation Enduring Freedom in Afghanistan, Gen. Tommy Franks, commander of the U.S. Central Command (CENTCOM), headquartered in Tampa, FL, required that decisions to attack targets be approved by CENTCOM. Consequently, this lag in decision time led to several important targets being lost. By the 2003 war in Iraq, Gen. Franks decided to delegate most of the authority to attack time-sensitive targets to the local air component commander, which led to a 50 percent improvement in effectiveness compared with operations in Afghanistan. See Amy Butler, "Moseley: Time Sensitive Targeting Improved from Afghanistan to Iraq," *Inside the Air Force,* June 20, 2003, 1.

25.   Barbara Opall-Rome, "Sensor to Shooter in 1 Minute," *Defense News,* October 2, 2006, 1. Opall-Rome reports "over 100" Hezbollah rocket launchers were destroyed. The figure, 125, is reported in No'am Ofir, "Look Not to the Skies: The IAF vs. Surface-to-Surface Rocket Launchers," *Strategic Assessment,* November 1–30, 2006, e-mail text published by the Jaffee Center for Strategic Studies, Tel Aviv, Israel.

26.   For an analysis of Global Strike and its pros and cons, see Hans M. Kristensen, "U.S. Strategic War Planning After 9/11," *Nonproliferation Review* 14, no. 2 (July 2007): 373–390.

27.   William M. Arkin, "Early Warning: Attack Iran? We're Ready," *Washington Post,* January 17, 2006, http://blog.washingtonpost.com/earlywarning/2006/01/attack_iran_were_ ready.html.

28.   The most prominent type of target mentioned by the Pentagon is terrorist related. See http://www.dod.mil/news/Mar2006/20060309_4439.html.

29.   See Dennis M. Gormley, "Conventional Force Integration in Global Strike," in James J. Wirtz and Jeffrey A. Larsen, eds., *Nuclear Transformation: The New U.S. Nuclear Doctrine* (New York: Palgrave, 2005): 53–68.

30.   See Steve Andreasen, "Off Target? The Bush Administration's Plan to Arm Long-Range Ballistic Missiles with Conventional Warheads," *Arms Control Today* 36, no. 6 (July/ August 2006), http://www.armscontrol.org/act/2006_07-08/.

31.   See Steve Andreasen, "The Ramifications of Making Ballistic Missiles More Usable," *San Francisco Chronicle,* February 14, 2006.

32.   For example, see Tom Sauer, "Limiting National Missile Defence," *Bulletin 22— Nuclear Policy, Terrorism and Missile Defence,* International Network of Engineers and Scientists Against Proliferation, http://www.inesap.org/bulletin22/bul22art31.htm. Among others, Sauer cites arms control specialist Jack Mendelsohn who argues that Russia remains concerned about America's capacity to employ powerful ground- and space-based radars and infrared sensors to greatly improve prospects for thick missile defenses.

33.   The characterization "rush to failure" came from a panel chaired by Gen. Larry Welch, U.S. Air Force (retired), which met in late 1997 to investigate ways of reducing risk in missile defense flight testing. For the full panel report, see http://www.fas.org/spp/starwars/program/ welch/.

34.   If it can be accomplished, boost-phase intercept offers many operational advantages. Obviously, destroying the enemy missile before it reaches its mid-course phase, when it can deploy decoys, eliminates that countermeasure challenge. Moreover, if chemical or biological payloads are involved, they descend on enemy rather than friendly territory. The rub is in designing a fast enough interceptor to do the job within perhaps 30 to 90 seconds after missile launch and getting close enough to the launch site to do the job within that narrow timeframe.

35.   John Liang, "DoD Finds Cruise Missile Defense 'Gaps,'" *InsideDefense.com News-Stand,* August 17, 2006, http://www.military.com/features/0,15240,110199,00.html

36.   Jack Mendelsohn, "The Impact of NMD on the ABM Treaty," in Joseph Cirincione et al., *White Paper on National Missile Defense* (Washington, DC: Lawyers Alliance for World Security, 2000).

37.   See Keir A. Lieber and Daryl G. Press, "The Rise of U.S. Nuclear Primacy," *Foreign Affairs* 85, no. 2 (March/April 2006) and Aleksandr Sharavin and Mikhail Lukan, "Russia's Underarmed Forces," *Trud* (in Russian), August 23, 2007 (Foreign Broadcast Information Services [FBIS] translated).

38.   See Dennis M. Gormley, "Thwarting U.S. Missile Defense From Within the Missile Technology Control Regime," in Davis Bobrow, ed., *Modification and Resistance to American Foreign Policy* (Pittsburgh: University of Pittsburgh Press, forthcoming in 2008).

39.   Striking the wrong target not only wastes attack resources but it could also entail friendly-fire consequences (a bus-load of children or civilians, for example). On "look-alike" population increases, see Gregory DeSantis and Steven J. McKay, *Unmanned Aerial Vehicles: Technical and Operational Aspects of an Emerging Threat,* PSR-Veridian Report 2869 (Arlington, VA: Pacific-Sierra Research-Veridian Corporation, 2000).

40.   The academic literature, particularly in regard to the U.S.-Soviet competition, is large. But nothing better captures the importance of recalling that intelligence assessments will inevitably be fraught with more noise than unambiguous signals than Roberta Wohlstetter, *Pearl Harbor: Warning and Decision* (Stanford: Stanford University Press, 1962).

41.   For two excellent if divergent treatments of the problem and challenges of establishing norms for missiles, see Aaron Karp, "Going Ballistic? Reversing Missile Proliferation," *Arms Control Today* 35, no. 5 (June 2005) and Mark Smith, "Pragmatic Micawberism? Norm Construction on Ballistic Missiles," *Contemporary Security Policy* 27, no. 3 (December 2006).

42.   Nina Tannenwald, "Stigmatizing the Bomb," *International Security* 29, no. 4 (Spring 2005), 8, as cited in Smith, "Pragmatic Micawberism? Norm Construction on Ballistic Missiles" (see Chap. 8, n. 41). For the Canadian view of its Foreign Affairs and International Trade office, see http://www.dfait-maeci.gc.ca/arms/missile-en.asp.

43.   K. Scott McMahon and Dennis M. Gormley, *Controlling the Spread of Land-Attack Cruise Missiles* (Marina del Ray, CA: American Institute for Strategic Cooperation, 1995), 2 and 45–73.

44.   This certainly was the case during the first term of the Bill Clinton administration in official treatment of both missile nonproliferation and counterproliferation policy articulation. See ibid., 75–80. Yet, even more recently, the documentation pertaining to nonproliferation policy produced by important MTCR members comes up short on emphasizing the fact that both ballistic and cruise missiles are covered under the regime. See, for example, "UK's Strategic Nuclear Deterrent: Memorandum submitted by the Ministry of Defence," November 2005, http://www.publications.parliament.uk/pa/cm200506/cmselect/cmdfence/uc986-i/ucm0102.htm. In addressing the MTCR in the memorandum, the ministry describes Category I systems as follows: "These comprise complete rocket systems . . . " suggesting that

complete unmanned aerial systems, including cruise missiles, were not included. Perhaps the ministry should have chosen the verb "include" rather than "comprise" in describing Category I systems.

45.　See http://www.mtcr.info/english/press/helinski.html.

46.　For a copy of the Code, the Netherlands' Foreign Ministry press release, and selected statements by governments, see http://www.acronym.org.uk/docs/0211/doc13.htm.

47.　Louis René Beres, "Israel's Uncertain Strategic Future," *Parameters* 37, no. 1 (Spring 2007): 37–54. Other members of the study group included Naaman Belkind, a retired engineer who worked for Israel's Atomic Energy Commission and Ministry of Defense; Dr. Isaac Ben-Israel, Maj. Gen. (Reserve), Israeli air force; Dr. Rand H. Fishbein, former national security staff aid to Senator Daniel Inouye; Dr. Adir Pridor, a retired Lt. Col. and former head of military analysis for the Israeli air force; and Yoash Tsiddon-Chatto, Col. (Reserve), Israeli air force.

48.　Ibid., 37.

49.　Ibid., 48–49.

50.　Ibid.

51.　Ibid., 52.

52.　See Hans M. Kristensen, "The Role of U.S. Nuclear Weapons: New Doctrine Falls Short of Bush Pledge," *Arms Control Today* 35, no. 7 (September 2005), http://www.armscontrol.org/act/2005_09/Kristensen.asp. On the doctrine's cancellation, see "Pentagon Cancels Controversial Nuclear Doctrine," http://www.nukestrat.com/us/jcs/canceled.htm.

53.　For a comprehensive listing of published documents pertaining to U.S. nuclear weapons guidance, see http://www.nukestrat.com/us/guidance.htm.

54.　"Iran Seeks Cruise Missile to Support Shihab," *Middle East Newsline,* June 10, 2004.

55.　Saeed Barzin, "BBC Monitoring Analysis" (in English), September 6, 2007 (FBIS transcribed).

56.　Hali, "Exercise Vajra Shakti" (see Chap. 8, n. 1).

57.　Unless otherwise indicated, the discussion of Operation Parakram and its implications depends on Sharad Joshi, *The Practice of Coercive Diplomacy in the Post 9/11 Period,* Unpublished PhD dissertation, Graduate School of Public and International Affairs, University of Pittsburgh, December 2006.

58.　See White House "Fact Sheet: United States and India: Strategic Partnership," March 2006, http://www.whitehouse.gov/news/releases/2006/03/20060302-13.html.

59.　Rajat Pandit, "IAF Plans War Doctrine to Expand 'Strategic Reach,'" *The Times of India* (internet version, in English), August 2, 2007.

60.　Vishal Thapar, "Pakistan Flaunts N-Missile, Catches India Unawares" (television report, in English), Noida CNN-IBN, April 5, 2006.

61.　"No Time to Lose," *New Delhi Force* (internet version, in English), March 9, 2005 (FBIS transcribed text).

62.　"Cruise Control: Missile Deal Can Boost Tech Capability," *The Tribune* (online edition), September 7, 2006, http://www.tribuneindia.com/2006/20060907/edit.htm#top

63.　July 2007 e-mail interview with a former French export control official, who did not have knowledge of the incident but speculated along the lines suggested here.

64.　Hali, "Exercise Vajra Shakti" (see Chap. 8, n. 1).

65.　Indian navy Chief Admiral Arun Prakash has essentially argued as such. See television report by Vishal Thapar, "Pakistan Flaunts N-Missile" (see Chap. 8, n. 60).

66.   Quoted in Minnie Chan, "PLA to Have Missile Ascendancy Over Taiwan by 2010, Expert Says," *South China Morning Post* (internet version, in English), April 25, 2007 (FBIS transcribed).

67.   Ibid.

68.   Wendell Minnick, "Taiwan Tests 'Brave Wind' Cruise Missile," *Defense News,* March 12, 2007, http://www.defensenews.com/story.php?F=2610742&C=asiapac.

69.   *FY04 Report to Congress on PRC Military Power* (Washington, DC: Office of the Secretary of Defense, 2004), 53–54.

70.   Holmes Liao, "Taiwan's Strategy on Cruise Missile Defense," Unpublished white paper, no date, mimeo.

71.   Ibid., 8.

72.   Kathrin Hille, "Taiwan Speeds Up Race to Match Beijing Missiles," *Financial Times* (Asia edition), September 25, 2004, 3.

73.   Liao, "Taiwan's Strategy on Cruise Missile Defense," 8 (see Chap. 8, n. 70).

74.   See, for example, Seoul *Dong-A Ilbo* (internet, text in English), October 24, 2006 (FBIS transcribed). As regards the 2001 agreement with the United States, "Although it is prohibited by the U.S. government to develop ballistic missiles with over 300 km missile range and 500 kg weight, the government can develop cruise missiles with no limitation on missile range as long as it [warhead] does not weigh over 500 kg." This South Korean interpretation is repeated almost verbatim in every story on Seoul's new LACMs.

75.   See, for example, *The Korea Herald* (internet version, in English), October 28, 2006.

76.   Kim Min-seok, "Seoul Feels Squeezed by Neighbors' Arms Race," *JoongAng Ilbo* (internet version, in English), March 28, 2007 (FBIS transcribed).

77.   For an appraisal of developments through mid-2006, see Daniel A. Pinkston and Kazutaka Sakurai, "Japan Debates Preparing for Future Preemptive Strikes against North Korea," *The Korean Journal of Defense Analysis* 18, no. 4 (Winter 2006): 95–121.

78.   Martin Sieff, "Japan Debates First Strike Idea," *United Press International,* July 24, 2006, http://www.spacewar.com/reports/Japan_Debates_First_Strike_Idea_999.html.

79.   See, for example, "Japan's Strategic Realignment," *IISS Strategic Comments* 11, no. 9, November 2005.

80.   Hideaki Kaneda, "Is It Possible for the SDF to Attack Enemy Missile Bases?" *Sekai no Kansen* (in Japanese), February 1, 2007 (FBIS translated text). Other advocates include retired General Toshiyuki Shikata and former Japan Defense Agency Director General Fukushiro Nukaga.

81.   Yoshiyuki Komurata, "Nukaga Suggests 'Discussion' on Possessing Tomahawks," *Asahi Shimbun* (morning edition, in Japanese), May 3, 2007, 4 (FBIS translated text).

CHAPTER 9

1.   Dennis M. Gormley, *Dealing with the Threat of Cruise Missiles,* Adelphi Paper 339 (Oxford: Oxford University Press, 2001), 11.

2.   Roberta Wohlstetter, *Pearl Harbor: Warning and Decision* (Stanford: Stanford University Press, 1962), 387.

3.   Gormley, *Dealing with the Threat of Cruise Missiles,* Chapters 4 and 5 (see Chap. 9, n. 1).

4.   Indirect evidence of Rumsfeld's concern about the cruise missile threat was reflected in the strategy review he instituted at the start of his posting as Defense Secretary. See Gormley, *Dealing with the Threat of Cruise Missiles,* 96 (see Chap. 9, n. 1). Nearly a year after the terrorist attacks of September 11, Rumsfeld was reported to have sent a classified memo to the

White House warning of the spread of cruise missiles and urging a major effort to improve defenses against them. See Bradley Graham, "Rumsfeld: Cruise Missile Threat Rises," *Washington Post*, August 18, 2002, A1.

5. Richard Speier, "Can the Missile Technology Control Regime Be Repaired?" in Joseph Cirincione, ed., *Repairing the Regime* (Washington, DC: Routledge, 2000), 202–216.

6. Frederick J. Hollinger, "The Missile Technology Control Regime: A Major New Arms Control Achievement," in U.S. Arms Control and Disarmament Agency, *World Military Expenditures and Arms Transfers 1987* (Washington, DC: Government Printing Office, 1998), 26.

7. Dinshaw Mistry, *Containing Missile Proliferation* (Seattle, WA: University of Washington Press, 2003), 96. Mistry states that the policy declaration that Washington negotiated with Seoul included a tradeoff provision allowing South Korea to develop 500-km-range LACMs with a lighter 400-kg warhead. South Korean press reports, however, uniformly indicate that the agreement placed no restriction on the range of cruise missiles as long as the payload remained under 500 kg. See, for example, "Korea Test Fires 1000 km Cruise Missile," *Dong-A Ilbo* (internet version, in English), October 24, 2006, which states that "Although it is prohibited by the U.S. agreement to develop ballistic missiles with over 300 km missile range and 500 kg weight, the government can develop cruise missiles with no limitation on missile range as long as it does not weigh over 500 kg." The weight referred to in this quotation relates to the payload, not to the gross weight of the missile.

8. Mistry, *Containing Missile Proliferation,* 95 (see Chap. 9, n. 7).

9. See the MTCR's technical annex, http://www.mtcr.info/english/index.html.

10. Dennis M. Gormley and Richard Speier, "Controlling Unmanned Air Vehicles: New Challenges," *Nonproliferation Review* 10, no. 2 (Summer 2003), 75.

11. Bradley Graham, "Terrorist Air Assault Caught the Pentagon Napping," *International Herald Tribune,* September 17, 2001, 3.

12. Richard A. Muller, "The Cropdusting Terrorist," *Technology Review,* March 11, 2002, http://muller.lbl.gov/TRessays/02_Cropduster_Terrorism.htm.

13. Dennis M. Gormley, "UAVs and Cruise Missiles as Possible Terrorist Weapons," in James Clay Moltz, ed., *New Challenges in Missile Proliferation, Missile Defense, and Space Security,* Occasional Paper No. 12 (Monterey, CA: Monterey Institute's Center for Nonproliferation Studies, 2003), 3–10, and Dennis M. Gormley, "Globalization and WMD Networks: The Case of Unmanned Air Vehicles as Terrorist Weapons," *Strategic Insights* 5, no. 6 (July 2006), http://www.ccc.nps.navy.mil/si/2006/Jul/gormleyJul06.asp.

14. "Nonproliferation: Assessing Missile Technology Export Controls," Hearing Before the Subcommittee on National Security, Emerging Threats and International Relations of the Committee on Government Reform, House of Representatives, 108th Congress, 2nd Session, March 9, 2004, Serial No. 108–165. See my testimony at http://www.cns.miis.edu/research/congress/testim/testgorm.htm.

15. See http://www.mtcr.info/english/Annex2005-002.doc. The new provision is found as item 19.A.3.

16. See the MTCR annex for 2006 at http://www.mtcr.info/english/annex.html. Propulsion systems are covered under Item 3, while navigation technology is addressed under Item 9.

17. The testimony of Vann Van Diepen on this subject is instructive. See "Nonproliferation: Assessing Missile Technology Export Controls," 162–163 (see Chap. 9, n. 14).

18. See the testimony of Lisa Bronson, "Nonproliferation: Assessing Missile Technology Export Controls," 154–160 (see Chap. 9, n. 14).

19.   William A. Schoneberger, "Backfitting Stealth," *Journal of Electronic Defense* 21, no. 3 (March 1998): 33–37.

20.   While the United States might tightly control the export of such unique countermeasures equipment, there is palpable value in bringing these devices under the aegis of the MTCR. Assuming that the MTCR states could reach consensus on their incorporation, their control would be effectively broadened to include 33 other states, many of which are capable of producing not only LACMs but also endgame countermeasures tailored to the signature of the supported LACM.

21.   "National Security Presidential Directive/NSPD-23 on National Policy on Ballistic Missile Defense," December 16, 2002, http://www.fas.org/irp/offdocs/nspd/nspd-23.htm.

22.   Amy Svitak and Gopal Ratnam, "Missile Defense Vs. Non-Proliferation," *Defense News,* July 14, 2003, 1.

23.   See, for example, Mitchell Kugler, "Missile Defense Cooperation and the Missile Technology Control Regime," in Henry Sokolski, ed., *Taming the Next Set of Strategic Weapons Threats* (Carlisle, PA: Strategic Studies Institute, U.S. Army War College, June 2006), 53–60.

24.   Dana Milbank and Dafna Linzer, "U.S., India May Share Nuclear Technology," *Washington Post,* July 19, 2005, A1. In a May 2007 interview I conducted in Vienna, Austria with a non-U.S. official who was privy to recent MTCR deliberations, the official stated that the United States had yet to acknowledge that it had made an exception permitting the sale of Arrow to India.

25.   Amy Svitak, "New U.S. Policy Paves Way For Predator Sale to Italy," *Defense News,* April 15–21, 2002.

26.   Dennis M. Gormley and Richard Speier, "New Missiles and Models for Cooperation," in Sokolski, ed., *Taming the Next Set of Strategic Weapons Threats,* 121–150 (see Chap. 9, n. 23).

27.   Ibid., 145–150. The idea of UAV services is the brainchild of Dr. Richard Speier, a former Pentagon official and one of the principal architects of the MTCR in 1987.

28.   David A. Fulghum, "Israeli Company Is Conducting Surveillance for the Military," *Aviation Week & Space Technology,* June 16, 2003.

29.   Perry Sims, "PACAF Considering Leasing Australian UAV," *Journal of Aerospace and Defense Industry News,* November 1, 2002.

30.   In 2006 the United States attempted to change the MTCR's currently simple criteria for determining a Category I cruise missile or UAV. Although I am not privy to the precise details of the attempted reformulation, a November 2006 interview with a non-U.S. official familiar with MTCR deliberations indicates that the U.S. position reflected a desire to loosen controls on large UAVs while tightening them on supersonic LACMs that fall just under the MTCR's Category I range and payload thresholds (such as the BrahMos). Naturally, such a proposal was not likely to elicit the support of Russia and it appears that the proposal did not achieve the necessary consensus among MTCR member states.

31.   See the Department of Commerce, Bureau of Industry and Security Annual Report-FY 1999, https://www.bis.doc.gov/News/Publications/99AnnReport/Ann99Chap4.html and Van Diepen, "Nonproliferation: Assessing Missile Technology Export Controls" (see Chap. 9, n. 14).

32.   Donald MacKenzie, "Theories of Technology and the Abolition of Nuclear Weapons," in Donald MacKenzie and Judy Wajcman, eds., *The Social Shaping of Technology* (Philadelphia: Open University Press, 1999), 425–426. The transfer of tacit knowledge skills requires time for learning from a master. This differs from the release of technology covered under the "deemed export" rule of the U.S. Export Administration Regulations. An export

of technology is deemed to have taken place when, say, blueprints or the oral transfer of technical information to a foreign national takes place within the United States. For details on deemed exports, see http://www.bis.doc.gov/deemedexports/deemedexportsfaqs.html#1.

33. I am grateful to Sonia Ben Ouagrham-Gormley, a senior researcher at the Center for Nonproliferation Studies, for information on Russian policy related to retired defense industry specialists. On the Federal Security Service's strong-arm attitude, see "Russian Chemist Accused of Divulging State Secrets," *International Export Control Observer* 6 (April 2006): 10–12.

34. Michael Beck and Igor Khripunov, "U.S.-Russian Engagement in Space: Space Cooperation and Nonproliferation," Unpublished paper submitted to the Eisenhower Institute, June 12, 2002.

35. See "Proliferation Security Initiative (PSI) At a Glance," Fact Sheet, Arms Control Association, http://www.armscontrol.org/factsheets/PSI.asp.

36. For a keen appraisal of UNSCR 1540's implementation challenges, see Peter Crail, "Implementing UN Security Council Resolution 1540: A Risk-Based Approach," *Nonproliferation Review* 13, no. 2 (July 2006): 355–399.

37. On the utility of the EXBS program, see Sonia Ben Ouagrham-Gormley, "An Unrealized Nexus? WMD-Related Trafficking, Terrorism, and Organized Crime in the Former Soviet Union," *Arms Control Today* 37, no. 6 (July/August 2007): 6–13.

38. For an exhaustive study of the general prerequisites for the implementation of a successful technology denial strategy, see National Academy of Sciences, *Finding Common Ground: U.S. Export Controls in a Changed Global Environment* (Washington, DC: National Academy Press, 1991).

39. Of course, there are those who would prefer not to include proliferators because they are likely to make reaching consensus on important new regime initiatives problematic. See Speier, "Can the Missile Technology Control Regime Be Repaired?" (see Chap. 9, n. 5).

40. Anupam Srivastava, "China's Export Controls: Can Beijing's Actions Match Its Words? *Arms Control Today* 35, no. 9 (November 2005), http://www.armscontrol.org/act/2005_11/NOV-China.asp.

41. Ibid.

42. Also worthy of consideration is the use of the MTCR's outreach activities to help China with its enforcement challenges. The good offices of the European Union also ought to be brought to bear to work with China on its enforcement weaknesses.

43. Victor Zaborsky, "Does China Belong in the Missile Technology Control Regime? *Arms Control Today* 34, no. 8 (October 2004), http://www.armscontrol.org/act/2004_10/Zaborsky.asp.

44. Albert Wohlstetter, Foreword to K. Scott McMahon and Dennis M. Gormley, *Controlling the Spread of Land-Attack Cruise Missiles* (Marina del Ray, CA: American Institute for Strategic Cooperation, 1995), v.

45. For details including a full listing of commissioners, see the WMD Commission web site, http://www.wmdcommission.org/sida.asp?id=1.

46. See *Weapons of Terror: Freeing the World of Nuclear, Biological and Chemical Arms,* Synopsis, May 2006, 15, http://www.wmdcommission.org/files/english.pdf.

47. Surely strong supporters of LACMs and UAVs as highly discriminating conventional weapons will argue against the Code's broadened scope. I would also anticipate that they would argue that many UAVs are entirely benign reconnaissance or surveillance systems, not weapons. But the important point to note is that the Hague Code does not prohibit the spread

of such systems. The Code grew out of the MTCR, but it does not, like the MTCR, specify range or payload thresholds for the missiles it addresses. Thus, UAVs under the Code should be seen broadly in much the same way they are viewed in the MTCR's Category I and Category II treatments of UAVs.

48.   Section 274 of the *National Defense Authorization Act for Fiscal Year 1996* (Washington, DC: Government Printing Office, 1995), 59–60.

49.   See Bryan Bender, "Defense Science Board Report Brands Cruise Missiles Increasing Threat," *Inside the Army* 7 (January 30, 1995), 1, and Richard Lardner, "Cruise Missile Defense Group Recommends AWACS, E-2C Upgrades," *Inside Missile Defense* 1, no. 4 (November 4, 1995), 1, 6–7.

50.   For rumors of the organization's termination, see Daniel G. Dupont, "Joint Theater Organization May Be Terminated," *Inside Missile Defense* 6, no. 17 (August 23, 2000), 3–4. For a descriptive profile of JTAMDO's budget and programs, see http://www.dtic.mil/descriptivesum/y2006/TJS/0605126J.pdf.

51.   Bradley Graham, "Rumsfeld: Cruise Missile Threat Rises," *Washington Post*, August 18, 2002, A1.

52.   Of course, none of this information was terribly new. See Gormley, *Dealing with the Threat of Cruise Missiles*, especially Chapter 2 (see Chap. 9, n. 1).

53.   On U.S. air defense development, see William P. Delaney, "Air Defense of the United States: Strategic Missions and Modern Technology," *International Security* 15, no. 1 (Summer 1990): 181–211.

54.   Timothy J. Biggs and Raymond V. Stuchell, "Capability-Based Acquisition: Key Factor in Meeting 21st Century Threats," *Program Manager*, September–December 2003, http://findarticles.com/p/articles/mi_m0KAA/is_5_32/ai_111506013.

55.   Robert W. Brinson, Jr., William Jones, Jr., and Patrick Kelly, "Reforming the Joint Acquisition Process," Paper prepared for Class #06–4, Joint Forces Staff College, Joint and Combined Warfighting School, August 25, 2006.

56.   CDI Missile Defense Update #7, August 10, 2006, http://www.cdi.org.

57.   Standard Missile-2 and -3 are earmarked for fleet and extended area defense and ballistic missile defense, respectively. The navy plans eventually to deploy the Standard Missile-6, called the Extended-Range Active Missile, for defense against LACMs. The missile will combine the Standard Missile-2's airframe and the seeker from the air force Advanced Medium-Range Air-to-Air Missile, or AMRAAM.

58.   AWACS performance is derived from Irving Lachow, *GPS-Guided Cruise Missiles and Weapons of Mass Destruction*, RP-463 (Santa Monica, CA: The RAND Corporation, 1995), 11–13.

59.   Gormley, *Dealing with the Threat of Cruise Missiles*, Chapter 4 (see Chap. 9, n. 1).

60.   See Bender, "Defense Science Board Report Brands Cruise Missiles Increasing Threat" (see Chap. 9, n. 49) and Lardner, "Cruise Missile Defense Group Recommends AWACS, E-2C Upgrades" (see Chap. 9, n. 49) for Defense Science Board recommendations in the mid-1990s. For one of several think tank contributions, see David Tanks, *Assessing the Cruise Missile Puzzle: How Great the Defense Challenge?* (Washington, DC: Institute for Foreign Policy Analysis, 2000).

61.   David A. Fulghum, "Stealth, Cheap Technology Complicate Defense Schemes," *Aviation Week & Space Technology*, July 14, 1997, 47, cited in Lt. Col. Phil Tissue et al, "Attacking the Cruise Missile Threat," Paper prepared for Class #03–3, Joint Forces Staff College, September 8, 2003, 19.

62. The DARPA study is referred to in Gregory DeSantis and Steven J. McKay, *Unmanned Aerial Vehicles: Technical and Operational Aspects of an Emerging Threat,* PSR-Veridian Report 2869 (Arlington, VA: Pacific-Sierra Research-Veridian Corporation, 2000), 9. The cost of $4 million per kill includes the cost of missiles fired and assets (like launchers) used. It is conservative in that today's cost of Patriot interceptors has risen significantly since the study was conducted.

63. Ravi R. Hichkad and Christopher Bolkcom, "Cruise Missile Defense," CRS Report to Congress, May 2, 2005, http://fas.org/sgp/crs/weapons/index.html.

64. David A. Fulghum, "Radar Threatens Stealth," *Aviation Week & Space Technology,* June 18, 2007, 132.

65. On the fate of E-10 and JSTARS, see Loren B. Thompson, "Fate of Secret Radar Reflects Transformation's Waning Role," Issue Brief, Lexington Institute, Arlington, VA, August 11, 2006. On the various antenna sizes of the MP-RTIP, see David A. Fulghum, "E-10 Takes Shape," *Aviation Week & Space Technology,* June 13, 2005, http://integrator.hanscom.af.mil/2005/July/07072005/07072005-15.htm. The JSTARS radar would not perform as well as the E-10's because the antenna's dimensions limit its ability to detect and track LACMs by virtue of less altitude discrimination.

66. Thompson, "Fate of Secret Radar Reflects Transformation's Waning Role" (see Chap. 9, n. 65).

67. Mickey McCarter, "Boost for Cruise Missile Defense," *Military Aerospace Technology* 3, no. 2 (June 25, 2004), http://www.military-aerospace-technology.com/article.cfm? DocID=521.

68. The cost figure cited is taken from Tanks, *Assessing the Cruise Missile Puzzle,* 28 (see Chap. 9, n. 60).

69. Bradley Peniston, "Navy E-2Cs Eye New Niches," *Defense News,* April 27–28, 2006, http://www.defensenews.com/promos/conferences/cmd/1735997.html.

70. Tanks, *Assessing the Cruise Missile Puzzle,* 19 (see Chap. 9, n. 60).

71. John Liang, "DoD Finds Cruise Missile Defense 'Gaps,'" *InsideDefense.com News-Stand,* August 17, 2006, http://www.military.com/features/0,15240,110199,00.html

72. Michael Sirak and Daniel G. Dupont, "Experts: US Not Prepared for Cruise Missile Attacks," *Inside Missile Defense* 4, no. 26 (December 23, 1998), 1, 13–15.

73. Interview with senior defense industry engineer familiar with cruise missile defense issues, September 2007.

74. Senior Pentagon officials reportedly were attempting, in September 2007, to make major changes in the policy planning process within the Pentagon in order to align acquisition more sensibly with national strategy. See John T. Bennett, "DoD Seeks Sweeping Changes to Policy Planning Process," *Defense News,* September 24, 2007, 1.

75. For a useful if broader approach to confronting proliferation challenges, see Dana Allin et. al., *Repairing the Damage: Possibilities and Limits of Transatlantic Consensus,* Adelphi Paper 389 (New York: Routledge, 2007), Chapter 2.

76. "USAF Theater Missile Defense Attack Operations, Briefing to Mr. Dennis Gormley," Headquarters, U.S. Air Force/XORT, January 21, 1999, mimeo.

77. For a critical appraisal of the adverse impact of the attempt to arm Trident missiles with conventional warheads, see Charles D. Ferguson and Dinshaw Mistry, "Moving Away From Missile Programs," *Boston Globe,* June 19, 2006.

78. Quoted in Dennis Ross, *Statecraft* (New York: Farrar, Straus and Giroux, 2007), 328–329.

Selected Bibliography

Alberts, D. J. *Deterrence in the 1980s, Part II: The Role of Conventional Airpower,* Adelphi Paper 193. London: International Institute for Strategic Studies, 1984.

Allen, Kenneth W., Glenn Krumel, and Jonathan D. Pollack. *China's Air Force Enters the 21st Century.* Santa Monica, CA: The RAND Corporation, 1995.

Allin, Dana, et al. *Repairing the Damage: Possibilities and Limits of Transatlantic Consensus,* Adelphi Paper 389. New York: Routledge, 2007.

Andreasen, Steve. "Off Target? The Bush Administration's Plan to Arm Long-Range Ballistic Missiles with Conventional Warheads." *Arms Control Today* 36, no. 6 (July/August 2006).

———. "The Ramifications of Making Ballistic Missiles More Usable." *San Francisco Chronicle,* February 14, 2006.

Andreasen, Steve, and Dennis Gormley. "Edging Ever Closer to a Nuclear Death Row." *Minneapolis Star-Tribune,* March 29, 2006.

Barrie, Douglas. "Downing Street Will Have to Sign Off on Releasing the Storm Shadow." *Aviation Week & Space Technology,* May 7, 2007.

———. "Indian Air Force Proceeds with Test Plans for a Supersonic Land-Attack Program." *Aviation Week & Space Technology,* February 27, 2006.

Benjamin, Daniel, and Steven Simon. "The Worse Defense." *New York Times,* February 20, 2003.

———. *The Age of Sacred Terror.* New York: Random House, 2001.

Ben Ouagrham, Sonia, and Kathleen M. Vogel. *Conversion at Stepnogorsk: What the Future Holds for Former Bioweapons Facilities,* Occasional Paper #28. Ithaca: Cornell University Peace Studies Program, 2003.

Ben Ouagrham-Gormley, Sonia. "An Unrealized Nexus? WMD-Related Trafficking, Terrorism, and Organized Crime in the Former Soviet Union." *Arms Control Today* 37, no. 6 (July/August 2007): 6–13.

Beres, Louis René. "Israel's Uncertain Strategic Future." *Parameters* 37, no. 1 (Spring 2007): 37–54.

Berman, Robert P. *Soviet Air Power in Transition.* Washington, DC: The Brookings Institution, 1978.

Betts, Richard K. (ed.). *Cruise Missiles: Technology, Strategy, Politics.* Washington, DC: The Brookings Institution, 1981.

Biggs, Timothy J., and Raymond V. Stuchell. "Capability-Based Acquisition: Key Factor in Meeting 21st Century Threats." *Program Manager,* September–December 2003.

Blank, Stephen J. *The Dynamics of Russian Weapon Sales to China.* Carlisle, PA: Strategic Studies Institute, U.S. Army War College, 1997.

Blinken, Antony J. "From Preemption to Engagement." *Survival* 45, no. 4 (Winter 2003–04): 33–60

Boot, Max. "The American Way of War." *Foreign Affairs* 82, no. 4 (July/August 2003): 41–58.

Bracken, Paul. *Fire in the East: The Rise of Asian Military Power and the Second Nuclear Age.* New York: Harper Collins, 2000.

Buchanan, Mark. *Ubiquity: Why Catastrophes Happen.* New York: Three Rivers Press, 2001.

Burt, Richard. "Local Conflicts in the Third World." In *Cruise Missiles: Technology, Strategy, Politics.* Richard K. Betts, ed. Washington, DC: The Brookings Institution, 1981.

Butler, Amy. "Pentagon to Announce JASSM Decision in 2008." *Aviation Week & Space Technology,* July 20, 2007.

Campbell, Kurt M., Robert J. Einhorn, and Mitchell B. Reiss (eds.). *The Nuclear Tipping Point: Why States Reconsider Their Nuclear Choices.* Washington, DC: The Brookings Institution Press, 2004.

Carus, W. Seth. *Ballistic Missiles in the Third World: Threat and Response.* Westport, CT: Praeger, 1990.

———. *Cruise Missile Proliferation in the 1990s.* Westport, CT: Praeger, 1992.

Chun, Clayton K. S. *Thunder Over the Horizon.* Westport, CT: Praeger Security International, 2006.

Cirincione, Joseph. "The Declining Ballistic Missile Threat." Carnegie Endowment for International Peace, January 25, 2005.

Cirincione, Joseph, Jon B. Wolfsthal, and Miriam Rajkumar. *Deadly Arsenals: Nuclear, Biological, and Chemical Threats.* Washington, DC: Carnegie Endowment for International Peace, 2005.

Cliff, Roger, et al. *Entering the Dragon's Lair: Chinese Antiaccess Strategies and Their Implications for the United States.* Santa Monica, CA: The RAND Corporation, 2007.

Cole, Bernard D. "China's Modernization and its Impact on the United States and the Asia-Pacific." Testimony before the U.S.-China Economic and Security Review Commission, March 29, 2007.

Comprehensive Report of the Special Advisor to the DCI on Iraq's WMD, Vol. II. Washington, DC: Central Intelligence Agency, September 30, 2004.

Crail, Peter. "Implementing UN Security Council Resolution 1540: A Risk-Based Approach." *Nonproliferation Review* 13, no. 2 (July 2006): 355–399.

Cummings, M. L. "The Double-Edged Sword of Secrecy in Military Weapon Development." *IEEE Technology and Society Magazine* (Winter 2003–2004): 4–12.

Delaney, William P. "Air Defense of the United States: Strategic Missions and Modern Technology." *International Security* 15, no. 1 (Summer 1990): 181–211.

DeSantis, Gregory, and Steven J. McKay. *Unmanned Aerial Vehicles: Technical and Operational Aspects of an Emerging Threat,* PSR-Veridian Report 2869. Arlington, VA: Pacific-Sierra Research-Veridian Corporation, 2000.

Eiseev, A. I. "On Certain Trends in Change in the Content and Nature of the Initial Period of War." *Voyenno-istoricheskiy Zhurnal* (November 1985).

Feickert, Andrew. "Iran's Ballistic Missile Capabilities." Congressional Research Service Report for Congress, RS21548 (August 23, 2004).

Ferguson, Charles D., and Dinshaw Mistry. "Moving Away From Missile Programs." *Boston Globe,* June 19, 2006.

Fetter, Steve. "Ballistic Missiles and Weapons of Mass Destruction." *International Security* 16, no. 4 (Summer 1991).

Freedman, Lawrence. *The Revolution in Strategic Affairs,* Adelphi Paper 318. Oxford: Oxford University Press, 1998.

Fulghum, David A. "Stealth, Cheap Technology Complicate Defense Schemes." *Aviation Week & Space Technology,* July 14, 1997.

Gill, Bates. "China's Military-Technical Developments: The Record for Western Assessments, 1979–199." In *Seeking Truth From Facts: A Retrospective on Chinese Military Studies in the Post-Mao Era.* James C. Mulvenon and Andrew N. D. Yang, eds. Santa Monica, CA: The RAND Corporation, 2001.

Gladwell, Malcolm. *The Tipping Point: How Little Things Can Make a Big Difference.* New York: Little, Brown and Co., 2000.

Gormley, Dennis M. "Conventional Force Integration in Global Strike." In *Nuclear Transformation: The New U.S. Nuclear Doctrine.* James J. Wirtz and Jeffrey A. Larsen, eds. New York: Palgrave, 2005.

———. "Cruise Control." *Bulletin of the Atomic Scientists* 62, no. 2 (March/April 2006): 26–33.

———. "Cruise Missile Threat Rises: U.S. Navy, Army Lag in Defense Preparations." *Defense News,* May 31, 1999.

———. *Dealing with the Threat of Cruise Missiles.* Oxford: Oxford University Press, 2001.

———. *Double Zero and Soviet Military Strategy: Implications for Western Security.* London: Jane's Publishing Co., 1988.

———. "Globalization and WMD Networks: The Case of Unmanned Air Vehicles as Terrorist Weapons." *Strategic Insights* 5, no. 6 (July 2006).

———. "Hedging Against the Cruise-Missile Threat." *Survival* 40, no. 1 (Spring 1998): 92–111.

———. "Missile Defence Myopia: Lessons from the Iraq War." *Survival* 45, no. 4 (Winter 2003–04): 61–86.

———. "New Developments in Unmanned Air Vehicles and Land-Attack Cruise Missiles." In *SIPRI Yearbook 2003.* Oxford: Oxford University Press for SIPRI, 2003, 409–432.

———. "Silent Retreat: The Future of U.S. Nuclear Weapons." *Nonproliferation Review* 14, no. 2 (July 2007): 183–206.

———. "Thwarting U.S. Missile Defense From Within the Missile Technology Control Regime." In *Modification and Resistance to American Foreign Policy.* Davis Bobrow, ed. Pittsburgh: University of Pittsburgh Press, forthcoming in 2008.

———. "UAVs and Cruise Missiles as Possible Terrorist Weapons." In *New Challenges in Missile Proliferation, Missile Defense, and Space Security,* Occasional Paper No. 12. James Clay Moltz, ed. Monterey, CA: Monterey Institute's Center for Nonproliferation Studies, 2003.

Gormley, Dennis M., and K. Scott McMahon. "Who's Guarding the Back Door?" *Jane's International Defense Review* 29 (May 1996).

Gormley, Dennis M., and Richard Speier. "Controlling Unmanned Air Vehicles: New Challenges." *Nonproliferation Review* 10, no. 2 (Summer 2003).

———. "New Missiles and Models for Cooperation." In *Taming the Next Set of Strategic Weapons Threats.* Henry Sokolski, ed. Carlisle, PA: Strategic Studies Institute, U.S. Army War College, June 2006.

Haffa, Robert P., and Jasper Welch. "Command and Control Arrangement for the Attack of Time-Sensitive Targets." Northrop Grumman Analysis Center, November 2005.

Hewson, Robert, and Andrew Koch. "Pakistan Tests Cruise Missile." *Jane's Defence Weekly,* August 17, 2005.

Hichkad, Ravi R., and Christopher Bolkcom. "Cruise Missile Defense." CRS Report to Congress, May 2, 2005.

Hilal, Khalid, and Jack Boureston. "Iran's Announcement of a Space Rocket Test: Fact or Fiction." *WMD Insights* (April 2007).

Hollinger, Frederick J. "The Missile Technology Control Regime: A Major New Arms Control Achievement." In *World Military Expenditures and Arms Transfers 1987.* U.S. Arms Control and Disarmament Agency, Washington, DC: Government Printing Office, 1998.

Hughes, Jr., Wayne P. *Fleet Tactics: Theory and Practice.* Annapolis. Naval Institute Press, 1986.

Huisken, Ron. "The History of Cruise Missiles." In *Cruise Missiles: Technology, Strategy, Politics.* Richard K. Betts, ed. Washington, DC: The Brookings Institution, 1981.

Isby, David C. "Cruise Missiles Flew Half the Desert Fox Strike Missions." *Jane's Missiles and Rockets.* February 12, 1999.

Joshi, Sharad. *The Practice of Coercive Diplomacy in the Post 9/11 Period,* Unpublished PhD dissertation, Graduate School of Public and International Affairs, University of Pittsburgh, December 2006.

Joshi, Sharad, and Peter Crail. "India Successfully Tests Agni-III: A Stepping Stone to An ICBM?" *WMD Insights* (May 2007).

Kan, Shirley A. *Taiwan: Major U.S. Arms Sales Since 1990.* RL30957. Washington, DC: Congressional Research Service, July 12, 2007.

Karp, Aaron. "Going Ballistic? Reversing Missile Proliferation." *Arms Control Today* 35, no. 5 (June 2005).

———. *Ballistic Missile Proliferation: The Politics and Technics.* Oxford: Oxford University Press, 1996.

Kass, Lee. "Syria after Lebanon: The Growing Syrian Missile Threat." *Middle East Quarterly* 12, no. 4 (Fall 2005).

Keaney, Thomas A., and Eliot A. Cohen. *Gulf War Air Power Survey: Summary Report.* Washington, DC: Government Printing Office, 1993.

Keller, William W., and Gordon R. Mitchell, (eds.). *Hitting First: Preventive Force in U.S. Security Strategy.* Pittsburgh: University of Pittsburgh Press, 2006.

Koch, Andrew. "Pakistan's Aerial Target Could Spawn Cruise Missile." *Jane's Defence Weekly,* October 23, 2002.

Kristensen, Hans M. "U.S. Strategic War Planning After 9/11." *Nonproliferation Review* 14, no. 2 (July 2007): 373–390.

———. "The Role of U.S. Nuclear Weapons: New Doctrine Falls Short of Bush Pledge." *Arms Control Today* 35, no. 7 (September 2005).

Kueter, Jeff, and Howard Kleinberg. *The Cruise Missile Challenge: Designing a Defense Against Asymmetric Threats.* Washington, DC: The Marshall Institute, 2007.

Kugler, Mitchell. "Missile Defense Cooperation and the Missile Technology Control Regime." In *Taming the Next Set of Strategic Weapons Threats.* Henry Sokolski, ed. Carlisle, PA: Strategic Studies Institute, U.S. Army War College, June 2006.

Lachow, Irving. *GPS-Guided Cruise Missiles and Weapons of Mass Destruction.* RP-463. Santa Monica, CA: The RAND Corporation, 1995.

Ladwig, III, Walter C. "A Cold Start for Hot Wars? The Indian Army's New Limited War Doctrine." *International Security* 32, no. 3 (Winter 2007/08): 158–190.

Lambeth, Benjamin. *NATO's Air War for Kosovo.* Santa Monica, CA: The RAND Corporation, 2001.

Leitenberg, Milton. *Assessing the Biological Weapons and Bioterrorism Threat.* Carlisle, PA: Strategic Studies Institute, U.S. Army War College, 2005.

Lennox, Duncan. "China's New Cruise Missile Programme 'Racing Ahead.'" *Jane's Defence Weekly,* January 12, 2000.

Levite, Ariel E., and Elizabeth Sherwood-Randall. "The Case for Discriminate Force." *Survival* 44, no. 4 (Winter 2002–03): 81–98.

Lieber, Keir A., and Daryl G. Press. "The Rise of U.S. Nuclear Primacy." *Foreign Affairs* 85, no. 2 (March/April 2006).

MacKenzie, Donald. *Inventing Accuracy: A Historical Sociology of Nuclear Missile Guidance.* Cambridge, MA: MIT Press, 1990.

———. "Theories of Technology and the Abolition of Nuclear Weapons." In *The Social Shaping of Technology.* Donald MacKenzie and Judy Wajcman, eds. Philadelphia: Open University Press, 1999, 425–429.

MacKenzie, Donald, and Graham Spinardi. "Tacit Knowledge, Weapons Design, and the Uninvention of Nuclear Weapons." *American Journal of Sociology* 101, no. 1 (July 1995): 44.

McCarter, Mickey. "Boost for Cruise Missile Defense." *Military Aerospace Technology* 3, no. 2 (June 25, 2004)

McMahon, K. Scott. *Pursuit of the Shield: The US Quest for Limited Ballistic Missile Defense.* Lanham, MD: University Press of America, 1997.

McMahon, K. Scott, and Dennis M. Gormley. *Controlling the Spread of Land-Attack Cruise Missiles.* Marina del Rey, CA: American Institute for Strategic Cooperation, 1995.

Medeiros, Evan S., Roger Cliff, Keith Crane, and James C. Mulvenon. *A New Direction for China's Defense Industry.* Santa Monica, CA: The RAND Corporation, 2005.

Mendelsohn, Jack. "The Impact of NMD on the ABM Treaty." In *White Paper on National Missile Defense.* Joseph Cirincione, et al. Washington, DC: Lawyers Alliance for World Security, 2000.

Minnick, Wendell. "China Tests New Land-Attack Cruise Missile." *Jane's Missiles and Rockets,* October 1, 2004.

Mistry, Dinshaw. *Constraining Missile Proliferation.* Seattle: University of Washington Press, 2003.

Muller, Richard A. "The Cropdusting Terrorist." *Technology Review,* March 11, 2002.

Mulvenon, James C., and David M. Finkelstein, (eds.). *China's Revolution in Doctrinal Affairs: Emerging Trends in the Operational Art of the Chinese People's Liberation Army.* Alexandria, VA: CNA Corporation, 2005.

Mulvenon, James C., Murray Scot Tanner, et al. *Chinese Responses to U.S. Military Transformation and Implications for the Department of Defense.* Santa Monica, CA: The RAND Corporation, 2006.

Nativi, Andy. "Lockheed Martin Bets on New Concepts to Shore Up Weapons Business." *Aviation Week & Space Technology,* May 28, 2007.

Naylor, Sean D. "Iraqi Ultralights Spotted Over U.S. Troops." *Army Times,* March 29, 2003.

Nicholls, David J. *Cruise Missiles and Modern War: Strategic and Technical Implications,* Occasional Paper No. 13. Maxwell Air Force Base, AL: Center for Strategy and Technology, Air War College, 2000.

Nolan, Janne. *Trappings of Power: Ballistic Missiles in the Third World.* Washington, DC: The Brookings Institution, 1991.

"Operation Iraqi Freedom Theater Air and Missile Defense History." 32nd Army Air and Missile Defense Command, Ft. Bliss, TX, September 2003.

Panofsky, Wolfgang K. H. "A Damaging Designation." *Bulletin of the Atomic Scientists* 63, no. 1 (January/February 2007): 37–39.

Pant, Harsh V. "India-Israel Partnership: Convergence and Constraints." *Middle East Review of International Affairs* 8, no. 4 (December 2004).

Petersen, Phillip A., and John R. Clark. "Soviet Air and Antiair Operations." *Air University Review* (March–April 1985).

Pinkston, Daniel A. "South Korean Response to North Korean July Missile Exercise Includes Unveiling of New Cruise Missile." *WMD Insights* (October 4, 2006).

Pinkston, Daniel A., and Kazutaka Sakurai. "Japan Debates Preparing for Future Preemptive Strikes against North Korea." *The Korean Journal of Defense Analysis* 18, no. 4 (Winter 2006): 95–121.

Polanyi, Michael. *Personal Knowledge.* London: Routledge and Kegan Paul, 1958.

Ricks, Thomas E. *Fiasco: The American Military Adventure in Iraq.* New York: Penguin Press, 2006.

Ross, Dennis. *Statecraft.* New York: Farrar, Straus and Giroux, 2007.

Roy, Denny. "The Sources and Limits of Sino-Japanese Tensions." *Survival* 47, no. 2 (Summer 2005): 191–214.

Rubin, Uzi. *The Global Reach of Iran's Ballistic Missiles,* Memorandum 86. Tel Aviv: Institute for National Security Studies, November 2006.

Russell, Richard. *Weapons Proliferation and War in the Greater Middle East: Strategic Contest.* New York: Routledge, 2005.

Sahni, Varun. "India and Missile Acquisition: Push and Pull Factors." *South Asian Survey* 11, no. 2 (2004).

Scheffran, Jurgen. "Missiles in Conflict: The Issue of Missiles in All Its Complexity." *Disarmament Forum* 1 (2007): 11–22.

Schoneberger, William A. "Backfitting Stealth." *Journal of Electronic Defense* 21, no. 3 (March 1998): 33–37.

Shichor, Yitzhak. "Israel's Military Transfers to China and Taiwan." *Survival* 40, no. 2 (Spring 1998).

Sidorenko, A. A. *The Offensive.* Moscow: Voyenizdat, 1970. Translated and published by the U.S. Air Force. Washington, DC: Government Printing Office, 1974.

Smith, Mark. "Pragmatic Micawberism? Norm Construction on Ballistic Missiles." *Contemporary Security Policy* 27, no. 3 (December 2006).

Sokolovskiy, V. D. *Soviet Military Strategy,* 3rd ed. Harriet Fast Scott, ed. New York: Crane, Russak, 1975.

Speier, Richard. "U.S. Space Aid to India: On a 'Glide Path' to ICBM Trouble." *Arms Control Today* 36, no. 2 (March 2006).

———. "Can the Missile Technology Control Regime Be Repaired?" In *Repairing the Regime.* Joseph Cirincione, ed. Washington, DC: Routledge, 2000.

Srivastava, Anupam. "China's Export Controls: Can Beijing's Actions Match Its Words? *Arms Control Today* 35, no. 9 (November 2005).

Stokes, Mark A. "The Chinese Joint Aerospace Campaign: Strategy, Doctrine, and Force Modernization." In *China's Revolution in Doctrinal Affairs: Emerging Trends in the Operational Art of the Chinese People's Liberation Army.* James Mulvenon and David M. Finkelstein, eds. Alexandria, VA: CNA Corporation, 2005.

———. *China's Strategic Modernization: Implications for the United States.* Carlisle, PA: Strategic Studies Institute, U.S. Army War College, 1999.

Surikov, B. T. *Combat Employment of Ground Forces' Missiles.* Moscow: Voyenizdat, 1979.

Tanks, David. *Assessing the Cruise Missile Puzzle: How Great the Defense Challenge?* Washington, DC: Institute for Foreign Policy Analysis, 2000.

Tannenwald, Nina. "Stigmatizing the Bomb." *International Security* 29, no. 4 (Spring 2005).

Tissue, Phil, et al. "Attacking the Cruise Missile Threat," Paper prepared for Class #03–3. Joint Forces Staff College, September 8, 2003.

Treverton, Gregory F. *Reshaping National Intelligence for an Age of Information.* New York: Cambridge University Press, 2003.

———. *Framing Compellent Strategies.* Santa Monica, CA: The RAND Corporation, 2000.

U.S. Congress. Senate. Committee on Armed Services. *Soviet Military Developments and NATO Antitactical Ballistic Missile Defenses: Hearings Before the Committee on Armed Services.* S. HRG. 99–804, PR 4. 99th Congress, 2nd session, January 30, 1986.

Van Diepen, Vann. "Missile Nonproliferation: Accomplishments and Future Challenges." *International Export Control Observer* 5 (March 2006): 16–18.

Vogel, Kathleen M. "Bio-securization: A Constructivist Approach to Assessing Bioterrorism Threats," Unpublished manuscript dated March 30, 2007. Provided courtesy of the author.

———. "Framing Biosecurity." *Science and Public Policy* (forthcoming).

Wagner, Alex. "Washington to Sanction China, Pakistan for Missile Cooperation." *Arms Control Today* 31, no. 7 (September 2001).

Watts, Barry, and Williamson Murray, "Military Innovation in Peacetime." In *Military Innovation in the Interwar Period.* Williamson Murray and Allan R. Millett, eds. Cambridge, UK: Cambridge University Press, 1998.

Willett, Lee. "TLAM and British Strategic Thought." *Undersea Warfare* 2, no. 3 (Spring 2000).

Williams, Mark. "The Missiles of August—Part II." *Technology Review,* August 29, 2006.

Wohlstetter, Roberta. *Pearl Harbor: Warning and Decision.* Stanford: Stanford University Press, 1962.

Wortzel, Larry M. "Comments on 'China's Military-Technical Developments: The Record for Western Assessments, 1979–1999.'" In *Seeking Truth from Facts: A Retrospective on Chinese Military Studies in the Post-Mao Era.* James C. Mulvenon and Andrew N. D. Yang, eds. Santa Monica, CA: The RAND Corporation, 2001.

Yuan, Jing-Dong. "Effective, Reliable, and Credible: China's Nuclear Modernization." *Non-proliferation Review* 14, no. 2 (July 2007).

Yung, Christopher D. *People's War at Sea: Chinese Naval Power in the Twenty-First Century.* Alexandria, VA: Center for Naval Analyses, 1996.

Zaborsky, Victor. "Does China Belong in the Missile Technology Control Regime?" *Arms Control Today* 34, no. 8 (October 2004).

Index

ABOUT THE AUTHOR

DENNIS M. GORMLEY is a Senior Fellow at the Monterey Institute's James Martin Center for Nonproliferation Studies in Washington, D.C. and a member of the faculty of the Graduate School of Public and International Affairs at the University of Pittsburgh. Mr. Gormley has chaired or served on numerous Department of Defense and intelligence community advisory panels and has frequently testified before Congressional committees on missile nonproliferation issues. He is the author of three books and has contributed frequently to leading journals and newspapers.